MORTGAGING THE EARTH

MORTGAGING THE EARTH

THE WORLD BANK
Environmental Impoverishment and the Crisis of Development

BRUCE RICH

EARTHSCAN

Earthscan Publications Ltd, London

First published in the USA in 1994
by Beacon Press, 25 Beacon Street,
Boston, Massachesetts 02108-2892

First published in the UK by
Earthscan Publications Limited
120 Pentonville Road, London N1 9JN

A catalogue record for this book is available from the British Library

ISBN: 1 85383 221 9

Printed in the USA

Cover design by Elaine Marriott

Earthscan Publications Limited is an editorially independent subsidary of Kogan Page Limited and publishes in association with the International Institute for Environment and Development and the World Wide Fund for Nature.

For Paul John Rich, Jr.,
and Doris Miller Rich

Contents

Preface

This book is one person's attempt to understand our world as the twentieth century draws to an end. Its subject is the World Bank, which, with the collapse of the communist bloc, has become a truly global institution. The history of the Bank is a particularly instructive case study in many of the philosophical, political, and economic assumptions and currents that have shaped the modern world—and how they have gone awry. These assumptions and currents can be summarized in one word—development. Economic development is now the organizing principle for almost every society and nation on the planet. But it is a relatively new idea in history, spreading from Western Europe in the seventeenth century to conquer the world over the next three centuries. Max Weber observed that this great transformation spurred two universal trends that often exist in uneasy tension with one another: bureaucratization and democratization.

We now are learning that economic development entails a third: a slowly building world ecological crisis. A phrase, a bit glib, was coined over a decade ago to suggest the way out of our global environmental predicament—sustainable development. But this crisis has been a long time brewing, and perhaps we need to rethink what societies and humankind really seek through development, sustainable or otherwise.

In trying to develop the world we have so changed it that at the moment when the ideals of modernity have conquered every cultural and natural niche of the planet, its assumptions and methods aren't performing as well as they used to. We are beginning to realize that the effects of our actions are much more complex and far less predictable than we thought. Centralized universal institutions like the World Bank aren't working very well, nor is the nation-state in many parts of the world. Such institutions seem at the same time too big and too small to deal with a new kind of challenge: a proliferation of local problems the repercussions of which are increasingly global. Nowhere is this more evident than in the world environmental crisis: building a polluting coal-fired power plant in India or burning the rainforest in a remote corner of Brazil are local occurrences with worldwide consequences, such as the acceleration of the warming of the earth's climate. Finding more flexible, responsive, and effective international approaches to deal with such problems is one of the great challenges of the end of this century and the beginning of the next.

At the same time, nongovernmental movements have burgeoned all over the world, especially in developing countries. This book reflects in part my experience with a number of these groups over the past decade, and their efforts to promote public accountability and ecological responsibility in public international financial institutions like the World Bank. All over the world, nongovernmental organizations are questioning the adverse environmental and social consequences of existing development efforts, and they are seeking alternatives at the local, national, and international levels. This is an extraordinarily important and hopeful phenomenon, and one quite unprecedented in history.

Mortgaging the Earth is about all these issues, and more. The World Bank is its focus not just because of the Bank's financial and political power, or its impact on the global environment, but above all because it mirrors the crisis of many of our institutions and values as we approach a new millennium on an uncomfortably small planet.

A Few Words on Method

Mortgaging the Earth is not a comprehensive, all-encompassing analysis and history of the World Bank. Such a book would of necessity be much longer, and much narrower in perspective. I have tried to explore essential themes underlying the Bank's institutional dynamics, to look for continuities beneath the evolution in policies and approaches of this half-century-old bureaucracy. To uncover these themes, *Mortgaging the Earth* examines the World Bank's relation to the environment. This inquiry takes us to the heart of what is one of the twentieth century's quintessential institutions. It also leads to questions about the assumptions underlying the dominant economic and political culture of the planet. I believe that today the environmental challenge is the preeminent one for all organizations, public and private, involved in international development. The environmental failure or success of public development institutions is the threshold question we must ask in deliberating whether they are worthy of taxpayer support.

Some will differ strongly with my characterization of change within the Bank. They would argue that the proliferation of environmental policies and staff, and of new kinds of projects has been substantial over the past several years, while conceding that more needs to be done. In fact, I agree with them, and add that by the norms of international bureaucracies, the changes are major. Indeed, this is precisely the issue, and the problem.

We may be too inclined to evaluate large organizations on the basis of process rather than substance. It is all too easy to mistake internal bureaucratic changes for what they produce (and fail to produce), to accept what institutions say about themselves as a substitute for an independent evaluation of their effects on the world.

It would be a mistake to assess an automobile company with a reputation for declining quality by its claims to have carried out bureaucratic restructuring, issued new corporate policies and hired new staff, or by advertisements that quality is its number one priority. Instead, one should ask people who actually buy the company's cars, and others affected by the company's product—those who work in garages, repair shops, etc.— whether they think it's still making the same old clunkers. Unlike visitors at company headquarters or showrooms, they are not fooled for long by new model designs and glossy brochures.

The World Bank tries to produce something called development, packaged mostly in specific projects. The closest we may get to listening to the equivalent of a car owner or a garage mechanic in the case of the World Bank is hearing what community and nongovernmental organizations in developing countries affected by Bank projects say about its product. This is an important part of the approach of this book, particularly because in the case of the World Bank, unlike that of the car company, poor product quality does not show up on the bottom line. Totally government financed and guaranteed, the Bank has no bottom line. Instead, it makes one up and redefines it as it goes along.

The lack of independent accounts on the effects of World Bank activities from the perspective of those who are on the receiving end is especially acute. The Bank produces most of the information that exists about it. It publishes only what management deems acceptable for public consumption, and keeps secret almost all of the documents it generates. The most serious social and environmental consequences of its lending often take place in remote rural areas in scores of developing nations around the globe. The people who are most affected are often the poor, the illiterate, the voiceless and powerless in their own national societies. Obtaining, not to speak of generating, independent information on what is really going on is often daunting.

The temptation for many researchers, I believe, is analogous to the situation of the drunken sailor whom a passerby finds in the middle of the night searching under a street lamp for his lost billfold. "Where do you think you lost your money?" the passerby queries. "About a mile from here," the sailor replies, but, he explains in response to the astonishment of the bystander, he is looking under the lamp because it is the only place there is any light. If our hypothetical researcher is the sailor, it is the Bank and its member governments that decide where to put the streetlights. The expanse of darkness is much more extensive than the islands of light. This book does not dwell only on the locales where Bank management has provided illumination, but also on areas it would prefer remained in obscurity.

The first two chapters of *Mortgaging the Earth* introduce the reader to the Bank and to the profound human and ecological damage caused by its lending, as well as to the protests of those made worse off by some of its projects. Are these problems of recent origin, or can they be traced to more fundamental dilemmas? In an attempt to find some answers, Chapter 3 and Chapter 4 turn to the history of the Bank from its founding at Bretton Woods in 1944 through the end of Robert McNamara's presidency in 1981. Chapter 5 examines the rise of an international grass-roots movement in the 1980s to prod the Bank into making environmental reforms, while Chapter 6 examines the credibility of some of these reforms. Chapter 7 brings together issues introduced in earlier chapters, examining the contradictory internal and external pressures that make it difficult for the Bank to carry out its environmental policies and commitments.

Can one fully understand an institution so central to the values of modern culture as the World Bank by limiting one's purview to the Bank itself? Chapter 8 speculates on more profound historical and social forces that made its creation—and current crisis—inevitable: the unfolding since the seventeenth century of the modern ideal of development, an evolution that may be approaching an end as we stand on the threshold of a postmodern epoch. With this deepened perspective, Chapter 9 turns to the issues underlying the 1992 Rio Earth Summit, and the key role of the Bank in its outcome. Chapter 10 contrasts the approach of Rio—global centralized environmental management—with the countervailing forces of what I call "emerging global civil society" (both are leitmotifs that run through the book) and suggests possible alternatives and reforms. However, the Bank may be unreformable without greater public pressure on its member governments to either radically reinvent the institution or stop funding it. It is my hope that after reading this book readers will be moved to exert such political pressure through their elected representatives and the executive branches of their governments.

More than a decade ago an official of the United Nations Environment Program called the lending practices of the World Bank and similar institutions "biological deficit financing." After nearly fifty years of such financing, the World Bank has left a mortgage on the earth we shall all be paying for a long time to come.

Acknowledgments

I wish to thank my publisher, Beacon Press, whose staff was enthusiastic about this project from the beginning, a tremendous morale booster for an author. I owe a special debt of gratitude to my editor, Deanne Urmy, whose insightful suggestions improved the original drafts a great deal. I can't praise enough the professionalism, sensitivity to language, and obsession with quality of my copy editor, Chris Kochansky. Thanks go to my agent, Meredeth Bernstein, whose encouragement spurred me to write the original proposal. Dan Guttman, after listening to me talk about the book I wanted to write once too often, prompted me to buy the laptop computer on which I wrote it and put me in touch with Meredeth.

I owe a special intellectual debt to Marshall Berman, whose examination of modernity in *All That Is Solid Melts Into Air* inspired much of my literary and historical discussion of development. Sometimes a serendipitous conversation or two can critically influence the evolution of a book. I was prodded to read Berman, and many other sources, after several immensely stimulating talks with Gustavo Lins Ribeiro of the University of Brasília's anthropology department.

Special thanks go to the following individuals who have spent many hours reading the manuscript in part or in its entirety: Luiz Fernando Allegretti, Pat Aufderheide, Don Babai, Chip Barber, David Batker, Anne Bichsel, Scott Hajost, Kevin Healy, Korinna Horta, Mimi Kleiner, Howard Kreps, Juliet Majot, Ray Mikesell, Patti Petesch, Paul Rich, Heffa Schucking, Steve Schwartzman, Paul Sweeney, Susan Swift, Ann Danaiya Usher, Peter van Tuijl, Ken Walsh. Their critical input has made the book much better than it would have been.

I am greatly indebted to several World Bank staff members who also reviewed the manuscript. Together, these individuals, who work in several different divisions of the Bank, have more than a century of cumulative firsthand experience of its operations. Their assistance has been invaluable.

The help and suggestions of all of the people mentioned above have been extraordinarily important, but, naturally, I alone am responsible for the content of this book as well as for all errors.

I am extremely grateful to my employer, the Environmental Defense Fund, for allowing me to spend much of my time last year researching and completing this project. EDF is a remarkably creative institution, one with rare tolerance and flexibility. I would like to emphasize that the opinions and views expressed in *Mortgaging the Earth* are my personal ones and in no way necessarily represent those of the Environmental Defense Fund, its staff, national membership, supporters, or board of directors. EDF is a refreshingly diverse organization, and among the many individuals associated with it one can find a variety of viewpoints on numerous issues, including the ones I address in this book.

Washington, D.C.
June 1993

The Dwelling Place
of the Angels

It was Bangkok, the humid summer rainy season of 1991. Thousands of workers toiled day and night on the most expensive public building ever constructed in Thailand, a country of 54 million people. The finance minister was anxious. The government had spent $100 million, and after nineteen months of around-the-clock work, the gleaming, modernistic palace of concrete and glass still was unfinished. Only a few weeks remained until "the meeting," and national face was at stake.

The minister had other reasons to be worried; despite a special government allocation of an additional $17 million for meeting-related expenses, there was one problem that no amount of money could cure in a few weeks. The Queen Sirikit Conference Center had to be built in the Sukumvit Road area, a new, rapidly growing part of town; no other place so central could be found to build such a large building, covering well over half a million square feet. But in a city with some of the worst traffic jams on earth, Sukumvit was one of the most congested areas of all. It could take two hours during morning rush hour to get there by taxi from one of the luxurious downtown hotels, and another two hours to return in the evening. Bangkok had quadrupled its population to more than 10 million in less than a generation, and the number of automobiles had increased over tenfold; the city was asphyxiating on its own growth. The traffic would be made worse during the three days of the meeting by the traditional insistence of many of the thousands of delegates on being chauffeured around town in private limousines. The vision of delegates from all over the world choking on smog in stalled limousines evoked consternation. What to do?

The government, installed by a February 1991 army coup, appreciated the virtues of military-like decisiveness: it would stop traffic and smog by shutting down most of the city. The prime minister announced that October 14 and 15, 1991, would be special national holidays in Bangkok, where more than 50 percent of the country's economic activity takes place. All banks, government offices, schools, and state enterprises would be closed.

This was just the beginning. The government set up a special medical system comprising a helicopter, two ambulances, and 830 doctors, nurses, and technicians, on call day and night, to provide free medical care to the delegates and their families. Bangkok's eight leading hospitals would be placed on emergency alert, and each of the seventeen luxury hotels lodging the delegates was matched with one of them. The director of the Bangkok General Hospital soberly assessed the health risks such a giant meeting would pose: "Our preparations have emphasized heavily . . . treatment of heart diseases, as they must be attended to urgently. All these meetings about money may create anxiety among delegates, many of whom are quite old."[1]

Solving these problems only seemed to uncover more, many of them linked to Thailand's remarkable success in the past twenty years as a model of dynamic, export-oriented economic growth. The country's economic transformation had uprooted millions upon millions of people from the Thai countryside. Many of them had come to Bangkok. The city has an estimated half-million prostitutes—women, men, and children—of whom a third may be already HIV positive.

Bangkok's thousands of nightclubs and massage parlors offer one of the most lurid spectacles on the planet. International sex tourism is big business in Thailand, and an important source of foreign exchange. Two-thirds of the country's five million visitors per year are men, and great numbers of them come for sex, many from Germany, Japan, and Australia. In the brave new era of the global—the global economy, the global environment, and global competitive advantage—Bangkok has become the global brothel.[2]

But would the delegates appreciate—or want to be seen appreciating—all this? Rumors abounded that the glossy German weekly *Stern* was sending its own delegation of photojournalists to stalk the city's most notorious clubs and whorehouses in the hope of catching delegates cavorting at German taxpayers' expense. NBC sent a team to film the meeting. Not just the image of the delegates, but that of the country was at stake. The government sent discreet orders to precinct police to ensure that dancing girls and boys were clothed during the meeting. The minister of health, an avuncular man popularly known as "Mr. Condom,"[3] would circulate at the conference center, handing out souvenir key chains with prophylactics encased in transparent plastic as a warning that the nation faced an AIDS holocaust.* And then there were Bangkok's tens of thousands of sidewalk vendors and hawkers, a clamorous, enterprising bunch. Some in the military and the government felt uneasy with the superficial aura of anarchic unruliness that teeming hordes of street vendors presented—it seemed somehow underdeveloped, at least in comparison with the crystal palace of the new conference center. So the government forbade street vendors from selling their wares around the conference center and the delegates' hotels for the duration of the meeting.

As the countdown to the great meeting continued, there remained the most intractable, embarrassing problem of all. On three sides of the conference center sprawled clusters, indeed whole neighborhoods, of wood and cardboard shacks with corrugated metal roofs—slums—really not so bad compared with those of many other developing countries (the Philippines and India, for example), but squalid and unsightly nevertheless. One could see thousands of the unseemly poor camped on the very ramparts of the new conference center. Like the hapless armies of prostitutes and street vendors, they were rural refugees, many from Thailand's poorest region, the northeast. Fifteen thousand influential people were to fly to Bangkok for a three-day meeting to discuss money and growth—and every time they looked out a window they would see poor people going about their daily life in makeshift shacks of broken wood and corroding zinc.

This was a job for the army, the finance ministry decided. There were over one million slum dwellers in the capital, many of whom had been relocated repeatedly for new construction. The fate of another two or three thousand should pose no new problems. Finance ministry officials proposed to the Thai cabinet in late June that the communities in sight of the conference center be removed by August; the Thai National Housing Authority would provide new housing, eventually, in another neighborhood miles away. The people would be better off—and out of sight.

But the slum dwellers didn't agree; those who could find work were street vendors and day laborers in markets near the conference center; relocating them miles away would destroy the little access they had to a precarious livelihood. They appealed to the prime minister, who arranged a compromise. A total of 647 families in two slums, Duang Pitak and

* In May 1991, almost 3 percent of Thai army recruits and 1 percent of all women attending prenatal clinics tested HIV positive. By the end of the decade, the minister of health estimates, two to four million Thais will be infected.

Klong Paisingto, would have to relocate ("voluntarily," the prime minister insisted), but hundreds of others would be allowed to remain in three other slum neighborhoods. Those who remained would be enlisted along with army brigades in a "beautification" program to plant trees and grass and otherwise improve the appearance of their dwellings for the aesthetic gratification of the foreign dignitaries.[4]

In early August, the prime minister toured the conference building for the first time. He was very proud; no one could deny that it was attractive and well designed, and it had been conceived and built entirely by Thais. Outside the entrance, a quarter-of-a-million-dollar gold statue, an abstract sculpture vaguely resembling a giant burning bush, would greet the delegates. According to official accounts, it symbolized prayer. But the prime minister's fancy was particularly captivated by the lavish bar, where so much important business would be conducted. He told reporters how much he appreciated the view from the corners of the barroom and the cafeteria—most of the slums adjacent to the conference center were still visible, thanks to his intervention. Thailand was still a poor country—why should it be ashamed of its own people? The areas to be bulldozed were across the street, not visible from the inside of the building; the delegates could reflect tranquilly on poverty, economics, and money while they munched hors d'oeuvres and sipped Singapore Slings—or could they? The prime minister announced to the Thai press that "the [bar] stools are too small. Foreigners who have big frames may find it uncomfortable to sit on them. I myself had difficulty sitting on them."[5]

Days later, the army moved in to evict hundreds of families from Duang Pitak; most had no more than a week's notice. Much of the vacant land would be used to build a special access road to the conference center to improve traffic circulation. As September approached, electricity and water were cut off to pressure those who still refused to move. Forty-three families huddled in the community school after their homes had been bulldozed away. By October most of Duang Pitak had been razed, and the stragglers were relocated.

The foreigners began to arrive, at first by the scores and then by the thousands and thousands, in the second week of October. The government assigned 6,365 police to ensure security and to guard against terrorism, and a special security budget of nearly $3 million was allotted to cover the extra cost. Bangkok cops called it "the mother of all meetings." By Sunday, October 13, nearly 15,000 officials, dignitaries, and bankers from 156 different countries would convene in Bangkok.

Meanwhile, a few hundred yards from the convention center, seventy families huddled in army tents underneath an elevated expressway. In one of the tents Kusuma Wongsrisuk tended her two-month-old daughter,

Ploy, who coughed and cried incessantly. Ploy had fallen ill after Kusuma and her family were relocated from the Duang Pitak slum. Ploy's older brother, Tha, had also fallen ill with respiratory problems. Kusuma told a reporter that their illness was no surprise—the area under the expressway was dark and damp, and the air was noxious, filled with dust and exhaust. The army tents had no insulation from the humid ground. The families were cut off from electricity and water, and lived by candlelight. Each family received $240 as compensation, not enough to cover the cost of the new houses they were helping one another build. Many of the men would lose their jobs as day laborers and vendors when they moved to the new houses, and some families could not borrow enough to move; the leaky Thai army tents would be their homes for the foreseeable future. Kusuma was bitter about the money the government had spent for the three-day meeting of well-heeled foreigners. She told a reporter that the compensation the displaced families received was "too small to even pay for their hotel room for a single night."[6]

Across town, another meeting had begun, much different from the one that would take place in the Queen Sirikit Conference Center. At Chulalongkorn University, more than a thousand people, mostly Thais but also sympathetic foreigners, were gathered in a "People's Forum." It was October 8, the first day of a series of alternative meetings that would take place over the next ten days. The People's Forum had been organized by a coordinating committee of more than 200 Thai nongovernmental organizations (NGOs) concerned with the environment, social equity, and alternative economic development.

In the 1980s, NGOs had burgeoned in Thailand, responding to growing social and ecological problems accompanying the country's export-oriented economic growth. The groups were typically small, focusing on specific problems such as health care, village development, and human rights, with staffs of fewer than ten persons, many of whom were volunteers or students. Their annual budgets of a few thousand dollars a year would hardly cover the expense of a couple of short trips to Thailand by one of the development bureaucrats employed by international agencies. Some groups were national in focus, like the Project for Ecological Recovery, which has played a lead role in documenting the ecological cost of government-sponsored development.[7]

Three hundred and fifty villagers from all over Thailand had come to Bangkok for the People's Forum, and they were joined by representatives of Bangkok's street vendors, slum dwellers, numerous students and academics, and spokeswomen for the country's prostitutes. One of the first speakers was a feisty middle-aged woman named Roy Srihaphong, well known as a vocal community organizer and affectionately called "Auntie

Roy." Auntie Roy explained that she lived in Klong Toey, one of the slum neighborhoods adjacent to the Queen Sirikit Conference Center.[8]

Before the packed conference room, Auntie Roy described how she had come from the poor northeast twenty-eight years earlier in search of a better life. After all these years she was no better off, and her makeshift shelter was threatened with demolition. Auntie Roy's voice rose as she described her feelings over the past months as the conference center was built:

I pass it every day, I can see it from my window. It looks like the dwelling place of the angels. We have tried to imagine these thousands of angels arriving in their flying boats—that's what we call airplanes—and we ordinary people wonder if we will ever be able to sit in that meeting room.[9]

The World Bank and the International Monetary Fund were coming to town.

Rich Nomads and Poor

Jacques Attali, longtime advisor to François Mitterrand and president of the newly formed European Bank for Reconstruction and Development (EBRD), had just arrived in Bangkok. Attali had recently published *Millennium: Winners and Losers in the Coming World Order,* in which he portrayed the triumph of the global free market economy in terms both enthralling and distressing. With the demise of the Soviet Empire, the whole world was united by now irresistible multinational economic forces. The market-oriented production of commodities and the forces of consumption reigned over the entire planet more totally than any previous political order or religious movement in history. The new world order described by Attali would be based in the political sphere on pluralism and democracy, a fitting culmination of the past two or three hundred years of Western history.[10]

But the French economist saw a dark side to the glorious commodification of the globe, one that threatened the prosperous beneficiaries of the global consumer economy:

From their privileged technological perches, they will preside over a world that has embraced a common ideology of consumerism but is bitterly divided between rich and poor, threatened by a warming and polluted atmosphere, girdled by a dense network of airport metropolises for travel, and wired for instant worldwide communication. Money, information, goods, and people will move around the world at dizzying speeds. . . . Severed from any national allegiance or family ties by micro-chip based gadgets . . . the consumer-citizens of the world's privileged regions will become "rich nomads". . . . These wealthy wanderers will everywhere be confronted by roving masses of "poor nomads"—boat people on a planetary scale—seeking to escape from the destitute periphery, where most of the earth's population will continue to live. . . .

And they will know that the prosperity that is not theirs partly comes at the price of their well-being and at the price of the environment's degradation.[11]

At the apex of this economic world order are situated a number of unique public international financial institutions, of which the most important are the World Bank and the International Monetary Fund (IMF).* The Bank and the Fund were established at an international monetary conference of the incipient United Nations, held in 1944 at the New Hampshire resort town of Bretton Woods. Linchpins of the post–World War II international economic order that produced unprecedented global growth, the Bank and the Fund have become the most important public institutions affecting economic development in the world. The IMF mainly lends to countries over the short term to remedy balance of payments deficits, and requires in exchange rigorous macroeconomic policy measures from the borrowing nations to cut internal expenditures and increase exports. In the 1980s, the Fund took on a related but new role in managing and partly financing international debt reschedulings between Third World countries and private international banks.

The World Bank lends about $24 billion a year to more than a hundred countries to support economic development projects and programs, the total cost of which is over $70 billion annually.** It manages a port-

---

* The other major public international financial institutions include three regional multilateral development banks (MDBs)—the Inter-American Development Bank, the Asian Development Bank, and the African Development Bank—as well as the newly created (1990) European Bank for Reconstruction and Development (EBRD). The regional multilateral development banks were founded in the 1960s to lend money to developing countries for large-scale economic development projects in their respective regions. Their structure and operations are largely modeled on the World Bank. The EBRD was established at the initiative of the French government and Jacques Attali to lend to the new market economies developing in Eastern Europe and the former Soviet Union. It too is a public international financial institution, conceived along the lines of the World Bank and regional MDBs. Chapter 3 discusses in more detail the origins and functioning of the World Bank, the IMF, and the post–World War II international economic system.

** The total cost of a project that the Bank supports is typically two to three times greater than the amount of a Bank loan, because of cofinancing from local governments, private banks, and other bilateral and multilateral development assistance agencies (such as the regional MDBs, the U.S. Agency for International Development, and the foreign aid agencies of Japan and the Western European nations). Disbursements on new World Bank loans typically extend over several years, so the actual amount of money the Bank annually pays out is less than the amount of new lending commitments. In 1992 the Bank disbursed $16.43 billion.

folio of outstanding loans totaling $140 billion, financing development schemes totaling over a third of a trillion dollars. The World Bank operates on a larger scale than any of the other so-called public international financial institutions. More than any other entity on earth, the Bank shapes the worldview of proponents of big international development, and the Bank is its biggest funder.

The annual meeting of the two Washington-based financial behemoths typically attracts the financial elite of the entire planet: the finance ministers and central bank presidents of the 176 nations (as of 1993) that are members of the Bank and the Fund, as well as high-ranking representatives of the world's leading private commercial banks and investment banking firms. The delegates to the meeting discuss the global economy and international finance, particularly with respect to developing nations. The meetings are above all an unprecedented opportunity for the world's bankers, public and private, to cut deals among themselves and with governments.

An overriding theme of many of the annual meetings in the 1980s was the Third World debt crisis. The response of the industrialized world, led by the United States, was to use the World Bank and the IMF to lend more money to the biggest debtors, such as Mexico and Brazil, while simultaneously promoting loan conditions the objective of which was to push indebted countries to reduce domestic expenditures and to export more. The impact of these policies on the poor in many countries was devastating: real wages dropped, and government health and education services were slashed.* In countries like the Philippines and Brazil, many of the impoverished became shock troops of tropical deforestation, vainly seeking to eke out a living on poor rainforest soils. The goal of the creditor countries was to avoid major debt forgiveness or loan defaults by pressuring poorer nations to earn more foreign exchange to service their debts. The terms for these policies had a sanitized ring to them that gave little hint of their tremendous social impact: officials spoke of "structural adjustment," "policy reform," and "stabilization." In 1991, in Bangkok, the new challenge was to incorporate Eastern Europe and the former Soviet Union into the World Bank/IMF realm.

Two years out of three the annual meeting takes place in Washington. Every third year a foreign city is chosen to host the event. In 1988, it was Berlin. Many Bank and Fund officials remembered Berlin as a uniquely unpleasant place. Mobs of young Germans gathered night after night outside the city's luxury hotels pummeling drums and clanging pots and pans to deprive the delegates of sleep. The lucky few who were lodged in what

---

* For more detail on the Bank's role in adjustment, see Chapter 5 and Chapter 7.

was still East Berlin could sleep and move around much more freely, thanks to the solicitous East German security forces. Demonstrators staged a sit-down blockade of the limousine convoys, and most of West Berlin's taxi drivers went on strike for an afternoon as an expression of solidarity. There were several alternative meetings involving tens of thousands of participants, including the convocation of a "Permanent People's Tribunal" to try the World Bank and IMF for crimes against humanity.

The greatest number of police since the Second World War—some 17,000 from all over Germany—were deployed to guard against potentially violent demonstrations and possible terrorism. Irritated Berliners complained that the meeting had transformed their city into "Bullenhauptstadt Europas"—the "cop capital of Europe." On the opening day of the official meetings, 80,000 demonstrators marched through the center of Berlin to protest the policies of the World Bank and the IMF. They carried banners alleging that the Bank and the Fund were destroying global ecological stability through their shortsighted development policies, and "organizing the poverty of the World's peoples."[12]

In Berlin, and now in Bangkok, the planetary boat people and marginalized urban nomads of Attali's nightmarish vision pressed alarmingly close. It was disturbing to think that their existence somehow had something to do with destruction of rainforests and global warming, not in a direct sense, but as simultaneous phenomena emanating from a common source or shared global system. They were an ontological eruption, a rude one at that. It was not so much the people themselves who were threatening, but the untidy and not very understandable reality they appeared to come from. No place was foreseen for this reality in "the dwelling place of the angels." Two worlds were colliding.

What on earth was happening?

Development or Destruction?

After Auntie Roy finished her short speech before the People's Forum on the morning of October 8, others told their stories. A former artillery officer spoke of how his life had been ruined by Thailand's first hydroelectric dam, Bhumibol, financed by the World Bank in 1964. More than 3,000 people were displaced by the dam, and the government-controlled Electrical Generating Authority of Thailand (EGAT) promised the displaced people new arable land and houses, with water, electricity, and a road. The officer, Lert Techa-in, had served his country for thirty years. But EGAT gave him and the others nothing, and twenty-seven years later Lert Techa-in accused EGAT of destroying the economic basis of many lives: "We still don't have electricity or water despite the fact that the site is only one kilometer from the reservoir and 36 kilometers from the power plant at Bhumibol."[13] Bhumibol was only one of the first of numerous World Bank loans to EGAT for large-scale dams and power plants: sixteen loans amounting to nearly $700 million were approved by 1991.[14] Other dams that followed in the 1970s and 1980s had names little known outside Thailand: Sirindhorn, Sirikit, Sri Nakharin, Khao Laem. The Sirindhorn dam also displaced thousands, who were resettled on infertile land and suffered increased poverty. The Sirindhorn refugees have been asking for adequate rehabilitation since 1967, to no avail.

In the course of these forced displacements of the poor, EGAT had created a legacy of secrecy and contempt for local opinion, and mistrust among people affected by its projects. EGAT is largely a World Bank creation; in fact, back in the late 1950s, the Bank insisted that the Thai government create an autonomous, independent power agency, which later became EGAT, as a condition for future power loans. The Bank was not only directly responsible for EGAT's birth, it was EGAT's main source of external financing, and thus exercised an important influence in its attention—or lack of attention—to environmental and social matters over the years.[15]

In 1980, the Bank promulgated a policy on rehabilitation of populations displaced by large infrastructure projects such as dams (although the Bank insisted that the policy was not retroactive, so it took no responsibility for the thousands of rural Thais it had helped to impoverish through negligent resettlement in earlier projects such as Bhumibol and Sirindhorn). The 1980 policy on its face is an equitable one: the Bank requires borrowers to prepare at an early stage in project preparation a resettlement and rehabilitation plan in consultation with, and acceptable to, the people who will be displaced. The plan must put the "project-affected population" in as good an economic situation as they were beforehand, and preferably in a better one.

At the 1991 People's Forum, though, there were scores of villagers and activists from the vicinity of the latest dam project in Thailand that the World Bank was planning to finance, Pak Mun, for whom the Bank's resettlement policy was little more than a public relations hoax. They claimed the Bank was still ignoring its resettlement guidelines, as well as violating the most basic criteria of environmental assessment. A relatively small project by World Bank standards, Pak Mun was becoming a rallying cry in Thailand for opponents of high-handed technocratic negligence. The dam was to be built in northeast Thailand, near the mouth of the Mun River, the largest tributary of the mighty 4,000-kilometer Mekong. Pak Mun was a 135-megawatt "run of the river" scheme, that is, the dam would create a reservoir no higher than historically recorded maximum flood levels of the river itself. The Bank and EGAT claimed the project would adversely affect the land of no more than 5,000 people, and require the resettlement of about 2,000 at most. The dam would be built in the middle of Kaeng Tana National Park, one of whose main attractions was the spectacular rapids downstream and upstream of the proposed dam. The Bank and EGAT insisted that the dam would not destroy the rapids.

But EGAT's history of withholding information and its high-handed treatment of villagers affected by its projects fostered tensions that prompted growing civil resistance. In March 1991, villagers from the proposed Pak Mun dam and reservoir area presented the World Bank resident representative in Bangkok with a petition of over 12,000 signatures protesting the project. The villagers asserted that EGAT had threatened them with retaliation if they continued to raise objections—not idle talk in a regime established a month before by a military coup.

In early May 1991, EGAT started building the dam, and on May 21 more than 800 villagers gathered near the site to protest the bulldozing of a small shrine in the construction area. Several arrests were made, and Thai authorities asserted that large public gatherings were illegal under martial law. Later that month, protesters rallying against Pak Mun near the dam site were fired upon by unidentified gunmen.[16] Although an environmental assessment of the project had been prepared in the early 1980s, EGAT continued to refuse any public access to the environmental studies, despite several protests by Thai NGOs to the World Bank, and to EGAT itself.

Finally EGAT agreed, on June 19, to allow a major Thai environmental group, the Project for Ecological Recovery, to view the environmental assessment documents (in English) in an EGAT library 500 kilometers from the dam site. But what EGAT granted on one occasion EGAT would refuse two months later: in August, a delegation of villagers affected by the dam traveled to the EGAT head office in vain to try to view for themselves the environmental assessment.[17]

As approval of the World Bank Pak Mun loan became imminent in the autumn of 1991, academics and scientists in Thailand and abroad attacked the assessment as incompetent, but World Bank officials claimed it was a worthy example of sound environmental planning. University of California biologist Walt Rainboth, one of the world's leading experts on the fishes of the Mekong River basin, obtained a copy leaked to U.S. environmental groups by the U.S. Treasury Department. "Although the perception of this report might be as a travesty or caricature," Rainboth wrote, "I suggest it is much more. Based on the importance of the project and the capacity for irreversible damage, the report is *criminal* [emphasis in original]. If something like this were submitted to Congress in order to solicit funds, its fraudulent nature would deserve criminal indictment."[18]

Rainboth, who had spent years studying the Mekong ecosystem, noted that its fish fauna is among the richest in the world, and that the Pak Mun dam would destroy untold identified and unidentified species. He asserted that the preparers of the assessment not only had undertaken grotesquely inadequate studies of the fish in the Mun River, but were so incompetent that they had misidentified the few species for which they did collect samples.[19] Public health organizations and doctors inside and outside Thailand assailed the assessment for greatly underestimating the risks and magnitude of parasitic diseases, particularly schistosomiasis, that might spread with the creation of the dam reservoir.[20] (Schistosomiasis is caused by a liver fluke that has crippled and killed millions in the Third World over the past three decades. It is spread by snails that typically proliferate in large man-made reservoirs in the tropics.) The Bank flatly asserted that the risk would not be greatly increased, and that the project would enhance health precautions.

EGAT and the World Bank had much deeper problems to explain away. According to a study of the Project for Ecological Recovery, twenty-six large irrigation and hydroelectric dams have been built in Thailand since 1957, most with the financial support of the World Bank and other international donors. The same study revealed that the nine major irrigation dams in Thailand have actually provided water to only 42.13 percent of the original planned command area (irrigation area) of the projects. Not a single dam achieved its projected irrigation capacity and targets, the best performance being 69 percent of the target area. Only one of Thailand's numerous major hydroelectric dams has achieved or exceeded its projected power benefits during the past decade. Two of the more notorious World Bank–financed projects, Bhumibol and Sirindhorn, are operating at 66.47 percent and 48.61 percent, respectively, of their targeted electric generating capacity.[21]

Moreover, there had been alternatives to many of these projects. At the People's Forum, a representative of the Washington- and Bangkok-based International Institute for Energy Conservation (IIEC) revealed the results of a recent study conducted by the IIEC under the sponsorship of the U.S. Environmental Protection Agency. Investments in energy conservation and end-use efficiency* could free up over 2,000 megawatts of power in

---

* "End-use efficiency" refers to investments in energy use and consumption that reduce total demand for power while achieving the same goals of industrial production, lighting, heating, etc. The power that is freed up can be supplied to new users and thereby replaces power that otherwise would have to be produced through investments in new generating facilities such as hydroelectric dams and coal-fired plants. In newly industrializing nations

Thailand at a fraction of the cost it would take to build fifteen dams like Pak Mun.[22]

In August 1991, the U.S. Agency for International Development sent a researcher, Mark Rentschler, to Thailand to investigate the Pak Mun controversy. He discovered that the World Bank's own project documents for Pak Mun estimated that the amount of power produced by the dam could be provided at less than a quarter of the cost by energy efficiency and conservation measures. In fact, in 1989 the Thai National Energy Administration prepared an $8-million three-year plan to free up 160 megawatts (26 megawatts more than Pak Mun) by January 1993, almost two years before the scheduled completion of Pak Mun. But the plan did not receive the needed funding, while the World Bank and EGAT prepared a $55-million loan to support Pak Mun and the expansion of heavily polluting lignite-fired power plants in Thailand's north.[23]

Given EGAT's record of technocratic high-handedness and compulsive secrecy, it is no wonder that Pak Mun was the fifth major dam project in three years to be the subject of massive grass-roots protest in Thailand. As a result, the four previous dams were indefinitely postponed: the Nam Choan, Kaeng Krung, Kaeng Sua Ten, and Haew Narok dams. And the Thai activists at the 1991 People's Forum contended that EGAT was only one of numerous Third World offspring of the World Bank, one which the Bank itself claimed was among its better pupils. In Thailand alone, 101 World Bank loans, totaling some $4.374 billion, had fostered the creation and expansion of several powerful, semi-autonomous, state agencies besides EGAT: the Industrial Finance Corporation of Thailand (IFCT), the Thai Board of Investment (BOI), and the National Economic and Social Development Board (NESDB).[24] The first two agencies are among the most important entities promoting and subsidizing industrial development, and the NESDP oversees all public investment planning. Thai NGOs asserted that the World Bank had undermined the already weak representative institutions of the country by setting up agencies acting as surrogate governments,* technocratic autocracies unaccountable to democratic political channels.[25]

As the Thai People's Forum continued on into its second and third days, the focus turned to destructive World Bank–fostered agricultural

---

such as Thailand, the cost per unit of power for such "demand-side" energy investments is often a fraction—one-third or one-quarter—of the cost of new "supply-side" power plants. The World Bank's negligence of end-use efficiency and conservation investments is discussed in more detail in Chapter 6.

* The Thai groups rightly identified one of the more ubiquitous World Bank mechanisms for influencing developing-country economic policies and circumventing democratic institutions. We shall return to this issue in Chapter 2 and Chapter 3.

policies. Over the past thirty years, the activists alleged, the Bank had promoted programs that encouraged the conversion of huge areas of forest into large-scale exploitations for export crops such as sugar cane, palm oil, cassava, rubber, and, of course, timber.* A typical example is the World Bank's lending for the Rubber Replanting Promotion Fund, starting with a loan of $50 million in 1976, continuing with loans of $142 million in 1982 and $60 million in 1986. Through this fund the Thai government provides subsidies for farmers to convert agricultural land, forests, and smaller, traditional rubber estates into large-scale industrial plantations. Starting in the late 1970s, over twelve years the land area of rubber plantations tripled to over 1.7 million hectares, more than 5 percent of the entire land area of the country. Ninety-five percent of the rubber produced is destined for export, of which half goes to Japan.[26] A Moslem farmer from Thailand's south described the impact of the Bank's policy before the People's Forum:

I am so angry about this fund. It promotes the destruction of all kinds of plants. . . . They had been promoting rubber for years, but in 1985 a new government regulation actually forbade farmers to have any other species of tree on land being subsidized by the fund. If they find a mango or jack fruit tree, they charge people about 250 Baht [ten dollars] per tree.[27]

Fishermen and small-scale rice farmers described the destruction of the coastal ecosystems on which their livelihoods depend, promoted by government tax incentives for export-oriented shrimp farming. The large-scale expansion of industrial shrimp farming helped destroy nearly half the country's coastal mangrove forests between 1985 and 1990, devastating fish habitats and causing the salinization of water supplies for rice paddies.[28]

By 1988, some 15 million hectares, nearly half the entire land area of Thailand (totaling 31.7 million hectares) had been allotted to private logging concessions, and another tenth of the country—3.2 million hectares of forest and farmland—had been converted to export crop production.[29] Thailand's forest cover had declined from 53 percent of its area in 1961, to 28 percent in the late 1980s, setting the stage for widespread erosion.[30] In November 1988, heavy rains unleashed unprecedented floods in the south, where so much forest had been destroyed. Hundreds died, and a

---

* One authority on Thai forests, Larry Lohman, writes, "The economic policies promoted by the World Bank in Thailand, in short, could hardly have failed to promote uncontrollable deforestation, no matter how finely they were tuned" (Lohman, "Trees Don't Grow on Money" [see endnote 34], 1). On deforestation, growing social inequity, and the occupation of forests in Thailand and Southeast Asia by vested economic interests, see Gopal B. Thapa and Karl E. Weber, "Actors and Factors of Deforestation in 'Tropical Asia,'" *Environmental Conservation*, vol. 17, no. 1 (Spring 1990), 19–26.

national outcry led the government to proclaim a ban on all logging in January 1989.*

The Great Thai Enclosure

The People's Forum of 1991 portrayed a tremendous economic, social, and ecological transformation through which Thailand's natural resources and entire land area were increasingly organized for intensive exploitation with a heavy bias toward earning export revenue. The physical occupation of so much of the country's land by large-scale development schemes over the past two decades had created millions of landless farmers. Many ended up as urban refugees in Bangkok. An estimated 10 million landless were subsisting on land administered by the Royal Forest Department. Many of them had been evicted from their ancestral lands by dams, logging concessions, and large-scale agricultural and industrial undertakings, as well as by strategic resettlement programs organized by the military in past years against communist insurrections.

It was a process that was profoundly undemocratic, ecologically devastating, and politically regressive. More than one observer compared this transformation of the Thai countryside to the enclosure of half of England's arable land that began in the late Middle Ages.**

There was no better example of the "enclosure" of Thailand's rural lands than a huge scheme that the Thai Royal Forest Department and the military touted as an unprecedented reforestation project to benefit the environment. The goal of the Khor Chor Kor program (the Forest Reserve Agricultural Land Resettlement Project) was to free up huge tracts of land administered by the Royal Forest Department for tree replanting. The first phase focused on Thailand's impoverished, drought-prone northeast, where over 1.25 million people were to be resettled over a five-year period starting in 1991. They would be forcibly evicted from about 1.5 million hectares of land and resettled onto an area only half as large which was already occupied by more than 2 million other poor Thai farmers. The government would transfer the 1.5 million hectares to large-

* However, the ban was difficult to enforce, and some illegal logging continued. Thailand's loggers and military also began to seek forestry concessions in neighboring, more pristine countries such as Burma and Laos.
** The great lords, eager for cash revenue, fenced off huge areas of formerly common grazing and pasture lands, whose customary use was essential for the survival of most of the English yeomanry. The process of enclosure lasted hundreds of years, engendering poverty, uprootedness, and suffering for much of England's population; it forged the urban masses of eighteenth- and nineteenth-century Britain and the human raw material for the Industrial Revolution and the modern English working class.

scale private industrial owners, who would plant and manage eucalyptus plantations to produce paper pulp for export. Thai-Japanese joint ventures and Royal Dutch Shell were among the prospective investors.[31]

The villagers, supported by Thai academics and environmental activists, asserted that with much less expense and human suffering reforestation could be achieved through community forestry programs administered by and belonging to the farmers themselves, using local tree species. Large-scale eucalyptus plantations would be an ecological disaster, they argued, since the fast-growing exogenous trees destroyed soil fertility and depleted water tables in semi-arid regions like the Thai northeast. Furthermore, the eucalyptus monocultures were monotonous and poisonous green deserts, sustaining virtually no biological diversity; the leaves were noxious to most animals, and the hardy, fast-growing trees outcompeted all indigenous species of plants for nutrients and water. Worse, remaining areas of natural forest in the northeast were being illegally logged so they could be replanted with the profitable tree.[32]

In 1990 and 1991, sparks of resistance to the Khor Chor Kor scheme ignited. In the Pa Kham district of Buri Ram province, twelve villages with more than 2,000 families were surrounded in early 1991 by hundreds of soldiers who threatened to burn their houses if they refused to leave. The villagers argued that the Royal Forest Department was actually encouraging illegal logging in 12,000 acres of remaining natural forest in the area, so that the whole region could then be replanted. A local Buddhist monk, Phra Prajak Khuttajitto, led many of the protests. The villagers confronted the illegal loggers in nonviolent standoffs, and under the leadership of Phra Prajak ordained older trees with the saffron robes of the Buddhist priesthood in an attempt to make felling of the old forests literally a sacrilege. In the spring of 1991, Phra Prajak led a special ceremony over a period of months, in which hundreds of villagers encircled the entire Dong Yai forest with a continuous sacred Buddhist string that he had blessed. Through the spring and summer of 1991, there were continual skirmishes between villagers and the army, and Phra Prajak was arrested and released several times.[33]

In September, Phra Prajak was arrested again for leading a group of 400 people in a protest against a military incursion that was attempting to carry out Khor Chor Kor in a nearby village. He was manhandled, and several villagers were beaten by government troops. As the World Bank meeting approached, Phra Prajak went into hiding.

With the Khor Chor Kor program, too, the World Bank, together with other multilateral aid agencies such as the Food and Agriculture Organization of the United Nations (FAO), and the United Nations Development Program (UNDP), played an indirect but Mephistophelean role. The three agencies had generated an ambitious international effort in the late 1980s known as the Tropical Forestry Action Plan (TFAP), originally advertised as a plan to save the world's endangered tropical forests. The TFAP, of which the Thai "Forestry Sector Master Plan" was an offshoot, evolved into an unprecedented scheme to prepare forestry development plans for nearly all developing countries. With international funding, a giant Finnish pulp and forestry consulting company, Jaakko Poyry, was commissioned to prepare the Thai plan. Jaakko Poyry's worldwide experience includes numerous logging, pulp, and eucalyptus-planting schemes in the Brazilian Amazon, Malaysia, Burma, Indonesia, and numerous other countries. A main thrust of the plan's terms of reference (it will not be completed until late 1993) is to focus on expanding forestry production and on increasing Thai forest exports through support for eucalyptus plantations. According to one observer familiar with the plan, it "has suggested an eventual lifting of the 1989 logging ban."[34]

The Economics of the Global Brothel

Indeed, the impassioned and disturbing People's Forum seemed to confirm what the arriving World Bank delegates across town already knew; whether the topic was eucalyptus or prostitution, it all came down to a matter of growth. Thailand's economy had grown faster than that of any other nation on earth in the early 1990s; the country had also had one of the highest increases in prostitution. Speaking before the People's Forum, Nongyao Naowarat, an education professor from Thailand's north, laid out the economics that had transformed Bangkok into the planet's brothel.

Nongyao observed that the model of development promoted by the government and international agencies like the World Bank had increased the gap between rich and poor and deprived the poor of access to the natural resources on which their livelihoods depended. She noted that most of Bangkok's prostitutes came from poor rural families in the country's north and northeast. In the north, 30 percent of the rural population was landless, and another 20 percent of farm families owned less than one rai, two-fifths of an acre. Women working as day laborers on larger farms producing export crops were paid between $1.20 and $1.60 a day; in factories they earned between $.80 and $2.00 a day. Dozens of golf courses and vacation condominiums were being built in the north, many for Japanese businessmen, who found it cheaper to fly to Thailand to play golf over a long weekend than to pay the astronomical membership fees of Japanese golf clubs. Tending grass, working as waitresses, or caddying at golf clubs, a northern woman could earn between $32 and $60 a month. Prostitutes could average between $400 and $800 a month, and the younger, prettier, luckier ones in Bangkok could have several good years averaging over $20,000 annually. "These are the kind of jobs the government has presented to the women of the North. Which of these jobs should they choose?" Nongyao asked.[35]

Development as if People Mattered

Bangkok that week in 1991 was a tale not just of two cities, but of two separate planets. At the official meeting, the 156 governors of the Bank and the Fund—most of the world's finance ministers and central bank presidents—delivered, as in past years, stale canned statements on the need to spur expansion of the international economy and on the year's past events, namely the collapse of the communist world. The earth as seen from the Queen Sirikit Conference Center seemed a strangely featureless, homogeneous surface, where disembodied forces such as debt, adjustment, poverty, and the environment interacted with one another on a global scale; when something bad happened, it was called a trade-off. The only other identifiable actors were states. The fundamental solution to nearly every problem was growth, which, the speakers insisted, had to be sustainable. On this uncanny planet of the finance bureaucrats it was hard to detect individual human beings or communities making decisions or assuming responsibilities, and nonhuman forms of life, though known to predominate on Planet Earth, were strangely invisible.

The earth of the People's Forum seemed to be a different world: much of its land surface was occupied by people whose daily lives were linked to the existence of other species of animals and plants. Their livelihoods often depended on forests, watersheds, river valleys, and wetlands—which were increasingly threatened all over the world. Logically enough, their communities had often (but not always) developed practices that provided economic benefits, albeit on a local, modest scale, while ensuring ecological security. And they were fighting to safeguard this security.

In Thailand, for example, the movement to "ordain" trees and whole forests had spread all over the country; in more and more areas one could see large, old trees encircled by bright-orange monks' robes. Villages in many regions depended on and maintained traditional community forests that provided villagers with a variety of foods and medicinal herbs while protecting water tables and watersheds. One of the most interesting examples was a case study presented by the Project for Ecological Recovery on Thailand's traditional irrigation system, *muang phai* (which literally means "dam, channel".)[36]

In the hill areas of northern Thailand, nearly 80 percent of the rice fields are still being irrigated by *muang phai*. This technology is small in scale and simple: weirs are built of mud, logs, bamboo, and sticks to impede but not block the flow of streams and small rivers; a system of channels brings the water to the rice fields. The weirs are intentionally built to allow a continual flow of water, and of silt and sediment. This feature is a crucial one; small concrete irrigation dams built in the north by the government were actually ripped down in some cases by villagers because they rapidly accelerated the siltation of the irrigation reservoirs and channels behind them by not allowing sediment and sand to flow through.

The most critical features of *muang phai*, however, have little to do with technology and everything with social organization and local management. Each *muang phai* dam has a local user committee, with members responsible for its maintenance. The committee agrees on an equitable sharing of both water and work for upkeep, usually in a written or oral contract which the committee reviews every year. Most important from an ecological standpoint, the *muang phai* committee also assigns responsibilities to its members for the protection of critical upland community forests on the watershed of a given stream. Numerous movements against illegal logging in the north in the late 1980s were led by such *muang phai* community water organizations.

It is in this context that large irrigation schemes, many supported by World Bank loans for large multipurpose dams like Bhumibol and Sirikit, had a disastrous impact on what had been an integrated, sustainable local system for watershed management. Control of water and conservation of watershed forests were taken out of the hands of villagers and entrusted to government agencies, the Thai Royal Irrigation and Royal Forest departments, and to large private undertakings. In some instances, the Irrigation Department, with advice from organizations like the World Bank, tried to recreate "participatory" local water-user committees, since local participation and involvement were viewed as essential for the maintenance of the systems. But such clumsy top-down efforts failed, since it was difficult to interest local farmers in intensive management of resources over which they had lost all control.

The financial cost of this destructive approach to development is immense. The Royal Irrigation Department has been increasing its budget for maintenance every year, and its growing foreign borrowings to finance large dams can only be repaid through increased export earnings, or through further borrowing. Ironically, the *muang phai* committees collect voluntary contributions of both materials and labor from farmers for maintenance, at no cost to the government or to the national economy. In fact, construction and maintenance of the *muang phai* systems is for the most part not monetized or realized in the market economy.

The Bangkok People's Forum ended on Thursday, October 10, 1991, with a call to halt the destruction of the country's ecological stability and to reverse the ongoing economic and social marginalization of millions of Thais. The chairman of the forum, Professor Saneh Chamarik, singled out the World Bank and the IMF: "These agencies must stop thinking only about economic growth numbers because these numbers have destroyed people's lives as well as the environment." He condemned the secrecy of both organizations, and called upon them "to recognize people's basic human right of access to information about projects that will affect their lives." The Thai NGOs called for "development as if people mattered," which would put a priority on decentralized, local management of resources.[37]

The following week hundreds of representatives of nongovernmental groups from more than forty countries attended the continuation of the nongovernmental meetings, the International Forum. Speakers from India, Brazil, Bangladesh, Indonesia, the Philippines, Malaysia, and other developing countries presented more case studies of local resistance, and alternatives to large-scale internationally financed development gone awry.

The Ball of the Nomads

During the official meetings, the world's leading banks and investment firms hosted lavish evening receptions and buffets in Bangkok's luxury hotels, as they had done every year before in Washington, Berlin, and other cities. Many big Japanese and American financial concerns had something in common to commiserate about this year: the growing number of scandals and swindles that had clouded the image of both communities. While Michael Milken was a well-known name,* few had heard of Nui Onoue, an Osaka restaurant owner and spiritualist who had used forged certificates of deposit to obtain over $1.8 billion in loans from the Industrial Bank of Japan (IBJ), the country's most respected

---

* Michael Milken epitomized the "go-go eighties" on Wall Street: he earned $500 million in a single year and led his firm, Drexel Burnham Lambert, to unheard-of profits by virtually inventing and dominating the market for high-interest, high-risk corporate "junk bonds." Milken entered a federal prison on March 3, 1991, to begin serving a ten-year sentence, after having pleaded guilty to six felonies, including insider trading, fraud, and bribery.

financial institution. Onoue, a superstitious sexagenarian, had held seances with stockbrokers in the back of her Osaka tearoom to invoke other-worldly aid in stock picking. She was now in jail.[38]

If there was anyone who was happy to be in Bangkok that October, it was Yoh Kurosawa, IBJ's chief. In September he had spent two weeks hiding in a Tokyo hotel room, after sending his wife and children to Europe to escape a feeding frenzy of Japanese press who had encircled his house in a day-and-night siege, shouting questions about IBJ's losses every time he emerged.[39] The IBJ reception at the Bangkok Hilton International Hotel was one of the more lavish and elegant ones: there was the expected champagne and caviar, but also a string quartet in black tie that played Mozart and Handel.

The biggest scandal, however, had involved many of the institutions represented at Bangkok—including the World Bank—for the most part, but not entirely, unwittingly. Only three months before, banking regulators and bailiffs in more than fifty countries had shut down the Bank of Commerce and Credit International (BCCI), an international bank based in Luxembourg and the Caymen Islands that had perpetrated the greatest financial fraud in world history. BCCI, founded by a charismatic Pakistani con man named Agha Hasan Abedi, had been the world's fastest-growing bank for two decades; its miraculous development was made possible by fraudulently misrepresenting its largely fictitious capital of $20 billion and serving as a money-laundering conduit for, among others, the Medellin Cartel, General Manuel Noriega, the CIA, and the terrorist Abu Nidal. BCCI avoided collapse for so long by relentlessly seeking out new deposits from any source and by any means possible: one of its most important strategies was to bribe finance ministry and central bank officials of developing countries to deposit with it national hard currency reserves; another was to offer high-ranking government officials unrecorded secret accounts for moving capital out of their countries. Before BCCI's collapse, Bangladesh, Barbados, Belize, Cameroon, Guatemala, Mauritania, Nigeria, Saint Kitts and Nevis, Pakistan, Togo, Trinidad, Tunisia, Venezuela, and Zimbabwe had all entrusted some of their hard-earned foreign exchange to the rogue bank, and most of them—along with more than a million other depositors, many of them expatriate Third World workers in the Middle East and Europe—lost most of their money.[40] In the small southern African country of Swaziland, BCCI functioned *as* the central bank.[41]

Winning the confidence of and being associated with the World Bank was a critical element in BCCI's strategy. In fact, one of the main functions of the Washington office of BCCI was to cultivate relations with the Bank—with some success. The World Bank had what *Wall Street Journal* reporter Peter Truell and Washington journalist Larry Gurwin characterized as "a startling number of connections" with BCCI. The official who effectively ran the World Bank from 1988 to early 1991 was its senior vice-president for operations, Moeen Qureshi. BCCI had considered making Qureshi head of First American Bankshares, a Washington-based institution illegally and secretly controlled by BCCI. Just months before the Bangkok meeting, Qureshi's brother had applied for a banking license with BCCI in Pakistan. The vice-president of the World Bank for Latin America, Shahid Husain, according to Truell and Gurwin, "had close connections with Abedi and his crowd and discussed going to work for BCCI with [World Bank] officials," and BCCI directly employed several prominent former Bank executives.[42] The Bank used BCCI as its disbursing agent on occasion in several African countries.[43]*

BCCI would certainly be missed by some of the people at the Bangkok meetings. The last time the Bank and the Fund held their annual extravaganza in a developing country—in Seoul, Korea, in 1985—BCCI officers were indiscreetly handing out cash bribes on the spot to Nigerian Central Bank officials as they made the rounds.[44]

On Tuesday, October 15, 1991, the new head of the World Bank, Lewis Preston, delivered the traditional Bank president's opening address in the imposing grand hall of the Queen Sirikit Conference Center before 2,000 assembled delegates. This was the moment, if any, for which all the efforts of the past twenty months had been expended: the building of a $100-million conference center in record time, the eviction of nearly 2,000 slum dwellers, the unprecedented mobilization of medical teams and security police on twenty-four-hour alert. As befitted an ex-marine and former head of the Morgan Bank, the speech had a straightforward, upbeat tone. Listening to Preston, one realized that one lived in the best of all possible worlds, given the circumstances: the industrial countries were poised for more growth, the world was becoming an integrated global market, progress was being made in managing the debt of the poorer countries, and the fall of the Soviet Empire had led to "the broad convergence of development thinking which has replaced ideological conflict." He suggested that a global consensus—on the need for free markets, sustainable economic growth, and a proper balance between the role of government and the private sector—was enveloping the world.[45]

There were challenges, of course. "The pace and complexity of change

---

* These World Bank associations appear to be purely circumstantial. Many were fooled by BCCI, including Jimmy Carter and Andrew Young, and others were criminally indicted in connection with their association with the rogue bank, like Clark Clifford. There may be much more to uncover about World Bank–BCCI connections in the huge volume of documents that were seized from BCCI offices in Washington and are now dispersed among the U.S. Justice Department, the Federal Reserve, and the New York District Attorney's Office.

have been staggering in the last few years. The competition for capital and markets has increased. Nations of the world have become increasingly interdependent." He pointed out a paradox in this brave, uniform world, where expanding networks of communications and trade collapsed time and space to draw all places and people closer together: the new order engendered strong centrifugal forces within nations, and environmental problems that "have become steadily more urgent."[46]

But for what? And why? Why had all these important people come so far, at such great expense? Why the receptions, the cocktail parties, the canned speeches of the financial rulers of the world? Why did Thailand spend tens of millions of dollars for a three-day event? Why did this exotic and ostentatious bankers' potlatch take place every year? Was it a strange anthropological rite, a convocation of the new, rich global nomads? What to compare it with—the great camel fair at Pushkar in Rajastan, where thousands of livestock merchants and scores of castes from all over India gathered every year in a great ritual that was much more than a market or a meeting? And what was the purpose of this roller-coaster world the World Bank president painted—of growth, competition for capital and markets, integration and centrifugal forces? Why, in fact, had 2,000 slum dwellers been evicted from the Duang Pitak and Klong Paisingto shantytowns across the street in two and a half months? Why were seventy evicted families still living in tents 400 yards from the conference center as Lewis Preston gave his speech?

The World Bank's president told the assembled delegates why: "This morning I want to discuss how we can take advantage of the opportunities and deal with the challenges before us, so that we can make progress toward our ultimate objective—the reduction of poverty." In case anyone had any doubts, he restated the point: "Poverty reduction, to which I personally am fully committed, remains the World Bank Group's overarching objective."[47]

"And how do we plan to realize this objective?" Preston asked. First and foremost, the World Bank "must serve as a strong leader of the worldwide development effort." The Bank would "articulate the interests of developing countries" in countless international meetings and negotiations, and "help coordinate the efforts" of innumerable government agencies and nongovernmental organizations around the world. It would "take into account the interests of the poor so that growth is equitable; environmental aspects so that development is sustainable . . . and the role of women who are vital to the development effort." More concretely, Preston pointed out, the Bank needed more money. And to move more money, "we must speed up our decision making and improve our responsiveness."[48]

This vision—the bureaucratic, institutional memory of the World Bank, regurgitated and articulated by a committee of speechwriters—was giddying. Lewis Preston, Jacques Attali, Yoh Kurosawa, and 15,000 bankers and officials had come to Bangkok to help Auntie Roy, Kusuma Wongsrisuk, and 2 billion other poor all over the planet. And now, Lewis Preston told the representatives of 156 countries, the World Bank needed a lot more money to do it. Not to be outdone, Michel Camdessus, chief of the International Monetary Fund, emphasized in the conclusion of his speech the need for the major industrialized nations to support a $180-billion increase in the lending capital of his institution.

A few hours later, across town, 20,000 Thais peacefully marched, defying the warnings of the military, to protest the eight-month-old dictatorship and to demand a return to democracy.

"If People Mattered . . ."

The next day, Wednesday, October 16, 1991, numerous World Bank delegates departed; many had only stayed two or three days. The Thai government was content; "the meeting" had come off without many hitches, and the country's international image would be enhanced. More than a thousand delegates had availed themselves of the free health services offered by the meeting's organizers. There was only one death: a Turkish banker inadvertently killed himself with a self-administered heroin overdose.

The nongovernmental International Forum also came to an end. Activists from forty-three countries signed a declaration urging the rich nations of the world to reduce their financial contributions to the World Bank and the IMF. The declaration condemned the global development model promoted by the Bank and the Fund as environmentally disastrous, socially inequitable, and economically unsustainable. It reiterated the call of the Thai People's Forum the week before for democratic, locally based development "as if people mattered."

2

Decade of Debacles

The contrast between the official and nongovernmental meetings at Bangkok in October 1991 revealed the contradictions of a planetary social and ecological transformation that is without precedent. This transformation entails nothing less than the final physical occupation and domination of the entire surface of the earth. The processes that had transformed Thailand over the past decade were at work on a larger scale in much of the developing world. Massive internationally financed development schemes were unleashing ecological destruction and social upheaval in areas larger than many American states or European countries. Huge forests had been destroyed, gigantic river basins filled with dams, and vast agricultural expanses consolidated into larger holdings for export production at tremendous ecological cost. What was occurring was not a reasonable, measured process to increase economic welfare, but the destruction of natural and social systems whose endurance are the prerequisite, and the goal, of any sane project for longer term human development.

A large part of the earth's land surface had become a global battlefield where millions of species were being exterminated and tens upon tens of millions of the world's poorest people were being involuntarily uprooted and resettled. Ongoing World Bank projects were forcibly resettling more than one and a half million people worldwide, and projects in preparation would displace at least another million and a half people—appalling figures, given the Bank's poor record in dealing with resettlement. In India alone, officially sponsored development projects had evicted more than 20 million poor from their lands and homes, mostly without compensation, since independence in 1947—2.5 percent of the current population. Increasingly, the displaced and the uprooted were protesting, actors in a larger planetary drama in which the World Bank was a leading protagonist.

The presentations of nongovernmental groups in Bangkok only scratched the surface of what had been a decade of development debacles. To begin to understand the dynamics of what was happening on a global scale, it is worth examining in more detail just a few of these schemes that proceeded simultaneously on different continents. Their common denominator: the World Bank.

The Highway of Death

> Ladies and gentlemen, I am a seringueiro [rubber tapper] from Amazonas. I am here to speak about the tropical forest. The Amazon forest is being brutally destroyed by large projects, financed by foreign banks, and planned by Brazilian interests that do not take into account the living beings in the forest, projects that take away their right to life.[1] —Jaime da Silva Araújo

The annual World Bank meeting happened to take place every year at the height of the "burning season" in Brazil's Amazon forest, the dry period that lasts from July to November. In a single week in September 1991, Brazil's National Institute for Space Research, known by its Portuguese acronym as INPE, identified 88,414 separate fires in the region. INPE estimated that the fires spewed 6 to 12 million tons of ash into the atmosphere; the air over several Amazon cities was more polluted than that of the dirtiest industrial areas of Brazil, in São Paulo state. In what was still one of the largest wilderness areas on earth, airports had to be repeatedly closed because of the thick haze, and hospitals were crowded with sufferers from respiratory illnesses.[2]

Although by the early 1990s deforestation in the Brazilian Amazon had declined to half its 1980s rate (between 1978 and 1988 an incredible 22,000 square kilometers annually, equivalent to razing a forest the size of Massachusetts every twelve months), it is still an environmental and social tragedy of global dimensions.[3] (The rate could rapidly increase again since the recent decline, according to Brazilian government scientist Philip M. Fearnside, "has mostly been due to Brazil's economic crisis rather than to any policy changes.")[4] All through the 1980s and early 1990s deforestation was most intense in two regions: in Brazil's northwest, including both the state of Rondônia and northern Mato Grosso state, and in the southeastern Amazon rainforest, in Pará state. It was no coincidence that these regions were almost precisely the areas of influence of two gigantic World Bank infrastructure projects: Polonoroeste and Carajás. The first was a road-building and agricultural colonization

scheme, the second a mining development and railroad construction project. Together they catalyzed an unprecedented ecological and human
calamity that was continuing even after Bank loan disbursements were
completed.[5]

Between 1981 and 1983 the World Bank lent $443.4 million to Brazil
for the Northwest Region Development Program, known by its Brazilian
name as Polonoroeste (northwest pole). More than half of these loans
financed the paving of Brazilian national highway number 364 (BR-364),
a 1,500-kilometer dirt track that connected Brazil's populous south central region with the rainforest wilderness in the northwest. Most of the
rest of the money went for the construction of feeder and access roads at
the frontier end of the highway, and for the establishment of thirty-nine
rural settlement centers to consolidate and attract tens of thousands of
settlers. The plan was to support settlers in raising tree crops for export,
mainly cocoa and coffee. Over 10,000 Amerindians belonging to more
than forty tribal groups were thought to live in the area; in 1980, parts of
the region were so isolated and pristine that there remained several tribes
who had no contact with the outside world.

Although previous tropical forest colonization schemes in the Amazon
had a record of unmitigated disaster, the World Bank plunged into
Polonoroeste with reckless hubris.* The Bank justified its support for the
scheme with a questionable rationale: it argued that migration into the
region had been increasing in the late 1970s, and that its intervention
would make the colonization sustainable.

But once the project was underway, so many colonists migrated in such
a short time—nearly half a million between 1981 and 1986—that the
Brazilian land colonization agency, INCRA, was totally overwhelmed in its
efforts to provide them with legal title to parcels of land. Agricultural
extension services and credit that were supposed to support the colonists
in raising tree crops for the most part never materialized. To survive, settlers burned the forest and then tried to grow annual crops such as beans,
rice, and maize. But the nutrients from the ashes were soon exhausted,
and the crops failed after a year or two on the poor, exposed soils, forcing

* For example, in 1973 a study of twenty-four tropical agricultural colonization projects in
Latin America noted that "few spheres of economic development have a history of, or a reputation for, failure to match that of government-sponsored colonization in humid tropical
zones. . . . Horror stories abound about expensive ventures that resulted in colonies where
few if any settlers remained after several years. The evidence is irrefutable" (Michael A. Nel-
son, *The Development of Tropical Lands: Policy Issues in Latin America* [Washington: Johns
Hopkins University Press, 1973], 265). The study urged a moratorium on new colonization
schemes in tropical forests, and concluded that the support of international financing agencies for government-sponsored agricultural colonization made things worse, not better, by
further complicating the "execution of [already] overly complex projects" (ibid., 287).

the colonists to move on. Lucky ones made a small profit by selling the land to larger landowners for cattle ranching (a use which past experience in the Amazon has shown to be unsustainable after several years), who in turn benefited from subsidies granted by the Brazilian government for ranching in the rainforest. Sometimes the land changed hands several times, in a real estate bubble prompted in part by the hoped-for development that proximity to the World Bank–financed highway would generate. But the speculative craze was above all based on a national obsession with land as a refuge against Brazil's constantly devaluing currency, and an optimistic if irrational faith in still greater fools who would be coming down BR-364.

Polonoroeste transformed Rondônia—an area approximately the size of Oregon or Great Britain—into a region with one of the highest rates of forest destruction in the Brazilian Amazon, increasing its deforested area from 1.7 percent in 1978 to 16.1 percent in 1991.[6] By the mid-1980s, the burning of Rondônia's forests became a major focus of NASA research as the single largest, most rapid human-caused change on earth readily visible from space.

Life-threatening diseases ravaged the settlers and the indigenous population. The incidence of malaria approached 100 percent in some areas, and more than 250,000 people were infected. Some Indian tribes were menaced with physical extermination from measles and influenza epidemics, and infant mortality rates of 50 and 25 percent were reported in two recently contacted tribes.[7] A 1987 World Bank report on the situation of indigenous peoples in Rondônia, leaked to the Brazilian press, cited systematic pillaging of Indian lands, widespread corruption and fraud in the government Indian protection agency, FUNAI, and rampant epidemics of tuberculosis, measles and malaria in the indigenous areas.[8] To date (1993), many of the recognized Indian areas in the Polonoroeste area of influence have never received full physical protection.

In the late 1980s, more and more failed settlers began to return to the populated urban centers of south central Brazil, carrying a highly resistant and lethal form of malaria that spread to the poor *favelas* (shantytowns) that ringed Brazilian cities. The ill-fated colonization scheme had created a public health nightmare that was spreading all over Brazil. Something had to be done quickly. In 1989, the World Bank approved a $99-million loan to support a $200-million emergency project to deal with the malaria epidemic in the Amazon, most of which was focused on Rondônia. The Bank loan would help finance the spraying of 3,000 tons of DDT (banned in the United States and most other industrialized countries) in houses and buildings in the Amazon region to control *Anopheles* mosquitos, while Brazilian health officials attempted to devise a longer-term strategy.[9]

An increase in murders, death threats, and assaults was another impact of the accelerated "development" of northwest Brazil, catalyzed by the paving of BR–364, as land conflicts between rubber tappers, indigenous tribes, cattle ranchers, and colonists were played out in increasingly brutal terms. This contributed to growing rural violence all over the Amazon, where more than a thousand rural labor organizers, small-scale farmers, and activists for indigenous rights were killed during the 1980s. The highly publicized assassination of Chico Mendes in late 1988 is only the best known.

Pig Iron

At the other end of the Amazon basin, in southeastern Pará state, deforestation proceeded on an even greater scale than in Rondônia during the 1980s. By late 1990, about 150,000 square kilometers were deforested in a gigantic region known as the area of influence of the Greater Carajás Program. More than three-quarters of this destruction took place on either side of a 780-kilometer railway financed by the World Bank in 1982. The Bank lent $304.5 million to the Brazilian state mining company Companhia Vale do Rio Doce (CVRD) to build the railroad from the world's largest reserves of high-grade iron ore to the sea. Besides the railroad, the World Bank project supported the development of the Carajás iron ore mine at one end, and the construction of a deepwater seaport at São Luis, the terminus of the railroad. The World Bank initially touted the Carajás Iron Ore Project as an environmental model, since the Bank's loan agreement called for sound ecological management ("due regard to ecological and environmental factors") around the mine, as well as in a corridor of 100 kilometers on either side of the railroad. It included provisions to protect the environment in the heavily forested project area, as well as a "Special Project" to protect the more than 10,000 Indians in twenty-three groups who live in the area of influence of the mine and the railroad. The total cost of the project was over $3 billion. The World Bank required other international financing as a loan condition, and helped negotiate loans from other sources, including $600 million from the European Community and $450 million from Japan.

These huge infrastructure investments catalyzed an uncontrolled development rush into the region, with exponential expansion of cattle ranching, logging, shifting cultivation, and gold mining.[10] As deforestation and social chaos engulfed the greater Carajás area, CVRD carried out environmental research and the reclamation of degraded lands in the immediate vicinity of the mine, creating an environmental Potemkin Village in the heart of a broader ecological disaster for which it shared prime responsibility.

Once the mine, the railroad, and the port were near completion, the Greater Carajás Program proceeded with an ecological threat of still greater proportions: the proposed licensing and construction by private companies of thirty-four charcoal-burning industrial projects along the railway corridor, which would require 3 million tons of charcoal, or 14 million tons of wood a year for fuel. Most of these projects would produce pig iron for export; others would manufacture manganese and other alloys, and cement. Although in theory large eucalyptus plantations were to supply the charcoal, in practice huge areas of remaining tropical forest would be the fuel source. Many of the indigenous reserves in the project area (which were supposed to have been protected in the Special Project) have large areas of standing forest and are already partially occupied by desperately poor peasants. As the smelters went into operation, they threatened to degrade and destroy these forested Indian lands, as well as other remaining forest reserves, by attracting into them an army of small-scale charcoal producers desperate for income. By 1987, six of the industrial projects were already established, four of them pig-iron smelters; if all thirty-four were to be carried out, they would result in the deforestation of 1,500 square kilometers a year. At this rate, in ten years an area larger than Wisconsin would be denuded. The thirty-four projects were a model of economic folly and short-sighted rapacity: they could not exist without massive tax incentives, they used the native tropical forest as a free source of charcoal, and together they would exhaust this fuel source in as few as a dozen years.

Some charged that in Carajás the World Bank was a prime accomplice in a major international environmental crime. Was it? In August 1987, twenty-nine environmental and indigenous rights organizations from around the world, including ten Brazilian organizations, sent a letter to World Bank President Barber Conable calling upon the Bank to use its influence to halt the charcoal-fueled industrial schemes.[11] The Bank's response appeared to express concern but impotence: the World Bank was worried about the problem, the Bank's country director for Brazil replied, but he insisted that it had no control over the licensing of the huge smelting projects.[12] The director pointed out that it was not the Bank's borrower, CVRD, that licensed the charcoal-fueled projects but rather the Greater Carajás Program itself, over which the Bank, he asserted, had no leverage. As the devastation increased, the Bank insisted more and more strongly that the CVRD Carajás Iron Ore Project, which it financed, was environmentally sound, but that unfortunately the Greater Carajás Program, which covered a gigantic area of 895,000 square kilometers, was out of control. The Bank's contribution to a solution would be to give a little more money to CVRD to prepare a study on alternative fuel sources for the pig-iron smelters.

In fact, the Bank's responsibility was central, since it funded the basic infrastructure (the mine, the railroad, and the deep-water port), for the process of devastation that followed.[13] Its borrower, CVRD, had a monopoly on the iron ore supplies for the smelters, and also owned and operated the railroad the projects were to use. Each of the thirty-four charcoal-fueled industrial projects could go forward only with CVRD's approval of contracts for the sale of iron ore and the use of its railroad and seaport facilities. Many of these projects were within the legal area of influence of the World Bank loan—100 kilometers on either side of the railway—and the Bank would have been within its legal rights if it had obliged CVRD not to sell its iron ore or the services of the railway to the charcoal-fired smelters. The CVRD company was a co-owner of three of these smelters. Scientists in Brazil also warned Bank officials as early as 1982 of government plans for the smelters, but the Bank proceeded regardless.[14]

The World Bank's refusal to take actions against CVRD, such as halting remaining loan disbursements, was particularly negligent given that on April 7, 1987 (six months before the Bank's Brazil country director claimed that the Bank and CVRD had no leverage over the situation), the CVRD environmental superintendent wrote the company's management that

CVRD's responsibility is greatly increased by the fact that the company holds a monopoly on the minerals and rail transport. Any metals industry in the region can only exist with the support of CVRD. . . . It will be difficult for the company to defend itself from the accusation of being the principal agent responsible for the devastation of the tropical forests in its area of influence.[15]

By spring 1988, the Bank had made the last disbursements for its Carajás loan, and it added a new argument for its environmental inaction: the issue of CVRD's role was moot since in any case the Bank no longer had any financial leverage. This too, was disingenuous: CVRD and the Greater Carajás Interministerial Council, which granted the licenses for the smelting projects, were both entities of the Brazilian federal government. There remained numerous other mechanisms—particularly the prospect of other loans and the Bank's so-called policy dialogue with the government—through which it could ensure that the unfulfilled conditions of the Carajás Iron Ore Project would be met.

And indeed, just as in Polonoroeste, the situation was a shambles: besides the massive deforestation in the region, the Special Project for the protection of Indian lands was a failure. In early 1989, only twelve of twenty-five Indian landholdings that were to have been demarcated were fully guaranteed legally, and most of the Indian territory was subject to constant invasions from loggers, miners, cattle ranchers, and agricultural colonists. But through 1988 and 1989 the Bank continued to refuse to take meaningful action.

In May 1989, the European Parliament adopted by a large majority a resolution expressing concern at the disastrous impact of the Bank-financed Carajás Iron Ore Project on the environment and on numerous Indian communities. The resolution also condemned the role of the European Commission and the European Coal and Steel Community (the part of the commission which, with encouragement from the World Bank, extended a $600-million loan to CVRD) "for their extremely irresponsible attitude in not taking into account the direct and indirect environmental effects of the Carajas iron-mining project and the crucial role of this project in the Grande Carajas Program."[16]

A subsequent, January 1990 report of the European Parliament recommended a boycott of the European Community against iron ore imports from Carajás. It noted that much of CVRD's $60-million environmental budget—touted by the Bank as a model effort—was spent on public relations and on high-visibility gestures such as the establishment of a botanic garden and wildlife park near the CVRD company town, to the neglect of comprehensive environmental protection and education in the project's larger area of influence. The report condemned the European Commission for relying totally on the World Bank for environmental monitoring of the use of its funds in the Carajás Iron Ore Project, and asserted that the Bank's record showed it could not be trusted to ensure environmental quality.[17]

The European Commission ignored the May 1989 resolution of the European Parliament, as well as subsequent protests and recommendations. Carajás became another disturbing case study in the lack of accountability for foreign assistance channeled through multilateral institutions. Both the Bank and the European Commission had demonstrated their unparalleled capacity to catalyze ecological destruction, and their impotence and irresponsibility in taking measures well within their mandates to halt it.

While the Bank and the European Commission fiddled as the forests of Carajás burned, Brazilian nongovernmental groups desperately fought to stop the thirty-four charcoal-fueled industrial projects. In October 1988, Brazilian public interest lawyers, representing seventeen Brazilian NGOs, initiated a legal action against the government, maintaining that the twenty-one charcoal-burning projects that had been licensed were in flagrant violation of Brazilian environmental assessment and forestry laws.

The groups obtained an initial court ruling in their favor, and the case was referred to the state courts of Pará and Maranhão for further action. It was mainly the pressure of Brazilian public interest advocates, and the threat of the Brazilian environment secretary, José Lutzenberger, to resign, that finally spurred the Brazilian government to withdraw, in September 1990, financial and tax subsidies for twenty-one of the Carajás projects that had already been approved. This action, combined with declining pig iron prices, temporarily removed the economic incentive to complete the ones that had not yet been built. Nevertheless, in 1993 four completed smelters were continuing to operate, and it is feared that a recovery in pig iron prices could resurrect government plans for the others.[18]

The Fourth World

Statistics and bureaucratic accounts of World Bank and European Community machinations hardly do justice to what one might call the developmental impact of Carajás, that is, its impact on people.[19] Let us recall Lewis Preston's 1991 Bangkok speech, which echoed scores of other addresses of World Bank presidents over the past twenty years: the Bank's ultimate and overreaching objective was reducing poverty. So how are the poor faring in the Carajás Iron Ore Project?

Along the CVRD railway, 160 kilometers from its western terminus and in the heart of the World Bank project area, is a town called Marabá. Thanks to the Carajás Iron Ore Project and the railway it financed, Marabá was Brazil's fastest growing town in the 1980s, increasing from 60,000 to 260,000 people. The slum dwellers of Bangkok inhabit a paradise by Marabá standards. Let us summarize a report of the Brazilian Catholic church's Grass Roots Educational Movement (or MEB, as it is known by its Brazilian acronym), as described in a 1990 special issue of the *National Catholic Reporter*: Seventy percent of Marabá adults are illiterate, completely or functionally, and 25,000 children have no schools. More than 60 percent of the houses are without running water, and less than a third have electricity—although the town is adjacent to the giant Tucuruí hydroelectric dam, which a 1985 World Bank Brazil Power Sector loan helped to complete in its very final stages. The sources of the city's water are contaminated with mercury used in gold mining. Hepatitis, typhoid fever, and various intestinal infections are rampant, and in 1989 the city had 6,000 cases of malaria and 7,500 people were suffering from either tuberculosis or leprosy. East of the city, forests are being cut to fuel cast-iron mills and the two pig-iron smelters that have been built in the city. CVRD is co-owner of one of them. The city is full of prostitutes and violent crime. South of Marabá and the railroad is the diocese of Conçeicão do Araguaia, which has the highest number of violent deaths from land conflicts in the Amazon region.

Less than 200 kilometers to the west is the company town of CVRD. Here, some 2,000 employees inhabit American-suburb-style homes. They have swimming clubs, a zoo, a modern clinic, and live in a special "ecological zone" surrounded by armed security guards.

The *National Catholic Reporter* concludes that

for the MEB team, the Fourth World situation of Marabá is the result, intensified by violent and corrupt local politicians, of the federal government's plans to "develop" the Amazon. The priority of the modern dams, factories and mines is to satisfy Brazilian and foreign investors, and few profits are plowed back into the region. The Amazon exports raw materials and imports ecological problems.[20]

Transmigration

Brazil is not the only place where the World Bank sponsored gigantic agricultural resettlement schemes in pristine rainforests. Between 1976 and 1986, the Bank lent $630 million* to support the most ambitious resettlement project on earth—Indonesia Transmigration.[21] The project's goal was simple: to move millions of poor Indonesians from the country's densely populated inner islands—Java, Lombok, Bali, and Madura—to the outer islands, principally Kalimantan (Borneo), Irian Jaya (Indonesian New Guinea), and Sumatra. Indonesia's outer islands contain 10 percent of the world's remaining rainforests and are inhabited mainly by non-Javanese indigenous tribes. Indonesia Transmigration shared many analogies with Polonoroeste: the resettlement was supposed to be voluntary, and the settlers, at least in the later projects, were to receive agricultural support and extension services, mainly to grow tree crops such as cacao, coffee, and palm oil for export. The $630 million in World Bank loans attracted tens of millions of dollars in further support from numerous other bilateral and multilateral aid sources such as the German, Dutch, and U.S. governments and the Asian Development Bank, United Nations Development Program, and World Food Program. Through 1983, an additional $734 million in World Bank agricultural loans for so-called nucleus estate projects,** supported, in part, additional resettlement in pristine tropical rainforest.[22]

---

* Approximately $130 million of these loans were subsequently canceled, reducing total Bank funding to about $500 million.
** In subsequent years, $227 million of these loans were never disbursed or were canceled, reducing the total loan commitments for "nucleus estates" to about $507 million. Typically,

The Bank claimed that the goals of Indonesia Transmigration were to alleviate population pressure and unemployment on Java and the other inner islands, and simultaneously promote the economic development of the receiving areas. And indeed, Java—with a population of 105 million in an area the size of New York State—is one of the most densely populated places on earth. Yet environmental and human rights critics both outside and inside Indonesia alleged that the project was a developmental fraud whose main goal was geopolitical. Indonesia, ruled by General Suharto since 1967, was a corrupt military dictatorship where 90 percent of the land area was inhabited by a largely non-Javanese and therefore politically unreliable population. In Irian Jaya, local tribespeople had been waging a guerrilla insurrection for twenty years against the 1969 Indonesian annexation of this western half of New Guinea, which its inhabitants call West Papua. Indonesia Transmigration was General Suharto's Star Wars,* the country's number-one national security priority.[23]

In terms of economically efficient, rational development, the scheme appeared to make little sense. The average cost of resettling a family in the mid-1980s, according to the World Bank's own figures, was approximately $7,000, about thirteen times the per capita income of most poor families in the inner islands.[24] The soils in the outer islands in most of the prospective receiving areas are among the poorest on earth, considerably worse on average than those of the Brazilian state of Rondônia. Indigenous tribal peoples claimed customary rights to many of the prospective resettlement sites in Irian Jaya and Kalimantan.

One thing was certain: World Bank participation in the scheme helped catalyze an almost exponential increase in its scale. From 1950 through 1974, the Indonesian government resettled 664,000 people through Transmigration. With World Bank support, over the next decade and a half nearly 3.5 million people were moved, and another 3 to 3.5 million migrated on their own, spurred and induced by official publicity but without direct government support (these were called "spontaneous transmi-

---

these projects involved planting new areas with cash crops—most often oil palms or rubber—with the plan that the land (80 percent of the project area) surrounding a government or privately owned "nucleus" would eventually be transferred to small-scale farmers. In many cases farmers never got the land.

* Robert NcNamara was president of the World Bank when it began to support Transmigration. According to his biographer, Deborah Shapley, "McNamara knew that Suharto's resettlement program was politically inspired and entailed some brutality, but the role McNamara had carved out . . . of making the Bank 'of' the Third World—and his everlasting zest for action—propelled him to buy the program. To influence it, he hoped. General Suharto needed the Bank's Good Housekeeping seal of approval to win international respectability" (Shapley, *Promise and Power: The Life and Times of Robert McNamara* [Boston: Little, Brown and Company, 1993], 537).

grants"). World Bank Transmigration and "nucleus estate" loans went directly to resettle 71,000 families, or about 355,000 people, in Sumatra and Kalimantan. More critically, Bank loans financed the planning and site selection for the resettlement of 400,000 families, or at least 2 million additional people. In total, the World Bank can take credit for assisting in the "official" resettlement of 2.3 million people, and for catalyzing the resettlement of at least 2 million more "spontaneous" migrants.[25]

Indonesia Transmigration left a legacy of environmental ruin. World Bank documents suggest that since the beginning of its own involvement, in the late 1970s, the program has cleared between 15,000 and 20,000 square kilometers of forest. In reality, the area is probably at least 40,000 to 50,000 square kilometers, representing over 4 percent of the forested area of Indonesia and .3 percent of the remaining tropical forests on earth.[26] A 1989 Indonesian government study indicated that sponsored and unsponsored resettlement in Indonesia's mangrove forests and swamps—the most extensive in the world—had converted about 35,000 square kilometers of wetlands alone.[27] A later World Bank study estimated that in the late 1980s deforestation in Indonesia was proceeding at a rate of roughly 10,000 square kilometers a year; one-quarter of this was caused by development projects, both public and private, and half by conversion of forests in the outer islands for agriculture, of which by far the most important cause was Transmigration.[28] (The remaining deforestation resulted from logging and fires.)

The social and developmental record of Indonesia Transmigration is equally dismal. By the late 1980s it had become abundantly clear that the scheme had made millions of poor people worse off. Resettlement sites in cleared mangrove forests and wetlands were beset by environmental calamities of biblical dimensions: acidic peat soils, flooding, paltry agricultural yields, and plagues of insects, rats, and wild boars. And these problems were compounded by the results of totally inadequate planning, such as poor access to markets. As in Polonoroeste in Brazil, promised agricultural extension services and inputs failed to materialize, and many people ended up trying to practice subsistence agriculture on some of the poorest soils on earth, garnering occasional cash income in the growing slum cities of the outer islands. In wetland and swamp areas, 40 to 50 percent of the settlers simply abandoned the sites.[29]

By 1986, the World Bank's own review of Indonesia Transmigration indicated that 50 percent of the households living on project resettlement sites were living below the poverty level*—estimated at the time as an

* The Bank argues that since the transmigrants are drawn from the poorer segments of the population, they are on the whole better off because 50 percent are now above the poverty line. (World Bank, *Indonesia Transmigration Sector Review* [see endnote 21], xiv–xv.)

income of $540 per year—and 20 percent were living below the subsistence level.[30] This was an astounding result, given that the average cost of installing a household, if given as a handout, would have kept a household above the poverty level for at least thirteen years. In the late 1980s, a French survey revealed that 80 percent of Indonesia Transmigration sites failed in terms of improving the living standards of their inhabitants.[31]

The most distressing situation was in Irian Jaya, where part of the World Bank Transmigration V loan planned and identified relocation sites for at least 15,000 families, or more than 75,000 people. For each "sponsored transmigrant," the government hoped to attract an equal number of "spontaneous" settlers, and by 1990 more than 300,000 Javanese had moved to Irian.[32] Irian Jaya is one of the world's great reservoirs of biological and cultural diversity. Most of its 417,000 square kilometers is pristine rainforest and wetlands, and of its 1.2 million inhabitants, 800,000 are tribal Melanesians, speaking at least 224 distinct languages. Here, critics argued, Indonesia Transmigration was little more than a strategic military program to "Javanize" an ethnically and politically unreliable province in which a guerrilla insurrection had festered ever since the Indonesians annexed it from the Dutch in 1969. Many of the resettlement sites were near the border with Papua New Guinea—a rather suspicious placement, given that this was precisely the area where the Free West Papua Movement, the OPM, focused its activities, using the hinterland in Papua New Guinea as a safe refuge from Indonesian troops.[33]

Irian Jaya's cities—Merauke and Jayapura—filled with refugees from the failed resettlement sites. Only a third of Merauke's inhabitants were Irianese, and many among the swollen, ex-transmigrant population had turned to the occupations of the poor in Java—prostitution and the scavenging of tobacco from discarded cigarette butts. Indonesia Transmigration was evicting the Irianese from their land, and violent conflicts erupted. At a site called Arso IV in the north, local Irianese massacred thirteen settlers and wounded many others in an incident in 1988, and further assaults and killings took place at two other resettlement sites (Arso I and II) in 1989.[34]

Through the 1980s, numerous nongovernmental groups around the world called upon the World Bank and other development agencies to halt their support for Transmigration. Indeed, Indonesia's growing network of nongovernmental groups was particularly courageous in publicly calling upon the Bank to at least reconsider its approach to the program, and to focus future funding on rehabilitation of existing settlement sites rather than promoting their expansion. This was not an easy position, given the Indonesian's military regime's focus on Transmigration as a national security priority.

In the late 1980s, the World Bank changed its priorities along the lines of what many Indonesian and international NGOs had suggested. This change was belated; already, in 1985, a study prepared by Indonesia's environment, forestry, and interior ministries in collaboration with the London-based International Institute for Environment and Development had concluded that the economic and ecological collapse of existing Indonesia Transmigration sites was so widespread that it posed a potential threat to national security through social and political unrest. The study estimated that 300,000 people were living in collapsing resettlement sites.[35] The World Bank's response was to approve in 1985 the $160-million Transmigration V loan to identify and select new resettlement areas for another 300,000 families, or 1.5 million people—although these ambitious targets were later greatly reduced, and the Bank belatedly reprogrammed part of the loan to shore up existing sites in lieu of planning for new ones. In the early 1990s the Bank embarked on a new strategy to support "Second-Stage Transmigration." "Second-stage" projects will continue to try to salvage already existing resettlement sites in former forests and swamplands, where hundreds of thousands of hapless colonists are threatened by the ecological and economic collapse of a scheme that from the beginning was environmental folly.

Meanwhile, more and more evidence came in on the failure of Transmigration. In autumn of 1991, the Indonesian Journalists Association held a seminar in Jakarta, where Indonesian academics concurred on the debacle: the project had redistributed rather than alleviated poverty, at an enormous cost—30 to 40 percent of the entire economic development budget of the outer islands in some years—and with widespread environmental destruction and social conflict as a bonus.[36]

The Inferno

Singrauli, the "energy capital" of India, stinks. It stinks of human degradation and it stinks of the negligence of the Indian Government and the World Bank which have together created an environment described here as the lower circle of Dante's Inferno.[37]
—Shahnaz Anklesaria Aiyar, Indian journalist

Have any of them ever had the experience of being thrown out of a comfortable house and existence and reduced to impoverishment? Have they ever had to see any of their children subsisting in hovels and slums?[38]
—Nirendra Nirau, Indian journalist

The early 1990s saw the demise of Cold War geopolitics. The Second World ceased to exist, and the countries of the former Third World were increasingly differentiated in terms of income and economic growth. But what the Catholic church in Brazil called the Fourth World—the global netherworld of increasingly marginalized, impoverished refugees *created* by massive development programs—was growing. And nowhere more than in India.

Ninety miles south of India's holiest city, Varanasi, is Singrauli, the site of one of the Third World's most ambitious energy development programs. There are five giant coal-fired power plants at Singrauli, with six more planned, as well as twelve huge open-pit coal mines. One of the mines is the second largest in Asia. Together, the power plants, if they all are completed, will be one of the largest sources of greenhouse gas emissions on earth. Most of the power plants and some of the coal mines have been financed by international aid agencies, with the World Bank in the lead. Singrauli is also the site of more than 300,000 displaced people, some of whom have been forcibly resettled without compensation four or five times over the past twenty-five years.

Up to thirty years ago, the area was not pristine, but it was nevertheless ecologically rich: rich tropical forests remained—habitat for tigers, wild boar, bears, deer, and a wide variety of other fauna. Hundreds of thousands of villagers, mainly tribal people, practiced a traditional subsistence-oriented agriculture. In the early 1960s their misfortunes began. In 1962, independent India's first prime minister, Jawaharlal Nehru, inaugurated the Rihand dam, one of the major projects which Nehru vowed would be "the temples of modern India."* He envisaged intensive industrial development for the Singrauli region, which would turn it into "a Switzerland." Indeed, huge coal deposits were developed in the 1970s, and the dam's reservoir created an ideal cooling source for the gigantic coal-fired power plants that were built around it. Roads and railway lines were constructed to facilitate the movement of coal, and a number of energy-intensive industrial developments—an aluminum smelter, a chemical plant, a cement plant, etc.—were constructed.

The World Bank was a lead investor, beginning in 1977 to commit four loans totaling $850 million for the construction of the Singrauli

* Nehru made this oft-cited observation first in 1954 at the inauguration of the Nangal canal in Punjab, part of the large Bhakra dam and irrigation project: "When I walked around the site, I thought that these days, the biggest temple and mosque and gurdwara is the place where man works for the good of mankind. What place can be greater than Bhakra Nangal, where thousands of men have worked or shed their blood and sweat and laid down their lives as well? Where can be a holier place than this; which we can regard as higher?" (Quote from Darryl D'Monte, *Temples or Tombs? Industry Versus Environment: Three Controversies* [New Delhi: Center for Science and Environment, 1985], 1.)

Super Thermal Power Plant, for the development of a huge open-pit coal mine called Dudhichua, and for electric transmission lines. Bank participation in Singrauli helped attract billions in loans and grants from Germany, the United Kingdom, Japan, and France for the construction of other power plants and industrial facilities. Even the Soviet Union financed a power plant, adjacent to the World Bank project.

But the planners and financiers of what Nehru called the Switzerland of India forgot two things: the people who lived there and the very existence of the land, air, and water except as abstract industrial inputs. The obliviousness was almost metaphysical: the builders and financiers of Singrauli never really had to see it or live in it; for them it was an empty, fungible space, distinguished only by conveniently located supplies of coal and water. To see Singrauli today is to witness a nihilistic negation of nature and humankind.

Incredibly, with billions of dollars of investment in foreign aid, the situation of many of the hundreds of thousands of the local inhabitants has degenerated from traditional poverty in what was a society based on subsistence agriculture thirty years ago to absolute destitution. Each time they were forced to move without compensation or rehabilitation they became poorer. Enormous quantities of coal dust and ash pollute the air. Eight cement plants and thousands of stone crushers release over a thousand tons of cement and rock dust daily into the atmosphere. The five thermal coal plants belch out huge quantities of sulfur dioxide—none are equipped with scrubbers—and emit over 1,650 pounds of mercury a year into the atmosphere. The Rihand dam reservoir and the land around it are poisoned by dangerous concentrations of mercury, fluorine, and chromium, and as a result the crops and fish that the half-million people in the Singrauli area consume are in many cases unfit for human consumption. The productivity of the land has been destroyed, the once drinkable groundwater is contaminated, and 70,000 contract laborers now work in semi-slave conditions under corrupt labor contractors for 8 to 10 rupees (65–80 cents in the late 1980s) a day in the coal mines and construction sites.

Many of the displaced live in unspeakable hovels and shacks on the fringes of the huge infrastructure projects in the area, including the World Bank–financed power plant and coal mine. Some are living in makeshift hovels *inside* the open-pit coal mines. The World Bank projects directly resulted in the forcible resettlement without economic rehabilitation of 23,000 people. The leading cause of death is tuberculosis, followed by chloroquine-resistant malaria.

It is true that in this huge scheme the Bank was only one aid donor among many, but its lead role was critical in catalyzing the support of others for the projects, and it could have been critical in funding any possible future remedial measures. It is also true that the Indian government, and its borrowing agencies in Singrauli, the National Thermal Power Corporation (NTPC) and Northern Coal Limited, were first and foremost responsible for the debacle. But the World Bank had played a key role in shaping the development of these agencies over previous years, particularly NTPC, which, in the decade after its creation in 1975 borrowed more money— over $2.6 billion—from the World Bank than any other agency of the Indian government.[39] India in turn was the Bank's most important borrower country.

In fact, the Bank proudly viewed the NTPC as one of its best pupils, and liked to think that NTPC, thanks to Bank influence, was more efficient and better managed than other parts of the Indian government bureaucracy. In numerous countries, Bank lending had encouraged the growth of carefully cultivated semi-autonomous technocratic development bureaucracies like NTPC or Thailand's EGAT.

When high-ranking Bank executives visited India in the late 1980s, the Bank's resident office staff in New Delhi showed them a model project— Singrauli. On a hill several hundred feet above the giant Singrauli Super Thermal Plant is a flower-bedecked heliport which welcomes visiting dignitaries. A ceremonial walkway leads from the heliport to an overlook on the power plant; on either side are young Ashoka crown trees, planted by such visitors as the energy minister of the USSR and David Hopper, vice-president of the World Bank for Asia in 1986. At the entrance to the ceremonial walkway, adjacent to the heliport, is a small plot with a large sign that reads, "NTPC Vegetable Garden." Below are the hovels of tens of thousands of displaced people; they blend in with the brown-and-black, scarred, denuded earth. They are so far away you can see them only with binoculars.

In 1987 and 1988, the displaced people at Singrauli started to organize to lobby for their rights, aided by local public interest lawyers and by national human rights and environmental organizations in Delhi. They brought lawsuits against the managers of the World Bank–financed power plant at Singrauli. Indian environmental groups condemned the scandalous neglect of basic human rights and environmental concerns at Singrauli in the Indian press. In the United States, the Environmental Defense Fund exposed the scandal in congressional hearings and called upon the World Bank to undertake emergency remedial measures with the Indian government and other aid agencies to mitigate the environmental and social disasters at Singrauli. Mass demonstrations and hunger strikes took place, including a protest of over 15,000 people on February 5, 1988, in the streets of Singrauli town.

In response to this criticism and pressure, Bank staff acknowledged neglect and sent several missions to Singrauli to investigate the situation. The Bank used remaining Singrauli disbursements to finance a $4.9-million environmental assessment of the region, conducted by the French national electricity company, Électricité de France. In 1989, both a World Bank vice-president and the director of the Bank's Environment Department made site visits to Singrauli and met with representatives of local nongovernmental groups. In 1989, the Bank began to prepare a "cleanup" project to remedy, retroactively at least, some of the social and environmental disruption in its Singrauli projects, as well as to promote environmental and resettlement rehabilitation for the entire Singrauli region. It was a hopeful moment, and the displaced poor of the region, after years of desperation and isolation, thought that the World Bank and the NTPC were finally becoming concerned. But the Indian government and the NTPC refused to borrow more money for the proposed Singrauli Environmental Rehabilitation Project, and it was stillborn.

Meanwhile, within the Bank, its tiny sociological staff (consisting of one senior sociologist and a couple of assistants) was concerned that there might be other Singraulis; discreetly, they queried the India country department about other coal-burning power plants the Bank had financed. Shocking evidence emerged that Singrauli was only the tip of the iceberg. In a single decade, from the late 1970s to the late 1980s, the World Bank had financed the construction of twelve gigantic coal-fired power plants all over India, of which Singrauli was only one. Unbeknownst to the international community, for eight other plants besides Singrauli the Bank had completely ignored the issue of resettlement. No one knew how many tens of thousands of poor had had their homes and livelihoods destroyed (one internal estimate is 75,000–100,000 people; another is 26,600 households, which could mean anywhere from 100,000 to over 200,000 people), but at one plant alone—Farakka, for which the Bank lent NTPC $300 million in 1984—more than 50,000 had been either forcibly resettled or dispossessed. Attempts to encourage NTPC and the Indian government to consider environmental and resettlement rehabilitation programs for some of these projects also failed.

In 1993 the Bank approved a new, $400-million loan to the NTPC to finance the first stage of a gigantic, $4-billion investment plan to intensify coal mining and expand coal-fired production of electricity in nine super thermal power plants all over India. Other loans are to follow. Under the investment plan, 3,750 megawatts of new generating capacity will be built at Singrauli alone. In the new loan virtually no funds are allocated for compensating and rehabilitating the hundreds of thousands of people forcibly resettled or otherwise adversely affected by previous Bank-financed NTPC projects.

A World Bank vice-president and its environment director had gone to Singrauli and left, Bank staff had raised expectations, and millions have been paid to foreign consultants for studies, but there have been few tangible improvements for the development refugees of Singrauli. Their desperation has only deepened.[40]

Streak of Gold

Imagine people encircled by water from all sides, running for [the] safety of their lives. Many of them climbed over trees. Their houses and other properties washed away. Boribinda, Gopalpur, Durrie and Birdih are a few villages among 52 villages in the state of Bihar which were submerged during August 26–27 [1991] due to the ongoing construction of the Chandil dam . . . a part of the Subernarekha Multipurpose Project . . . funded by the World Bank.[41]

—Kavaljit Singh, Director,
Public Interest Research Group, New Delhi

From September 25 to 28, 1991, a young Indian public interest activist, Kavaljit Singh, together with a medical doctor and a journalist, visited a huge irrigation and power scheme in northeastern India that the World Bank had been funding for nearly a decade. They witnessed the aftermath of a horrendous incident: A month before, heavy monsoon rains led to the rapid rise of water behind the nearly completed Bank-financed Chandil dam, and the livelihood of thousands of people was destroyed in hours with little warning. Dam officials, local villagers asserted, refused to open the sluice gates. Six villages were totally inundated, and dozens of others lost all or part of their agricultural land. A pregnant woman and her husband were drowned as they tried to save their belongings. Government bureaucrats claimed it was an unavoidable natural disaster, but the villagers pointed out that this could not be so since the only part of the entire river valley affected was the area directly behind the dam. Singh would report that more than 10,000 people had been turned into refugees, and many, marooned in waterlogged villages, were suffering from destitution and starvation.[42]

The Subernarekha River flows through India's northeastern states of Bihar, Orissa, and West Bengal for nearly 700 kilometers before it debouches into the Bay of Bengal. The river valley is rich in resources—forests, copper, iron, and auriferous sand from which the valley's inhabitants extract gold. Indeed, *subernarekha* means "streak of gold." Hundreds of thousands of tribal people, India's original indigenous inhabitants, live in the valley: the Gonds, the Ho, the Santhal, the Bhumij, and others. There are more than 65 million tribal people in India, and since the great Indo-Aryan invasions of 1500 B.C., they have been pushed into the most remote and marginal ecosystems in the country: tropical and upland forests, arid regions, isolated rural areas. Without caste in a civilization built on caste for 3,500 years, these people suffer tremendous social discrimination and political disenfranchisement.

In August 1982, the World Bank approved a $127-million loan for the Subernarekha Multipurpose Project, a massive irrigation and water-supply scheme that involved the construction of two major dams, Chandil and Icha, two smaller barrages, and seven canals with a total length of 342 kilometers. If the whole scheme is completed, some 120,000 people will be forcibly displaced, most of them tribal. The Chandil and Icha dams alone would displace 68,000 people and inundate 30,000 hectares of farmland and forest. Although the stated purposes of the project were to provide water for irrigated crops and for industrial and urban use, and to promote flood control, many Indian critics alleged that most of the water will go for industrial development and for cash crop production benefiting richer farmers.[43]

A project of this scale involves enormous environmental impacts: it would submerge some of the richest remaining sal forests in Asia; the dam reservoirs could provide habitats for the spread of waterborne diseases such as schistosomiasis and malaria; massive waterlogging of lands and salinization of soils to be irrigated could undermine the agricultural goals of the project; and movement of seawater into the mouth of the river could seriously affect the livelihood of populations downstream from the dam. There would also be a need to prevent erosion and deforestation on the watershed of the dam reservoirs, to prevent their siltation. All of these issues needed comprehensive studies, which normally should be undertaken before major construction begins. Although the World Bank issued its first environmental review guidelines in 1984, an environmental assessment for the project was not completed until 1990, twelve years after construction began on the Chandil dam, and nearly a year after the last funds from the Bank's $127-million 1982 loan were disbursed. The Bank itself acknowledged that the study was totally inadequate; it was based mainly on old government data rather than scientifically competent field work, and ignored a number of major issues.[44]

The environmental issues were linked to a more dramatic situation—the fate of the tens of thousands of tribal people whose homelands would disappear forever. They began to protest the project from its inception in 1975, when survey work began. In 1978, more than 10,000 people protested at the Chandil dam site as construction began. In April 1978, hundreds of villagers began a Ghandian fast at Chandil to protest the project, and on April 29 the police attacked the fasters and arrested them. The next day, over 8,000 tribal people gathered at the site, protesting the police action and vowing to continue the fast. This time the police returned en masse and opened fire on the unarmed crowd, killing four. The project continued, and two years later the World Bank found it worthy of support and began preparing the $127-million loan. In the spring of 1982, as the World Bank was in the final stages of appraisal for its loan, more violent police interventions against protests led to the killing by police of one of the leaders of the anti–Icha dam movement, Gangaram Kalundia.[45]

By the summer of 1988, the gates of the Chandil dam had closed, threatening some 10,000 hapless Indian tribal poor stranded without viable alternative means of subsistence. Thirty thousand others faced displacement by inundation within another twenty months, as the reservoir filled. Reports from researchers at a regional university and from the Indian press described scenes of mass misery and suffering, and one World Bank official reported back to Washington that the situation required the emergency intervention of the International Red Cross.[46] Belatedly, on October 8, 1988, the Bank suspended loan disbursements, and postponed again the closing date for the project. The Bank recommenced funding in 1990, arguing that there had been sufficient improvement in the resettlement situation to justify renewed support for the project, and started to prepare two new loans for Subernarekha, totaling $375 million.

Local researchers and community activists continued to argue that the project authorities and the Bihar state government did not comply with either Bank or Bihar policies concerning resettlement, or with minimal human rights standards. The World Bank's recommencement of disbursements and preparation of new loans was abetting an unconscionable social and environmental disaster. In December 1990, a University of Pennsylvania researcher described the scene:

The poor are turned first into shifting refugees—they leave the [Chandil] reservoir area during the seasonal rise of water and return after the monsoon to cultivate their bits of land. When the dam is finished . . . they will all have to go.

News has gone around that sites selected for relocation are stony and infertile, and there are no plans for their reclamation. When the reservoir first started filling, 16 villages were evacuated. The 2120 families [about 12,000 people] of this first batch were to be relocated in 22 selected sites, but only ten percent went there, and of that number half returned to their old villages as soon as the water seasonally went down. The other 90 percent of this first batch of oustees slipped quietly away into the vastness of Indian humanity. . . .

The settlers have no way to earn a living and have to subsist mostly as shifting population with seasonal work. They have to travel 40 km to the project office repeatedly to make their claims. Most of the promised infrastructure, such as health and educational facilities, is not provided. . . .

And where rising water did force people out, there was evacuation in a crisis atmosphere. No compensation was ever paid for standing crops, which was another concern for the oustees' great anger. . . . They have no hope of fighting the authority of government, so they quietly drift off as refugees in India's crowded, impoverished society.[47]

Construction continued, the Bank continued to disburse funds, and civil disorder grew as local authorities escalated violence against the poor. On April 5, 1991, approximately 500 people, mainly tribal, began a sit-in at the other Subernarekha dam, Icha in Bihar state. They were protesting both its construction and the lack of minimal resettlement provisions for the 30,000 additional people it will displace, mainly of the Ho tribe, living in some 61 villages. On April 9, police arrested and detained about 250 of the protesters, including women and children, as well as a locally well known social activist, Kumar Chandra Mardi. Most were released five weeks later, but only after more than 10,000 people marched on the capital of Bihar, Patna, on May 13, protesting the actions of the police and project authorities and demanding the release of the detainees. Ten Indian local and national NGOs that work with the poor alleged that the project was rife with corruption and misuse of funds on the part of contractors and officials.[48]

As all this was occurring, the World Bank still forged ahead in preparing huge loans for two new projects to complete the scheme, the Subernarekha Irrigation Project and the Subernarekha Multipurpose II Project. The new loans would reward the project authorities and Indian officials who have created an environmental and human rights nightmare with well over a third of a billion dollars. In spring 1993, the Bank withdrew these projects from its lending pipeline. However, new irrigation consolidation projects for the states of Bihar and Orissa are in preparation which could support the completion of the new projects.

The Revolt of Local Knowledges

We don't have anything written, we don't have anything made in a government office, we don't have any run of the mill platitudes. We bring you something concrete—reality—because we live in it.[49]

—Jaime da Silva Araújo

In the 1980s, in the Amazon, in India, in Thailand, and in many other parts of the developing world, local populations long relegated to the margins of power and history began to mobilize to defend the ecological balance of the resources on which their survival depends. Such struggles, community-based in origin, were joined at the national and international level by environmental, social justice, and human rights groups around the world.[50]

In huge internationally financed development projects like Carajás, Singrauli, and the others we have examined, two universes collide, two ways of knowing and of being in the world. One is that of government planners and World Bank project officers, of Jacques Attali's affluent global nomads, rooted ultimately if imperfectly in a geometric, Cartesian vision of the availability and basic interchangeability of different spaces and times, which are viewed as the physical playing fields for economic development. It is a world of a ceaseless quest for more intensive economic use of the earth's space and time, a world conceived as an abstract expanse, which through the correct method can be controlled and manipulated. A forest in central India can be developed as a coal mine—or flooded as a dam reservoir, or chopped down and replanted with fast-growing, commercially useful eucalyptus, or demarcated as a nature reserve—depending on what "trade-offs" are involved.

The tribal people displaced by dams and coal mines in India, and the Brazilian rubber tappers threatened by deforestation, are not oblivious to this vision; they experience it as an everyday reality and are revolting against it. They are not opposed to all economic development; they desire it, but on different terms. Their world is locally rooted, grounded in the history, culture, and cry for survival of threatened peoples and places. Their survival depends on their parts of the earth being conserved as Earth, as a functioning, stable ecosystem.

Searching out and joining forces with national and international environmental groups, local campaigns in Brazil, India, Thailand, and other countries began to give local ecological concerns a global political significance in the 1980s. Around the world raged the insurrection of a thousand local realities based on as many local knowledges. To the planet's leading financial bureaucrats and bankers who attended World Bank annual meetings, this revolt appears uncompromising and therefore irrational, even if based in legitimate local social and environmental concerns. But for many in the developing world, global integration means local destitution, and the marginalization of hundreds of millions to a "Fourth World" at the very moment when the Second and Third Worlds are being absorbed into the global market. The new world order and its global promise of consumer abundance and universal markets also threatens survival on a local and global scale: at stake is the future of cultures, languages, and indigenous peoples, the existence of whole ecosystems and millions of years of accumulated biological diversity, and, more and more, the ecological equilibrium of the entire planet.

Although public international financial institutions like the World Bank claimed they were promoting free enterprise, in many developing countries their loans strengthened the state and expanded the areas subject to its administration. Nongovernmental groups like the ones gathered at Bangkok in October 1991 sought a reduced, decentralized role for the state, and greater autonomy and control for the groupings and institutions of "civil society," such as local community organizations, local businesses, cooperatives and NGOs. They sought to retain and regain control over rural ecosystems that had often served as sustainably managed commons, like the community forests managed by villagers in the hills of northern Thailand and the Himalayas. These groups understand that the so-called "tragedy of the commons," the relentless exploitation and destruction of resources that belong to no one, occurs only after the village and communal social framework is destroyed.

Was this a one-sided view, that of the "losers" in the March of Progress? Were the worst projects of the World Bank and the governments of developing countries unfortunate but inevitable mistakes, the exceptions that nevertheless proved the rule that most projects were desirable? Didn't many multilateral bank–financed development projects benefit people? Aren't the World Bank and other multilateral banks not only taking into account environmental and social concerns, but even financing environmental protection projects? Didn't everyone agree now that development had to be sustainable—whatever "development" and "sustainable" mean? Can you make the omelette called development without breaking eggs? In short, which vision of the world was real? Or were they both real, since they described almost separate worlds that, increasingly, were colliding with one another?

A world is a human creation, the sum of an individual's or a society's assumptions, perceptions and life projects, rooted in foundations that are given by culture and history, epoch and place. It is not the universe, which we cannot know, nor the physical earth, on which all our worlds are based and depend for sustenance. Let us take a closer look at the world that created the World Bank, and the world it helped to create.

3

Brave New World
at Bretton Woods

> The creation of the Bank was an entirely new ven-
> ture. . . . So novel was it, that no adequate name could
> be found for it. . . . However it was accidently born with
> the name Bank, and Bank it remains, mainly because no
> satisfactory name could be found in the dictionary for
> this unprecedented institution.[1]
> —Georges Theunis, Bretton Woods
> Conference delegate

> We have perhaps accomplished here in Bretton Woods
> something more significant than what is embodied in
> this Final Act. . . . If we can so continue, this night-
> mare, in which most of us here present have spent too
> much of our lives, will be over. The brotherhood of
> man will have become more than a phrase.[2]
> —John Maynard Keynes

It was a cold winter Sunday, but the entire federal government of the United States was feverishly at work. The date was December
14, 1941, exactly one week after the Japanese attack on Pearl Harbor.
Secretary of the Treasury Henry Morgenthau was thinking not about the
world war but its aftermath. He directed his top advisor on international
economic affairs, Harry Dexter White, to draft a memorandum on a postwar "Inter-Allied Stabilization Fund" that would harmonize international
currency exchanges and promote trade. White was ready; he had been
at work on a much more ambitious scheme for a new world economic
order since the spring of 1941. Besides an international monetary stabilization fund, he envisaged the creation of a second institution, a "Bank
for Reconstruction and Development of the United and Associated
Nations."[3]

For nearly a year and a half, the Germans had been propagandizing a postwar "New Order" for Europe that had important international economic components. The German plan proposed an international multilateral trade system that would replace the economic chaos of the 1930s and bring a new era of prosperity to Europe. A regime of European free trade would be based on the reichsmark, and an international monetary clearing office in Berlin would coordinate stable exchange rates and assist national governments in managing balance of payments problems. Germany and Italy would cooperate to lead European reconstruction. "We will use the same methods of economic policy that have given such remarkable results, both before and during the war, and we will not allow the unregulated play of economic power, which caused such difficulties to the German economy, to become active again," proclaimed Walter Funk, Nazi minister for economic affairs. In the "New Order," Berlin would replace London as the world financial capital.[4]

The British ministry of information was concerned by the propaganda effect of Herr Funk's proposals, and asked John Maynard Keynes, Britain's most distinguished economist, to discredit them in a proposed November 1940 radio broadcast. The ministry suggested Keynes tout the virtues of the gold standard and of free trade as it had worked in the 1920s and early 1930s—a proposal Keynes viewed as hopelessly lacking in credibility. This was precisely the old international economic regime that had led to economic catastrophe in the 1930s through escalating bilateral trade wars and beggar-thy-neighbor competitive currency devaluations. Keynes replied, "If we have nothing positive to say, we had better be silent." He prepared the outlines of a counterproposal, which would be the "same as what Dr. Funk offers, except that we shall do it better and more honestly. . . . For a proposal to return to the blessings of 1920–1933 will not have much propaganda value." Indeed, as early as 1930 Keynes had suggested, in his *Treatise on Money,* the creation of a supernational bank, one which, however, would not be a bank to finance reconstruction or development, but a draft stabilization fund or clearing union to manage international currency exchange rates and balance of payments problems. At that time Keynes, according to one British official who knew him, "was not very keen on international investment, holding that the indebtedness thereby created was dangerous in relation to the balance of payments of the recipient countries."[5]

Keynes did not make public his counterproposal to Herr Funk's "New Order," but discussed it in meetings with American officials in 1941. While the United States remained a nonbelligerent, it could do little in the way of postwar international economic planning except to commit itself to the general principle of freer trade and to joint efforts with Great

Britain to promote expanded international production, employment, and exchange of goods. These principles for U.S.-British international economic cooperation and other war aims were set out in August 1941 in the Atlantic Charter, and in the Master Lend-Lease Agreement, signed by President Roosevelt in early 1942.[6] Pearl Harbor changed everything, and in response to Morgenthau's December 14, 1941, request, Harry White wrote in early 1942 his first version of the plan that launched the World Bank and the International Monetary Fund.

The dream of an international investment and development bank was not a new one. In nineteenth-century Paris, Henri Saint-Simon and his disciples had made several proposals for public international banks to promote the economic development of humanity; two Saint-Simonians, the Pereire brothers, established the first private international investment bank, the Crédit Mobilier.* For its founders, the Crédit Mobilier was not merely a financial institution, but "a center of administration and control which was to direct according to a coherent program the railway systems, the town planning activities and the various public utilities and other industries."[7]

The international financial conferences of the 1920s and 1930s also spawned a number of proposals that could be viewed as antecedents of the World Bank. In 1920, the Belgian prime minister, M. Delacroix, proposed to the recently formed League of Nations the establishment of an "International Bank of Issue" that would grant loans to member countries, borrow money through bond issues that would be backed by the membership subscriptions of governments, and generally promote European reconstruction and development. The bank would have some power to intervene in the economic policies of borrowing governments to ensure repayment. At the international financial conference held in Genoa in 1922, the German finance minister, Walter Rathenau, proposed the creation of a "Bank of Nations" formulated by one of his aides, Dr. Hans Heymann. Heymann's "Bank of Nations" would grant loans and credits to member countries, and in particular establish in borrowing nations "subordinated national trust banks to finance new productive enterprises—factories, soil reclamation, public utilities, etc.—and . . . maintain existing business and trade. Because of their productive character," Heymann suggested, "these banks shall be called Construction Banks."[8] These proposals and others were all stillborn for a variety of reasons, not the least of which was lack of interest by the country that was already the world's premier economic power and creditor, the United States.

One public international financial institution was established before

* Chapter 8 will discuss in more detail the historical and philosophical significance of the Saint-Simonians as harbingers of modern development.

Bretton Woods—the Bank for International Settlements. The B.I.S. was founded in 1930 as transfer agent to the allied powers for German war reparations and debts, but its main raison d'être vanished the following year when the German government permanently defaulted on most of these obligations. The B.I.S. demonstrated the remarkable resilience that has come to characterize international bureaucracies by not only surviving but flourishing in its other intended role as a coordinating center for national central banks. The B.I.S. charter members of Belgium, England, France, Germany, and Italy were eventually joined by other European nations, Japan, and the United States.[9]

The Father of the World Bank

Harry White delivered his 138-page "Proposal for a United and Associated Nations Stabilization Fund and a Bank for Reconstruction and Development of the United and Associated Nations" to Henry Morgenthau in April 1942. He urged Morgenthau to present it to President Roosevelt and to convoke a financial conference in Washington of the allies, now with increasing frequency referred to as "the United Nations." White and his colleagues at Treasury were particularly concerned that delay would lose them leadership of postwar financial planning for the administration, since the State Department, led by Cordell Hull, was developing its own plans for international economic cooperation,* much of which focused on arrangements for free trade.[10]

On May 15, 1942, Morgenthau met with Roosevelt and presented White's proposals, without any prior consultation with the State Department. The treasury secretary shunted aside Roosevelt's initial suggestion that Treasury first share White's plan with Cordell Hull, and the following day President Roosevelt endorsed Morgenthau's recommendations.[11] The U.S. Treasury had won the turf war of the century, and the State Department has been trying to regain influence in international economic affairs ever since.**

White's initial proposal for an international bank for reconstruction and development was extraordinarily ambitious, and proposed powers that

---

* According to one commentator, "The Secretary of State actually believed that the fundamental causes of the world wars lay in economic discrimination and trade warfare. Some of his aides went so far as to propose a trade agreement with Nazi Germany in 1939 as a means of avoiding the Second World War!" (Richard N. Gardner, "The Political Setting," in Acheson, Chant, and Prachowny, *Bretton Woods Revisited* [see endnote 4], 22).

** "Had Hull been Roosevelt's Duchess County neighbor instead of Morgenthau, we might have ended up with an ITO [International Trade Organization] and not an IMF!" (Gardner, "The Political Setting," in *Bretton Woods Revisited*, 23).

went well beyond the final charter of the World Bank that was ultimately approved at Bretton Woods. The proposed bank would lend for reconstruction and development in its member countries, and also guarantee private investments. It would help stabilize international commodity prices and issue its own international currency notes, to be called unitas, equal in value to ten U.S. dollars. It would have many of the functions of a world central bank. The bank also would finance international relief efforts in areas suffering from the devastation of war or natural disasters, and it would promote democratic institutions in its members. A Treasury memorandum called White's proposed international fund and bank "a New Deal in international economics."[12]

Morgenthau and White wanted to move quickly to prepare for a financial conference of the United Nations, but both the rearguard objections of the State Department* and concerns over the 1942 congressional elections led to a two-year process of technical consultation and revision with other Allied nations, including Australia, Brazil, Canada, China, Mexico, and the Soviet Union.[13]

Meanwhile, Lord Keynes prepared his own proposal, for an "International Clearing Union," which was shared with the United States in August 1942. The clearing union proposal was more ambitious and broadsweeping in its powers than White's stabilization fund. It included some of the functions of White's bank—such as the issuing of an international currency, the bancor, which would be based on gold—but Keynes made no mention of an international development, reconstruction, and investment bank, which remained exclusively Harry White's brainchild. Through 1942, 1943, and early 1944, and at the Bretton Woods Conference itself, the attention of financial and economic experts would be focused on resolving the differences between White's and Keyne's visions of the structure of what would become the International Monetary Fund; the World Bank, as has often been said, was almost an afterthought until the final days of the conference.

In November 1943, the Treasury made public a substantially modified version of White's plans for a United Nations bank and stabilization fund, which would serve as the main negotiating text for Bretton Woods. The revised proposal eliminated many of White's more broad-ranging ambitions for the bank, such as its issuing of a world currency, its financing of war and disaster relief, and its powers as a world central bank. Morgenthau and White were wary of what could be sold to Congress and the American people—isolationism was still a strong undercurrent in American politics, particularly in the Republican party, and the private commer-

* The State Department viewed a conference in 1942 as premature until the Allied military position improved, and advocated closer collaboration with Britain in planning.

cial banking establishment opposed any government-funded competition with their business, domestic or international.

After further consultations with the British and other allies, and the beginning of a campaign by the administration and sympathetic members of Congress to prepare the American public for a new era of economic internationalism, all was in place. On May 26, 1944, President Roosevelt formally invited forty-three nations to attend the United Nations Monetary and Financial Conference to be held at the Mount Washington Hotel in Bretton Woods, New Hampshire, beginning on July 1. Rather than in humid Washington, the conference would take place in a scenic New England mountain resort, partly in deference to Lord Keynes's preference for a cool meeting place that would not exacerbate his heart condition.[14]

In late June, more than 700 delegates traveled to the United States for the conference; a number of them, including Keynes, Morgenthau, and White, met in the Claridge Hotel in Atlantic City to hammer out last-minute details. On the evening of June 30, two special trains left Washington and Atlantic City filled with hundreds of well-dressed men (there were few women—the U.S. delegation had only one, an economics professor from Vassar) in conservative suits, conversing in numerous European languages. Reporters dubbed the remarkable procession "the Tower of Babel on Wheels."[15]

Birth of a New World Order

The Mount Washington Hotel was built in 1902 to resemble a sumptuous Spanish Renaissance palace, and was incongruously plunked down in the middle of the million-acre Mount Washington National Forest in New Hampshire's White Mountains. The inaugural session took place in the Grand Ballroom, which easily held the hundreds of delegates. Henry Morgenthau, president of the conference, read a welcoming message from Franklin Roosevelt. Morgenthau's opening speech set the tone for and indeed embodied the spirit of the gathering. He reminded the delegates of "the great economic tragedy of our time," the Depression, and recalled how the resulting "bewilderment and bitterness [became] the breeders of fascism and finally, of war."[16]

Morgenthau envisaged

[the] creation of a dynamic world economy in which the peoples of every nation will be able to realize their potentialities in peace . . . and enjoy, increasingly, the fruits of material progress on an *earth infinitely blessed with natural riches*. This is

the indispensable cornerstone of freedom and security. All else must be built upon this. For freedom of opportunity is the foundation for all other freedoms. [Emphasis added.]

He exhorted the conference to focus on an important "elementary economic axiom . . . that *prosperity has no fixed limits*. It is not a finite substance to be diminished by division." [Emphasis added.][17]

Morgenthau concluded, "The opportunity before us has been bought with blood. Let us meet it with faith in one another, with faith in our common future, which these men [the soldiers of the United Nations] fought to make free." The 700 delegates arose to leave the Grand Ballroom, as the band—yes, there was a band—played "The Star-Spangled Banner."[18]

Here then, in a nutshell, was the shared vision of Bretton Woods. In the wake of the greatest economic collapse and most catastrophic war in history the representatives of the United Nations sought world peace, freedom, and security. Global economic growth integrating countries in a world market would be the means to achieve these goals—growth based on the "axiom" of infinite natural resources feeding limitlessly increasing prosperity. The Bretton Woods institutions, the World Bank and the IMF, would be the critical instrumentalities.

Keynes expressed similar sentiments. He chaired one of the three commissions of the conference—Commission II, on the Bank—where much of the technical work was to be carried out. (Commission I concerned the Fund, and Commission III other financial arrangements.) In his opening remarks before the second commission, he stated, "In general, it will be the duty of the Bank, by wise and prudent lending, to promote a policy of expansion of the world's economy. . . . By 'expansion' we should mean the increase of resources and production in real terms, in physical quantity, accompanied by a corresponding increase in purchasing power."[19]

After three weeks of intensive work, on July 22, 1944, the hundreds of delegates gathered for the closing plenary session. The views of White and the Treasury Department had largely prevailed over those of the British and all others, as a simple consequence of the unique and unprecedented economic and military predominance of the United States at that moment in history. The United States accounted for half of world economic production and had the only internationally viable currency. The Bank was entirely White's idea, and the conference in its final act adopted the proposed charter, or Articles of Agreement, with relatively few modifications. Much more time was spent drafting the articles of the Fund, although the British had already abandoned the more ambitious proposals that Keynes had envisaged in his earlier draft plan for an international clearing union.

Henry Morgenthau, in his capacity as president of the conference, delivered the farewell address. It was to have been preceded by a "Resolution of Thanks" delivered by the head of the Brazilian delegation, but Morgenthau announced that "we have time on the radio for the United States beginning in two minutes and Mr. Souza Costa [the Brazilian representative] has very kindly permitted me to make my address to you now before he gives his. So would you mind just relaxing until the Columbia Broadcasting Company is on the air." Seven hundred people in the Grand Ballroom waited in silence for two minutes.[20]

"I am gratified to announce that the Conference at Bretton Woods has successfully completed the task before it," Morgenthau began.

What we have done here is devise a machinery by which men and women everywhere can freely exchange, on a fair and stable basis, the goods which they produce through their labor. And we have taken the initial steps through which the nations of the world will be able to help one another in economic development to their mutual advantage and for the enrichment of all.

The International Monetary Fund would further the first goal, and the World Bank the second. Morgenthau, perhaps playing to the national radio audience, recalled the New Deal ideals that infused the U.S. government's conception of Bretton Woods. "I take it as an axiom that after this war is ended no people—and therefore no government of the people— will again tolerate prolonged and widespread unemployment."[21]*

The Brazilian delegate, Souza Costa, finally delivered the "Resolution of Thanks," musing that the proposed Fund and Bank were "inspired by a single ideal—that happiness be distributed throughout the face of the earth."[22] The delegates rose to their feet as the band played "The Star-Spangled Banner" for the last time. John Maynard Keynes moved toward the exit, and spontaneously all the hundreds broke out in applause and sang "For He's a Jolly Good Fellow."[23]

"An Entirely New Venture"

The International Bank for Reconstruction and Development (IBRD)—or the World Bank, as it came to be known—was indeed an

---

* If freedom and full employment were among the ideals of Bretton Woods, bought, as Morgenthau proclaimed, with the blood of Allied soldiers, it would be interesting to speculate on what he would have thought of the Bank and the Fund in later decades, when they supported brutal dictatorships and economic adjustment programs that increased unemploy-

unprecedented institution. Although it has grown immensely over the decades, the fundamental structure set out in its Articles of Agreement remains unchanged. The charter described the most general organizational principles and goals, and left most of the details of operations to be worked out by the Bank's management and Board of Executive Directors. The main purposes of the Bank are "to assist in the reconstruction and development of territories of members by facilitating the investment of capital for productive purposes," and "to promote the long-range balanced growth of international trade . . . by encouraging international investment . . . thereby assisting in raising productivity, the standard of living and conditions of labor" (Article I). It would do this by guaranteeing private investments as well as lending directly from its own capital. Reconstruction and development were to be of equal priority in the Bank's activities.

The original capital of the Bank was set at $10 billion, the equivalent of at least $70 or $80 billion in 1993. This was indeed a "huge sum," as one of the Bretton Woods delegates observed, which "far exceed[ed] anything the world has ever known in this field."[24] Twenty percent of the capital subscriptions would be paid in by member countries, and the remaining 80 percent of the capital would be "callable" as a guarantee. The ratio of "paid-in" to callable capital has decreased over the years; as of 1993, the Bank's total capital was $165.59 billion, of which only $10.53 billion was paid in.[25] This guarantee by major industrialized nations (the Bank's callable capital) allows the Bank to raise money for lending by borrowing in international capital markets; the Bank charges borrowers a rate of interest typically .5 percent above its own cost of borrowing, pocketing the difference to pay its own operating expenses and to add to reserves. Membership in the International Monetary Fund is a prerequisite for joining the Bank.

The Bank would lend only for "specific projects"—in practice, dams, highways, power plants, etc.— "except in special circumstances" (Article III, Section 4 [vii]). The Bank must "ensure that the proceeds of any loan are used only for the purposes for which the loan was granted, with due attention to considerations of economy and efficiency and without regard to political or other non-economic influences or considerations" (Article III, Section 5[b]). The prohibition on consideration of "political" and "non-economic" considerations in the Bank's operations has proven to be one of the most important provisions in the charter, and is repeated more strongly in Article IV, Section 10: "The Bank and its officers shall not

---

ment and lowered wages in real terms for hundreds of millions of poor in the developing world. But we are getting ahead of our story.

interfere in the political affairs of any member; nor shall they be influenced in their decisions by the political character of the member or members concerned. Only economic considerations shall be relevant to their decisions, and these considerations shall be weighed impartially to achieve the purposes [of the Bank] stated in Article I."

The governance of the Bank (and of its sister, the International Monetary Fund) is also unique. All the powers of the Bank are vested in the Board of Governors, one governor representing each member country. The governors of the Bank (and Fund) are usually the finance ministers or central bank presidents of their respective nations; the first U.S. governor of the World Bank was Treasury Secretary Henry Morgenthau. The governors formally choose the Bank's president, but in reality, since the president is by custom an American, he is chosen by the U.S. government, usually by the Treasury Department. (The head of the IMF is traditionally a European.) The annual Bank/Fund meetings are the occasions at which all the governors of both institutions convene. On a day-to-day basis most of the powers of the governors are delegated to the Board of Executive Directors.

Originally there were twelve executive directors of the Bank, representing its forty-four founding member countries. The Bank's charter provides that the five biggest shareholders of the Bank each appoint their own executive director; the remaining directors represent several countries each, and are elected by those countries. As the Bank added new members (they totaled 176 in 1993), the number of executive directors has grown to twenty-four. Their voting power is roughly proportional to the amount of money the member countries they represent contribute to the Bank. The U.S. vote originally counted for 36 percent; it is now down to about 17.5 percent. In 1993, the ten richest industrialized countries controlled 52 percent of the votes. The executive directors reside in Washington, meet frequently (at least weekly) and must approve every loan and major policy of the Bank. Normally decisions by the Executive Board require a simple majority of votes, but today any action to change the Articles of Agreement requires the approval of at least three-fifths of the members and 85 percent* of the total voting shares.[26]

The Bank could only begin business after member countries whose voting shares totaled at least 65 percent had endorsed the charter, which would remain open for signature until the end of 1945;[27] in practice this

---

* In 1946, when the United States had 36 percent of the Bank's voting shares, only 65 percent were needed to change the charter. As its percentage of total Bank funding decreased, the United States succeeded in amending the Articles of Agreement to retain its veto power over changes—most recently in the 1989, when the percentage of votes needed to change the charter was increased from 80 to 85 percent.

meant the Bank would be stillborn without the approval of the U.S. Congress.[28]

The Selling of Bretton Woods

> We have to go out from here as missionaries, inspired
> by zeal and faith. We have sold all this to ourselves. But
> the world at large still needs to be persuaded.[28]
> —John Maynard Keynes

Nowhere would the selling of the Bank and the Fund be more difficult than in the United States. Isolationist sentiment still was strong, and some administration officials recalled the Senate's rejection twenty-five years before of U.S. membership in Woodrow Wilson's League of Nations. The U.S. domestic debate over Bretton Woods is worth recalling, since it articulated several of the more problematic questions that to this day remain unresolved within the public international financial institutions, and with respect to international development efforts in general. Debate had already begun after the publication of White's plan in November 1943.

Since the United States had the only viable international currency and credit, the early lending of the Bank would probably be limited to the amount of the U.S. capital subscription. In late 1943, a National City Bank of New York (today Citicorp) vice-president, Wilbert Ward, raised a question that nearly fifty years later remains unanswered: "If you are going to set up a bank you should set up an organization to finance transactions that will in the end liquidate themselves. Otherwise it is not a bank. . . . Where can we loan thirty to fifty billions around the world with any prospects of its being repaid?"[29]

The *New York Times* echoed this question in an editorial on December 4, 1943, recalling the massive defaults on loans given by private banks (many to Latin American countries) before the war, suggesting that government-sponsored and -guaranteed loans through the Bank would be of even lower quality than private loans, since "people are far more likely to be careful in lending their own money than in lending other peoples' money." If creditor governments attempted to exert "control over the internal policies of the debtor Governments, there would be more sources of international friction and bitterness," the *Times* added. It expressed skepticism about White's underlying assumption that "the world can be saved only by increased governmental management, by increased government power."[30]

With the hindsight of the 1990s, we see that these were not idle specu-
lations: a new developing-country debt crisis, recalling in some respects
that of the 1920s and 1930s, exploded in the 1980s.* A major concern of
the Bank from the late 1950s on has been the need to increase its lending
to heavily indebted countries that have few prospects of ever repaying
their international indebtedness, either to private banks or to public international financial institutions. Increasingly intrusive and controversial
intervention in the domestic policies of borrowing governments, with the
goal of increasing their foreign exchange earnings to service debt, became
a mainstay of the World Bank and IMF lending policies in the 1980s.**

In preparation for congressional hearings that would take place in the
spring and summer, Treasury launched in early 1945 what has been characterized as "one of the most elaborate and sophisticated campaigns ever
conducted by a government agency in support of legislation." It hired a
New York public relations firm, mobilized the support of academics and
churches, and sent government officials off to make countless speeches
and hold luncheons, meetings, and seminars around the country. Treasury
helped prepare radio scripts, booklets, and magazine articles, and "even
subsidized short moving pictures."[31] It promoted the Independent
Bankers' Association, which supposedly represented thousands of small-
town banks all over the nation. In a House of Representatives hearing, the
secretary of the association, who claimed he was one of the twelve best
economists in Sauke Center, Minnesota (ironically, the hometown of Sin-
clair Lewis, and the source of much material in his novels castigating the
hypocrisy of "Main Street" America), conceded that the Independent
Bankers' Association's report backing Bretton Woods had been written by
none other than Harry Dexter White.[32] The *New York Herald Tribune*
called it "the most high powered propaganda campaign in the history of
the country."[33]

It was the Senate that Treasury feared, particularly the Republican
leader, Robert Alfonso Taft. Taft was a remarkable politician who refused
to compromise on principle, even—or especially—in the face of certain
defeat. The son of William Howard Taft, the only man to have been both
president and chief justice of the United States, Robert Taft was a formidable intellectual opponent, first in his class at Yale, first in his class at
Harvard Law, relentlessly rigorous and probing.[34] The administration

---

* Although the debt crisis appeared to have abated by the early 1990s, it was by no means
resolved. See, for example, Nathaniel C. Nash, "Latin Debt Load Keeps Climbing Despite
Accords," *New York Times*, 1 August 1992, 1.
** The principal instruments for this intervention were—and continue to be—nonproject
"sector adjustment" and "structural adjustment" loans. The adverse social and environmental consequences of these loans are discussed in Chapter 7.

would take no chances—the Articles of Agreement of the Bank and the Fund would not be submitted to the Senate as a treaty, requiring ratification by two-thirds vote; U.S. membership in both organizations would be proposed through an executive agreement, requiring only majority approval by both houses of Congress.[35]

Taft made his stand against Bretton Woods in Senate hearings in early June 1945, and in a historic one-hour speech on the floor of the Senate on July 12. His objection to Bretton Woods focused on the Bank, which, he observed,

has not received one-tenth the attention . . . given the fund. I doubt if a single Senator has read the articles of agreement for the bank. Yet, this agreement embarks the United States on a permanent policy of foreign lending and investment by Americans in huge sums, sponsored and to a large extent guaranteed by the Federal Government. The bank is proposed, not as a relief organization, but as a permanent institution involving this Government in a permanent policy.[36]

If relief and reconstruction for war-torn Europe were the goals, Taft argued, another, temporary organization for funneling assistance would be more appropriate.

Taft foresaw that the permanent policy on which the U.S. government was embarking was development lending to poorer countries, and he questioned the fundamental assumptions behind such lending. He noted that the World Bank would be able to make foreign loans using government support and guarantees that individuals and companies in the United States could not obtain for purposes at home—raising questions about both the soundness of the loans and the domestic equity of such a policy. He cited a 1932 study that wholeheartedly endorsed Keynes's earlier skepticism over the virtues of large-scale foreign lending: "To lend large sums abroad for long periods of time without any possibility of redress is a crazy construction, especially in return for a trifling extra dividend." The study's author was none other than Harry Dexter White.[37]

The senator questioned the assumption that large-scale foreign lending and investment would automatically promote peace and security:

I do not think that history shows anything of the kind. Ordinarily after an investment is obtained, the people of a country are likely to regard its owners as absentee landlords concerned only with draining away the assets of the country. Foreign investors are likely to be regarded as exploiters of natural resources and cheap labor. . . . Their activities are likely to build up hostility to the United States. . . . Witness the agitation against American sugar investments even in Puerto Rico and Cuba.[38]

Taft foresaw, too, that Wall Street, as opposed to Main Street, would welcome the Bank. After all, he observed, "it is almost a subsidy to the business of investment bankers, and will also undoubtedly increase the business to be done by the larger banks."[39] Taft also warned that the new system would foster "the domination of international trade and investments by governments," with the World Bank at the apex, choosing which governments to lend to in larger or smaller amounts.[40]

Finally, he questioned the fundamental assumption that the transfer or lending of large amounts of money from a rich country like the United States to poorer nations can really promote development over the longer term:

I think we overestimate the value of American money and American aid to other nations. No people can make over another people. Every nation must solve its own problems, and whatever we do can only be of slight assistance to help it over its most severe problems. . . . A nation that comes to rely on gifts and loans from others is too likely to postpone the essential, tough measures necessary for its own salvation.[41]

On July 19, 1946, the Senate endorsed U.S. participation in the Bank and the Fund by a vote of sixty-one to sixteen. It was, as one Senator put it, "an economic charter for the world."[42] Taft's fight on the Senate floor had been a vain one, but it had the great merit of identifying critical long-term implications inherent in the creation of the World Bank. In the 1960s, Taft's critique of the Bank would be praised for its prescience— not by conservatives, but by the New Left.[43]

In the 1990s, the questions raised by Robert Taft remain as troubling as ever. The Bank and the Fund are seemingly permanent, eternally expanding institutions, and there is little possibility that most developing countries will ever pay off their burgeoning debts. The "solution" has been to lend them more and more, and to postpone the ultimate day of reckoning. The charge that the Bank and the Fund are using taxpayer support to subsidize and manage the foreign debt exposure of private international banks is a highly credible one, made by (among others) Professor Jeffrey Sachs* of Harvard and Congressman David Obey (Democrat), the chairman of the House Subcommittee on Foreign Operations, which must approve every year all U.S. funding for the Bretton Woods institutions.[44] And the success of Bank attempts to promote development through large loans to governments in many parts of the world is abysmal—if one reads the literature not prepared by the Bank or under its sponsorship.[45]

---

* "The taxpayers are picking up a part of the bill [of the debt crisis] for the commercial banks . . . through official lending by the IMF and World Bank, much of which is effectively recycled into commercial bank interest payments," writes Sachs. "Note that the $75 billion [1988] General Capital Increase of the World Bank is an explicit taxpayer contribution [to] this process" (Sachs, "New Approaches to the Latin American Debt Crisis" [see endnote 44], 19).

Finally, Taft was right to question the role that the Bank would play in promoting international peace and security. Certainly it cannot be accused of intentionally fostering war or violence. But there is a significant literature that associates much Bank-sponsored development, including specific projects, with increasing inequality and exacerbated social and ethnic tensions in developing nations. Even more seriously, the Bank has been accused of systematically increasing its financial support for violently repressive military dictatorships in the developing world at the critical moment of their ascension to power—an accusation that is incontrovertible in the cases of Brazil in 1964, Indonesia in 1965, and Chile in 1973.

But these issues would come to the fore only years later; the early history of the Bank posed at the outset other fundamental, still unresolved questions of political accountability and the ethos of technocracy.

The Triumph of Technocracy

> We attach . . . a lot of conditions to our loans. I need hardly say that we would never get away with this if we did not bend every effort to render the language of economics as morally antiseptic as the language the weather forecaster uses in giving tomorrow's prediction. We look on ourselves as technicians or artisans. Words like "savings" and "investment," "efficiency," and "productivity" are tools of our trade, and like good artisans we try to develop proper standards for their use.[46]
>
> —Eugene Black (third president of the World Bank), 1962.

The Bank was very much a product of the New Deal and of a pioneering optimism about the ability of government and centralized planning to manage economic forces and cycles. It was conceived, negotiated, and promoted by economists and financial technicians as an institution that, along with the Fund, would operate on an apolitical, unbiased basis where "only economic considerations" would be relevant. It was the first, and remains the preeminent, global technocracy. Little thought was given to the political and moral risks associated with such an enterprise, though the literature of modernity from Max Weber onward is replete with warnings of the human consequences of bureaucratic rationality divorced from political and social accountability.

No one embodied this technocratic faith more than Keynes, who envisaged the Bretton Woods institutions as virtual technocratic priesthoods, beyond the vulgar machinations of national politics that had led to so

much grief in the past. But to vest institutions with unprecedented financial and political power without corresponding accountability to those
who are affected by their decisions is a dangerous path indeed, and technical reason cannot legitimize power—it only rationalizes and magnifies the
consequences of its exercise.

With historical hindsight, these were the fundamental issues at stake at
the March 1945 inaugural meeting of the World Bank and the IMF, which
took place at the General Ogelthorpe Hotel on Wilmington Island, Georgia, near Savanah.[47] Thirty-four nations had ratified the Bretton Woods
Agreement and sent to the meeting their newly chosen governors for the
Fund and the Bank. Ratification had been a formality, based on little knowledge on the part of the public or parliamentarians in participating countries
concerning the strange new institutions that were being established.[48]

The agenda was to discuss and adopt the bylaws for the new institutions. Superficially, two of the main issues to be decided appeared to be
technicalities: the location of the Fund and the Bank, and the determina-
tion of the exact functions and salaries of the executive directors. Richard
N. Gardner, in his classic study *Sterling Dollar Diplomacy,* summarized
their deeper implications: "Were the Fund and Bank purely financial institutions whose direction could be entrusted to a group of international
civil servants? Or did their operations have such economic and political
implications as to require close control by the member governments?"[49]

Keynes and the British delegation lobbied for locating both bureaucracies in New York (at Bretton Woods, Keynes had already lost the fight to
locate the Fund in London), removed, in Keynes's words, from "the politics of Congress and the nationalistic whispering gallery of the Embassies
and Legations."[50]

For similar reasons, Keynes envisaged a restricted role for the executive
directors: the job would be part-time, and would not reside all the time at
Bank and Fund headquarters. He had also argued at Bretton Woods that
the executive directors should, like the staff and management of both
organizations, function as international civil servants with no allegiances
except to the Bank and the Fund.[51] Keynes stoutly maintained that if the
two new institutions were "to win the full confidence of the suspicious
world[,] it must not only be, but appear, that their approach to every
problem is absolutely objective and ecumenical, without prejudice or
favor." He delivered a highly ironic speech at the Wilmington Island
meeting, based on the tale of Sleeping Beauty, referring to the "curses"
that a "malicious fairy" might pronounce on the two multilateral
foundlings, "Master Fund" and "Miss Bank": "You two brats shall grow
up politicians; your every thought and act shall have an *arriere-pensee;*
everything you determine shall not be for its own sake or on its own mer-

its but because of something else."[52] The U.S. delegation head, Treasury Secretary Fred Vinson, was not amused.

The United States was contributing most of the usable resources* of both organizations, and the Bank and the Fund had mandates for which the policy implications were too important not to be closely watched by the U.S. government, through its executive directors at both institutions. Moreover, Morgenthau and White thought that putting Bank and Fund headquarters in Washington, D.C., would finally break the thralldom of U.S. foreign economic policy to Wall Street and private vested financial interests.[53] Of course the U.S. prevailed, as it had on other issues. The Fund and the Bank were housed in a new building in Washington, originally intended for the State Department, at 1818 H Street—a five-minute walk from the White House. And in the Bretton Woods Agreement Acts, authorizing U.S. participation in the new organizations, Congress expressly stated that the U.S. executive directors would be first and foremost representatives of the U.S. government, rather than international civil servants.[54]

At first blush, Keynes might seem the hero in this debate over the "politicization" of the Bank (and Fund), the purist defender of a vision of a world in which enlightened, selfless international civil servants would create a harmonious, ecumenical supranational order above venal nationalism and vested interests. This was a vision shared by White and Morgenthau, whatever their differences with Keynes. But it was a dangerous, if seductive, mirage. Great power—financial, economic, or other—can never be separated from politics or the interests of one social entity or another, be it a local community, a region, a nation, or group of nations. To pretend otherwise is to create a very dangerous mystification, one which promotes the de facto concentration of power and its isolation from countervailing views and restraining forces. The resulting lack of accountability and public access to information ultimately breeds corruption, if not material, then of a much more dangerous kind—intellectual and ethical. At the very least, then, better to make the Bank accountable to its member governments, rather than simply to itself.

Moreover, as first-term Senator William Fulbright had pointed out the year before, in the June 1945 Senate hearings on Bretton Woods, "It does not seem . . . that in the future we can isolate the economic from the political: and [referring to Morgenthau's earlier testimony] in stating sev-

---

* At the end of World War II only the U.S. dollar, and to a limited extent, the British pound, were internationally accepted currencies; the capital contributions of other members were in local currencies that other nations would not accept for loans and purchases. The same distinction continues today between the "hard" money of the Western industrialized nations and Japan, and the national currencies of most developing nations and the countries of the former Soviet bloc.

eral times that this must be done without regard to politics, that is not quite correct." He added, "I think politics is not such a disreputable thing that it cannot be accepted in this or any other international organization."[55] Indeed, if one thinks of politics in its root sense, as the democratic life of the *polis,* that is, of the city or community as the Greeks conceived it, to exclude political accountability from the first supranational economic organizations would be a tragic mistake, a negation of the very values of democracy and Western civilization that the founders of Bretton Woods sought to rescue from the abyss of the Great Depression and World War II. Perhaps the root problem was that already in 1946 the nation-state had demonstrated its inadequacy as the sole representative of democratic values.

In any case, one consequence of Bretton Woods and the inaugural meeting was that accountability in the Bank (and Fund) to member nations, and indeed to the rest of the world, would be exercised through only one locus, the Board of Executive Directors. And after an initial battle during the short reign of the Bank's first president, accountability would be weakly exercised when at all.

The Fathers of Bretton Woods: Postscript

On the train back from Georgia to Washington, Keynes suffered a heart attack. He recovered, returned to Britain, and a little more than a month later collapsed and died from a second attack, provoked, according to some, by his disappointment with U.S. dominance of the proceedings at Wilmington Island.[56]

Fate dealt Harry White a bitter, almost savagely uncharitable end. President Truman appointed White to be the first U.S. executive director of the International Monetary Fund, a post he held through May 1947. In 1947 and 1948, Whittaker Chambers and Elizabeth Bentley, former communists and key inquisitors of the McCarthy era, accused White of being a communist and a Russian agent. The charges prompted a federal investigation in 1947 and a failed effort to bring a grand jury indictment; White suffered a severe heart attack in September. The House Committee on Un-American Affairs held hearings in the summer of 1948, where Bentley and Chambers further castigated White, and he asked for the opportunity to vindicate himself. On August 13, 1948, he testified—obviously ill, requiring an impromptu recess at one point—and delivered a resounding declaration of his innocence and belief in American principles, bringing the public gallery to its feet at one point with applause. Three days later he was dead.[57]

Early Years

The Bank's first president was Eugene Meyers, publisher of the *Washington Post*. Meyers's tenure was short and unhappy, marked by a constant battle with the strong-minded Board of Executive Directors over how much respective authority they would have in running the Bank. Meyers resigned in December 1946, after serving only six months. As 1947 began, the new institution was in trouble; it had not made a single loan and was looking for a new president.

The choice was John J. McCloy, a prominent Wall Street lawyer who would subsequently earn the sobriquet "Mr. Eastern Establishment" as Allied high commissioner for Germany and director of the C.I.A. McCloy's tenure launched the Bank as a viable operation after a false start, and marked the first years of the Bank as conservative ones, oriented toward winning acceptance on Wall Street as a top-quality lending and borrowing institution. It was the confidence of Wall Street that the Bank needed first and foremost, since its main source of financial resources would be Wall Street–syndicated international borrowing, guaranteed by the callable capital of its most important member, the United States.

McCloy's first challenge was to set ground rules that would allow internal management and staff to run the Bank, and contain the executive directors in a role of passive oversight and supervision. As a condition for accepting the presidency, McCloy had issued a virtual ultimatum to the Executive Board that it not interfere in the Bank's operations and management. He won, establishing the Bank as a management-driven institution, a situation that has continued to this day. Although the executive directors were full-time officials, answering first to their member nations, one could argue that Keynes's vision of an apolitical international economic technocracy finally prevailed in practice, at least in part.[58]

It was a general expectation that the Bank's early activities would focus on European reconstruction, and that its most important function would be that of guaranteeing private investment; it was thought that direct lending would be at best a secondary activity.[59] These proved to be false assumptions, and this was to prove extraordinarily important to the Bank's evolution and its longstanding dilemmas.

Reconstruction in Europe required not interest-bearing loans for specific projects involving lengthy preparation, but the rapid disbursement of grants and highly concessional loans (that is, loans with very low or no interest), to be used for balance of payments support and desperately needed imports for basic needs. The Bank made only four reconstruction loans, all in 1947. These four, to France, the Netherlands, Denmark, and

Luxembourg, totaled $497 million, and were "nonproject" program loans allowed under the "special circumstances" exception of Article III, Section 4 (vii) of the charter.[60] The enormous, quickly disbursed grants of the Marshall Plan made the Bank as an agent of reconstruction virtually irrelevant: by 1953 the Bank had lent only a total of $1.75 billion (of which $497 million was for reconstruction), while the Marshall Plan had transferred $41.3 billion.[61]

The expectation of an important loan guarantor role for the Bank was based in part on the assumption of an immense postwar shortage of capital for large-scale reconstruction and development projects; people like White feared the demand for such projects would far exceed the willingness and capacity of both governments and the private international banking and business establishment. It could be argued that the anticipation of this demand was the single most important assumption behind the creation of the World Bank.[62]

But from the early years on, the Bank was plagued by an embarrassing lack of quality, "bankable" projects to be submitted for prospective loans—and there was still less demand for it to guarantee the loans of private banks.* The Bank's third annual report, for the year 1947–48, related that "the number of sound, productive investment opportunities thus far presented to the Bank is substantially smaller than was originally expected."[63] It put the blame on lack of technical and planning skills and on economic, financial, and political instability in its potential borrowers.

McCloy's successor, Eugene Black, reiterated before the United Nations Economic and Social Council in 1950 that the reason the Bank had made so few loans was "not the lack of money but the lack of well-prepared and well-planned projects ready for immediate execution."[64] His successor, George Woods, was of the same view, and Warren Baum, who would hold high-ranking positions in the Bank through the 1980s, admitted in 1970 that the Bank had to actively stimulate and help design projects in a ceaseless struggle to keep the money flowing: "We do not get enough good projects to appraise unless we are involved intimately in their identification and preparation."[65]

This problem—the inability to find quality projects—only became worse as the years went on and the Bank greatly accelerated its lending to Third World nations in the 1970s. Many of the environmental and social difficulties that came to characterize Bank projects can be attributed to

---

* In practice, it soon became apparent that there were several reasons why direct loans were easier for the Bank to prepare than guarantees: there were legal complications with guarantees; the Bank had to establish first its financial credibility on Wall Street for its bonds and guarantees; and direct borrowing was less expensive and more attractive to borrowers. (Eckes, *Search for Solvency* [see endnote 4], 221.)

this fundamental flaw, which became apparent soon after the Bank's very founding. Particularly from Robert McNamara's tenure on, it resulted in an internal "pressure to lend" that militated against all considerations of project quality.

The surprising lack of demand for the Bank's services can also be seen as an ironic and embarrassing reflection on its very rationale for existence. For the Bank, it posed a constant challenge to find new ways and reasons to justify increasing its capital.

The first signs of other fundamental problems in the Bank's operations emerged in McCloy's tenure, with the $195-million reconstruction loan to the Netherlands, approved on August 7, 1947. Holland was already on the road to economic recovery, but nevertheless was strapped for resources, with production at 90 percent of its 1939 level.

Since August 1945—when nationalists proclaimed the Republic of Indonesia—Holland, a small nation of 10 million, had been faced with a revolt in its huge overseas empire in the East Indies. Seventeen days before the Bank approved its loan, the Netherlands unleashed a war against anticolonialist nationalists with massive air and ground attacks in Java. In the two-year conflict that followed, the Netherlands committed 145,000 troops, supported by considerable air power and mechanized tank forces. After an initial U.N. cease-fire in 1948, the Dutch launched a total economic blockade of nationalist-held areas, causing widespread hunger and health problems among a considerable number of the colony's 70 million inhabitants. Later that year the Netherlands unilaterally broke the U.N. cease-fire with a second series of massive surprise air and land attacks. Critics in the United Nations charged that the Bank loan provided the Dutch government with the resources it needed to both continue its economic recovery program and launch a full-scale war halfway around the world.[66]

The Dutch loan raised two fundamental quandaries which through the years have only become more troubling. First was the alleged inability of the Bank to adequately supervise and monitor the real end use of its money. Closely related is the fungibility question: the Bank may lend for a specific project, but money, by its nature, is interchangeable for different purposes. It has been argued that in reality Bank lending provides governments with the extra foreign exchange to finance their most economically marginal and dubious activities.*

* This is a complicated issue, which could be the subject of a much longer analysis. In later years the Bank would require submission of receipts for specific foreign exchange purchases in many projects and sector loans; thus, with scrupulous monitoring and supervision (a big assumption, since this has been a weak area for the Bank), the Bank could assert that its money was used only for the specific purposes intended. The "fungibility" critics maintain

In the United States, domestic critics made these arguments about Marshall Plan aid to the Netherlands. A number of Republicans in the Senate took the lead, forcing the State Department to modify its position and to notify the Dutch in 1949 that Congress would cut off aid unless the Netherlands respected the U.N. cease-fire and reached an agreement with the Indonesian nationalists. It is worth recalling the words of Senator Wayne Morse in this regard, since they apply with equal force to the World Bank loan: "I do not see how we can escape the conclusion that to whatever extent we have been helpful to the Dutch economy under the Marshall Plan, we necessarily thereby have been helpful to the Dutch Government in carrying out its violations of what I consider to be one of the most basic principles of our pledges under the United Nations Charter."[67]

The threats of the U.S. Congress to halt Marshall Plan aid to the Netherlands, along with increasing criticism in the U.S. press, played a critical role in prompting the Dutch to halt the war, and to grant Indonesia its independence in 1949.[68] It was the first major example of the democratic exercise of accountability for the use of foreign aid—and in retrospect underscores the relative lack of accountability inherent in the structure of then new multilateral organizations like the World Bank.

In 1947, the Bank negotiated and signed a controversial agreement with the fledgling United Nations that set the tone for its relations with other international agencies: it was as much, or more, a declaration of independence from the U.N. as an agreement to work together.[69] Of particular significance is the agreement's treatment of information, since it declares the Bank's right to withhold from the U.N. not only all information it deems "confidential," but all information that "would otherwise interfere with the orderly conduct of its operations."[70]

This early U.N. agreement was an important step in the Bank's establishing operating procedures of blanket confidentiality and secretiveness. It withholds most of its official project documents and background studies and memos not only from the United Nations, but from the public, and from democratically elected legislatures of all its members—including the U.S. Congress. Bank management does not allow the Board of Executive Directors access to information in its files (even though the charter vests the directors and the Board of Governors they represent with all ultimate authority!), nor does it allow them to examine draft project documents, not even for projects in the later states of elaboration.

The official culture of secretiveness was only exacerbated by the Bank's

---

that governments in many cases would undertake the Bank-financed projects anyway, and thus the extra resources provided by World Bank loans permit them to finance other schemes the Bank would not support.

bureaucratic growth. Edward Mason and Robert Asher observed only half facetiously in their twenty-five-year history of the Bank that when a public bureaucracy grows beyond 1,000 employees, the staff members begin to spend much more time communicating with one another than with the outside world. The World Bank reached the 1,000-employee level in the mid-1960s.[71]

The Bank's carte blanche to ignore, indeed defy, the United Nations when it saw fit, was tested in the mid-1960s when the U.N. General Assembly passed resolutions calling on all its specialized agencies, in particular the World Bank and IMF, to withhold financial and technical assistance from Portugal and South Africa. Portugal's colonial domination of Angola and Mozambique, and South Africa's apartheid policy were, the resolutions declared, flagrant violations of the U.N. Charter. Following the passage of the U.N. resolutions in late 1965, the Bank approved in 1966 loans of $10 million to Portugal and $20 million to South Africa.* The Bank argued that Article IV, Section 10, of its charter, prohibiting interference in the political affairs of any member, legally obliged it not to follow the U.N. resolutions.[72]

The incident elucidated more than the relation of the Bank to the United Nations; like the 1947 Dutch reconstruction loan, it cast light on the questionable hypothesis—one of the pillars of the Bank's construction of itself—that economic and political matters exist in separate, walled-off spheres. In a memorandum justifying the World Bank's position, the Bank's general counsel referred to the "technical and functional character of the Bank as it is established under its Articles of Agreement," claiming that its members intended it as a "financial and economic agency and not a political one."[73] But the same members had also signed the U.N. Charter, and were committed to upholding it and to complying with the resolutions of the General Assembly. The Bank was claiming the right to defy the will of most of its shareholders whenever it saw fit—since this will, expressed, for example, in U.N. resolutions, could always be characterized as political by definition.

McCloy left the Bank in 1949 to become high commissioner of Germany, a post he esteemed more important and prestigious. He was succeeded as president by Eugene Black, a Georgia native and Chase Manhattan Bank senior executive before he became U.S. executive director at the World Bank during McCloy's term. The Bank under McCloy's tenure had made its first loans and gained the confidence of Wall Street, which underwrote its bond offerings. The role of the Bank would be in the

---

* This brought cumulative Bank lending to South Africa to $241.8 million through 1966. (Mason and Asher, *Since Bretton Woods* [see endnote 3], 588.)

development of poorer countries, not reconstruction. But McCloy had labored under an illusion against which both Wilbert Ward of the National City Bank of New York and Robert Taft had warned: he thought the Bank's lending for development eventually would be self-liquidating, as the private sector increasingly responded to the need for capital and members paid back their loans.[74]

Dreams of Development

> The pedigree of Development Economics reads "by Colonial Economics out of Political Expediency."[75]
> —Gerald M. Meier

Over the next twenty years, under Black and his successor, George Woods, World Bank loans supported large infrastructure projects in what came to be known as the Third World. The Bank's lending was mainly for electric power projects, especially large dams, for transportation (first railroads and then, increasingly, highways), and cash crop agriculture (e.g., cacao, rubber, and livestock). Many of these projects had very adverse environmental and social consequences, which were almost totally ignored.

In its 1947–48 annual report the Bank set out the practical development philosophy that would characterize its lending for the next two decades. The report pointed out the disparity in productivity and standard of living between poor countries and developed ones in North America and Europe,* and concluded that increasing production and incomes in underdeveloped nations required technological development and increased capital investment as well as increased trade. The Bank's strategy would be to invest in carefully planned and prepared projects in critical areas "relatively less attractive to private capital" and this would catalyze the flow of additional capital into other sectors of the economy. Specifically, this meant focusing on transportation, communications, and power facilities, which along with other infrastructure activities "form the basis for the development of all other sectors of the economy." In addition, the

---

* An inequality that by the 1990s had greatly grown for the poorest countries. The 1947–48 annual report lists average income per head as $1,300 in the U.S., between $500 and $750 in Western Europe, and "around $100" in most underdeveloped countries—a disparity of thirteen to one. By 1989, the richest countries had per capita incomes of over $20,000, while the forty-one poorest countries—with 56 percent of the world's population—had per capita incomes between $300 and $350, a ratio of between fifty-seven and sixty-six to one. (World Bank, *World Development Report 1991* [New York: Oxford University Press], 204–5.)

report observed that "large irrigation and reclamation projects, public utilities, health and training programs, and migration schemes" are less attractive to private investment and thus would be especially deserving of Bank support. The Bank declared that technical assistance and intellectual leadership would be equally important in its relations with underdeveloped nations: its technical aid would "define the shape of a sound over-all development program."[76]

Development theory in the 1950s and 1960s emphasized this capital-intensive approach (though the Bank's exclusive focus on specific projects was a subject of some debate). Walt Rostow spoke of the economic "take-off" that would occur once the catalytic effect of capital investments had spurred increased productivity and growth; Paul Rosenstein-Rodan, who was head of the economics advisory staff of the World Bank between 1947 and 1953, coined the term "Big Push" to characterize the critical mass of investment, national economic planning, and programming to achieve the take-off.[77]

Whatever the theory, in practice early Bank lending was biased not toward the needs of borrowing countries, but toward what was easiest for the Bank to lend for. Power and transportation projects were easily appraised, involved technology transfer and planning that appeared to be the same all over the world, and at least partly filled the dearth of "bankable projects."[78] This would be a constant theme in the development of the Bank: what was convenient for the institution and its staff in preparing projects and moving money would often weigh as heavily as the rather abstract (viewed from Washington) and complicated development needs of the Third World.

But the one-sidedness of the Bank's approach went much further. It combined blanket paternalism with breathtaking naiveté, rooted in a priori macro- and micro-economic assumptions, rather than in empirical understanding of local social, political, and economic realities.*

The distinguished economist Albert Hirschman recounts his experience in the early 1950s as an advisor to the newly created Colombian National Planning Council while he was working for the World Bank—"which," he observes, "had taken an active part in having the Planning Council set up

---

* Economist Paul Streeten reflected in 1984 that "the history of development economics can be regarded as a progress from large generalizations and high abstractions to greater specificity and concreteness. This applies to countries within the Third World, which was found more heterogeneous than originally thought" (Paul P. Streeten, "Development Dichotomies," in Meier and Seers, *Pioneers in Development* [see endnote 75], 341). This is almost a Scholastic, Aristotelean approach. That it took three decades for the proponents of development to admit timidly that three-quarters of the earth's land surface and population was "more heterogeneous than originally thought" speaks volumes about the cultural, historical, and biological ignorance of such an approach.

in the first place and then in recruiting me for it." Hirschman recollects that he

wanted to learn as much as possible about the Colombian economy . . . in the hope of contributing marginally to the improvement of policymaking. But word soon came from World Bank headquarters that I was principally expected to take, as soon as possible, the initiative in formulating some ambitious economic development plan that would spell out investment, domestic savings, growth and foreign aid targets for the Colombian economy over the next few years. All of this was alleged to be quite simple for experts mastering the new programming technique: apparently there now existed adequate knowledge, even without close study of local surroundings, of the likely ranges of savings and capital-output ratios, and those estimates, joined to the country's latest national income and balance of payments accounts, would yield all the key figures needed. . . .

One aspect of this affair made me particularly uneasy. The task was supposedly crucial for Colombia's development, yet no Colombian was to be found who had any inkling of how to go about it. That knowledge was held only by a few foreign experts.[79]

Although the Bank obviously became more sophisticated in later years, its basic approach has changed surprisingly little.* With unintended irony, a Stanford economics professor reflected, "Rather oddly, in retrospect, most of those who began theorizing about underdeveloped countries were citizens of the developed countries."[80]

Walt Rostow, reminiscing in 1984, spoke of the development experts and bureaucrats of the 1950s as "crusaders" in an effort that was "rapidly exposing previously apathetic peoples to the possibility of change."[81] "We were in the line that reached back a century and more to the missionaries from Western societies who went out to distant and often obscure places, not merely to promulgate the faith but also to teach and to heal."[82]

The Politics of Influence

Since the demand for development projects the Bank could finance was less than expected, the Bank's strategy from the 1950s onward was to create it. A primary focus was institution building, most often taking the form of promoting the creation of autonomous agencies within governments—EGAT in Thailand and the NTPC in India are typical

---

* Of course there was much that appeared to change. Every decade the Bank declared new rationales for its lending and it experimented with new kinds of projects and issued new policies. But the continuities were even more profound: the top-down, technocratic methods, the obliviousness to local ecological and social realities, the reliance on foreign experts and plans, and above all, the constant pressure to lend. See, for example, the discussion at the end of this chapter, and Chapter 6.

examples—that would be continual World Bank borrowers. Such agencies were intentionally established to be relatively independent financially from their host governments, as well as less accountable politically—except, of course, to the Bank.[83]

The political consequences of this strategy were far-reaching. A case study prepared by the International Legal Center (ILC), in New York, of the World Bank's involvement in Colombia revealed that between 1949 and 1972, thirty-six of the Bank's fifty-one loans to that country supported autonomous agencies that the Bank had either established or strengthened. The Bank's interventions had a profound impact on the political structure and social evolution of the entire country. According to the ILC study, they weakened "the political party system and minimiz[ed] the roles of the legislature and the judiciary." Indeed,

given the unequal power of the Bank and the borrowing government and the Bank's technocratic bias, an international decision making process evolved which, at the international level, gave the Bank some of the powers of a surrogate government and, at the national level, built up a powerful segment of the administrative arm of the government but bypassed non-technocratic decision making, including the legislative and judiciary branches.[84]*

The Bank, backed by the intellectual influence of some of the economists it employed in the 1950s, such as Paul Rosenstein-Rodan, also played an important role in promoting the establishment of national planning offices and long-term country economic programming in developing nations. Hirschman's experience in Colombia was only a harbinger.[85]

The Bank exerted increasing influence over the evolution of critical economic sectors such as agriculture by linking loans for specific projects to the acceptance of technical packages of fertilizers, pesticides, and technical training, provided mainly from the outside. The effect, of course, was the international economic integration, and dependence, of formerly self-sufficient economic activities.

With considerable financial assistance from the Ford and Rockefeller foundations, the Bank created in 1956 the Economic Development Institute (EDI) to offer six-month training courses in theory and practice of development for senior officials from borrowing countries.** In subsequent years EDI expanded its offerings to include more practical instruction on World Bank techniques for project appraisal and country pro-

---

* Mason and Asher go even farther, and argue that "the Bank's traditional emphasis on insulating the institutions [it supports] from domestic politics can result in institutional behavior so at variance with dominant thinking in the borrowing country as to contribute to the downfall of the government" (Mason and Asher, *Since Bretton Woods,* 702).
** The two foundations provided half of EDI's budget for the first three years (Mason and Asher, *Since Bretton Woods,* 326).

gramming (long-term country lending strategies).* By 1971, more than 1,300 officials had passed through EDI, a number of them already having risen to the position of prime minister or minister of planning or finance in their respective countries.[86]

Another mechanism that amplified the Bank's influence is its practice, starting in the late 1950s, of mobilizing other aid agencies into country consortia or consultative groups, whose purpose is to coordinate and program all foreign assistance to a given country. These country consortia and groups include as members the national foreign aid agencies of industrialized nations, such as the U.S. Agency for International Development and the German Corporation for Technical Assistance (GTZ), as well as other multilateral development banks and the multilateral aid agencies of the United Nations (e.g., the U.N. Development Program and its Food and Agriculture Organization). They meet annually or semiannually, often in Washington or Paris. By 1971, the Bank chaired sixteen of these country aid coordination groups, including those for India, Pakistan, Thailand, Malaysia, and East Africa, and participated in several others, such as that for Indonesia. Whether it chaired the groups or not, the Bank quickly assumed the role of financial and intellectual leader in setting development assistance priorities for most of the nations concerned.[87]

For a critical observer, the World Bank's definition of "politics" and "political influence" appears to come straight out of *Alice in Wonderland:* whatever it does is by definition not political because it says so. Yet, from the beginning, the Bank's use of political leverage and pressure went considerably beyond simple loan conditions relating to specific projects, to broad questions of national economic and social policy. According to Mason and Asher's 1973 history, the Bank characteristically would support the executive branch of a government against elements in the parliament, or the interest of one ministry (finance or energy, for example) against the rest of the government.[88] Equally critical, the Bank would back politicians and bureaucrats amenable to its prescriptions; its ability to favor specific ministries and autonomous agencies with loans was and is a powerful lever of patronage. Thus, by 1970 the Bank had established unique and unprecedented mechanisms for continual political intervention in the internal affairs of borrowing countries. In the words of Mason and Asher, "In the typical case . . . the Bank finds itself supporting certain elements in the government or in the community against others."[89] It would be hard to find a more succinct definition of politics.

The original International Bank for Reconstruction and Development (or IBRD, which, as we have seen, was the first and official name for the

* Country programming became particularly important under the presidency of Robert McNamara (see Chapter 4).

World Bank) was augmented by the establishment of two affiliates, the International Finance Corporation (IFC) in 1956 and the International Development Association (IDA) in 1960. Together, the IBRD, IFC, and IDA would subsequently be referred to as the World Bank Group. IDA and the IBRD share the same staff and management, but the IFC's staff is separate. All three have the same president and the same board of executive directors, who review and approve their policies, loans, and investments. Both the IDA and the IFC have separate articles of agreement, which with minor differences mirror the charter of the IBRD.

The International Finance Corporation is the private-sector branch of the Bank; rather than lending to governments and government agencies, it engages mainly in joint investments with private corporations in industrial and commercial ventures in developing nations. The initial capital of the IFC was quite small, only $100 million, and its investment commitments have remained at a level of about 10 percent to 12 percent of total World Bank Group loans. The IFC's Articles of Agreement contain a proviso that limits it to investing in private projects only "where sufficient capital is not available on reasonable terms" (Article I [i]). The charters of the IBRD and IDA similarly enjoin them to lend only for projects where "private capital is not available on reasonable terms." (IBRD Article I [ii]). For the entire World Bank Group this means that the most economically viable and attractive investments, capable of attracting sufficient private investment, are off limits by definition. Combined with the chronic lack of bankable projects presented to the Bank to begin with, it is hardly any wonder that project quality has been a problem over the years. The IFC's mandate appears particularly dubious: it must find viable, productive private-sector projects that the private sector alone has found unworthy of investment.[90]

Much more critical for the Bank's future was the creation of the International Development Association, which gives long-term loans (now typically thirty-five or forty years) at no interest (but with a .75 percent annual "service charge") to the Bank's poorer members. The IDA came to be as a result of lobbying led by India, Chile, and Yugoslavia in the United Nations in the 1950s for a "Special United Nations Development Administration." Poorer nations in the U.N. proposed an institution separate from the Bank to provide "soft," low-interest loans for development purposes. The industrialized nations, led by the United States, at first resisted the proposal, but eventually agreed, provided that the new fund be administered by the World Bank, which they controlled.[91]

The creation of the International Development Association had several critical consequences. It made the World Bank still more of an institution with "development" (whatever that might be) as its mission, as opposed to a bank or merely a lending agency for large infrastructure projects. IDA's charter specifies that it (like the IBRD) is to finance "specific projects" except in special circumstances, but adds that these shall be "of high developmental priority" (Article V, Section 1[b]). Second, for some countries the World Bank Group would be able to put together combined financial packages of both IBRD loans and IDA credits (as the IDA loans are called). The combined lower interest rates associated with such packages would make borrowing more attractive for these nations, although the number of countries qualifying for both IBRD and IDA assistance was limited.*

Most importantly, IDA financing was completely different from that of the IBRD; it had to be fully replenished with hard funds every three years by the major industrialized countries. The IBRD raised most of its resources by borrowing in international capital markets, using the guarantee of the callable capital of the major industrialized nations. True, to increase its borrowings the IBRD eventually has to request a capital increase from its members, but this occurs less frequently than IDA replenishments. The triennial IDA replenishment obliges the Bank to make its case not just before the Board of Executive Directors (giving them, at least potentially, more direct power over the president and management),[92] but also before the public and the legislatures of its most powerful members. In the United States, this gives the Congress, and several key subcommittees, more continual control over the Bank's purse strings. In the late 1980s, for example, U.S. congressional appropriations for IDA averaged about a billion dollars a year, whereas the annual contribution of the United States to the IBRD's paid-in capital was less than $100 million a year.** Many IDA replenishments came to be characterized by strained relations between the U.S. Congress and the Bank.

The Specter of Net Negative Transfers

An institution limited to a zero net transfer of capital can hardly be characterized as a development institution.[93]   —Edward Mason and Robert Asher, 1973

From its early years to the present, there have been two main factors behind the pressure to lend within the World Bank. One,

---

* In 1964, IDA established an income test; as of 1992, only countries with per capita incomes of $610 or less qualified for IDA credits.
** For each dollar of paid-in capital, the U.S. Treasury commits itself to back the IBRD with as much as $20 of callable capital. This guarantee does not appear in the budget figures; however, it is a potential government liability, if the IBRD were ever to encounter massive defaults by its borrowing nations. The analogy with the government's liability for savings and loans institutions has already been made by some authors.

already discussed, was the lack of quality, "bankable" projects. A second, even more serious pressure, began to appear at the end of the 1950s—net negative transfers from its borrowers; that is, some countries began to pay more money back to the Bank than the Bank disbursed to them in new loans.* For most banks this is not a problem, but a simple fact of life: disbursements from a lender to a borrower will be heavily in the borrower's favor in the early years of a loan; in later years, the flow reverses as the borrower pays the loan back. To keep increasing the volume of loans as time goes on to a borrower, so that net transfers over the short term from the bank to the borrower remain positive, is obviously building a house of cards; it sets up a situation that risks massive default later on as the debt service consumes increasing amounts of the borrower's income. But a well-run commercial bank does not face this prospect if it can recruit a constant stream of new customers to lend to, corporate or individual.

The World Bank, however, has a unique problem: its customer base is limited to a few score developing nations. At some point most countries start paying back more to the Bank than it lends, and the Bank eventually liquidates itself—as John J. McCloy, hardly a financial or political naif, indeed expected. This outcome can be averted only if the Bank keeps increasing the volume of lending to the same countries, piling on new debt, or, better, can obtain funds to disburse as grants or low-interest loans.[94]

Thus, in the 1960s, IDA, with its funding replenished every three years by the major industrialized nations, played an important role in alleviating, but not eliminating, the Bank's looming net negative transfer problem with poorer countries. The problem is that IDA replenishments must also constantly grow to stanch the flow of resources back to the Bank.**

* The term *net transfer* has been given a number of a times opaque technical definitions in the literature of international debt and foreign aid. Here, however, we are using it as Mason and Asher use it in their twenty-five-year history of the Bank: simply to indicate the relation between the amount of new inflows of money from the World Bank (including IDA) to a given borrowing nation (or group of nations) and the total repayment in the same time period (usually a Bank fiscal year) of principal and interest on previous loans. If a country is paying more back to the Bank than the Bank is disbursing to it, there is a net negative transfer to the Bank from the borrowing nation. (For more technical discussions, see Cheryl Payer, *Lent and Lost: Foreign Credit and Third World Development* [London, United Kingdom and Atlantic Highlands, New Jersey: Zed Books, Ltd., 1991], 10–15; and World Bank/IMF Development Committee, *Development Issues: Presentations to the 44th Meeting of the Development Committee, Washington, D.C.—September 21, 1992* [Washington, D.C.: World Bank, 1992], 53–54.)
** Writing in 1973, Mason and Asher described the net negative transfer specter haunting the Bank: "The most important fact to us at the moment is that without a further increase in the volume of IDA credits and in their proportion to total loans and credits from the Bank Group to less developed countries, the Group's *net* transfer of resources to those countries will probably become negative or negligible" (Mason and Asher, *Since Bretton Woods*, 418).

In 1961, developed countries were already paying more back to the Bank than it was lending them. This, of course, was expected, since there was no need for the Bank to continue lending to richer nations. But the same phenomenon would also be true in the future for the Bank's poorer members, whose borrowing was creating a debt that was contributing to their underdevelopment and dependence. The World Bank's annual report for 1963–64 expressed alarm: "The heavy debt burden that weighs on an increasing number of its member countries has been a continuing concern of the World Bank group."[95] In the 1960s, the Third World debt crisis became, according to the history that the Bank commissioned for its twenty-fifth anniversary, "a central preoccupation of the Bank." "The large increase in bilateral and multilateral development assistance flows in the 1960s had begun by 1970 to generate unmanageable demands for reverse flows," the same history adds.[96] In 1963, 1964, and 1969, India transferred more money to the World Bank than the Bank disbursed to it, despite large cash infusions from IDA.[97] In 1968, India was obliged to reschedule its long-term debt, followed by Indonesia in 1970. In 1970, debt service payments for developing countries already equaled 40 percent of the total transfer of funds to them from the industrialized north. That same year, the Bank had its first year of net negative transfers—borrowers paid more back to the Bank than the total amounts the Bank disbursed.[98]

Enter Robert McNamara.

4

The Faustian Paradox of Robert McNamara

The parable of the talents is a parable about power—about financial power—and it illuminates the great truth that all power is given us to be used, not to be wrapped in a napkin against risk.[1]
—Robert McNamara, September 30, 1968

A chain of marshes lines the hills,
Befouling all the land retrievement;
To drain this stagnant pool of ills
Would be the crowning, last achievement.
I'd open room to live for millions
Not safely, but in free resilience.
Lush fallow then to man and cattle yields
Swift crops and comforts from the maiden fields.[2]
—Goethe, *Faust*

More than any of his predecessors—or successors—Robert McNamara made the Bank into what it is today. In physical terms, he drove it to expand at a pace unprecedented for a large institution, at a rate that was clearly unsustainable for more than a few years: during his thirteen-year tenure from 1968 to 1981, lending increased from $953 million to $12.4 billion (sixfold, in real terms), and the Bank staff from 1,574 to 5,201.[3] Even more important, he brought a sense of moral mission to the Bank that has not been seen before or since. His fervor and single-mindedness, reflected in the Bank's astounding physical growth, was for the sake of development—"one of the biggest and the most important tasks confronting mankind in this century," as he declared in 1969.[4] Above all, he proclaimed, it was for the sake of the poorest of the poor.

It was McNamara, too, who created in 1970 an environmental office in the Bank, and who declared in Stockholm at the 1972 U.N. Conference on the Human Environment,

The question is not whether there should be continued economic growth. There must be. Nor is the question whether the impact on the environment must be respected. It has to be. Nor—least of all—is it a question of whether these two considerations are interlocked. They are.

The solution of the dilemma revolves clearly not about whether, but how.[5]

McNamara asserted in Stockholm that the environmental office reviewed "each project processed by the Bank" and conducted "careful in-house studies" of the ecological components, using comprehensive environmental criteria embodied in checklists that "encompass the entire spectrum of development." In two years' time, he claimed, the Bank had established a formidable environmental record, which, he implied, was worthy of emulation: "While in principle the Bank could refuse a loan on environmental grounds . . . the fact is no such case has yet arisen. Since initiating our environmental review, we have found that in every instance the recommended safeguards can and have been successfully negotiated and implemented."[6]

Let us examine, then, the Bank's poverty agenda in the McNamara period, as well as some of its environmental implications. After all, at Stockholm in 1972, Indira Gandhi of India declared that poverty itself was the greatest polluter in developing nations. This theme would be repeated by McNamara's successors, who argued that by helping the poor the Bank was also helping the environment.

A Matter of Morality

McNamara presented an intriguing paradox. Many thought of him as the quintessential technocrat. The former chief of the Ford Motor Company and U.S. secretary of defense during the Vietnam War, he had an almost obsessive faith in quantification, rationalism, and control, in universally valid managerial methods that could be brought to bear on any problem.* "Running any large organization is the same,

---

* McNamara, in the words of his biographer Deborah Shapley, "stood for quantification and technology when American romance with both was at its height" (Shapley, *Promise and Power* [see endnote 7], x). McNamara was converted to this faith in the modern mission to control economic and social development through quantitative analysis and method at Harvard Business School in the 1930s; it was an approach developed in the first decades of the twentieth century by Alfred P. Sloan, Jr., at General Motors and by the Dupont Company. Called "financial control, management control, statistical control, or control accounting" (Shapley, 21) at different times for different applications, it dominated the management of

whether it's the Ford Motor Company, the Catholic Church, or the Department of Defense," he observed in the early 1960s. "Once you get the certain scale, they're all the same."[7] His top-down vision of social and economic development had at times echoes of the modernizing heroism of Peter the Great and other benevolent despots of the European Enlightenment. "Management," he declared in 1967, "is the gate through which social and economic and political change, indeed change in every direction, is diffused throughout society."[8]

But McNamara forcefully made it clear that his personal goals, and those of the World Bank under his tenure, were moral and ethical. He told the assembled Board of Governors of the Bank and Fund in Nairobi in 1973 that although there are many justifications for development aid (expansion of trade, international security, reducing social tensions, etc.),

the fundamental case for development assistance is the moral one. The whole of human history has recognized the principle—at least in the abstract—that the rich and the powerful have a moral obligation to assist the poor and the weak. That is what the sense of community is all about—any community: the community of the family, the community of the village, the community of the nation, the community of nations itself.[9]

Would the Bank under McNamara evolve from the bloodless financial technocracy of Eugene Black's tenure into the global economic church of the poor and the weak? In that same 1973 Nairobi speech McNamara set out the institution's new agenda: Bank lending would continue to grow at the phenomenal rate of 14 percent a year; more importantly, an increasing portion of loans would be targeted to alleviate what McNamara called "absolute poverty," a condition he had defined the year before as affecting 40 percent of the total population in developing countries, some 700 million people who, left behind by economic growth, "remained entrapped in conditions of deprivation which fall below any rational definition of human decency."[10]

Most of these people lived in rural areas, McNamara stated, and the Bank's poverty strategy would focus on an initial goal: to increase production on small farms (less than 5 hectares) so that by 1985 their output would grow at an annual rate of 5 percent.[11] The strategy comprised several key elements, all targeted, in theory, to aid the poor: promoting land reform; ensuring better access to credit for poor farmers; making available more water for irrigation and family use; expanding agricultural extension services and agricultural research; and increasing access to public services,

---

American industry for decades to come, as well as the organization of other large-scale efforts, such as procurement and logistics for the U.S. government in World War II. (See Shapley, 20–57.)

particularly health and education. "Most critical of all," McNamara emphasized, the Bank would support new rural institutions and organizations that would devote more attention to improving the productivity and potential of the poor than to "protecting the power of the privileged."[12]

Robert McNamara concluded his Nairobi address with an almost ecclesiastical exhortation:

All of the great religions teach the value of each human life. In a way that was never true in the past, we now have the power to create a decent life for all men and women. Should we not make the moral precept our guide to action? The extremes of poverty and deprivation are simply no longer acceptable.

It is development's task to deal with them.[13]

The Alleviation of Poverty: Theory

The most important single assumption in the Bank's poverty strategy, set out in a 1974 report entitled "Redistribution with Growth," was that there would be no, or very little, trade-off between social equity and economic growth; it was thought that not only did the two goals not conflict, but the same policies could promote both simultaneously. The Bank's strategy would direct investment toward poorer groups, with the goal of promoting national economic growth; it would avoid the thorny question of redistribution of income or assets.[14] In practice, however, these assumptions would be contradicted by increasing relative economic inequality in the 1970s and 1980s within a number of rapidly growing countries favored by the Bank, such as Chile and Thailand.

In the McNamara years, the Bank continued its traditional lending for infrastructure—about half to two-thirds of its portfolio included the typical projects of the 1950s and 1960s, like big dams and highways—but the proportion of "new-style" poverty projects grew much more quickly. The main focus was on rural development and agriculture, a sector which grew from 18.5 percent of Bank lending in 1968 (with $172.5 million in loans, and IDA credits) to $3.8 billion in 1981, or 31 percent of annual loan commitments.[15] Urban poverty-alleviation projects (usually involving upgrading of slums, i.e., installing water pumps, electricity, etc.), and education and health projects also became for the first time a significant part of the Bank's portfolio.

McNamara's ambitious make-over of the Bank went further than a huge increase in lending with a reorientation toward targeting investment to benefit the poor; he initiated an ambitious intensification of Bank research and long-term planning, the ultimate goal of which was to shape aggressively the future evolution of scores of developing countries with most of the world's population. In a speech at Columbia University in February 1970, McNamara declared:

To provide a solid foundation for consultation and action by both developed and developing nations, in the whole field of development strategy and administration of aid, we plan a new and expanded program of Country Economic Missions. These will be regularly scheduled, thoroughly staffed, comprehensive missions whose mandate will be to assist the member government to draw up an overall development strategy which will include every major sector of the economy, and every relevant aspect of the nation's social framework. . . .

Once the mission is completed, we will promptly produce for use by all of the parties concerned a thorough Country Economic Report which will serve as a profile of the country's progress and of its overall development plan.[16]

The Bank would also prepare five-year master country lending plans, set out in "country programming papers" (CPPs); the CPPs set targets and priorities for all Bank lending in a given nation, based on the work of the country economic missions and ensuing reports. It goes without saying that these economic reports and CPPs ranked among the most confidential and closely held documents in the Bank, apart from internal memoranda. In some cases, even ministers of a nation's cabinet could not obtain access to these documents, which in smaller, poorer countries were viewed as international decrees on their economic fate.* The CPPs were the master planning documents for the Bank's entire lending portfolio, but the Bank refused to allow the executive directors to see them, as well as many other documents.[17] The directors were reduced to a rubber stamp; McNamara would not even allow them to review in advance his major policy speeches at the annual Bank/Fund meetings.[18] As never before, the Bank was accountable only to itself.

Here, then, was a vision of global central planning, based on an extraordinary presumption: the staff of the World Bank would, through visits ("missions") of a few days or weeks, combined with desk research, take the lead in gathering data to prepare a development plan for "every relevant aspect" of a "nation's social framework." The Bank would go on to lead scores of governments in formulating these plans, which, it goes

---

* This was the author's experience as a conservation consultant to Belize in 1982, where government officials complained about their inability to obtain a recently completed World Ban country economic memorandum for the newly independent nation. They would have found it interesting: Belize is the last relatively forested country in Central America, a region plagued by deforestation caused in large part by cattle ranching. Nevertheless, the Bank's country economic memorandum recommended investments for expanding cattle raising.

without saying, would attempt to regulate "every relevant aspect" of society. Based on the Bank's gathering, filtering, and organizing of information, other international agencies would help to finance the elements of the development blueprints formulated under the Bank's aegis.

This vision assumed and greatly reinforced the notion of the state as an entity that by right plans and directs all "relevant" aspects of social, economic, and political evolution. Critical to this project is the systematic shaping of information, in this case under the aegis of the Bank, in a form that can be used as an instrument of social control and domination by pliant governments in the developing world. The role of the private, of the nongovernmental, of the local or national community, of everything that is characterized as civil society, is absent in this vision; at its limit, it proposes a world in which all that happens is permitted to happen because it has been officially studied, officially sanctioned, and officially planned. The vision constantly invoked the welfare of the poor, but had no place for political or civil accountability to the people affected by Bank lending in borrowing countries, nor to the public of its donor nations. The possibility of open debate about alternative social, economic, and political priorities was excluded from this brave new order.

Last, but not least, under McNamara the Bank's expanded planning ambitions embodied deep-rooted assumptions about the "knowability" of complex human social systems and their interactions with nature. The Bank would guide the generation of such knowledge in order to plan; implicit in the planning is control, and in control domination—over the evolution of human beings and nature on a planetary scale. It is no exaggeration to call such a project Faustian.

The Alleviation of Poverty: Practice

The notion that rural development can be engineered through an appropriate mix of financial and technological inputs, irrespective of the social structure and political norms of the host country, does not withstand rational scrutiny.[19]
—René Lemarchand, Belgian anthropologist

We have seen that McNamara's development vision appeared idealistic, indeed, moralistic, but the means were infused with a disquieting lack of accountability, a structure of top-down control, and a thrust toward domination. In practice, McNamara's approach greatly exacerbated already existing trends in the Bank which reinforced the growth of its own institutional power while ignoring the complex and diverse social and natural reality of developing nations.* First and foremost, the McNamara years were characterized by an unprecedented and tremendous pressure on staff to increase lending to meet publicly announced rates of expansion. The old problem of lack of bankable projects, however, had not gone away. On the contrary, it was worse than ever. The solution was the intensification of an across-the-board technocratic approach. Easily quantifiable targets were defined as indicators of progress, and complex social realities were reduced to "figures and numbers of target groups, beneficiaries, incremental output, improvements in productivity, changes in incomes, and so forth."[20] The same technologies were applied everywhere, with predictable results: they were usually inefficient at best, and often so environmentally and socially inappropriate as to foreordain many projects to failure.

The Bank's approach to poverty also assumed that powerful elites in developing nations, who were well ensconced in siphoning off the benefits of development aid from government ministries, could be induced to make institutional and structural changes for the benefit of the poor and powerless.[21]** Lack of informed consultation with, or the participation of,

---

* The literature on the McNamara years is not as extensive as one might expect. Several books reach the same conclusion, that the Bank by its very nature (top-down, technocratic, closed) and programs (lending to governments controlled by corrupt elites) not only did not improve the lot of the poor in the 1970s, but actually contributed to increasing inequality. See Aart Van de Laar, *The World Bank and the Poor* (The Hague: Martinus Nijhoff, 1980), written by a Dutch economist and former Bank staff member; Cheryl Payer, *The World Bank: A Critical Analysis* (New York: Monthly Review Press, 1982), a Marxian critique, but well-researched, with conclusions similar to those of other critical researchers; Tatjana Chahoud, *Entwicklungsstrategie der Weltbank: Ein Beitrag zur Ueberwindung von Unterentwicklung und Armut?* (Saarbruecken and Fort Lauderdale: Verlag breitenback, 1982), a 500-page German study which concludes that the World Bank is not helping the poor; Rainer Tetzlaff, *Die Weltbank, Machtinstrument der USA oder Hilfe fuer die Entwicklungslaender?* (Muenchen: Weltforum Verlag, 1980), another lengthy German study with highly critical conclusions; Zaki Laidi, *Enquête sur la Banque Mondiale* (Paris: Fayard, 1989), a recent French study that concludes that McNamara lending did not reach the poor.

Robert L. Ayres's, *Banking on the Poor* (Cambridge, Massachusetts and London, England: MIT Press, 1984) contains a number of damning criticisms, but the author concludes that difficulties in reaching the poor should not be blamed on McNamara's policies or on the Bank, but on the international and national constraints the Bank has to operate under. Though the constraints are real, they should not and cannot serve as a blanket alibi for the Bank (see Chapter 7).

** Chahoud examines as a case study the Bank's Brazil Rio Grande do Norte Rural Development Project, approved in 1975. Its principal goal was to double income from cotton cultivation in Brazil's impoverished northeast; it included a public health component, as well as agricultural credit and extension services. According to Chahoud, most of the benefits of the project were from its very inception targeted toward richer farmers and large landowners, and largely excluded the majority of the poor, sharecroppers and the landless. (Chahoud, *Entwicklungsstrategie der Weltbank* [see endnote 23], 298–320.)

the putative beneficiaries (that is, the poor) of the huge increase in Bank lending was also the rule.[22]

Other critics pointed out that even in theory the whole approach was fatally flawed: of the 700 to 800 million poorest-of-the-poor who were the targets of the Bank's poverty strategy, 60 to 70 percent were landless farmers, agricultural laborers, or so poor they were unable to obtain credit under any circumstances. The McNamara strategy of targeting investment to benefit small-scale landowners to increase their production would—if and when it worked—reach the minority that needed help least.[23]

From the standpoint of the environment, the social and technological inappropriateness of Bank policy compounded the ill effects of fundamentally destructive strategies. A major focus of the so-called new-style projects of the 1970s was the opening up of "new lands" for agriculture, commercial forestry, and cattle ranching, often in tropical forests, often involving large-scale resettlement. Capital-intensive, Green Revolution agricultural technologies were promoted, requiring increasing use of chemical fertilizers and pesticides. Ironically, in the name of the poor, development Bank-style resulted in increased domination of powerless social groups and increased occupation of natural areas and spaces.

How the Bank and its borrowers often transmuted McNamara's uplifting rhetoric on poverty and the environment into its opposite in practice is best seen in specific examples.

The all-too-typical diversion of Bank loans from the poor to local political and economic elites is well illustrated in a case documented by two American researchers, Betsy Hartmann and James Boyce, who experienced firsthand the effects of an IDA project that financed the installation of 3,000 tubewells in northwestern Bangladesh. The project was supposed to benefit cooperatives of twenty-five to fifty farmers, specially formed for the purpose of buying the wells. In the village where the Americans lived, the tubewell was purchased by the richest landlord of the region (a man named Nafis), who collected a few bogus signatures to indicate to project authorities that he was the "manager" of the irrigation cooperative.[24]

Nafis got the $12,000 tubewell by spending about $300 in bribes to local officials and installed it in the middle of his own 30-acre tract. This is only half the size of the area capacity of the tubewell, but the price Nafis planned to charge neighboring small farmers for use of the water is so high that the well will not be used to its full capacity. Nafis is the *only* beneficiary of the project in his village, and he will probably use his enhanced income to purchase plots to add to his own, driving the previous owners into landlessness.[25]

India is a particularly important case of the combination of corruption and the deflection of benefits from the poor, since it was (and continues to be) the Bank's biggest borrower, and contains more of the absolute poor than any other nation. Indian agriculture, particularly irrigated agriculture, was the foremost battlefield of the McNamara poverty war.

In 1982, British researcher Robert Wade described the systemic corruption in the irrigation administration in an unnamed state of South India; citing this example, he argued that in many countries there is no justification for assuming that irrigation systems are built and operated in the interest of small farmers. Instead, Wade suggests, chronic underperformance of irrigation projects may often be a result of their operation and maintenance "so as to raise large amounts of illicit revenue for their staff and for politicians."[26] In his South Indian case study, he notes that as much as 50 percent of maintenance funds were simply siphoned off in corruption and that the irrigation engineers had a vested interest in actually creating scarcity and uncertainty in water supplies, cutting off supplies to vulnerable villages until they paid the requisite extortion. "Bribes are high where uncertainty [of water supply] is high," Wade concludes.[27] Other studies indicated the problem was actually worse elsewhere: in the Kosi canal system in Bihar, in northeast India, an estimated 50 to 60 percent of project funds illicitly disappeared into the hands of contractors, corrupt officials, and local politicians.[28] The scale of this corruption explains in part what Wade calls "the consistent political commitment to irrigation investment, which in some Indian states accounts for over half the state's development budget."[29]

The World Bank might have had a role in reducing mismanagement of such projects; in reality, the enormous pressure to increase lending in the McNamara years had the opposite effect in many cases. Wade noted in 1982 that the official position of international agencies like the Bank was "to concern themselves with increasing the inputs to development, while it is for the host government to worry about the outputs from development projects."[30] In fact, according to Wade, the Bank's approach in the 1970s was to blame the farmers for the chronic underperformance of irrigation projects in India.

The key to more efficient and more equitable irrigation systems lies in reform of management, and in taking into account local social and political factors; in fact many traditional irrigation systems in Asia achieved more efficient water use at less cost than Bank-financed projects. But Wade concludes that the World Bank emphasized massive, expensive programs reflecting the engineer's bias of its South Asia irrigation division toward "big and complex hardware. The problem is that what is good for the Bank, as a lending institution, is not necessarily good for adoption in the borrowing country as a general recipe."[31]

Agricultural extension was another critical component of the Bank's agriculture strategy in India and some two dozen other countries. The Bank touted its "Training and Visit" agricultural extension system (T & V), which promoted a centralized system of transfer of knowledge from field extension agents to a select 10 percent of farmers, called "contact farmers." Typically, village extension agents would meet every two weeks with the contact farmers to disseminate a preprogrammed lesson, and the contact farmers in turn were responsible for spreading the word to the other ("follower") farmers in their area.

Though simple and attractive in theory, the T & V approach in practice was another matter. According to British researcher Mick Moore, in India it had little effect in improving the quality of agricultural extension services, but was successful in committing the central and state governments of India to increase recurrent expenditures to maintain a greatly expanded extension system.[32] The village extension agents simply did not do their jobs; the fortnightly training sessions were often empty, formalistic exercises; and, most critically, the contact farmers did not pass on their knowledge to the "follower" farmers, or did not even know that they were "supposed to be contact farmers in the first place."[33] The Bank promoted T & V in India on a grand scale; between 1977 and 1982 it approved twelve loans and credits totaling $200 million (with the Indian government throwing in another $200 million) to promote the new extension system in thirteen Indian states, mainly in the "command areas" (that is, the areas to be served) of large irrigation projects.[34] Most of this money went for buildings, vehicles, and staff salaries, and, naturally enough, created a big lobby in Indian state agriculture departments for the new system.

Why was T & V so ineffective? According to Moore, the Bank applied a standardized system in "disregard of the heterogeneity of local ecological and institutional considerations." Local ecology and cropping patterns, community institutions, and sociological factors were largely ignored. Moreover, Moore charges, the Bank exerted considerable pressure on Indian officials to declare the system a success and actively squelched questioning and criticism:

As one source put it to this author, the World Bank "preached T and V like a religion." No questioning of the concept was permitted, and the Bank used its considerable resources and propaganda apparatus simply to persuade. The author's own recent experiences suggest that this observation is still to a large extent true.[35]

Moore concludes that the Bank played a deeply disturbing and counterproductive role in its promotion of T & V in India: a single extension model "had been introduced, probably inadvisedly, to a wide variety of agricultural situations." The specific needs of local farmers and the constraints of local ecologies had little place in a universal model that was to be applied everywhere. The whole system was driven by the career interests of Bank staff and of Indian agriculture officials, rooted in the complementary interests of both to move as much money as possible.* The suppression of criticism and questioning was a logical and characteristic corollary.[36]

Perhaps the most disturbing charge of critics of the McNamara years is that rhetoric notwithstanding, Bank poverty-oriented agricultural lending actually promoted the destruction of smaller local farms and the displacement of hundreds of millions of peasants around the world. Beneath the uplifting rhetoric, McNamara's poverty strategy in practice only accelerated a process of agricultural modernization and integration into the global market that in the view of many researchers *increased* inequality** and *produced* poverty and underdevelopment by displacing rural people formerly rooted in traditional subsistence-farming communities.*** It was an economic process of appropriation of smaller farms and common areas that resembled in some respects the enclosure of open lands in Britain prior to the Industrial Revolution—only this time on a global scale, intensified by the economic concentration fostered by Green Revolution agricultural technology.[37] Subsistence farmers and tribal, indige-

* Moore apportions the blame equally between Indian officials and the World Bank, observing that the Bank is "as much victim as aggressor. Its ability to support institutional change has been severely circumscribed by its own internal imperatives to be seen to be running a successful and fast-expanding programme and by its dependence on Indian allies who have material interests of their own" (Moore, "Institutional Development" [see endnote 32], 31).

** In the words of a classic study on the Green Revolution by Keith Griffin, "The changes which are at present occurring tend to increase relative inequality" (Keith Griffin, *The Political Economy of Agrarian Change: An Essay on the Green Revolution* [Cambridge, Massachusetts: Harvard University Press, 1974], 73).

*** Cynthia Hewitt de Alcantara's *Modernizing Mexican Agriculture 1940–1970: Socioeconomic Implications of Technological Change* (New York: United Nations Research Institute for Social Development, 1976) is a classic study of this process. She concluded that the Green Revolution in Mexico (which received considerable financial and policy support from the World Bank) worsened the absolute living standards of most of Mexico's poor rural population, reduced domestic production of food crops, and raised the price of food, resulting in *increased* hunger and greater concentration of poverty in the countryside. Most benefits were deflected to the cities. Traditional Indian communities such as the Yaqui in northwest Mexico were "undeveloped" by the whole process: local traditions of economic and social democracy in the formerly self-governing communities were destroyed as they were reduced to greater dependency on the outside and suffered increasing poverty and marginalization. Ironically, as their nonmonetized material and cultural wealth was destroyed, their per capita income increased somewhat due to their fuller integration into a money economy.

Her conclusion is an epitaph not only on the World Bank, but on distorted goals of the global economy: "There would thus seem to be no necessary correlation in the Mexican countryside between monetary income and basic wellbeing, as there has unfortunately been no necessary correlation between modernization and development" (Hewitt de Alcantara, op. cit., 319–20).

nous peoples were often the first victims, pushed from poverty to destitution. Researcher Tina Wallace concluded that in northern Nigeria, although Bank-financed irrigated agriculture projects were

supposed to benefit ordinary peasant farmers[,] [i]n practice they do anything but. Many are resettled and in the process lose some of their acreage. . . . Others downstream of the schemes have lost the annual flooding that made their land fertile. Even those on the irrigated plots often cannot afford the extra costs of this new commercial farming and rent out their land or sell it.[38]

Even projects that the World Bank claimed as among its most successful proved to have created greater inequality and worsened the lot of the landless poor. A classic case is that of the Malaysia Muda Irrigation Project, which, according to a 1975 Bank completion report, doubled average farm incomes in its area of influence between 1965 and 1974, increased rice production two-and-a-half-fold, and achieved an economic rate of return of 18 percent as opposed to the expected rate of 10 percent.[39] Yale political scientist James C. Scott lived in a small village affected by the project between 1978 and 1980 and discovered a much more ambiguous situation. While average prosperity had increased for a majority of households, "a substantial minority—perhaps 35–40 percent—have been left behind with very low incomes which, if they are not worse than a decade ago, are not appreciably better."[40] Small tenants who had half the income of landowners when the project began had a quarter of their income after its completion, and by 1979 had lower real incomes than when the project began in 1966.[41] The state, which before was "largely [a] bystander or mediator in relations [of farmers] with nature and the private sector . . . is now a direct participant, decision maker, allocator, and antagonist."[42]

Scott documented a pattern of growing passive resistance by the village's poorer population in the mid-1970s, including numerous incidents of sabotage of large harvesting combines. According to Scott, the combines eliminated two-thirds of the wage-earning opportunities for the poor in the village area.[43] He concluded that "as in so many other 'green revolutions' the rich have gotten richer and the poor have remained poor or grown poorer."[44]

The Bank's urban poverty projects, which focused on upgrading slum neighborhoods, suffered similar problems of deflection of benefits despite laudable intentions. In the South Indian city of Madras, for example, a study by two Dutch development workers concluded that a Bank-financed slum improvement project, and others like it, hardly ever reached the poorest fifth of the population; worse, such projects spurred increasing land prices and rents, resulting in the eviction of poorer families.[45] Analogous problems occurred in what was supposed to be a model urban shelter project financed by the Bank in Dar es Salaam, Tanzania.[46]

In not a few cases, Bank poverty projects not only increased inequality, but exacerbated ethnic conflicts—as with the Rwanda Mutura Agriculture and Livestock Development Project. Financed in the 1970s, its goal was to help 9,000 poor and landless families through an ambitious program of agricultural settlement and the establishment of cattle ranches over a total project area of 51,000 hectares. A Belgian anthropologist, René Lemarchand, was hired by the Bank in 1978 to help appraise a second loan for the project, which had been underway since 1974. Lemarchand warned that the project ignored critical ethnic and political factors: following a 1973 military coup, the Hutu tribal majority, 85 percent of the population, had wrested power from the long-dominant Tutsi minority. The project area covered a region traditionally inhabited by the Hima and Tutsi peoples, though by 1978 the land was mostly occupied by Hutu settlers. The project itself was a typical top-down undertaking, and its main consequence was not to alleviate poverty, but to establish a system of political patronage and spoils, administered by the Hutu, which

for the Hima and Tutsi . . . has meant little more than a thinly disguised attempt to reduce their resource-base (both in terms of the size of their herds and the extent of their grazing areas) and a reshaping of their pastoral way of life in such a way as to increase their economic and political dependence on the Hutu.[47]

The fatal flaw of the Mutura project, endemic in most Bank poverty alleviation efforts, was to virtually ignore the social and political dynamics of the local situation—dynamics which "proved largely incompatible with the very objective of rural development as defined by the Bank, in effect denying the poor access to the resources, services and institutional support structure that might have allowed them to move up the economic and social ladder."[48] Lemarchand's warnings were ignored: "My contribution to the project eventually appeared in the Bank Staff Appraisal Report reduced . . . to two pages of largely innocuous verbiage, properly asepticized."[49]**

* The distortion, indeed suppression of information generated by Bank consultants is a recurring theme in projects in the 1970s and 1980s. Claude Reboul, an agricultural specialist affiliated with the French National Institute for Agronomical Research (INRA), was hired by the World Bank in 1974 to prepare a study on agriculture in the West African country of Senegal. Reboul's conclusions confirmed those of other researchers: the Bank's poverty strategy was making the already better-off farmers richer and marginalizing still further the poor. Reboul xeroxed fifty copies of his report to distribute to his colleagues at INRA. World Bank officials not only rejected his analysis, but wrote Reboul that "we oppose any dissemination of this report and demand that all existing copies be destroyed" (René Dumont, *Pour l'Afrique, j'accuse,* Annexe IX, "L'Inquisition Ressuscitée: La Banque Mondiale Ordonne La Destruction d'un Rapport de Claude Reboul" [Paris: Plon, 1986], 367–72). See also the

Ambitious land-clearing and settlement projects were another important component of the Bank's purported poverty alleviation strategy. One year after the Mutara project, the Bank approved a $21-million Rwanda Forestry and Livestock Development Project to establish pastures, new agricultural settlements, and commercial timber plantations in 37,000 acres of the virgin Gishwati forest.[50]

In Malaysia, the Bank supported with numerous loans the massive forest-clearing and agricultural settlement activities of the Federal Land Development Authority (FELDA)—an autonomous development agency of the kind fostered by Bank "institution building." The Bank approved three loans between 1968 and 1973 for the Jenka Triangle land settlement scheme, involving the clearing of about 100,000 acres of prime tropical rainforest in central peninsular Malaysia, and the resettlement of 9,600 families to grow oil palms and rubber trees. In 1973, the Bank approved another $40-million loan to FELDA for clearing 81,000 acres of tropical forest to establish oil palm estates in the Jahore region in southern peninsular Malaysia. The project resettled 7,550 families and constructed eight villages and five palm oil mills. The 1975 Keratong Project loan of $36 million financed the clearing of tens of thousands of acres of tropical forest in south-central Malaysia for the planting of more oil palm estates, and the 1978 FELDA VI Land Settlement Project provided $28 million for the clearing of 72,000 acres of tropical forest for rubber, cocoa, and annual crops, and the resettlement of 6,200 families.[51]

It is significant that the Bank viewed its FELDA projects as unusually successful: they met or overfulfilled quantitative goals of land clearing, crop production, and settlement. In the words of a 1982 post-project evaluation report prepared by the Bank's Operations Evaluation Department (OED),* "With more than 1.3 million acres developed and 72,600 families settled since 1960, FELDA is undoubtedly one of the most important and efficient settlement agencies in the world."[52] Altogether these 1.3 million acres covered 4 percent of the entire land area of peninsular Malaysia and accounted for the destruction of about 6.5 percent of its remaining forest cover in the 1970s.[53] Another OED report proudly asserted that "early and continuing Bank financial support has provided FELDA enormous momentum."[54] But the total cost per family of these forest-clearing and settlement schemes was astronomical: U.S. $23,000 per

---

discussion concerning David Price in my Chapter 6, and the section on the Morse Commission report in Chapter 9.

* The Operations Evaluation Department was established in 1974 to prepare independent evaluations of completed Bank projects for the Board of Executive Directors and Bank management. Its functions, and lack of success in influencing Bank operations, are discussed in Chapter 5 and Chapter 6.

family (in 1981 dollars; nearly $40,000 in 1993 dollars) for the Johore settlement project, and only slightly less in the three Jenka Triangle projects.[55] In contrast, the much more publicized and criticized Indonesia Transmigration and Brazil Polonoroeste projects of the 1980s were relative bargains, averaging $6,000 to $8,000 per family resettled.

The most severe environmental consequence of these Malaysian land settlement schemes was intentional: the clearing of huge areas of intact tropical rainforest. But there were other effects. Massive pollution from Bank-financed palm oil factories was one; the project appraisals had ignored all provision for pollution control. The rapid decimation of forests in the Bank project areas also created widespread difficulties with rampaging wild elephants, boars, and porcupines. The elephants, deprived of their forest home, stampeded onto the newly established oil palm and rubber estates; in the Johore project, 46 percent of the oil palm stands were destroyed by rampaging pachyderms, sometimes in repeated targeted attacks which, in the opinion of some observers, bore signs of uncanny purpose and intelligence. Nearly a hundred miles of electrified barbed-wire fences had to be constructed to keep the elephants at bay so that the palms could be replanted, and the project encountered a 96 percent cost overrun.[56]

The proliferation of land settlement projects in the McNamara years increasingly resembled a war against the earth's rapidly dwindling tropical forests. The Colombia Caqueta Land Colonization Project attempted to promote spontaneous migration of settlers to the Colombian Amazon rainforest through the construction of 200 kilometers of roads and the promotion of subsidized agricultural credit for cattle ranching.[57] The Cameroon Niete Rubber Estate Project was the first of two Bank loans (in 1975 and 1980) to clear and develop 37,000 acres of tropical forest in southwestern Cameroon for rubber plantations. The deforestation proceeded so crudely that logs were not even salvaged for commercial use. The description from the Bank's completion report for the project conveys the approach: "The land was prepared mechanically using D8 crawler tractors equipped for deforestation work. The felled vegetation was then windrowed using bulldozer blades and root rakes." The project also financed a master plan for the twenty-five-year development of tree crop plantations and agro-industrial complexes in a largely forested area of a quarter of a million acres in southwest Cameroon.[58]

The deforestation and the destruction of indigenous communities unleashed by the Bank's Polonoroeste and Carajás projects had been preceded on a smaller scale by the Brazil Alto Turi Land Settlement Project, a scheme approved in 1972 to promote the settlement of some 5,200 families in a 9,390-square-kilometer area covered by primary and secondary tropical forests in the northeast Amazon state of Pará. The project contributed to the deforestation of most of this area, as well as to the outbreak of violent conflicts, including casualties, between settlers and Indians.* The project encountered cost overruns of nearly 200 percent.[59]

In the Nepal Settlement Project, approved in 1974, a surrealistic pattern emerged that characterized bigger Bank environmental debacles in the 1980s—the financing of "cleanup" projects to alleviate the disastrous environmental effects of a preceding Bank loan. The original project objective was to raze 43,472 acres of tropical forest in Nepal's low-lying Terai region, to construct twenty-six sawmills, and resettle 7,900 families on the cleared land. Perversely, most of these families were already environmental refugees from the deforestation, erosion, and soil exhaustion of Nepal's mountain and highland areas. The project (fortunately in retrospect) only cleared 18,000 acres and resettled 2,781 families; this was largely due to the Nepalese government's shift to forest conservation policies while the project was being carried out.[60] Nevertheless, the consequences were bad enough: the logged areas were clear-cut, without regard for leaving trees on slopes and other areas subject to rapid erosion in a monsoon climate, and the transplanted settlers were clearing more forests every year. What for Nepal was a disaster was from the Bank's standpoint an opportunity for a new loan:

> The September/October 1980 supervision mission took note of the adverse environmental impact of the project and underscored the need for ascertaining [the] future role of [the] forestry sector in the Terai. A subsequent mission in November/December 1980 noting that the forest land in the Terai had dwindled from estimated 52.6% of total area in 1964 to 22.4% in 1972 (some estimates put it at 19 percent) suggested that priority should be given to the identification of a comprehensive Terai Forestry Project for implementation in 1982 or early 1983. Forest Department predictions indicate that the current forest conversion and exploitation place the forest resource of the Terai . . . heavily in deficit from 1980 onwards and it will disappear within 20 years.[61]

In 1983, Nepal borrowed $18 million for a second forestry project, in part to help reforest the Terai.

Already by the late 1970s the Bank's own internal post-project audits began to confirm many of the criticisms of outside researchers. The first

---

* Once again, it is illuminating to read the post-project audit report, prepared in 1982, knowing that the Bank had just approved hundreds of millions in loans for Polonoroeste: "The audit mission noted, while driving on the BR-316 and project area roads, the nearly continuous area of secondary shrubs and bushes; only a few blackened remnants of tall tropical trees remained. In the knowledge that this area was only recently covered by tropical forests, the visual impression forcefully underscores the environmental impact of this and similar projects" (IBRD, OED, PPAR, *Brazil Alto Turi Land Settlement* [see endnote 59], 18).

public (and somewhat sanitized) annual review of project audit reports of the Bank's Operations Evaluations Department, published in 1978, reviewed nine poverty-oriented agriculture projects, most of which were completed between 1973 and 1975.* Three of these projects were total failures and were canceled before their completion. Of the remaining six, four, rather than benefiting the poor as intended, mainly assisted better-off landowners. The other two supposedly benefited both the target group of the poor and the richest landowners, to the detriment of economically middling farmers.[62] But according to a German researcher, even in these two projects Bank financing went mainly for credit to the tenants of rich farmers, credit not available to independent peasants, thereby mainly benefiting, once again, the large landowners, who were able to increase rents and income.[63]

By the late 1980s it became clear that the performance of Bank agriculture projects during the McNamara period was abysmal in the Bank's own terms of meeting appraised economic rates of return, avoiding huge cost and time overruns, and reaching the poor. The OED's 1989 annual review of evaluation results examined eighty-two Bank agricultural projects, most of which were approved between 1975 and 1982—the prime years for "new-style" poverty lending. Nearly 45 percent were judged to be unsatisfactory.** In nine of a total of twenty-one irrigation projects reviewed, "agricultural production declined after investment phase was completed, and the physical infrastructure financed appears less durable than expected." Of the seventeen of these irrigation projects in Asia, ten were considered overall to be failures.[64]

One of the most important regions for McNamara-style poverty projects was Brazil's northeast. The World Bank approved more than half a dozen projects*** in the late 1970s to support the Northeast Integrated Area Development Program (POLONORDESTE), an ambitious agricultural

---

* The entire report reviewed seventy-two projects, of which twenty-one were in the agriculture sector (of which in turn only nine were explicitly targeted to help poor farmers).
** It is worth noting that among the agricultural *successes* cited by the 1989 OED report were projects heavily criticized by NGOs and community groups in developing countries for their adverse environmental and social consequences. The Thailand Second Tree Crop Project, for example, overfulfilled most of its quantitative targets, but was part of the Bank-financed rubber tree replanting program condemned at the Bangkok People's Forum in 1991 (see Chapter 1). (*Evaluation Results 1989* [see endnote 64], 3-2.) The same report lauded the success of Bank social forestry projects in India that in fact were the subject of widespread protests by poor farmers and tribal people throughout the 1980s. (Op. cit., 2-8.)
*** For example, the Rio Grande do Norte Rural Development Project (1975), the Ceara Rural Development Project (1977), the Paraiba Rural Development Project (1978), the Bahia Rural Development Project (1978), the Seripe Rural Development Project (1979), the Pernambuco Rural Development Project (1979), the Second Ceara Rural Development Project (1980).

and livestock development scheme that purported to target the landless and poor, small-scale farmers in a 500,000-square-kilometer area covering nine states in northeastern Brazil. It soon became clear that POLONORDESTE was a debacle; let the Bank's Operations Evaluation Department speak for itself:

By 1980 . . . only 37% of the projected number of farmers had actually been assisted, 18% had received credit, fewer than 6% of the anticipated land titles had been distributed and less than a third of the planned health posts and water supply systems had been built. Benefits, moreover, had for the most part been monopolized by 100,000 owner occupiers, with the bulk of the program's three million low-income rural families, especially landless farmers, being largely excluded from credit and agricultural services. . . . In addition, the program was excessively "top-down," allowing virtually no local participation in the design of its components and individual investments.[65]

For India, the vanguard country of the World Bank's agricultural poverty-alleviation projects, much of the record reveals an even greater fiasco. In 1991, the Bank's India Agriculture Operations Division completed its own confidential review of irrigated agriculture for its largest borrower. It noted that of nine large projects completed in 1989, just two had economic rates of return "above the estimated opportunity cost of capital in India of 12%." Seven of the nine projects had capital investment overruns ranging from 49 percent to 147 percent, as well as considerable delays in completion. Moreover, the report concluded that economic rates of return had been overestimated for earlier Bank irrigation projects in India (1970–84), and that "the most reasonable conclusion is that project performance and economic viability have been poor all along for most projects."[66]

Worse,

rapidly rising recurrent expenditure on unproductive staff costs is squeezing out genuine investment in the sector . . . and is throwing the sector into financial crisis. . . . Sooner, rather than later, the burden will be financially unsustainable, and infrastructure will be physically unsustainable due to declining construction and maintenance standards. The situation is compounded in some areas by environmental degradation.[67]

The cause? "With the focus centered on construction, the broader management needs of the sector were neglected, and the cumulative costs of this neglect are now apparent."[68] Indeed, the Bank noted that weak management was "overwhelmed by the growing complexity of the sector in the face of limited institutional adaptation and encroachment of rent-seeking and often disruptive political pressures [i.e., corruption]."[69]

There is just one final observation missing from this evaluation: over the preceding two decades the World Bank was by far the most important external funder and promoter of the approach its India Agriculture Operations Division castigated, an approach that emphasized grandiose, complex, and costly infrastructure over improved management and sensitivity to local ecological and social concerns. The Bank continually financed new schemes rather than completing the growing backlog of half- or two-thirds-completed projects. Nor did it heed the warnings of researchers like Wade and Moore that its irrigated agriculture strategy in India and elsewhere was socially and ecologically inappropriate, and was committing governments to snowballing recurring costs they could not bear over the longer term.*

Model Countries

There was a more sinister side to the McNamara years, one that went beyond wasted money and environmental devastation. On July 18, 1977, Senator James Abourezk of South Dakota, a liberal Democrat, rose on the U.S. Senate floor to denounce what he and others characterized as the World Bank's predilection for increasing support to military regimes that tortured and murdered their subjects, sometimes immediately after the violent overthrow of democratic governments that the Bank had previously refused to lend to. The senator charged that in its fiscal year 1979 the Bank intended "to increase loans to four newly repressive governments twice as fast as all others. These governments—Chile, Uruguay, Argentina, and the Philippines—have all received major new loans since the onset of torture and repression and are tentatively scheduled to get $664 million." He read into the record a leaked confidential preliminary 1979 loan list of the Bank, and criticized "that institution's excessive secretiveness." He reminded his colleagues that in appropriating funds for the World Bank, "we vote the money, yet we do not know where it goes."[70]

Abourezk entered into the record a human rights report by a Washington think tank, the Center for International Policy, which conveyed a damning picture indeed of World Bank lending priorities in the 1970s. The report noted that the Bank had refused to lend to the democratically elected Goulart government in Brazil in the early 1960s, but following the 1964 military coup (which installed a twenty-year military dictatorship), lending rose from zero to average $73 million a year for the rest of the 1960s and reached levels of nearly half a billion dollars a year by the

* There are striking similarities here with the criticisms of Bank-financed irrigated agriculture in Thailand voiced by Thai NGOs and community groups at the Bank/Fund 1991 annual meeting in Bangkok (see Chapter 1).

mid-1970s. Chile under the democratically elected regime of Allende received no Bank loans, but following the Pinochet coup in 1973 the country suddenly became creditworthy, despite a worsening economic situation. Indonesia under Sukarno—an autocrat, but at least a civilian—received no World Bank loans; Sukarno was overthrown by an extraordinarily bloody military uprising in 1965, which included the mass murder of more than half a million alleged communists, many of whom in fact were ethnic Chinese. The Bank approved its first loans to Indonesia in late 1968, and McNamara made increased lending to General Suharto's regime a priority in the 1970s, reaching levels of $600 to $700 million annually by the end of the decade. The report noted that "fifteen of the world's most repressive governments will receive $2.9 billion in World Bank loans in fiscal 1979," about a third of the Bank's entire proposed new loan commitments for that year. President Carter and Congress had cut off all U.S. aid for four of the fifteen—Argentina, Chile, Uruguay, and Ethiopia—for flagrant human rights violations.[71]

Was this what the Bank's ambitious country-by-country economic studies and loan programming finally amounted to? Whatever the reasons, the lending patterns spoke with a blunt and brutal finality. The report of the Center for International Policy concluded that not only did the Bank "obviously undermine" the Carter administration's international human rights policy, it encouraged the spread of repressive regimes.* "Ironically, in the name of stability and economic development, the World Bank has sacrificed human rights—the end purpose of economic development."[72]

Ceaucescu's Bank

Democratic centralism entails popular participation in formulating the plan at the enterprise level.[73]
—World Bank Romania country report, 1979

In 1972, while the Bank was cutting off all loans to Allende's Chile, it geared up to lend to its newest member, Romania, at McNamara's personal urging. Indeed, the Bank made several unprecedented exceptions for the Ceaucescu regime. The secretive Romanian government refused to share information on key economic indicators with

---

* The standard Bank riposte to these charges was that first (recalling the dispute with the United Nations in the mid-1960s over lending to South Africa and Portugal), its charter forbade it from taking into account the human rights violations of potential borrowers, since this was a "political" rather than an economic concern. Second, the Bank claimed that its loans, particularly in the McNamara years, were aimed at poverty alleviation, and that arguably the poor under a repressive regime needed such assistance even more urgently.

the first Bank economic mission to the country, and the Bank could not even determine Romania's creditworthiness according to customary criteria.[74] The World Bank started lending to Romania, even though the country did not settle its outstanding World War II debts with foreign creditors until 1975; the Bank had refused to lend to Chile for several years in the late 1940s for precisely the same reason.[75]

Some in the Bank's senior management had trouble seeing the economic logic of lending to Ceaucescu. According to former Bank staff member Aart Van de Laar, at one meeting McNamara responded to questions on Romania with a statement that he had "great faith in the financial morality of socialist countries in repaying debts." At which point a Bank vice-president acerbicly observed that "Allende's Chile had perhaps not yet become socialist enough."[76]

In any case, Romania quickly became one of the Bank's bigger borrowers. Over eight years (1974–82) it received $2.364 billion.[77] In 1980 it was the Bank's eighth biggest borrower out of a total of nineteen; in 1982 it received $321 million, making it the eleventh biggest borrower for that year out of a total of forty-three.[78] After 1982, Ceaucescu's alarm at the size of the country's foreign debt led him to refrain from further borrowing and to undertake a uniquely harsh austerity program to prepay the country's loans, politically possible only in a total police state.

Romania was one country where the Bank's predilection for large infrastructure loans was identical with the government's priorities; massive power projects, heavy industry, irrigation, and agro-industrial schemes predominated. Interestingly enough, Bank lending coincided with a marked increase in state centralization of planning and control in what was already one of the most centralized and planned economies on earth.[79]

In 1979 the Bank published, in a sanitized form, its country economic study on Romania. It is an astounding document, even without the historical hindsight of the 1990s. A section entitled "Importance of Centralized Economic Control" approvingly cites Ceaucescu's pronouncements on the necessity of state planning, and accepts uncritically the government's prediction that per capita income in 1990 would reach $3,000 in 1963 terms, or over $15,000 in 1993 dollars.[80] In fact, Romania emerges in the Bank report as a virtual model for achieving economic growth. "It remains probable that Romania will continue to enjoy one of the highest growth rates among developing countries over the next decade and that it will largely succeed in implementing its development targets," states the report, and it concludes that "if all plans are fulfilled, Romania will have 'taken off' and become an industrialized economy by 1990, on a level with many other countries considered to be developed."[81]

A section in the Bank's country report entitled "Development of Human Resources" is Orwellian in its obliviousness to the human suffering and repression exacted by one of the most tyrannical regimes in recent history:

To improve the standards of living of the population as a beneficiary of the development process, the government has pursued policies to make better use of the population as a factor of production. . . . An essential feature of the overall manpower policy has been . . . to stimulate an increase in birth rates.[82]

The regime's policies to boost population growth not only forbade all abortions, but limited the availability of contraceptives to women, with disastrous consequences for tens of thousands of unwanted, abandoned children condemned to vegetate in state orphanages.

Another section, on "Environmental Considerations," noted the disastrous environmental implications of the regime's plans to shift the country's main energy source from natural gas and petroleum to coal and lignite. Hundreds of square kilometers of prime agricultural land were being turned into open-pit mines, and numerous villages resettled; the shift to lignite was already causing severe air pollution in numerous towns and cities. By 1979, the Bank had lent $130 million in two loans for a giant coal-fired thermal power plant, and in 1980 it would approve another $125-million power loan. The Romania country report accepted the regime's environmental claims with the same credulity it gave to its growth projections and its policies for "development of human resources": "Remedial measures to minimize the environmental consequences of large-scale mining and power generation are being undertaken. . . . To prevent atmospheric pollution in urban areas from becoming worse during the current five-year plan, countermeasures are planned."[83]

"Learning by Doing"

By the end of the 1970s, the World Bank had become an institution where policy pronouncements and rhetoric were largely dissociated from reality.[84]

There were several hypotheses to explain the Bank's behavior. Many speculated that the institution was driven by an unwritten agenda of increasing support to countries favored by U.S. foreign policy and cutting off those who incurred the wrath of Uncle Sam.* Equally important, per-

---

* Doing away with Allende was an obsession of the Nixon administration, and the United States and NATO were anxious to lure the independent-minded Ceaucescu regime farther away from the Warsaw Pact. Securing Indonesia—the fifth most populous nation on earth—

haps, was the need of the Bank in the eyes of McNamara and his acolytes to be a universal, global institution; new opportunities to increase lending were worth the bending of a few rules and precedents. But the only fully consistent hypothesis to reconcile the discordant elements of the Bank's actions, performance, and stated goals was that of a bureaucracy that had become an end in itself, driven by an institutional culture of expansion and a will to power for its own sake.

Two other trends emerged in the McNamara years that reinforced this premise. First was a growing bias of the Bank, almost missionary in its hubris, to assume that its intervention in a given situation in a borrowing country would almost always, whatever the problems, leave a situation better than it would be without the Bank's involvement. This bias was compounded by an institutional culture that makes it difficult, if not impossible, in the words of one former Bank employee, "for Bank staff to show pessimism once management has gone on public record" on the viability of a particular project or lending strategy.[85] Worse, this penchant for intervention, coupled with the greatly increased pressure to lend, prompted some Bank staff to fabricate or invent information to satisfy their statistics-obsessed president: "Without knowing it," said one of the World Bank's highest ranking officials, McNamara "manufactured data. If there was a gap in the numbers, he would ask staff to fill it, and others made it up for him. The practice was not widespread, but it was habitual."[86]

The second tendency was even more disquieting; the World Bank characterized it as "learning by doing."[87] The Bank approached its projects increasingly as experiments in "development," an undertaking which, as experience grew, perversely appeared more and more shaky and undeveloped itself in its empirical and theoretical foundations.

Unfortunately, the objects and pawns in these experiments were hundreds of millions of the poorer and more disenfranchised human beings on our planet—as well as untold species and unstudied ecosystems the destruction of which, when a development experiment goes awry, is irreversible. The risks for poor people and the ecosystems they depended on were sometimes absolute, for Bank staff—if their experiments should go awry, as they often did—trifling. In their sealed offices in Washington, or in their short stays in five-star hotels in tropical capitals, many staff and the executive directors were so removed from the consequences of their

---

in the Western camp became a greater priority in the 1970s as the United States withdrew from Vietnam. But the Bank's continued financial courting of the developing world's major human rights violators during the Carter years seemed to contradict at least part of the Carter foreign policy agenda.

actions that they acted as if they were dealing with a make-believe world on another planet than the one they inhabited, one that could be put back together again after their mistakes.

The Faustian Legacy

To state that the World Bank under McNamara was a Faustian enterprise is more than a literary metaphor; his development crusade at the Bank bears uncanny analogies with the actual plot as well as the themes of the concluding acts of Goethe's play. In recent years critics and social scientists have rediscovered the fourth and fifth acts of the second part of *Faust* as one of the most powerful prophecies in Western literature of the dilemmas of twentieth-century development. Goethe's vision, inspired by the dawn of the industrial age,* was of "the tragedy of development," of "the city in which mankind shall have to live in future time," a city that awaited Robert McNamara to try to build it on a global scale.[88] To understand the ultimate paradox of McNamara's years at the Bank, it is worth taking a short concluding journey into the symbolism of Goethe's tragedy.

In the last two acts of the play, Faust tries to achieve fulfillment through the domination of nature and the unleashing of large-scale economic development.[89] The setting is at the very dawn of the modern age, sometime in the early sixteenth century (the period of the historical Faust, a shadowy alchemist who was reputed to have promoted his magical powers before Holy Roman Emperor Maximilian I). In act 4, Faust, with Mephistopheles at his side, surveys the sea, lamenting its unused power, and dreams of giant development and reclamation projects. Faust and Mephistopheles help the (unnamed) Emperor win a civil war (a war unleashed, ironically, by social disintegration caused by hyper-inflation after Faust and Mephistopheles convince the Emperor to issue paper money). As a reward, the Emperor grants Faust a huge virgin domain along the seashore, as well as virtually unlimited resources and workers.

Titanic development projects are soon under way day and night— canals, dams, ports—but at a heavy cost in human suffering.

* While writing the last two acts of *Faust*, Goethe confided to his friend and biographer Eckermann his visionary enthusiasm about new proposals for gigantic development works; his source for many of these ideas was the Saint-Simonian journal *Le Globe*. "One of the standard features of *Le Globe*, as of all Saint-Simonian writings, was a constant stream of proposals for long-range development projects on an enormous scale" (Berman, *All That Is Solid Melts into Air* [see endnote 88], 72). See the discussion of the Saint-Simonians in Chapter 8.

> Where the flames would nightly swarm
> Was a dam when we awoke.
> Human sacrifices bled,
> Tortured yells would pierce the night,
> And where blazes seaward sped
> A canal would greet the light.[90]

Two indigenous inhabitants, an old couple, occupy the site of Faust's construction and colonization projects, which he calls "The masterpiece of sapient man, / As he ordains with thoughtful mind / New homestead for his teeming kind."[91] They inhabit a charming hamlet, vestige of a more harmonious age, that includes their cottage, a church, gardens, and linden trees. Faust offers them what he considers just compensation and a place to resettle, but they refuse. Exasperated, he tells Mephistopheles to get them out of the way as he can, and Mephistopheles razes the entire hamlet—cottage, church, trees—burning the old couple alive. Unaware, Faust surveys the charred trunks of the linden trees contentedly, believing that the old couple has been successfully resettled, "glad of my generosity."[92]

Only later does he discover the truth, but it is a minor accident in the realization of his grand vision: a new society and world of freedom for millions, driven by development and technology. In the last moments of the drama, Faust impatiently surveys the progress of his endless projects, this time of what he thinks is a drainage canal: "I want a tally, daily to be rendered, / How much the trench in hand is gaining room."[93]

He then ponders the limitless expanse of his works, "new homesteads," "a land of Eden":

> Such teeming would I see upon this land,
> On acres free among free people stand.
> I might entreat the fleeting moment
> Oh tarry yet, thou art so fair![94]

The parallels with McNamara's Bank are uncanny: the sweeping vision of new lives for millions, the huge dam, irrigation, and agricultural resettlement projects, the tragic displacement of indigenous peoples and the destruction of forests, to name a few. Here, too, is the obsession with statistical tallies and numerical data to measure progress.

McNamara's grandiose vision involved a wager that was indeed Faustian—a risky experiment with life and nature, using simplistic technologies, and a fatal hubris about the Bank's ability to know, plan, and direct the evolution of human societies and the natural systems they depend on. Secrecy, subversion of democratic institutions, and gross ecological negligence all became associated with the Bank in the name of the poor. The means were tragically Mephistophelean.

The end of the play evokes the fatal flaw that inevitably turns Faustian development to ruin. Faust, when he surveys the grandness and benevolence of his works in the passage cited above, is blind; he has been blinded in the previous scene by Care, whose power he refuses to recognize. His vision is oblivious to reality. And the canal whose deepening he directs is not a canal, it is his own grave, dug by the Lemures, spirits of the evil dead in classical mythology, here the cohorts of Mephistopheles.* He loses his wager** with Mephistopheles in the very moment he thinks he has realized his life's work of development, when he commands the moment—and the vision—to tarry. Mephistopheles in an aside tells us that nature itself works against Faust:

> For *us* alone is your commotion
> Your dams and all your care
> It is for Neptune you prepare,
> The Water Devil, a repast.
> You cannot do what you desire:
> With *us* the elements conspire
> And ruin reaps your crop at last.[95]

The most noble purpose cannot command or direct nature's elements; they work with the spirit, and further the self-contained ends of the means that are employed. The elements venge themselves on Faust's vision, which, scorning Care, is blind.

* "Critics have often neglected the absolute ironic contrast between Faust's vision and the agents of perverse and inhuman power which now [in the end] control his city. Mephistopheles has summoned forth the Lemures, who sing grotesque ditties as they dig Faust's grave. Nor is there any reason to doubt that they shall inherit the entire realm which Faust leaves behind. . . . The worldly city built by Mephistopheles and his henchmen at the instigation of Faust, which is surely meant to represent the city in which mankind shall have to live in future time—and all readers of *Faust* must also locate themselves there—is abandoned to the control of demonic and inhuman powers" (Cyrus Hamlin, "Interpretive Notes," in *Faust*, Arndt translation [see endnote 2], 343).
** The wager is that Mephistopheles—an embodiment of the devil—will be Faust's servant on earth, but will take Faust's soul upon his death. Faust agrees to perish if he ever finds a moment of life so beautiful or fulfilling that he wishes it not to pass.

5

Greens Lay Siege
to the Crystal Palace

> Then—this is all what you say—new economic relations
> will be established, all ready-made and worked out with
> mathematical exactitude, so that every possible question
> will vanish in the twinkling of an eye, simply because
> every possible answer to it will be provided. Then the
> "Palace of Crystal" will be built.[1]
> —Fyodor Dostoyevsky, *Notes from Underground*

At the beginning of the 1980s, the edifice appeared complete. In a world where the most widely shared political value was the virtue of economic growth, the World Bank had emerged as the Vatican of development, an intellectual mansion forty years in the building—but with much deeper historical origins—a crystal palace that beckoned to most of the earth's still developing nations.

The Crystal Palace is more than an evocative metaphor; it was an actual historical building, erected in London's Hyde Park in six months to house the first world's fair, the Great International Exposition of 1851. Constructed of then revolutionary industrial materials, iron and glass, the Crystal Palace was one of the great wonders of the age; Dostoyevsky visited it in 1862. The building had what sociologist Marshall Berman has called an "extraordinary psychic impact" on Russian thinkers, symbolizing the "specter of modernization haunting a nation that was writhing ever more convulsively in the anguish of backwardness."[2] For some Russians, obsessed with the fate of the nineteenth century's prototypal underdeveloped nation, the Crystal Palace embodied the promise of technology and development. For Dostoyevsky, it presaged a new social and political order that subsumed human freedom to a single project—the absolute rationalization of social organization to promote economic growth.[3] He shuddered before the vision of a world that enshrined rather than questioned what he characterized in *Notes from Underground* as the human "predilection for systems and abstract deductions," a predilection so great that man "is ready to distort the truth intentionally, he is ready to deny the evidence of his senses only to justify his logic."[4]

Dostoyevsky feared that the project of Western economic development entailed not only the suppression of freedom in the name of reason and progress, but also, as an inexorable corollary, the abolition of history.* His underground antihero protests against "a palace of crystal that can never be destroyed. . . . And perhaps that is just why I am afraid of this edifice."[5] After all, history is the arena where alternative scenarios of human development are played out, where the free choice of human communities and individuals is both a deciding factor and the ultimate stake.

Another prophet of the new world heralded by the Crystal Palace was the great turn-of-the-century German social scientist Max Weber. Much of Weber's lifework was given to analyzing what he saw as the universal rationalization and bureaucratization of Western society in the service of technology and economic growth. Profoundly pessimistic, Weber envisaged the future as an "iron cage" in which human activity would be increasingly subject to instrumental, rationalized domination by fundamentally unaccountable bureaucracies.[6]

Both Dostoyevsky and Weber realized that the triumph of technology and the centrality of economic, material growth as the basis of all modern societies created a unique rationale for new forms of political and social domination. For both, the project of modern development evolved with a menacing paradox at its heart—increasing rationality in form accompanied by ultimate unreason and nihilism in its consequences.

A Certain Amount of Faith

As Keynes once remarked, if capitalists foresaw all the uncertainties to which their investments would be subjected, they would probably not have invested in the

---

* See, for example, Francis Fukuyama's *The End of History and the Last Man* (New York: Free Press, 1992), where the neo-Hegelian thesis is advanced that with the collapse of communism, global economic and political development is achieving its logical culmination—the reign of a global market economy and liberal, Western democracy. But Fukuyama's vision of democracy accepts as a premise and inevitability a single path of global modernization in which "all countries . . . must increasingly resemble one another," sharing a "universal consumer culture" (pp. xiv–xv). "Rather than a thousand shoots blossoming into as many different flowering plants, mankind will come to seem like a long wagon train strung out along a [single] road. . . . To get through the final mountain range they all must use the same pass" (pp. 337–38).

first place. . . . Since the Bank is using other people's
money . . . [w]hat is required is a certain amount of
faith in the development prospects of a country—a faith
that transcends the expectations that can certainly be
associated with particular projects.[7]
—Edward Mason and Robert Asher

When A. W. "Tom" Clausen, former president of the Bank
of America, assumed the presidency of the World Bank from McNamara
in 1981, he could rightfully boast that it had "become the world's largest
and most influential development institution."[8] Virtually no one questioned his assertion that the Bank was "widely respected for the quality of
its work because its standards for the identification, preparation, appraisal,
implementation and supervision of development projects are recognized
as among the most rigorous and exacting in the world."[9] Within the
Bank, few paid attention to the internal project audit reports that cast
doubts on its claims with regard to poverty alleviation and successful
development; fewer still heeded the occasional case studies in development periodicals that documented from the field the disastrous environmental and social consequences of Bank projects. These consequences
often eluded the quantitative indicators the theologians of development
cited to show progress.*

The Bank faced a new challenge at the beginning of the 1980s: the
intractable net negative transfer menace that had plagued it for two
decades was only a microcosm of the relationship between developing
countries and their private and public creditors in industrialized nations.
For example, by 1976 gross disbursements from all public and private
lenders to Latin America totaled $31.387 billion, of which nearly half,
$15.194 billion, was transferred back to service previous debts; by 1981,
three-quarters of the more than $72 billion lent to Latin countries imme-
diately returned to the North. The following year, when the debt crisis
exploded with the threat of Mexican default in August 1982, Latin countries borrowed only $49.63 billion, but paid back to the North $66.811
billion, a net negative transfer of over $17 billion.[10]

Throughout the 1970s private international banks—with Mr. Clausen's
Bank of America in the forefront—had encouraged major nations like
Mexico, Brazil, Argentina, and Nigeria to engage in the most extravagant
borrowing binge in history. The World Bank's approach contributed to
the problem: in the 1970s it lobbied its donors for huge capital increases,

---

* See, for example, the extraordinary collection of environmental disasters, some financed
by the Bank, documented in Mitaghi Farvar and John P. Milton, *The Careless Technology: Ecology and International Development* (Garden City, New York: Natural History Press, 1972).

and, as we have seen, increased its lending more than tenfold. This improved the short-term foreign exchange balances of many borrowers, but helped set them up for an even bigger crisis in the early 1980s.

Now, as major countries threatened to default in succession like a row of tumbling dominos, private banks lost all inclination for further lending. The U.S. Treasury and other creditor-nation finance ministries pushed the World Bank and the International Monetary Fund to take up the slack in lending as much as possible; even more critical for containing the crisis, the Bank and the Fund were to pressure borrower countries to reduce domestic imports and expenditures, and to export more to earn the foreign exchange to continue servicing their debts. This new approach was called "structural adjustment."

World Bank structural adjustment loans were tailored to help avoid a debt meltdown: they were huge (typically $100 to $500 million) and fast disbursing, providing massive quick fixes of foreign exchange. The loans did not finance specific projects (the Bank's Executive Board decided it could lend up to 25 percent annually for so-called non-project adjustment loans and not violate its charter).* But in exchange, the recipients of adjustment loans had to relinquish important parts of national sovereignty, basically agreeing to revamp their economies into foreign exchange–earning, export-oriented machines, often to the detriment of long-term domestic social and environmental needs.**

Adjustment loans alone were not enough to stanch the crisis. In the early 1980s Clausen also initiated a "Special Action Program" which accelerated ongoing World Bank loan disbursements to major debtors like Brazil and Mexico, regardless of quality or implementation problems in specific projects. And Clausen called for, and obtained in 1982, a doubling of the Bank's capital, an infusion of more than $30 billion in cash and guarantees.

Thus, the pressure to lend had increased exponentially since the beginning of the McNamara era. The old problems of the lack of bankable projects and the threat of net negative transfers were bigger than ever. The most basic economic efficiency criteria were often ignored: many Bank loans supported massive government programs in the agriculture and energy sectors that were thoroughly permeated with grossly wasteful subsidies for big users of water, power, and agricultural chemicals. But devel-

---

* I.e., the injunction of Article III, Section 4 (vii) that the Bank was to lend only for specific projects "except in special circumstances."
** For an indictment of the disastrous effect of World Bank and IMF adjustment policies and on the welfare of children in developing nations, see the UNICEF study *Adjustment with a Human Face*, Giovanni Andrea Cornia, Richard Jolly, and Francis Steward, eds. (Oxford: Clarendon Press, 1987), vol. 1, *Protecting the Vulnerable and Promoting Growth.*

opment lending, as Edward Mason and Robert Asher stated in their McNamara-commissioned history of the Bank, was above all an act of faith; what mattered in Bank project appraisals was theological adherence to the canon and credo, not necessarily their observance in everyday life.

Outside the gates of this secretive palace of crystal built on debt, green heretics were beginning to suspect the emperor had no clothes.

Questions and Doubts

> For a decade now, the Bank has required, as part of project evaluation, that every project it finances be reviewed by a special environmental unit. . . . Nearly two thirds of the projects reviewed have raised no serious health or environmental questions, and I'm pleased to say that it has been possible to incorporate protective measures in all the projects we have financed over the past decade.[11]   —A. W. Clausen, November 12, 1981

The above statement was an untruth, one repeated by two presidents of the World Bank for nearly a decade. It is difficult to judge which interpretation is more disturbing: were Robert McNamara and A. W. Clausen consciously lying, or were they and Bank management simply so removed from the day-to-day reality of Bank projects that they actually believed what they were saying?

Several environmental advocates in Washington, working with groups such as the Natural Resources Defense Council, the Environmental Policy Institute, and the National Wildlife Federation* suspected there was little evidence to back the World Bank's environmental claims. Groups defending the human and cultural rights of tribal and indigenous peoples, such as London- and Washington-based Survival International and Cultural Survival in Boston, had criticized the destruction of tribal cultures by Bank-financed projects for several years, but with little tangible political impact.

In early 1983, the environmentalists began to investigate. The Bank's Office of Environmental and Scientific Affairs, which according to Clausen reviewed every project, numbered only six individuals out of a total Bank staff of 6,000 (of whom more than 3,500 were professionals). In fact, when McNamara first claimed in Stockholm in 1972 that the Bank's envi-

---

* Including the author, Brent Blackwelder (now vice-president of Friends of the Earth, U.S.), and Barbara Bramble, director of international programs at the National Wildlife Federation.

ronmental office evaluated each project and conducted "careful in-house studies" so that "in every instance" environmental safeguards were successfully negotiated and implemented, the office consisted of one person.

The head of the environmental office in 1983 was a well-meaning physician who disliked traveling to developing countries; one of his major professional interests was travelers' diarrhea. Three of the staff were concerned with vaguely defined research, public relations, and training functions in the area of science and technology (positions that were abolished in the mid-1980s). This left only three people to evaluate some 300 new lending operations totaling over $12 billion a year, in addition to monitoring hundreds of ongoing projects totaling tens of billions more. Only one of these three was actually devoting any significant time to reviewing the most environmentally sensitive lending sectors of the Bank (accounting for more than half of its loan commitments), agriculture, energy, and transportation. Not that more staff would have made much difference anyway, since the environmental office was only officially informed of projects at the appraisal stage, the final phase of project development, which typically came as much as two years after an investment proposal had been identified and in preparation. Changing or stopping a project at this point was virtually impossible; the environmental office was set up so that it would sign off on lending operations that were bureaucratic *faits accomplis.*

The Bank vaunted its publicly available environmental guidelines, checklists, and procedures, bound in two thick blue volumes. Indeed, scores of dust-covered sets sat in piles inside the offices of the environmental staff, available to anyone from the outside for the asking. In an institution that zealously kept its most trivial working documents secret, this was no anomaly: not only were the Bank's other 6,000 employees not required to use the guidelines in preparing projects, most of them were not aware of their existence. Indeed, it would have been senseless to require most Band staff to use them, since the guidelines focused on industrial and processing activities, a small part of Bank lending in comparison to agriculture, irrigation, dams, and roads—for which there were no guidelines whatsoever. In fact, many of the checklists and procedures had been collated together from various sources as a spare-time office hobby of one of the six environmental staff members, a Belgian specialist in industrial pollution who was near retirement.

Anyone could have discovered this state of affairs by spending an afternoon in the Bank's environmental office, questioning staff and reading the guidelines—but for over a decade, apparently, no one had. Those with whom the Bank shared some information were constrained by signed agreements not to cite documents, or even to fully disclose to the public the details of what they might find. The information the Bank cares to present to the public is carefully sanitized to avoid giving any controversial insight even into those problems Bank management is aware of. As former U.S. Senator Ernest Gruening complained in an early congressional study on foreign aid, "Publications by international organizations [are] virtually useless. Filled with euphemisms in order not to offend anyone, they become so bland and obfuscated as to be virtually meaningless."[12]

Many academics and research groups specializing in international development either had contractual relations with the Bank, were partly dependent on it and other international aid agencies for income, or looked to these agencies for future employment. In one of the few deeply researched, critical accounts of the Bank that has appeared, *The World Bank and the Poor*, Dutch economist Aart Van de Laar denounced the chilling effects on critical analysis of this patronage system, which, he charged, "regretfully . . . extends deeply into the academic world."[13] Development experts and overseas research councils would be the last ones to launch a reformation in the church from which they received so many indulgences.*

The Hearings Begin

In early 1983, the Washington environmentalists persuaded the House Subcommittee on International Development Institutions and Finance to hold the first oversight hearings on the multilateral development banks (MDBs) and the environment.[14] On June 28 and 29 of that year, Congress listened for two days to a litany of development gone mad.

On the first day, advocates from U.S. national environmental groups

---

* In the early 1980s, the only comprehensive outside study on the World Bank and the environment was that prepared by the London- and Washington-based International Institute for Environmental Development (IIED), an institution involved in a conflict of interest, since much of its work was dependent on paid contracts with the same aid agencies it purported to evaluate. The IIED report, called *Banking on the Biosphere?*, examined the environmental policies and procedures of nine multilateral aid institutions and focused on the World Bank, praising it for showing "since the early 1970s, a unique practical concern over the environmental impact of its lending" as well as "undoubtedly exert[ing] intellectual leadership in environmental matters in the entire international development community." The study did note that a "wide gap remains between the . . . concern of some individuals and the official response of most institutions," but that the World Bank and the IDB (Inter-American Development Bank) "have developed a greater environmental awareness and sophistication than other development organizations." In other words, though more needed to be done, there was no cause for alarm, the World Bank was leading the way. (Brian Johnson and Robert Stein, *Banking on the Biosphere?: Environmental Procedures and Practices of Nine Multilateral Development Agencies* [London and Washington: International Institute for Environment and Development, 1979], xiv, 11, 133.)

recounted what they had discovered: the World Bank's environmental office, though staffed by some dedicated individuals, was mainly a public relations sham, while the other MDBs did not even bother to undertake the charade of setting up an environmental staff. The witnesses recounted case after case of environmental and social disasters financed by the Bank and its sister institutions: huge dams that displaced indigenous peoples, botched irrigation schemes that contributed to the spread of waterborne diseases such as malaria and schistosomiasis, cattle ranching schemes that destroyed tropical forests, and massive resettlement projects, including the Polonoroeste and Transmigration programs, for which the World Bank had recently committed hundreds of millions of dollars.

The next day, representatives of indigenous peoples' rights organizations spoke. They charged that much development financed by the Bank in the name of the poor was a catastrophe for the earth's tribal peoples, verging in some cases on genocide. Rudolph Ryser of the National Congress of American Indians charged that "the economic and development policies of States . . . and international banking institutions like the World Bank . . . have a profound and frequently disastrous effect on the peace and well-being of more than 500 million indigenous peoples throughout the world." He cited examples of World Bank–financed dam projects in Costa Rica and the Philippines that threatened the livelihood of indigenous groups.[15]

The most disturbing account was that of a Cornell-based anthropologist, David Price, who had worked as a consultant for the Bank in 1980 on the preparation of the Polonoroeste loans. Price was the leading expert on the Indians in the Polonoroeste project area, particularly the Nambiquara tribe in Mato Grosso state, with whom he lived and studied while completing his thesis at the University of Chicago. The Nambiquara, who numbered 20,000 at the beginning of the century, had been reduced to about 650 individuals by the time the Bank appraised Polonoroeste in 1980. In 1968, the Brazilian government forcibly deported most of the Nambiquara from their traditional homeland in the Guaporé Valley (a relatively fertile area of the Amazon) into an adjacent area that was mostly infertile scrubland and sand. In the 1970s, much of the surviving population, particularly children, was decimated by epidemics of influenza, measles, and dysentery, the latter abetted by massive contamination of rivers in the region, caused by the widespread application by loggers and miners of Tordon 155-Br, a highly toxic defoliant, to open up the forest in the Guaporé Valley. In the mid-1970s, a group of doctors from the International Red Cross visited the Nambiquara and denounced to the world the slow genocide they witnessed: "The life of these Indians is a shame, not only to Brazil, but to all humanity."[16]

Price charged that the Bank hired him only after four other anthropologists unfamiliar with the area refused Bank offers; he learned that each of the four had told the Bank that Price was the qualified expert on the region. Price's report to the Bank contained grave warnings that the Brazilian government's Indian agency, FUNAI, was so weak and corrupt* that to go ahead with the massive land colonization scheme of Polonoroeste would threaten not just the welfare but the lives of the tribal groups in the area, particularly the Nambiquara. His report stated that information on the location of isolated tribal groups, the suitability of the soils for agriculture, and even on the distribution of land tenure arrangements was either absent or grossly deficient: "It would appear that over and over again there was inadequate information to decide legitimately on the feasibility of Polonoroeste."[17]

Price testified that the Bank deliberately suppressed and distorted his findings; he noted, for example, "I included in my report an allegation that one of the top men in the FUNAI has been positively identified as a former political torturer. In response, the World Bank suggests that the FUNAI needs to improve its image."[18] He told the Congress that "there is a tendency for the World Bank to become hermetic and monolithic—a law unto itself. If the rest of the world could see what goes on inside the World Bank, it might conduct its business more scrupulously."[19]

After Price and the other anthropologists concluded their statements, the congressmen questioned the witnesses. Congressman Jerry Patterson, a Democrat from California and chairman of the subcommittee, summarized the two days of testimony as "eye-opening" and "shocking," but expressed his concern that "I don't hear any support for any projects from any one of you in any of the testimony we have heard."[20] A moderate Republican sympathetic to the cause of foreign aid, Douglas Bereuter of Nebraska, put it more bluntly. "It is almost inevitable," he declared, "that the comments and remarks here today will be used by opponents on the floor and elsewhere against funding for the multilateral development banks." He questioned the impression the hearings had created that "the MDBs' projects have done more harm than good that they have done."[21] And, Patterson added, "the projects approved generally come from the country of origin," so it was the countries that bore the primary responsibility.[22]

---

* "The public record on what had been going on within FUNAI . . . which was available to anyone who wanted to read Brazilian newspapers, made it very, very clear . . . that it had been taken over . . . by military men with previous experience in intelligence and manipulation of public opinion, security, and that more than 50 sincere committed indigenists with a genuine concern for the welfare of the Indians had been systematically identified and weeded out" (Price [see endnote 17], 477).

Certainly the witnesses had made a powerful prima facie case that if "good" was being done, it was not for the environment or the world's remaining tribal peoples; the "good" the MDBs were doing was something called development. But what kind of development was it that so cavalierly destroyed the resource base on which all human activity—economic and otherwise—ultimately depends? What kind of poverty strategy was it that devastated the lives and cultures of a good proportion of the earth's economically poor, its indigenous peoples?* The witnesses at those two days of hearings in June 1983 knew that environmental and tribal peoples' issues are not adjuncts or economic "externalities" to human development in a world culture, they are at the heart of whatever our destiny is as a planetary species. In response to such arguments, economists in the MDBs often rejoined that there were necessary trade-offs to development. But what was being traded here was the future.

It was also indeed true, as Patterson observed, that borrowing countries bore the first responsibility for the environmental and social destruction caused by certain projects, but the Bank was a key accomplice through its eagerness to lend and look the other way when its loan conditions and policies were violated. Another congressman, Mike Lowry, a Democrat from Washington (who later was elected the state's governor), gently rebuked his colleagues for being "too defensive of these banks." "There is a way by which certain institutions work," he noted; perhaps it was not true of the MDBs, but "there is a mentality . . . which would cement the Grand Canyon if they would justify getting any jobs out of it, the contractors, the banks, and the aluminum companies, and anybody who says that does not exist, I want to disagree frankly with."[23]

Lowry's suspicions were at least partly justified. We have seen that from the 1950s on, the Bank found an embarrassing lack of demand for "bankable" projects which threatened it with irrelevancy unless aggressive countermeasures were taken. Over several decades it helped to stimulate borrowing demand for big projects through the creation of autonomous project authorities, "policy dialogue," and by encouraging "development-minded" functionaries in key ministries through what amounted to a global system of international financial patronage. The Bank financed by definition undertakings the private sector found unattractive. Many of the

---

* Moreover, critics like Aart Van de Laar and Cynthia Hewitt de Alcantara argued, we recall, that in practice Bank agriculture projects—the heart of the McNamara poverty strategy—were actually *creating* new hordes of displaced poor, rather than helping them. Van de Laar concluded in 1980 that "if, indeed, there is a growing body of evidence which indicates that the pattern of economic growth has been accompanied by growing unemployment, more pronounced income inequality, and continuation of mass poverty and disease, there is then a clear need for a different pattern of future growth and development" (Van de Laar, *The World Bank and the Poor* [see endnote 12], 1).

projects that the Bank funded, one could argue, were the very ones that developing countries and their populations *least* needed.

But the more fundamental answer to the questions of the congressmen was that the approach of the MDBs ignored the deeper, ancient ecological and social realities that are the basis of our world; these realities are veiled, or obscured, by the political and economic superstructure of nation-states that the banks deal with. Rudolph Ryser told Patterson and Bereuter:

Take a look at the world. What you see is a quilt divided up into various little pieces we call states. What we don't see from out there is an ancient world that has existed for thousands of years that has been covered up by that quilt and, in fact, divided up by the little pieces of string that make the quilt. Underneath that surface are the millions of indigenous peoples of ancient societies. . . . One of the problems I have alluded to for states' governments and the multilateral banks and multilateral institutions generally is that this quilt, string by string, is slowly but surely coming apart.[24]

The congressmen decided that the questions raised by the hearings were unusually important and had to be explored further. They requested that the Treasury Department forward all of the statements of the witnesses to the World Bank and its sister institutions, so that they might respond.

The Campaign Mounts

The presentations of the . . . witnesses at the hearings were, frankly, surprising and distressing. When we had an opportunity afterward to cross-check the information presented to the committee, we found substantial corroboration of the information presented by most of the witnesses.[25]

—James Conrow, Deputy Assistant
Secretary of the Treasury

In January 1984, the U.S. Treasury forwarded the rebuttals of the multilateral banks to the House Subcommittee on International Development Institutions and Finance—over 1,000 single-spaced pages, certainly the most comprehensive response of international agencies ever prepared to answer outside inquiries about their operations. But the replies were evasive and misleading. For example, in response to the charge that the Bank's Office of Environmental Affairs (OEA) was understaffed and impotent in changing Bank projects, the World Bank told the U.S. Treasury and Congress that "the World Bank, with its Office of Environmental Affairs, is the oldest, largest, and most experienced institution dealing with these issues."[26] The Bank repeated the claim that "every project proposed for financing comes to the attention of OEA early in the project cycle," and asserted that by the time of final appraisal "the environmental assessment will have been largely completed."[27]

Internal Bank files show that shortly after the Bank made these assertions to the government of its largest shareholder, some of its most senior management were fully apprised of precisely the contrary. On March 9, 1984, the "Operational Policy Subcommittee" of the Bank met and discussed, among other issues, "environmental aspects of bank work." Chaired by Ernest Stern, the senior vice-president for operations, the meeting was attended by four other vice-presidents of the World Bank, high-ranking Bank directors managing operations in Latin America and Asia, and James Lee, the head of the Bank's environmental office.* A March 30, 1984, Bank office memorandum cites Stern as asking those present

whether Bank staff know that they have a responsibility to consider environmental issues on every project, whether they do so, and whether management looks at these issues. The view was, as a matter of routine, environmental issues are not considered, but that they are taken into account in specific instances when environmental consequences are pointed out by the Bank's environment advisor, the press, or special interest groups in host countries.[28]

In other words, when there was a scandal in the press or strong opposition among local groups representing the people affected by a scheme, having an environmental specialist or two in house came in handy for damage control.

The Bank further claimed in its response to the U.S. Congress that nearly all projects cited by NGOs had been prepared several years before, creating a "misleading impression that past trends continue."[29] This was also inaccurate, since Indonesia Transmigration and Brazil's Polonoroeste, for example, were huge multi-loan programs that were just hitting their stride. Transmigration, the Bank claimed, was no longer "solely (or even mainly) designed to reduce population pressure in Java, but rather to develop natural resources that otherwise would be wasted."[30] Polonoroeste, the Bank asserted, was "an opportunity to develop sustainable agriculture" in areas with "relatively better soils" where settlement had already occurred.[31]

As for David Price, "most of Dr. Price's testimony is a matter of interpretation of facts and events surrounding tribal peoples to be affected by a

* The other vice-presidents present were Shahid Husain, the vice-president for operations policy; the vice-presidents for the South Asia region, and for energy and industry, David Hopper and Jean-Loup Dherse, respectively; and Warren Baum.

Bank-financed rural development project in Brazil."[32] Moreover, financing Polonoroeste was necessary because "the unavoidable alternative is to expose the region to continued shifting cultivation and land degradation."[33]

Here the World Bank repeated its standard justification for many of its controversial projects: that without multibillion-dollar investments in schemes like Polonoroeste and Transmigration, things would somehow be much worse. "Attention should be paid to the human and ecological costs of *not* going ahead with projects," the Bank asserted.[34] Another variant that officials repeated time and time again was that governments were determined to go ahead with such projects with or without Bank financing; Bank involvement ensured that more attention would be given to environmental and indigenous peoples' issues. As one U.S. Treasury official commented to the author in 1983, "What they're really saying is that there is no project so costly, and so disastrous, that the Bank won't throw hundreds of millions of dollars into it to try to make it better."[35] In fact, this rationale implied that the more disastrous the project, the more urgent the justification for Bank involvement.

The House Subcommittee on International Development Institutions and Finance hired a special staff assistant to evaluate the responses of the MDBs, and to prepare, in consultation with nongovernmental groups, a series of congressional recommendations for environmental reform of the multilateral banks. The recommendations were reviewed in draft in further hearings in September 1984,[36] and issued in December. The congressional recommendations numbered nineteen in all, and called for the United States to urge the World Bank and its sister institutions to greatly increase their environmental staffs, to consult with environmental and health ministries in preparing projects, to involve and share information with nongovernmental organizations, and to finance a greater proportion of smaller-scale, environmentally beneficial projects.[37] The Treasury Department agreed with most of the directives, and designated a full staff position in its Office of Multilateral Banks to review the environmental aspects of multilateral bank loan proposals.

It appeared to be a remarkable breakthrough; in the highly ideological, politically charged atmosphere of Reagan's first term, the administration and the Democrat-controlled House agreed on what was a bipartisan environmental policy for U.S. participation in the World Bank and its sister institutions. In late 1985, thanks to the initiative of Congressman David Obey, chairman of the House Appropriations Subcommittee on Foreign Operations, many of the recommendations would be enacted as law.

The United States was the largest shareholder in the Bank, but still it controlled only one-fifth of the Bank's voting shares. Would its influence be sufficient to promote the environmental reforms? The Washington environmental advocates began to expand their contacts to groups in the United Kingdom, Germany, the Netherlands, and Scandinavia, in the hope of promoting similar pressure for reform on other governments with large voting shares on the World Bank's Executive Board.

Nevertheless, the Washington-based environmental advocates thought they had won a decisive victory. They believed—naively in retrospect—that surely, now that the World Bank was publicly confronted with evidence of systemic problems in its projects, it would take actions to remedy them. Little did they suspect that the battle had just begun.

The Fight for Rondônia

Polonoroeste was to be the first test case. Through the summer of 1984, the author and a University of Chicago anthropologist recently returned from Brazil, Steve Schwartzman, gathered information on the huge road-building and rainforest colonization scheme that threatened the welfare of some 10,000 Indians and the integrity of a largely intact rainforest area three-quarters the size of France. At almost the same time, nongovernmental environmental and human rights groups in Brazil were becoming interested in expanding their international contacts to pressure the Brazilian government to protect the rights of threatened Indian tribes and to take measures to stop the accelerating deforestation of the Amazon rainforest. That summer, a research collaboration began between Washington environmentalists and Brazilian groups that would soon have international political repercussions.

Ironically, in the early 1980s the World Bank touted Polonoroeste as an ecological model; the Bank claimed that this was the first time that environmental considerations had played such an important role in what it characterized as a large-scale, integrated rural development program. The Bank conditioned its $457 million in loans for Polonoroeste on adequate demarcation and protection of over fifteen Indian reserves, and implementation of health measures to protect the Indians. The Bank also provided for setting aside two biological reserves, a national park, four ecological stations (which would also be protected natural areas), and national forest areas. In addition, one of the loan agreements between the Bank and the Brazilian government contained specific provisions in which the Brazilian government pledged that Polonoroeste settlements would not occur on unsuitable soils or soils of unknown quality, or menace the numerous areas to be protected.

But the research of the NGOs confirmed the direst warnings of anthropologists such as David Price that the Brazilian government had little capacity and even less political will to carry out the Indian protection and environmental components of the project. They documented that Polonoroeste was totally out of control, a cauldron of exponentially increasing migration, deforestation, disease, and violence.

As they were completing their own investigation, the Washington environmentalists convinced another congressional subcommittee—this one on agricultural research and the environment, chaired by James H. Scheuer, a Democrat from Queens—to hold a special hearing on Polonoroeste. They raised funds to fly to Washington José Lutzenberger, a Brazilian agronomist and Brazil's leading, most eloquent environmental activist. Lutzenberger had led successful campaigns in south-central Brazil in the 1970s to promote stronger state laws regulating pesticide use. In the repressive atmosphere of Brazil's military regime, he had been one of the few in the country unafraid to criticize the government. Lutzenberger's testimony before Scheuer's subcommittee on the morning of September 19, 1984, was taped by Brazilian national television for broadcast nationwide on the evening news that same day.

Lutzenberger began by pointing out that the purpose of the project was to transfer landless poor from rich agricultural areas mainly in south-central Brazil to tropical forest areas where the soils were relatively poor. In contrast to the feudalistic northeast of the country, large-scale landlessness in southern Brazil was a relatively recent phenomenon, brought on by massive concentration of landholdings, spurred in turn by government policies to convert Brazilian agriculture from smaller-scale, domestic food production to a capital-intensive, export-oriented model. These migrants were the descendants of "German, Italian and Polish immigrants . . . [who] produced a relatively healthy, permanently sustainable peasant agriculture in the last century which flowered into the fifties of this century."[38] Millions had been uprooted over the past twenty-five years to make room for giant export-oriented soya and citrus plantations. In fact, Brazil had become the world's largest exporter of soya beans and citrus fruit; much of the orange juice consumed in North America and Europe came from Brazilian groves, whose produce, even with transportation costs added, was still cheaper than that of farmers in Florida and Spain.

The Brazilian military government, Lutzenberger charged, viewed these uprooted and landless masses in the richer, more politically developed part of the country as a serious political threat, and advertised migration to Rondônia as an alternative to land reform. The wiry, intense scientist held up government advertising brochures before the subcommittee.

The glossy pamphlets, widely circulated in southern Brazilian cities, were dumped by unmarked cars belonging to Brazilian security forces at political rallies protesting landlessness; they urged migration to Rondônia, where there was "enough good land for everybody."[39]

Lutzenberger denounced the "pitiless" cultural and even at times physical destruction of the Indian populations of the northwest. He made a plea for all the traditional inhabitants of the rainforest—which included *caboclos* (small-scale farmers in the forest) and *seringueiros* (rubber tappers), whose ways of life are compatible with the survival of the forest. "Why can't we leave Amazonia to the Amazonians?" he asked.[40]

And then, before millions of television viewers in Brazil, Lutzenberger denounced the World Bank, not just for ignoring the Brazilian government's flouting of Bank loan conditions in Polonoroeste, but for abetting the underlying agricultural strategy behind the project.[41] Equally important, he made it clear that there was a new political force to be reckoned with in the closed world of international development finance—"the Brazilian environmental movement" and "citizen groups" around the world.

Several weeks after the hearing, on October 15, 1984, Congressman Scheuer wrote U.S. Secretary of the Treasury Donald Regan, urging the Treasury to push the World Bank to take immediate measures to deal with the disastrous deforestation and the threats to Indian populations that Polonoroeste had unleashed. Only three days before, thirty-two NGOs from eleven countries had sent their own letter on Polonoroeste to World Bank president Clausen; it summarized, and was accompanied by, the extensive research dossiers the author and Steve Schwartzman had prepared. Signatories included José Lutzenberger, the presidents of the American and Brazilian anthropological associations, the president of the Rio de Janeiro section of the Brazilian Bar Association, eleven members of the German Bundestag, and numerous environmental and indigenous rights groups in Brazil, the United States, and Europe. The letter called upon the Bank to enforce its loan covenants with the Brazilian government by immediately withholding disbursements for Polonoroeste, urged the Bank to prepare with the Brazilian government an emergency environmental and Indian lands protection program in order to deal with the rapidly deteriorating situation, and cited the debacle in Polonoroeste as an example of the Bank's need to "undertake concrete measures and commit real resources, such as more professionally trained staff, to improve the ecological design and review of its projects."[42]

About a month later, the chief of the World Bank's Brazil division sent a brief response (not much longer than a paragraph) to the thirty-two signatories of the NGO letter on behalf of President Clausen:

As you are aware, Polonoroeste is a carefully planned regional development program, which seeks to stabilize and maximize the economic development of the region, while minimizing the risks to the regional ecology and Amerindian populations. . . . You can be sure that the Bank is continuing to monitor the situation closely, and that your concerns will be considered as Polonoroeste continues.[43]

The Republican Senator, James Bond, and Casanova

Not only Polonoroeste, but the Bank itself appeared to be out of control, beyond accountability. Within a year and a half there had been a half-dozen special U.S. congressional hearings, nineteen congressional recommendations for environmental reform, a letter from the chairman of a congressional subcommittee, exhaustively documented dossiers on the Polonoroeste disaster endorsed by American and Brazilian NGOs as well as parliamentarians and academic experts from a dozen countries—and all of this could not spur the World Bank even to enforce its own loan conditions in a single, wildly destructive project.

Almost in desperation, in January 1985 the Washington environmentalists turned to the Republican-controlled Senate. The environmental groups hardly expected to find strong support for their cause among many of the Reagan Republicans who entered the Senate in 1980; there was one, however, Senator Robert Kasten of Wisconsin, who had seemed sympathetic when the author testified before the Senate Appropriations Subcommittee on Foreign Operations, which Kasten chaired, in the spring of 1984. When Kasten and his staff, Alex Echols and James Bond, saw the exchange of correspondence on Polonoroeste with the World Bank, they hit the roof; it seemed to confirm their worst suspicions about the arrogance and lack of accountability of multilateral institutions. Kasten sent a gruff letter to Clausen, describing the response as a "brush-off" and "an insult."

"As you know better than anyone else," the Senator chided Clausen,

securing support for U.S. contributions to multilateral development institutions is difficult at best. That the World Bank would respond in such a cavalier fashion to groups and individuals who would otherwise support their programs is most difficult to understand.

The questions and concerns raised in the [environmentalists'] . . . letter are legitimate and deserve a credible and responsive answer. I, therefore, put these questions and concerns to you and ask that you respond to me as Chairman of the Foreign Operations Appropriations Subcommittee.[44]

Kasten sent an even blunter letter to Secretary of the Treasury Donald Regan. "Dear Don," Kasten wrote, "the [Bank's] response . . . is an insult." It was "outrageous," reinforcing feelings "by many that international organizations such as the World Bank are arrogant and totally unwilling to receive constructive criticism." He asked Regan to take up the matter personally, and again stated that the Bank's attitude "obviously compounds our problems" in securing appropriations in the Senate.[45]

Not much more than twenty-four hours after the Kasten letter to Clausen went out, the author received a phone call from James Burnham, the U.S. executive director at the World Bank; he wanted to have lunch at a mutually convenient time, but preferably as soon as possible. The next day the U.S. executive director of the Inter-American Development Bank (IDB), a Cuban-American named José Casanova, called and announced he would attend also. At the lunch, Burnham rambled on at length about all of the important functions of the World Bank and its sister multilateral institutions—why, just a few hours before he had been on the phone with finance ministries in Europe to discuss how the World Bank could play its part in channeling more money into Brazil to deal with the debt crisis. The environment was important, and the Bank should pay more attention to it, but the Bank had bigger fishes to fry. It wouldn't be very good for the global environment or anyone else if the entire international financial system collapsed, would it?

It became clear that Burnham was troubled by the thought that Senator Kasten, as chairman of the key subcommittee that appropriated the U.S. funds for the banks every year, was in a position to single-handedly hold hostage one-fifth of the World Bank's funding. The Wisconsin politician might do the unimaginable—block World Bank appropriations on a pretext as silly as protecting tropical rainforests and the fate of a few thousand Amazonian Indians affected by a particular project. Burnham and Casanova concluded the lunch by stating their intention to raise environmental issues more regularly and seriously in the board meetings of the two multilateral banks. So cool it with Kasten, was the implication, you'll get action without him.

The idea of an alliance between a Reaganite Senator and a group of environmentalists and anthropologists to make the World Bank more accountable disturbed some people. These included World Bank staff who thought of themselves as 1960s-style "Great Society" liberals, congressional aides, other environmental groups, and a number of people who worked with think tanks that promoted—and partly depended on—foreign aid. Kasten, they argued, didn't really care about the environment, poor people in the Third World, or the indigenous inhabitants of the Amazon; he was—apparently a terrible epithet for some—a "Bank basher" who, like a number of his reactionary colleagues, was against foreign aid and was looking for a pretext to cut it. The environmentalists, in their naiveté, had handed it to him.

In reality, Kasten's personal interest and commitment to rainforest conservation and the fate of indigenous peoples would continue through the years.* But this was hardly the point. The perception that the senator was looking for a pretext to cut World Bank funding made the threat all the more effective. The Washington environmentalists argued that if indeed the senator was inclined to cut funds and was looking for an excuse to do so, the only solution for the World Bank was to clean up its environmental act as quickly as possible and deprive Kasten of his pretext.

Showdown on Polonoroeste

A few weeks later, in March 1985, Clausen's aides told Kasten that the environmentalists would get a credible response to their October 12, 1984, letter: a meeting with the president himself and the entire senior management of the Bank—who the Washington activists insisted be present—to discuss what the Bank was going to do about Polonoroeste.

The environmentalists had met Clausen once before, in the spring of 1984. They had requested the meeting before several of them were to testify in the Senate on appropriations for the "soft-loan" facility of the Bank, the International Development Association. That meeting was a fiasco. The president of the World Bank read in part from 3-by-5 note cards, and interrupted them before they could finish their presentations. "Don't hold IDA hostage to the environment," he interjected. "Think about poor people"—as if conserving the resource base and helping the poor were contradictory goals. He told them that the problem was that there was an inaccurate perception of the Bank's environmental record, and that he was not going to increase the Bank's environmental staff. When the environmentalists replied that they simply wanted more information so they could accurately testify on behalf of the more than five million members of their organizations, he shot back, "I resent the leverage"—an extraordinary statement for the head of an institution whose power largely rested on exerting leverage through its loan conditions.

At the second meeting with Clausen, a little more leverage made a world of difference. The meeting took place on the afternoon of May 22, 1985, in the large, wood-paneled meeting room adjacent to Clausen's

* One could argue, though, that it was easier for him or any other senator to take a strong stand on environmental issues that did not affect interests in his own constituency.

office. Besides the environmentalists,* Senator Kasten and his aide Alex Echols were present, as well as David Maybury-Lewis, the former chairman of Harvard's anthropology department and an advocate for indigenous rights. Clausen, seated at the head of the table, opened with a conciliatory statement in which he asserted that all present shared the same, mutually complementary goals of sustainable development and environmental conservation. He noted that the issue of the day was the Polonoroeste project, but that first, Bank senior management wanted to say a few words. To Clausen's right was Ernest Stern—senior vice-president for operations and the second-ranking executive in the Bank hierarchy. Stern, an American who had worked for U.S.A.I.D. before coming to the Bank more than a decade before, was the wizard of the World Bank, a consummate bureaucrat and all-powerful manager. It was obvious to many that Stern, with his encyclopedic knowledge of the Bank's unwritten history and rules, and his powerful web of internal contacts and allies, was the man who really ran the place. He rarely spoke in public, and it soon became apparent why.

Stern droned on in a low monotone, lecturing those present about the Bank's recent evolution, namely its shift in the early 1980s to devoting up to a quarter of its lending for structural adjustment. His monologue was disconnected from the subject of the meeting and redundant for anyone who followed the Bank at all closely. It appeared that a filibuster was taking place. Senator Kasten became increasingly impatient; he turned to Clausen, who was seated next to him, and whispered in his ear. Clausen immediately interrupted Stern, and gave the floor to the environmentalists, who demanded specifics.

So, eight months after their letter, a response: in March the Bank had halted remaining disbursements—totaling over a quarter of a billion dollars—on the Polonoroeste loans, pending the preparation and carrying out of emergency environmental and Indian lands protection measures by the Brazilian government. Brazil had agreed to halt its nationwide advertising campaign to attract new settlers; it would be taking new measures to demarcate and enforce the protection of natural areas and Indian lands; and so on. The Bank and Brazil were doing much of what the environmentalists had asked for in their letter. In a sense, the meeting was a belated formality, a symbolic political ballet, since the environmentalists had already known this information for two months, and Bank staff continued to insist on the peculiar fiction that they had not initiated the halt in funding, but that the Brazilian government had requested the Bank not to disburse, for a limited period, the remaining Polonoroeste loans.

* Including the author, Brent Blackwelder of the Environmental Policy Institute, and Barbara Bramble of the National Wildlife Federation.

Still, it was an extraordinary double precedent: for the first time, the Bank was forced to account to outside NGOs and a parliamentarian of a member country for the environmental and social impacts of a lending program, and for the first time a public international financial institution had halted disbursements on a loan for environmental reasons.

But Polonoroeste was only one project—what about the others? The author asked Ernest Stern how the Bank could be preparing hundreds of millions of dollars in new loans for the Indonesia Transmigration program, when Polonoroeste had turned out to be such a disaster. Why was the Bank continuing to finance dubious jungle colonization schemes— couldn't it surely find less risky and economically more promising investments elsewhere? Stern's response was remarkably candid and disturbing. "If we wanted to," he replied, "we could finance nothing but health and education projects. But we would be avoiding our responsibilities as a development institution."[46] He maintained that for the Indonesian government Transmigration was a major national priority, a project that would go ahead regardless of Bank support. It was important for the Bank to support programs like Indonesia Transmigration so it could influence them and continue to have a major impact on development in its major borrowing countries. This is the role of the Bank, not to be an observer on the sidelines.

The man running the World Bank had just explained his view of its raison d'être, one which had little to do with economics and rigorous cost-benefit analysis (not to speak of helping the poor or conserving the environment) and a lot to do with political power on a global scale.

Rubber Tappers and Environmentalists Join Hands

We became environmentalists without even knowing that word.[47]   —Chico Mendes*

Just as the World Bank suspended disbursements on its Polonoroeste loans in early 1985, the Inter-American Development Bank approved loans totaling $58.5 million for the paving of more than 200 miles of the extension of the Polonoroeste penetration road, BR-364,

* The best account of the struggle of the rubber tappers and their subsequent alliances with NGOs in Brazil and the United States can be found in Andrew Revkin's *The Burning Season: The Murder of Chico Mendes and the Fight for the Amazon Rain Forest* (Boston: Houghton Mifflin Company, 1990). Another excellent account is Adrian Cowell's *The Decade of Destruction: The Crusade to Save the Amazon Rainforest* (New York: Henry Holt and Company, 1990).

from Porto Velho, Rondônia, to Rio Branco, the capital of the state of Acre. Acre is a Maryland-sized state at the extreme northwest corner of Brazil, bordering on Bolivia. Acre and adjacent areas influenced by the road in the state of Amazonas are mostly pristine tropical forest, inhabited by some 10,000 Indians belonging to 39 different ethnic groups. The region is also inhabited by some 40,000 *seringueiros* (rubber tappers), forest-dwellers who depend on sustainable extraction of wild rubber, Brazil nuts, and other forest products for income.

This time something unprecedented happened: the information gathered by the environmentalists in Washington on the World Bank Rondônia disaster convinced the U.S. Treasury Department to abstain on approving the IDB Acre loans for BR-364, the first time the United States had ever not approved a loan to Brazil since the founding of the IDB in 1960.* The U.S. abstention prompted IDB management to withhold all disbursements on the loans until the Brazilian government agreed to and started to carry out an environmental and Indian lands protection plan for the project—the "PMACI" (Programa de Proteção do Meio Ambiente e as Comunidades Indígenas).

There are some 350,000 rubber tappers in the Amazon, descendants of thousands of workers who migrated to the rainforest in the great rubber boom at the end of the nineteenth century. The boom collapsed in the years before World War I, when the British successfully began to export rubber from plantations in Malaysia. The Amazonian rubber tappers stayed, but for decades remained subject to debt peonage to their rubber-baron patrons. After the middle of this century more of the *seringueiros* worked autonomously, but they often lacked secure land titles, and land conflicts with ranchers and large landowners increased. In the 1970s, the *seringueiros* began to organize in local unions with the aid of the Catholic church. The rubber tappers in Acre were the best organized in the entire Amazon region.

The lobbying of the Washington activists became known in Acre, where the *seringueiros* had a soft-spoken organizer—Chico Mendes. Mendes was a leader who arose not from the Westernized, urban, educated elites often cultivated by diplomats, conservation groups, and think tanks in North America and Europe, but from the rural poor whose survival depended on the conservation of their natural surroundings. A man who had worked full-time harvesting latex in the rainforest since the age

---

* There were three proposed loans, totaling $72 million. The U.S. abstention did not prevent the approval of two of the loans, which were "hard," with interest rates close to commercial terms, since the U.S. voting share in the IDB, 34.5 percent, was not sufficient to carry the vote. It did veto the third, "soft," no-interest loan of $13.5 million, for which the IDB's charter requires two-thirds of Executive Board votes for approval, rather than a simple majority.

of eleven, Mendes led the efforts of *seringueiros* in Acre to secure title to their lands and to conserve the forest as a base of extractive production.

Mendes and his colleagues had seen how the Polonoroeste debacle had destroyed the livelihoods of many rubber tappers in neighboring Rondô-nia; disillusioned refugees, as well as land speculators, were streaming into Acre over the still-unpaved extension of BR-364. The *seringueiros* intensi-fied their unique form of nonviolent resistance to deforestation, *empates,* which they initiated in the mid-1970s. *Empate* literally means "stale-mate," a standoff in which groups of *seringueiros* surround and peacefully confront landowner-employed laborers chopping down the forest. Like the activists of Chipko, the village-based women's movement to save Himalayan forests (see Chapter 10), the *seringueiros* literally put their bodies between the trees and those wielding axes and chainsaws.

In October 1985, some 120 rubber tapper leaders from all over the Amazon basin held their first national meeting in Brasília. Present, too, were environmental activists, researchers, and three people who would play a key role in helping the rubber tappers to form alliances inside and outside Brazil with other groups—Steve Schwartzman of the Environ-mental Defense Fund; Mary Helena Allegretti, who subsequently founded the Institute for Amazon Studies to promote sustainable use of the Brazil-ian Amazon; and Tony Gross, an Englishman who had worked with Oxfam in Brazil since 1980. The meeting was a watershed. The *seringueiros* formed a national organization, the National Council of Rub-ber Tappers. They called for a halt to agricultural colonization projects in intact forests and for the conservation of the forests they occupied. They insisted that local needs and knowledge be taken into account in future development projects in the Amazon, and that they be consulted and par-ticipate in the planning of projects that would affect them directly. And they proposed a new model for conservation of the Amazon rainforest—the setting aside of large areas of forest as protected "extractive reserves" under the management of local rubber tapper communities. In these reserves, the rubber tappers suggested, the forest would be conserved but also economically harvested in a sustainable fashion. Already, rubber tap-pers regularly gathered and sold more than a dozen rainforest products besides natural rubber and Brazil nuts.

Not long after their first national meeting, the rubber tappers formed an alliance with the Union of Indigenous Peoples, the umbrella organiza-tion representing most of the Indian tribes in Brazil. They called the new coalition the Amazonian Alliance of the Peoples of the Forest, and it too was unprecedented. Indians and *seringueiros* had often been at logger-heads in land conflicts in the Amazon, but now they were united against the exponentially growing threat to their forest home. The Alliance condemned the Brazilian government and the World Bank for the devastation of the forest exemplified in Polonoroeste, and called for a new Amazon development policy based on the principle of "Amazonia for the Amazonians."[48]

A highly effective collaboration evolved among the rubber tappers, their supporters in Brazil (groups affiliated with human rights organizations and NGOs like Mary Allegretti's Institute for Amazon Studies), and environmental activists outside Brazil, particularly environmental groups in Washington and the U.K. Over the next three years, Mendes and other Brazilian activists such as Mary Allegretti and Ailton Krenak, leader of the Union of Indigenous Peoples, traveled to Washington to lobby officials of the World Bank and IDB. Mendes met with Senator Kasten and other members of Congress and their staffs, and traveled to Miami in 1987 to lobby the governors and executive directors of the IDB at their annual meeting. He received two international environmental awards, one of them from the United Nations Environment Program.

Just before Christmas 1988, Chico Mendes was murdered, a death foretold. The patriarch and the son of a local ranching family had threatened to murder Mendes for nearly a year. Several of his predecessors, union leaders in Acre, had been murdered before him, and through the early 1990s the killings continued, part of an escalating dynamic of rural violence in the Amazon, exacerbated by the social tensions unleashed by the huge internationally financed development projects of the 1980s.

By the end of 1986, the intense public pressures of U.S. environmental groups on the World Bank and the IDB created a unique opportunity: the multilateral banks were eager to grasp any chance to show they were considering alternatives to their projects in northwest Brazil. Through that year, Steve Schwartzman and Mary Allegretti prepared a study on the economic, legal, and financial feasibility of setting up extractive reserves in the Brazilian Amazon. In early 1987, the Environmental Defense Fund (EDF) forwarded the report to the U.S. Treasury Department, which circulated it to the World Bank and the IDB. In a memorandum to the U.S. executive director of the World Bank dated April 2, 1987, none other than Ernest Stern wrote:

We fully endorse the recommendation of the report for the establishment of extractive reserves in the Amazon region. At present, these reserves are the most promising alternative to land clearing and colonization schemes, which are often questionable in environmental terms. The establishment of these reserves would permit the simultaneous conservation and economic development of large tracts of primary forests in the Amazon region, and, by attending to the long neglected needs of traditional rubber tappers, would have important social benefits as well.[49]

Stern's memo was a remarkable about-face. After all, the World Bank for over two decades had been the preeminent international funder of disastrous forest-clearing and colonization schemes, and not just in Brazil. Washington generates yearly thousands upon thousands of pages of reports and recommendations on foreign aid, international development, and the global environment, many of which are rarely read even by the staffs of the institutions that prepare them. If one were to take Stern's memo at face value, the short rough draft of a report authored by two anthropologists employed by environmental groups had convinced the operations chief of the world's biggest employer of development economists of the error of its ways.

In fact, public and congressional pressure was growing and the press was beginning to portray the World Bank as an environmental ogre, ruining fifteen years of Bank public relations work. Just as Samuel Johnson observed that nothing concentrates a man's mind so effectively as the prospect of being hanged in twenty-four hours, so it might be said that the attention bureaucracies are willing to give to outside proposals that they change their ways has a strong correlation with credible threats to their funding.

Following Stern's reversal, the Bank and the IDB began to consider reprogramming part of the remaining disbursements for Polonoroeste and the Acre road loans to support the creation of extractive reserves. The two institutions also reprogrammed funds to provide for increased protection of Indian lands. The constant threats to withhold funding, particularly from the IDB, by Senator Kasten and the new chairman of the Senate Subcommittee on Foreign Operations, Democrat Daniel Inouye of Hawaii, continued to play a critical role in focusing the attention of both institutions. The National Council of Rubber Tappers and Mary Allegretti's Institute for Amazon Studies would help Brazilian authorities draft a new law which permitted communities of rubber tappers to take control of and manage what was a totally new form of land tenure. By 1992, the Brazilian government would create nineteen extractive reserves in four different states of the Brazilian Amazon, covering an area of nearly three million hectares of tropical forest.

Closing the Circle

By first organizing nationally with Brazilian human rights groups and NGOs, and subsequently joining with the Washington environmentalists, the rubber tappers closed the circle between the highest levels of public international finance, the Brazilian national government, and local concerns. It was a novel form of international political action, linking formerly isolated constituencies. Once the World Bank and the IDB began to support the creation of extractive reserves in Acre, the political balance of power in the state was changed: the *seringueiros* were now joined to nongovernmental groups that could exercise political pressure nationally and internationally, and even more important, help channel international funding to Acre and other states in Brazil's Amazon to support conservation of the forest.

In at least one particular case, the top-down model of big international development appeared to be reversed. Local groups were taking the initiative in proposing a development alternative rooted in the ecological and social reality of the place they inhabited—and at least some people in the multilateral banks, the Brazilian government, and finally in the state government of Acre were listening and responding.* Or so it seemed.

The internationalization of local environmental controversies was only the last step in a burgeoning of social and community movements in developing nations in the 1980s. It was little known outside Brazil that by the middle of the decade there were hundreds of nongovernmental organizations in the country concerned with the environment. A few, like José Lutzenberger's AGAPAN, dated back to the worst years of military repression in the 1970s, when any criticism of the government was a physically dangerous proposition. Others, like OIKOS in São Paulo, led local neighborhood opposition to ill-conceived urban infrastructure projects; OIKOS, working with the Environmental Defense Fund in Washington, pressured the IDB to hold a local, public hearing that resulted in the IDB's withdrawal from financing a highway that would have violated one of the last park areas left in São Paulo. Some groups, like CEDI (the Ecumenical Council for Documentation and Information) and NDI (the Nucleus for Indigenous Rights), had developed remarkable research and social networking expertise that were the equal of those of most organizations in the developed world—all accomplished under conditions of financial and

---

* As Stephan Schwartzman points out, what was critical in the campaign of the rubber tappers was not the use of local knowledge, "but its application in the context of a campaign mounted by organizations with the political weight to gain a hearing in the [U.S.] Congress and the U.S. government agencies, and with the will to use their weight. The history of extractive reserves as a development alternative, proposed by the rubber tappers movement and eventually endorsed by the MDBs and the Brazilian government, is a history of making a specific cultural and historical reality comprehensible as a general principle" (Stephan Schwartzman, "Deforestation and Popular Resistance in Acre: From Local Social Movement to Global Network," *Centennial Review*, vol. 35, no. 2 [College of Arts and Letters, Michigan State University: Spring 1991], 420).

political uncertainty that would have done in many of their counterparts in North America or Europe.

Other circles began to close, in Indonesia, India, and elsewhere. Not only in Brazil were environmental and social action groups proliferating, but all over the developing world. Many of these NGOs became active in the late 1970s or early 1980s, when their existence was relatively unknown in the industrialized North. Their emergence was a consequence of several global trends.

The liberalizing and/or demise of military and dictatorial regimes in Latin America and Asia opened a political space for such groups. At the same time, the failures of Marxist ideology and socialist movements created a demand for new alternatives and strategies among those in many countries who organized to change society. The integration of many societies into the global market economy was accompanied by growing inequality and unprecedented ecological problems; these trends in turn created an acute need for debate on alternatives and practical ways to test them. By the late 1980s, the growing ease of private national and international communications through computer networks, faxes, and electronic mail made it possible for like-minded groups around the world to inform one another quickly of crises and to mount international letter-writing and lobbying campaigns in a matter of hours.

The collaboration of the rubber tappers and other Brazilian groups with the Washington environmentalists was really only the best-known example of the newly formed global networks between local groups in developing countries and environmental activists and advocates in the North. Often, but not always, World Bank or other international financing of destructive projects was the catalyst that spurred the creation of these networks.

In Malaysia, groups like Sahabat Alam Malaysia (SAM—Friends of the Earth, Malaysia) and the Consumers' Association of Penang were already extraordinarily active in researching and lobbying for change in their country and region, beginning in the late 1970s. In 1986, SAM coordinated the founding of two international environmental activist networks associating scores of environmental groups around the world: the Asia-Pacific Peoples Environmental Network, and the World Rainforest Movement. In early 1987, these networks became critically important in generating international support for tribal groups in Sarawak (one of two Malaysian states in North Borneo) who initiated massive, nonviolent blockades of Japanese-financed logging roads. In October 1987, the Malaysian government launched a nationwide crackdown on dissent, arresting tribal protesters in Sarawak as well as leading environmental and civil rights activists, including Harrison Ngau, a SAM activist and Penan tribal leader from Sarawak, and Meenakshi Roman, a leading public interest environmental lawyer for SAM.

In Indonesia—the world's fifth most populous nation—environmental action groups from all over the country formed WALHI, the Indonesian Environmental Forum, in 1980; by 1983 it had more than 320 participating organizations. In October 1982, more than a dozen other organizations formed SKEPHI, the Movement Against Forest Destruction.[50]

But environmental and human rights groups walked a precarious tightrope in Indonesia: General Suharto's military regime permitted their existence, but overly vigorous criticism of the government could lead to the banning of an organization, the arrest of its members, or worse. In this political atmosphere, foreign criticism of projects financed by the World Bank gave groups like WALHI and SKEPHI an opportunity to join in efforts to criticize destructive schemes such as Transmigration without directly attacking the government. In 1986 and 1987 WALHI, SKEPHI, the Indonesian Legal Aid Foundation, and other Indonesian groups sent joint letters and dossiers with over fifty NGOs in ten other countries to the World Bank, calling upon the Bank to halt the financing of new Transmigration sites in pristine tropical forests.[51] With the specter of another Polonoroeste not far behind, the Bank conceded in December 1986 that new loans for Indonesia Transmigration would indeed go only to consolidate existing settlements* rather than to open up new areas.[52] It appeared that on a case-by-case basis, in response to concerted international pressure, the Bank was getting out of the business of rainforest colonization.

The growing international links between Indonesian groups and NGOs abroad was also helping to create political space for freer expression and the development of civil society in an otherwise repressive regime. There was a need for more political space in the international aid deliberations on Indonesia, too. Indonesian NGOs linked up with groups in Europe and North America** to lobby at the annual meeting in The Hague of the international aid agencies with Indonesian officials to coordinate the next

---

* This meant that the Indonesian government, too, was reducing, if not eliminating, its expansion of Transmigration. With the collapse of oil prices in the mid-1980s, Indonesia—one of the world's largest oil exporters—was increasingly dependent on the foreign exchange provided by the World Bank; it could not finance large-scale expansion of Transmigration without further international funding.

** In the mid-1980s, the most active Indonesian NGOs institutionalized their relations with groups abroad through the creation of the INGI—the International NGO Forum on Indonesia. Formed with the support of Dutch church groups, the INGI grew to include more than twenty-five major NGOs from Indonesia and more than fifty non-Indonesian groups from eleven countries by the early 1990s.

year's development assistance. They tried to influence policy by preparing and circulating position papers on issues such as human rights, the need for environmental protection, and the role of women in development. But the aid agencies, led by the World Bank, refused to allow the NGOs to attend the meeting, and continued to withhold most information on their deliberations and decisions.

In no country was the depth and breadth of nongovernmental activism more impressive than in India. In the late 1970s and early 1980s, numerous Indian NGOs conducted a successful national campaign to halt a proposed dam that would have destroyed one of the biologically richest and most intact tropical forest areas left in the country—the Silent Valley in the southwestern state of Kerala. Saving Silent Valley became a national cause célèbre in India, prompting Prime Minister Indira Gandhi to intervene personally to halt the project in 1983.[53]

Silent Valley was the first victory of India's burgeoning "green" movement. Increasingly, Indian environmentalists formed alliances with local peoples protesting the destruction of their livelihoods and cultures by gigantic government-promoted mega-projects, often financed by the World Bank. As would occur in Thailand several years later, small farmers and landless tribal people also protested large-scale eucalyptus plantations for commercial forestry, often financed by the Bank and other international aid agencies. The aid agencies characterized these projects as "social forestry," since they were intended to provide at least in part for fuelwood and other basic needs of the poor; instead, the international aid went principally to support commercial tree farm schemes managed by state forestry agencies and benefiting more prosperous landowners. The large-scale monoculture of eucalyptus often left the land useless for other purposes, depleting soil fertility and draining water tables in arid regions.

In numerous industrialized countries, NGOs increasingly coordinated lobbying with their counterparts in developing nations. Groups in Britain, Germany, Scandinavia, the Netherlands, Italy, Canada, and Australia launched their own campaigns to pressure their governments to push for environmental reforms in the MDBs. Parliamentary inquiries and hearings were launched, and research dossiers prepared. Finnish groups, for example, prepared a particularly devastating critique of the World Bank–financed social forestry projects that were the subject of so much protest in India. Remarkably, several officials still in government positions dealing with international development in several countries, particularly in Northern Europe, began to discretely help the NGOs with leaked information and documents, which could have cost them their jobs.

Although the Bank reversed course in a few specific cases like Polonoroeste and Transmigration, overall it lumbered along unchanged, a juggernaut fueled by a seemingly unstoppable, hypertrophied propensity to move huge amounts of money quickly, whatever the consequences.

Further Follies in the Amazon

World Bank loans for huge dams in Brazil spurred still more organized resistance. Two Bank-financed projects completed in the early 1980s in northeastern and southeastern Brazil, the Sobradinho and Machadinho dams, had displaced some 70,000 rural poor without adequate consultation and compensation. These experiences had generated widespread bitterness and mistrust. Yet by 1986 the Bank was planning to finance the completion of another mega-dam in the northeast, Itaparica, which was well underway without adequate plans to resettle and rehabilitate the 40,000 people it would displace. But in this case most of the people to be resettled joined rural unions sponsored by church and labor organizers to protest and fight for their rights. Once again, an international coalition mobilized, involving EDF and Oxfam—which was working on the ground at Itaparica.

The Bank was preparing a huge $500-million "Brazil Power Sector" loan to finish not just Itaparica, but a score of other big dams. And the loan was intended to be only the first of several—to be handed out in half-billion-dollar chunks—to Brazil's national electric utility, Eletrobrás, to support a gargantuan power investment plan called the Plan 2010. The Plan 2010 called for the construction of 136 dams over a twenty-year period, of which 79 were in the rainforest; it would have destroyed the ecological and cultural integrity of much of the Amazon basin. The first Brazil Power Sector loan would help to complete and/or initiate the first 25 dams, which would flood an area the size of Connecticut and force over 90,000 people to resettle, including the 40,000 at Itaparica. As the loan was being prepared, the Bank's Energy Department was completing a study—with conclusions the Bank ignored—that indicated that in large countries like Brazil and India many if not most energy generating projects planned over the coming twenty years could be replaced by investments in end-use energy efficiency and conservation.[54]

Enough was enough; when the Bank's Executive Board met on June 18, 1986, to consider the Brazil Power Sector loan, U.S. Alternate Executive Director Hugh Foster and several other executive directors expressed grave concerns about the dams. The U.K. director, using information from Oxfam, insisted that a specific loan provision be included to insure decent resettlement and rehabilitation of the population threatened by Itaparica; if the Bank did not comply, he threatened, he could not approve the loan. Foster was more pessimistic: "Equally clear is the total absence of any possibility that the [Itaparica] resettlement will take place without extensive human suffering and bitter recriminations."[55] Sadly, events would prove him to be right.

Using information supplied in part by EDF, Foster went on to deliver a blistering condemnation of the loan before the Bank's management and Executive Board:

The Bank has been involved in regional planning in Rondonia for at least six years. One would hope at least that planning for the Indian protection aspects of projects in that state would have benefitted from the Bank's tribal people's policy and from the unfortunate experience in the Polonoroeste project.

We find instead a proposal which includes financing of the Gi-Parana Dam in Rondonia where there has been virtually no planning to address the needs of the Amerindian population or the need for protection of the environment in the immediate area of the dam. Furthermore, the dam will flood a portion of an Indian reserve which previous Bank financing helped establish. This is pure folly.[56]

The U.S. representative castigated the Bank for helping to complete other disastrous projects, like the "infamous Tucurui Dam," and, "to add another folly," he continued, "the investment program includes financing for what the [loan] Appraisal Report terms 'the notorious Balbina Dam.'" He directly questioned the credibility of Bank staff attempts to put environmental window dressing on the loan through an "Environmental Master Plan" to promote environmental assessment of future Eletrobrás projects: "How much confidence can we have that it will be carried out conscientiously when the same [Brazilian government] institutions will be implementing a series of environmental disasters at the very same time?"[57]

On June 19, 1986, a majority of the Bank's Executive Board approved the loan, but the United States voted against it. It was the first time any member of the World Bank had refused to approve a loan on environmental grounds. It would not be the last.

By late 1986, several countries, including Germany, Sweden, the Netherlands, and Australia were sending signals to their World Bank executive directors to press for environmental reforms that echoed those urged by the United States. In the United States, other groups formed to mobilize grass-roots action on international development and the World Bank. Randy Hayes, an environmental activist based in San Francisco, spurred the creation of the Rainforest Action Network, a group that was able to mobilize tens of thousands of letters of protest to the World Bank in solidarity with campaigns led by NGOs in the developing world. The International Rivers Network, also based in San Francisco, specialized in fighting dams all over the world and mobilized its own extensive network of activists abroad and in the United States. More radical groups, such as Greenpeace and Earth First!, also turned their attention to the Bank. At the annual Bank/Fund meeting in Washington in September 1986, U.S. NGOs coordinated the first annual alternative meeting of environmental, development, and human rights groups from around the world to protest the policies and projects of the Bretton Woods behemoths. A U.S. activist named Chad Dobson helped organize this first alternative meeting, and he would go on to found his own NGO, the Bank Information Center, which specialized in circulating confidential documents from the World Bank to groups around the world.

By late 1986, the World Bank began to resemble a fortress under siege: on September 30, coinciding with the Bank's annual meeting in Washington, Greenpeace, Earth First!, and Rainforest Action Network activists with rock-climbing expertise scaled the roof of a World Bank building in the middle of the day and hung out an immense banner, whose image was transmitted by photojournalists around the planet: "The World Bank Destroys Tropical Forests."

Besieged

In the United States the congressional hearings continued—more than twenty by 1987, held by six different subcommittees of the Senate and House. Robert Kasten called a special Senate hearing in May 1987 to record widening international criticism of the multilateral banks for their environmental negligence. Among the witnesses were nongovernmental representatives from Brazil, Indonesia, Canada, and the Netherlands. David Obey, the powerful House Democrat from Wisconsin, played a key legislative role, since he chaired the House of Representatives Subcommittee on Foreign Operations, which appropriated funds for the World Bank. Ironically, Obey and Kasten disliked one another ideologically and personally; each was particularly peeved when one would get media recognition for international environmental accomplishments and not the other. This antagonism spurred an intense rivalry and one-upmanship in their staffs, who competed to introduce every year increasingly stronger environmental reform legislation for the World Bank. Through a strange alchemy of antipathy, the two political enemies worked more effectively together to further international environmental concerns than if they had been allies and friends.

In the press and media the pressure also continued to mount. In 1986 and 1987, both the *New York Times* and the *Wall Street Journal* featured the campaign of the Washington environmentalists against the World Bank on their front pages and, perhaps more embarrassing for conscientious Bank staff, leading scientific journals such as *Nature* and *Science* carried news articles highly skeptical of the Bank's environmental record.

Two British documentary filmmakers played a unique role in stirring up international public opinion about the role of the multilateral banks in Brazil and other tropical countries. One, British producer Adrian Cowell, had traveled in and written about the Amazon forest and its inhabitants since he graduated from Cambridge in the mid-1950s. In 1980 he struck a deal with Britain's Central Independent Television Company that must have been the envy of every producer of documentaries in the world: over the next decade, Central would fund a series of films on the fate of the Amazon rainforest to be produced and directed by Cowell. "Imagine," Cowell told the Central Television executives, "if you could have had a filmmaker on site in the 1870s and 1880s to record the fate of the American West—here you have a chance to do this for the Amazon." The area Cowell chose to work in was Rondônia. More than two years into his cinematographic epic, Cowell realized that the fate of Rondônia was being decided as much in Washington, in the offices of the World Bank, as it was in Brazil.

By 1984, he was working closely with the environmental activists in Washington—Barbara Bramble, Steve Schwartzman, and the author. He filmed several of the congressional hearings, and worked closely with Chico Mendes, José Lutzenberger, and other Brazilian activists; both the making and the subsequent showing of the film series became important weapons in the fight to conserve remaining rainforests in northwest Brazil, and in helping the Brazilian activists strengthen their links with nongovernmental groups and sympathizers abroad. In the late 1980s and early 1990s, Cowell's five-hour series, *The Decade of Destruction,* would be shown in more than a dozen countries, including nationwide on PBS in the United States in October 1990.*

One of Cowell's assistants in the filming of the first episodes of *The Decade of Destruction,* Nicholas Claxton, was already an accomplished documentary filmmaker in his own right. He had won an Emmy in 1984 for *Seeds of Despair,* the BBC film that documented famine in Ethiopia and spurred the Live Aid movement of international rock concerts to raise emergency relief funds for Africa. Claxton found the theme of big interna-

---

* See Cowell's account of his experiences in Brazil during the 1980s, Andrian Cowell, *The Decade of Destruction: The Crusade to Save the Amazon Rain Forest* (New York: Henry Holt and Company, 1990).

tional development, the environment, and the multilateral banks compelling; he decided to make his own film on the subject, *The Price of Progress.*

The film was hard hitting and deeply disquieting: shot on site in Brazil, India, and Washington, with extensive footage from Indonesia and Africa, it portrayed giant, ill-conceived development schemes destroying the environment and indigenous cultures, all financed by the World Bank and other multilateral development banks. Claxton interviewed local activists in the developing world, academic experts, and World Bank executives; the contrast in sensibility was alarming.

One of those interviewed was Thayer Scudder, an anthropologist at the California Institute of Technology; he had the sad distinction of being the world's leading expert on forced resettlement of populations caused by large-scale development projects. Much of his experience was gained in over twenty years of consulting for the World Bank. His statements in Claxton's film were sobering: he could not point to a single project, World Bank-financed or otherwise, where a displaced population had been successfully rehabilitated. These populations are often tribal or traditional, he noted, and the effects of rapid, total uprooting are irreversible social disintegration, economic helplessness, and frequently a remarkable rise in mortality rates. Forcible resettlement, he concluded, "is the worst thing you can do to a people next to killing them."

The film showed an impassioned plea by Medha Patkar, the charismatic leader of the tens of thousands of tribal people in India, protesting their imminent displacement by the Bank-financed Sardar Sarovar dam; next, it turned to David Hopper, at that time the Bank's vice-president for South Asia. Hopper dispensed with the usual Bank rhetoric about helping the poor. "You can't have development without somebody getting hurt," he began. "We're going in as new carpenters and are likely to botch the first job, but we'll learn," Hopper noted when asked whether any populations had ever been successfully rehabilitated after being displaced by a Bank-financed project. "The tribals themselves, the oustees will learn," he added, as if there could be any comparison between what the "learning" entailed in real terms for an outcast Indian peasant and for World Bank staff who went home every night to comfortable suburban houses (in earlier years subsidized by the Bank with special low-interest loans for its employees). *The Price of Progress* was broadcast on national television in Britain and several other countries (though not in the United States), and shown before several national parliaments, including those of Sweden and Norway, and the U.S. Senate.

On Easter Sunday, 1987, the World Bank and the Polonoroeste debacle were the subject of an exposé on "60 Minutes," the most widely watched news program in America. It was a damning piece: correspondent Diane Sawyer presented dramatic clips of deforestation, migrants dying from malaria, and denunciations of Bank actions by José Lutzenberger and David Price. She interviewed the World Bank vice-president for external relations, José Botafogo. When Sawyer asked the hapless Botafogo how the Bank could proceed with such a project, he maintained that although the Bank knew there were risks, the Bank concluded, knowing what it did at the time, that it would be better for the environment, the Indians, and the migrants coming to the region if the Bank were involved. And then, before more than 20 million television viewers, Sawyer pulled out of her briefcase stacks of internal World Bank documents in which the Bank's own staff, between 1979 and 1983, continuously and consistently warned management that the project was a disaster in its very conception and predicted uncontrollable deforestation and virtual genocide of the Indians if the project went ahead.

The Bureaucracy of Destruction

> The management of the modern office is based upon written documents ("the files"), which are preserved in their original or draught form.[58]
> —Max Weber, *Wirtschaft und Gesellschaft*
> (Economy and Society)

What the "60 Minutes" documents revealed is negligence and knowing disregard by Bank management of the warnings of its own experts and consultants that the project would almost certainly result in human and ecological disaster. On January 8, 1980, for example, nearly two years before the first Polonoroeste loans were approved, the head of the Bank's then tiny Office of Environmental Affairs warned Mr. V. Rajagopalan, then a Bank department director who was his immediate superior, that "to use unproven technologies as a basis for agricultural settlement under extremely adverse soil conditions would be a highly risky undertaking and would prove disastrous for the settlers themselves."[59] As indeed it did. On February 25, 1980, J. C. Collins, a senior agricultural specialist in the Bank, wrote the environmental office that the proposed funding of "environmental" components of Polonoroeste (protected forest areas, ecological research stations, etc.) "in no way will . . . offset the possible harmful effects of project—deforestation, particularly of lands unsuitable for sustained agriculture, use of unsustainable agricultural production systems and the invasion of tribal reservations."[60]

On May 20, 1980, D. C. Pickering, assistant director for agriculture of the Bank's country policy staff, and James Lee, the Bank's head environment advisor, wrote a memorandum to the head economist working on Polonoroeste, D. J. Mahar. In their memo they questioned the "overoptimistic assessment of the agricultural potential of the area," noting that "at present the nature and extent of the various soils is [sic] not precisely known" and that it was "impossible to broadly identify the types and locations of the major soils." They concluded that "certainly there would seem to be better opportunities to increase agricultural productivity elsewhere, but there is no consideration of such alternatives in the report."[61]

On July 9, 1980, Collins wrote Mahar again to warn him that "very little is known about the land capability," reminding him that "the soils of the Amazon area as a whole are generally poor and, furthermore, highly variable. There is no evidence that the northwest is less variable, though it may have a somewhat higher proportion of soils with fewer limitations for agriculture." (These lands mostly were already occupied by ranchers and large landowners by the end of the 1970s.) "The tone of overall optimism," Collins warned, "does not seem warranted." Polonoroeste would be an economic debacle, Collins futilely protested:

It seems far from certain, at present, that the Northwest Region will either prove capable of sustaining any very significant volume of exports out of the region, or of providing a sustained livelihood for the anticipated large number of poor settlers without requiring a large and continuing Government subsidy.[62]

In November, 1980, Lee and Pickering again wrote Rajagopalan, Robert Skillings, the Brazil division chief, and Dennis Mahar, the Polonoroeste economist, that "the total milieux [sic] in which this development is being undertaken is hardly promising of success."[63]

Although the warnings of Lee, Pickering, and Collins did not seem to have any effect on the project, the Bank's management was, on the other hand, quite concerned about David Price, who was beginning to publicize his concerns about what he characterized as the genocidal implications of Polonoroeste for numerous Indian tribes.

On December 9, 1980, the director of the country department for Brazil, Enrique Lerdau, wrote a three-page background memorandum on Price, circulated again to Rajagopalan, Skillings, and others, noting,

Our most serious problem with Mr. Price's report was . . . that it was full of undocumented attacks and allegations against Brazilian officials which would certainly have a detrimental impact on our relations with the country and the officials concerned. Here are a few examples: . . .

Lerdau went on to quote Price's report:

". . . I was told that during the Medici regime, [a certain high official in FUNAI, the Brazilian Indian agency] belonged to the Burnier Squadron, which is reputed to have gotten rid of so-called communists by flying out and dropping them in the sea. One person who was arrested at that time has positively identified him as a torturer.

"To entrust their (the Indians) welfare to FUNAI as it is now constituted would be criminal."

In the same memo, Lerdau warned of

an adversary campaign against Brazil and the Bank being engineered by Mr. Price in complete disregard to . . . the assurances he gave us. . . . Mr. Price is certainly not foreign to a resolution critical of Brazil and the Bank (attached) passed by the American Anthropological Association council meeting on December 5, 1980. Mr. Price spoke in favor of this motion at the meeting. We should be prepared for more of such adverse manifestations from Mr. Price and his fellow anthropologists. . . . Mr. Skillings has been asked to discreetly warn the Brazilian authorities against Mr. Price's current activities.[64]

Lee, meanwhile, futilely wrote memos for the files. A memorandum dated December 19, 1980, records a telephone conversation on the subject of the fate of the Indians with Skillings, who was successfully ramming the project ahead despite Lee's objections.

Mr. Skillings indicated that he anticipates FUNAI will make an effort to better understand the needs and requirements of the tribal peoples in the area to be impacted by the proposed project, and to implement measures that will be responsive to the anthropological authorities.

He went on to state that the World Bank was above all else an economic development institution and should not align itself with or "take up" a cause such as the one under consideration. He cited drugs, urban crime, etc. as causes which could also merit the Bank's attention.[65]

By 1981, the warnings of the Bank's agricultural and environment staff became more urgent. They were ignored. An especially damning example is found in a memorandum of June 9, 1981, sent by Lee to a vice-president of the Bank, Warren C. Baum, through Lee's superior, Rajagopalan. The memo warns again of the risks, and cites still another consultant's report that "cast increasing doubt on the likelihood that the project will fulfill the expectations of both the Government and the Bank's advocates." Lee urged that at the very least the Bank should insist on stronger loan conditions concerning protection of the Indians and the environment.[66] Lee was appealing because he was powerless; only a commitment at a higher level by Baum or Rajagopalan could produce results.

The memo was returned to Lee the same day, with a hand-scribbled note by Rajagopalan: "Mr. Baum does not want these details to be discussed at the Vice-President's level—he believes that you should deal with these issues directly at the working level."[67]

On July 21, 1981, Bank agricultural specialist J. C. Collins received another memo, this time from a W. B. Peters, commenting again on a Bank assessment of soil suitability in the Polonoroeste region. "The information on soil physical properties is nil with nothing on the substrata. . . . In my view, the investigation of lands is presently inadequate to justify the Program."[68]

Not only did the Bank's Board of Executive Directors not see any of these memos, even today Bank management could bar their access to any of them. The criticisms of Lee, Collins, Pickering et al. (not to mention David Price) were omitted or reduced to vague mentions of "acceptable risk" in the appraisal documents.

So, on December 1, 1981, the World Bank's Executive Board unanimously approved the first three Polonoroeste loans, totaling $320 million. In fact, for the executive directors and the Bank's president, it was a model project, one of the best prepared in recent memory. The board minutes describe their enthusiasm:

Several [executive directors] congratulated the Bank staff and Brazilian authorities for their conception and design. Also, a speaker [executive director] and the Chairman [World Bank president] commented on the excellence of the staff's presentation of the projects to the Board. . . . Most of the speakers [executive directors] who supported the projects pointed to their truly integrated nature and the comprehensive approach to development they represented; they also cited the balance among infrastructure, agriculture, health and even ecology and Amerindian welfare.[69]

Alas, the Bank would approve over $200 million more in subsequent loans for Polonoroeste in 1982 and 1983, the 1983 loan supporting new agricultural colonization even as there was indisputable evidence that the project was catalyzing an ecological holocaust and economic debacle.

Collins and Lee would continue to protest, vainly. A July 29, 1983, memo sent from Collins to Shahid Husain, senior vice-president for policy and research and number three in the Bank hierarchy, warns Husain that the Polonoroeste Phase III loan for new colonization soon to be presented to the board also appears to be headed for disaster. The memo expresses "doubts . . . whether the Phase III project now being proposed will be any more successful in promoting viable, sustainable and environmentally sound cropping practices than has its predecessor."[70] Lee followed with a similar memo to Rajagopalan on August 5, 1983.[71]

In fact, as the new loan was being prepared, the Bank was sending urgent cables to the Brazilian cabinet in March 1983, protesting that "little progress has been made in demarcating Amerindian reserves, particularly those of the Nambikwara [*sic*] groups"—the very ones David Price was so concerned about.[72]

On October 27, 1983, a World Bank press release announced the approval of the Phase III Polonoroeste loan for $65.2 million. As for the Bank using its financial leverage on the Brazilian government to halt mounting threats to the Indians and the environment, the following statement speaks for itself:

As part of the World Bank's Special Action Program, disbursements for the first two fiscal years of project implementation will be accelerated. The Special Action Program was initiated by the Bank in February 1983, to help developing countries maintain economic momentum in the face of the current international economic crisis.[73]

The Greening of the Bank?

Something had to budge, and it was going to be the Bank. In July 1986, A. W. Clausen was replaced by Barber Conable as Bank president. Conable, a Republican congressman from western New York, had served on the House Ways and Means Committee for over twenty years and had earned universal respect for his integrity and competence. James Baker, secretary of the treasury during Reagan's second term, chose Conable in the hope he would be more successful than his predecessor in cajoling Congress to deliver the U.S. financial contribution to the Bank. There was no doubt that the environment had become the Bank's most prickly public relations problem. Republicans like Senator Kasten and James Conrow, head of the Office of Multilateral Development Banks in the Treasury Department began to sound like radical street agitators when queried on the subject. "When people find out what's been going on," Kasten expounded in late 1986, "you're going to see people out in the streets saying, 'My God, did you read this information. Why are our dollars being used to fund this kind of destruction?'" Not to be outdone, at about the same time Conrow told Nicholas Claxton, commenting on the failure of the Bank to consult those affected by its projects, "I think it's a disaster, it's a mistake, and it's been going on for years."[74]

Conable did not feel bound to the mistakes of the past, and he was more sympathetic to environmental concerns than Clausen, as well as to issues such as family planning and the role of women in development. He met with Washington-based environmentalists in the autumn of 1986 and told them that he was planning far-reaching environmental reforms in the

Bank. No one could doubt his good intentions, but at times he appeared befuddled, commenting at his early meetings with the environmentalists that he was told what was possible and what was impossible by long-entrenched senior Bank management, and that at times he had trouble himself figuring out who was running the institution he headed.

On May 5, 1987, in the ornate ballroom of the Sheraton-Carleton Hotel in downtown Washington, Conable unveiled a series of what appeared to be sweeping environmental reforms. Much of Washington's environmental community, as well as Senator Kasten and U.S. Treasury officials, were in the audience. Adrian Cowell was filming for posterity. Conable admitted that "the World Bank has been part of the problem in the past" as far as the environment was concerned, contradicting statements made by Robert McNamara, A. W. Clausen, and a host of Bank officials and public relations flunkies over the previous fifteen years. He admitted that it had "stumbled" in Polonoroeste: "The Bank misread the human, institutional and physical realities of the frontier."[75]

Unlike his predecessors, he went beyond rhetoric to outline a concrete program of environmental action. First, the Bank would greatly increase its still exiguous environmental staff in a new central Environment Department, and create four regional environmental units that would be watchdogs for every project prepared by the Bank in its four operations regions—Asia, Africa, Latin America and the Caribbean, and Europe and the Middle East. The total number of environmental staff positions would approach 100—a more than sixteenfold increase. The Bank would launch a series of environmental issues papers and action plans with the purpose of reviewing and addressing environmental problems in the most vulnerable developing countries. Conable also committed the Bank to financing new environmental programs of various kinds, the most important of which would be a plan to alleviate tropical deforestation through unprecedented increases in forestry lending. Finally, he called for greater involvement of nongovernmental groups of all kinds, in both borrowing and donor countries, in the Bank's operations.[76]

On the face of it, Conable's environmental reforms reflected much of what the environmental activists had been calling for; the major points also paralleled the legislation drafted by Congressman Obey and Senator Kasten. And indeed, many were optimistic; the head of the World Resources Institute, the environmental think tank at whose annual dinner Conable gave his address, called it "a charter for a new day at the World Bank."[77]

But a second reading of Conable's speech was less reassuring. Yes, the Bank had stumbled in Polonoroeste's implementation, but, Conable asserted, it was initially "an environmentally sound effort."[78]

And then, a vision that had elements of déjà vu and ruinous hubris: "A . . . basic truth is that development cannot be halted, only directed. And the Bank cannot influence progress from the sidelines. It must be part of the action. With the developing nations, we must go on learning by doing."[79]

6

The Emperor's New Clothes

Once it is fully established, bureaucracy is among those
social structures which are the hardest to destroy.[1]
> —Max Weber

In the field in actuality, all of those [the World Bank's]
assurances, those written assurances don't amount to a
hill of beans. They simply are not real. They don't even
exist for practical purposes."[2]
> —Representative James Scheuer, 1989

Barber Conable's promises to green the World Bank
aroused great hopes. For the first time the Bank began to finance a number of so-called free-standing environmental loans*: a $117-million
national environmental protection and research project to strengthen
Brazil's environmental agencies, for example, and an $18-million national
environmental management project for Poland.[3] Indeed, by 1989
Conable could claim that more than a third of the Bank's projects had
"significant environmental components," a proportion that Bank literature asserted jumped to 50 percent the following year.[4]

But many of the projects that now contained "environmental components" involved environmental disruption so severe that the Bank felt
compelled to incorporate some mitigating measures, however ineffective
or poorly carried out. It was becoming apparent that the debacles of the
past decade, such as Polonoroeste and Transmigration, were, bizarrely
enough, pioneers in this respect since they were among the first programs
in which the Bank gave special attention to attempted environmental miti-
gation measures. Indeed, by the early 1990s it became clear that many
new as well as ongoing projects were causing senseless environmental and

---

* I.e., loans for projects whose main purpose is supposedly environmental protection and
conservation.

social destruction, the Bank's greatly increased environmental staff and new policies notwithstanding. Although a minority of "free-standing" environmental projects lived up to their billing, on closer scrutiny many others turned out to be production-oriented forestry and agriculture schemes rebaptized in the midst of preparation as "natural resources management projects."

Beneath its long, self-proclaimed mission of banker to the poor, and behind the new green facade, the Bank continued to do what it had always done: move larger and larger amounts of money to developing-country government agencies for capital-intensive, export-oriented projects. One real innovation of the 1980s continued: large, fast-disbursing adjustment loans to promote more rapid integration of borrowing countries into global markets so they might earn still more hard currency to continue servicing their debts.

Signs that the Emperor's new clothes bore only faint traces of green appeared in September 1989, when the Bank's annual meeting was accompanied for the fourth year in a row by a counter-meeting of NGOs from around the world. During the counter-meeting, representatives of the groups appeared before a special hearing of the Human Rights Caucus of the U.S. Congress to lay down new allegations of continuing Bank violations of its own environmental policies and international human rights standards.[5]

One such example was the Kedung Ombo dam in Java, financed by a $156-million World Bank loan in 1985. Although the World Bank claimed it had gotten out of the business of expanding Indonesia Transmigration, Kedung Ombo was one of several Bank-financed dam sites where thousands of people were being coerced into resettlement on Transmigration sites.* The Indonesian government told the 20,000 villagers farming the area of the future reservoir that their only alternative to Transmigration was cash compensation at one-tenth the market price of equivalent land in central Java. Villagers were threatened with jail, and others were warned their identity cards would be branded with the initials E.T., signifying *ex-tapol,* that is, former political prisoner, if they would not transmigrate.[6]

In June 1987, a month after Conable's environmental mea culpa in

* An Indonesian environmentalist, Dr. Otto Soemarwoto, reported that a large majority of the villagers displaced by the Bank-financed Cirata and Saguling dams in Java had protested government efforts to resettle them as transmigrants. Saguling and Cirata were funded, respectively, by the World Bank's tenth and thirteenth Indonesia Power loans, approved in 1981 and 1983. Human rights activists also reported opposition to forced migration at seven other dam sites in Java. ("Land Dispute in Kedung Ombo," TAPOL *Bulletin* [bulletin of the Indonesia Human Rights Campaign, published by TAPOL, Thornton Heath, Croydon, Surrey, U.K.], no. 84 [December 1987], 24.)

Washington, six Kedung Ombo villagers traveled to Jakarta to plead their case before the Jakarta-based national Legal Aid Society. The Legal Aid Society wrote the World Bank office in Jakarta, pleading for Bank action. But the Bank ignored the letter, as well as accounts in the Indonesian press and the warnings of a consultant it sent to the site in June 1988.

On January 16, 1989, the Kedung Ombo reservoir started to fill. The scene was almost Dantesque. More than 5,000 people remained, and many were marooned on rooftops, clinging to trees, or waiting for boats to pick them up and take them to makeshift shelters on the temporary shore of the rising lake. They told local press that they would stay, even as the water rose, as an act of nonviolent civil protest against the government and the World Bank. University students all over Java took up the cause of the Kedung Ombo villagers and staged support rallies in several cities as well as near the dam site. The military surrounded the area and strictly controlled access by outsiders, particularly journalists. As the new lake created by the dam spread, the Bank asserted to concerned human rights and environmental groups that it was pressuring the Indonesian government to prepare some sort of resettlement plan in the area for those who remained.[7] A year and half later, 600 families were still living around the dam site and reservoir, and still insisted they had not received offers of fair compensation.*

Nongovernmental witnesses at the Human Rights Caucus documented other cases—the Ruzizi II Regional Hydroelectric Project in Zaire and Rwanda, one of Africa's poorest regions, where more than 2,500 people lost their farmlands and received virtually no compensation. And they cited the growing revolt against the Bank-financed Narmada Sardar Sarovar dam in India.

More than any other project, Sardar Sarovar came to embody the Bank's inability to change. By 1989, the Narmada River Valley and all of

---

* On April 6, 1991, only five weeks before the scheduled inauguration ceremony of Kedung Ombo, about twenty villagers met with World Bank officials in the Bank's Jakarta office. They protested that the remaining families were being offered compensation that was one-nineteenth of the market value of their land. They requested that the World Bank postpone the imminent official inauguration of the project until their fate was redressed in an equitable way. One again, the World Bank promised it would look into the situation and contact Indonesian government officials; it could not and would not postpone the inauguration.

On May 18, 1991, under tight military security, the Indonesian head of state, President Suharto, the commander of Indonesia's armed forces, cabinet members, World Bank officials, and the Japanese ambassador participated in the Kedung Ombo inauguration. Suharto warned those villagers who refused to leave the dam and reservoir area "would have no future." The villagers are still waiting. ("Farmers Meet with the Banks, But the Inauguration Goes On . . ." *Setiakawan* [published by SKEPHI, the NGO Network for Forest Conservation in Indonesia], no. 6 [July 1991], 40–41.)

India were aroused by years of broken promises by the Indian government and the World Bank, which had failed to prepare critical environmental plans and a resettlement program for the 90,000 rural poor the dam's 120-mile-long reservoir would displace. Most of those threatened were tribal people, stigmatized by the Hindu caste system. Their village headmen and leaders vowed to die on site rather than move. The poor and powerless of the Narmada Valley found an impassioned leader and advocate for their cause in Medha Patkar, a fiery orator and organizer among the tribal villages. In 1989 her movement—Narmada Bachao Andolan, or the Save Narmada Movement, was joined by one of India's holiest saints, Baba Amte, a charismatic figure in his seventies who had founded and run a leprosarium for the poor in Bengal state. Baba Amte moved to the Narmada Valley and stated quite simply that he would die on the banks of the Narmada rather than move.

Just ten days before the Human Rights Caucus hearing, on September 18, 1989, 50,000 villagers and activists from all over India gathered in protest at the town of Harsud in the Narmada Valley in Madhya Pradesh state. Harsud is a small city of more than 23,000 that would be totally inundated by the next dam that the World Bank was planning to finance in the Narmada scheme—the Narmada Sagar Project, which altogether would displace another 110,000 people in addition to the 90,000 from Sardar Sarovar. Medha Patkar and Baba Amte spoke at the giant rally, and then an intense, wizened woman from Rajasthan, Srilata Swaminadhan:

I have come all the way from Rajasthan to tell you something. They built dams in Rajasthan, too. There too they promised all sorts of things—land for land, compensation in the thousands, everything. The people trustingly gave up everything they had. Do you know where they are now? Scrounging around in the garbage heaps of big cities, hoping to snatch a morsel of food for their hungry bellies—believe me, I work with these people. That's why I have come to tell you, don't believe this government. Don't even listen to their promises. Above all, don't allow this dam to come up and flood you out of your hearths and homes. Tell me, will this dam be built?

Thousands of voices echoed back, "Nahin, kabhi nahin [No, never]," shaking the very earth.[8]

It was a strange contrast. The highest World Bank officials had often pleaded a strange powerlessness in supporting projects like Narmada, claiming "development cannot be halted, only directed" and that the Bank "must be part of the action." Two-and-a-half years after the Bank painted itself green, thousands of the poorest people on earth—alleged beneficiaries of its lending—were literally willing to die to demonstrate the contrary.

The Harsud rally was a historic watershed, for it was not a protest against the Narmada dams alone, but a "national rally against destructive development," the beginning of a nationwide campaign of India's burgeoning green movement against large-scale, capital-intensive, economically wasteful development, inappropriate and inequitable for Indian conditions. To the rally thronged displaced people from Singrauli, Subernarekha, and many other Bank-financed development disasters. Present, too, were activists and leaders of tribal people and the poor who were fighting to defend the ecological basis of subsistence all over India— Sunderlal Bahuguna, for example, one of the best-known figures of the Chipko movement in the Himalayas, which had begun in the 1970s when tribal village women formed human chains around trees to block loggers from illegally cutting communal forests.

In October 1989, Medha Patkar and a human rights lawyer representing the Narmada villagers, Garesh Patel, traveled to Washington to testify before still another congressional oversight hearing, this time focusing exclusively on the continuing scandal of Sardar Sarovar. The hearing was convoked by Representative James Scheuer, chairman of the House Subcommittee on Agriculture Research, Environment, and Natural Resources. Scheuer, a Democrat from Queens, was Conable's former colleague in Congress, and had chaired the 1984 special hearing at which José Lutzenberger documented the destruction caused by Polonoroeste.

Patkar, Patel, and Lori Udall of the Environmental Defense Fund told how from the project's inception the Bank had ignored both its own loan conditions and environmental policies, and India's. In 1985, India's Department of Environment and Forests refused to grant legal clearance for Sardar Sarovar because eight requisite environmental and social studies—dealing with issues such as the need for afforestation of the reservoir watershed, public health, and resettlement—were never completed. The World Bank pressed on and negotiated and approved the loans anyway. Once the loans were approved, agricultural interests in Gujarat state and finally Prime Minister Rajiv Gandhi himself exerted tremendous political pressure on the Indian Department of Environment and Forests to grant a "provisional clearance" that allowed construction to proceed even though the studies still had not been prepared. By 1989, with the dam more than one-third built, the studies were still incomplete.*

The World Bank's policy on resettlement required the Bank to ensure that a comprehensive resettlement and economic rehabilitation plan,

---

* Yet, the World Bank's own loan conditions for the Sardar Sarovar project required that several of these reports—on public health and forests and wildlife, for example—be completed by December 1985, along with schedules for implementation of action plans based on the still nonexistent studies. To this date (June 1993) they have not been completed.

acceptable to those who would be displaced, be prepared before the loan was approved. But there was no resettlement plan when the Bank approved the Sardar Sarovar loans, and there was still no plan after Barber Conable's 1987 environmental speech, while the Bank continued to disburse funds for the project. Between November 1988 and October 1989, the World Bank laid down several deadlines for the resolution of specific resettlement and environmental issues—each time with weaker requirements—and all passed with negligible compliance with the required measures. And the Bank continued to pour money into the project.

Scheuer was appalled by the record of continuing human rights abuses, gross violations of World Bank environmental policies and loan conditions, immense cost overruns, and grossly inflated cost-benefit estimates. He and seven other U.S. representatives and senators subsequently wrote the World Bank asking it to reconsider its involvement—to no avail.

Medha Patkar and Garish Patel returned to India. In December 1989, they met in Bhopal with a number of environmental and social activists from all over India to found the Movement Against Destructive Development, Jan Vikas Andolan. This movement, its founders declared,

[is] against the development paradigm being practiced in post-independence India whereby a narrow elite primarily benefits at the cost of a very large population that continues to be marginalized, displaced and pauperized, along with large scale degradation and plundering of our natural resource base. The movement . . . is not against development. Rather, it maintains that much of what today goes under the name of development is not genuine development but is in fact socially disruptive, biologically and genetically homogenizing and environmentally destructive. The Andolan's demand is for real development, in which the over-riding objective is not just a higher growth rate regardless of its human and environmental cost, but the fulfillment of basic human needs and the creation of just and human conditions of life for all our people.[9]

Flaws in the Crystal: The World Bank and Late Modernity

Senior Bank officials continued to argue that ongoing problems in projects like Sardar Sarovar or Kedung Ombo were "historical" (i.e., rooted in projects designed and approved years before the Bank's heightened environmental awareness) or "anecdotal," and did not accurately reflect on the Bank as a whole. But environmentalists characterized the Bank's escalating rhetoric as "Greenspeak," a new Orwellian dialect in which ecological destruction was rebaptized as "sustainable natural resources management."

The Bank's flawed lending operations were a microcosm of a larger ecological and political crisis. This crisis is in fact a worldwide one, linked to the expansion of a single global system of market-based development. Current patterns of development place increasingly insupportable pressures on local and global ecosystems. These threats include the ongoing extermination of half the planet's species through rainforest destruction, increasing desertification, and global warming. The political aspect of the crisis, related to and feeding into the ecological dilemma, is provoked by the adoration of economic development and its technological handmaidens as secular gods, ignoring the need for accountability, democratic participation, and the moderating influences of civil society. At the heart of this political predicament is the inability of centralized bureaucracies like the World Bank to reconcile their internal "institutional rationality" with external political pressures and with ecological and social needs.

The institutional rationality in question is that of bureaucratic modernity, first described by Max Weber. It is characterized by the dominance of instrumental reason, and treats the elements of nature and society as objects for management and administration. The insulation of decision makers from the direct consequences of their actions and the substitution of technical rationality and procedural correctness for moral responsibility are other traits. It is a world—our world—where enormous advances in the organization of technical means contrast with ends that become so far removed and ill-defined that they approach the vanishing point. The proliferation of increasingly fragmented, rationalized, self-contained spheres of human activity contrasts with the increasing irrationality, not to say violence and destructiveness, of the cumulative social and ecological effects of these activities.

A closer look at the Bank's attempts at environmental reform in the late 1980s and early 1990s provides an illuminating case study for these issues. The Bank's environmental failure is systemic and rooted in deep institutional contradictions, not limited to individual "problem projects." In more than one sense, the Bank's environmental quandary is a journey into the political and cultural schizophrenia of late modernity.

We shall first examine three areas of critical importance: the Bank's continued difficulties in dealing with the forcible resettlement of populations displaced by its projects, its forestry lending, and its energy lending. The World Bank's policy on resettlement is the oldest, and arguably most important of the Bank's officially stated environmental and social policies, which numbered twelve by 1992.* Increased forestry lending was the

* The others address critical environmental and social issues such as the treatment of tribal peoples (official policy statement dated 1982, revised 1991); wildlands conservation (biodiversity, 1986); preservation of cultural property (archaeological and historic patrimony); pes-

centerpiece of Conable's environmental program to fund new projects to protect the environment, while energy has been and continues to be one of the Bank's top two lending areas. We shall then turn to the World Bank's ability to learn from past experience—institutionalized in its Operations Evaluation Department—and finally, to its new role as the central repository of international environmental funds through the creation of the Global Environment Facility in 1990.

Superfluous People

Much of the history of Western economic development has also been the history of the production of huge masses of superfluous people—the creation of a new class of poor, uprooted from every traditional link to the land and the local community. The market-driven rationalization and administration of the earth's surface and natural resources for economic production has had a brutal corollary: the uprooting and depossession of huge rural populations from their less efficient modes of production. The great enclosures in seventeenth- and eighteenth-century Britain were an early example of this process at work on a national scale. But in the past thirty years the process has accelerated with almost demonic intensity. In Brazil, the government's planned, concerted efforts to modernize and rationalize agriculture from small holdings producing food for domestic consumption into a capital-intensive, export-oriented machine for earning foreign exchange resulted in the uprooting of 28.4 million people between 1960 and 1980—a number greater than the entire population of Argentina.[10] In India, large-scale development projects have forcibly displaced more than 20 million over the past forty years.[11]

Although population growth and poverty are often blamed for the growing masses of uprooted people in the developing world, in many countries economic development as it has been practiced is as much the cause of such poverty as a solution. A confidential 1990 World Bank analysis aptly describes the phenomenon in Brazil:

The central point to be made here is that *increasing capitalization of agricultural production reduced the physical and social space available to small-scale producers of all types* in south central Brazil. . . .
The analysis of extensive rural outmigration during the past several decades, in

ticides (1987); dams and reservoirs (irrigation and hydro, 1989); and environmental assessment (1989, revised 1991). (Robert J. A. Goodland, "Environmental Priorities for Financing Institutions," *Environmental Conservation*, vol. 19, no. 1 (Spring 1992), 9–21; table 3, p. 11.)

short, indicates that this phenomenon was not so much a response to relative levels of poverty in the various parts of Brazil as it was a reflection of the timing and rhythm of agricultural modernization. In this connection, it is significant that the rural exodus of the 1970's occurred first and most intensively in the more developed areas of Sao Paulo, Parana and Rio Grande do Sul, where modern agricultural technology is most prevalent. [Emphasis added.][12]

A disproportionate number of these "development refugees," as anthropologist Thayer Scudder calls them, come from the marginalized peoples of the earth: tribal and indigenous groups, the harijans (outcastes) in India, the landless and homeless—all those who increasingly fall outside the mainstream of the modern market economy. Jacques Attali's vision of a planet overrun by hordes of global nomads is no mere nightmare, but one possible outcome of the historical project of Western development.

The World Bank does not advertise that forced displacement of millions of the earth's poorest and most marginalized people is a consequence of its style of development—but this has been a subject of internal concern for years. The Bank's capacity and willingness to enforce its resettlement policy goes to the heart of the institution's proclaimed development mission of assisting the poor. The resettlement policy was the Bank's very first binding internal environmental directive, issued in 1980, and subsequently strengthened in 1986 and 1990. Its essence, as mentioned above, was the minimum of human decency—quite simply, that borrowing governments prepare and implement in a timely fashion rehabilitation plans for people displaced by Bank-financed projects so that they are at least no worse off than before.

Yet by September 1989, when the U.S. Congress Human Rights Caucus held its hearing on the issue, the Bank and leading experts could not point to a single project where, over the long term, displaced groups had been successfully rehabilitated.[13] The hearing revealed that 1.5 million people were being displaced by ongoing Bank projects, with more than another 1.5 million threatened by projects in preparation. Indeed, for over a decade internal staff reports warned management that the policy was not being implemented successfully—but to little avail. A 1986 study prepared by the Bank's Agriculture and Rural Development Department revealed that fully three quarters of the Bank projects involving forced relocation that the study reviewed did not even include resettlement experts on their appraisal missions.[14] And the number of people displaced and impoverished by Bank projects continued to grow after Conable's 1987 environmental reforms reaching nearly 2 million in the early 1990s.

Even in the minority of projects where Bank staff tried to comply fully with the policy, the very nature of forced resettlement of traditional peoples tied to the land made rehabilitation a chimera. No one has described this tragedy better than Thayer Scudder (who, we recall, after twenty years of consulting to the World Bank was the world's leading expert on the subject):

During a transition period which follows relocation you can predict that death rates, [and] the rates of illness among the relocatees will go up, especially among the elderly, who are very tied to the land, and often among women and children, too. . . . There's a whole bunch of reasons for this. . . . There is psychological stress. You can break that down into two components. [One is] anxiety about the future—what's going to happen to me?—especially where government planning is poor. You've been given a little money, [but] it's insufficient to buy land. . . . What's going to happen? And there's grieving for a lost cause.

And then the third component is what we call social-cultural stress. The food economies of these people are tied to a given habitat, given soils, knowledge of given resources. Much of that information is not going to be good in the future. At the same time the leadership of people is undermined. If the leaders try to oppose the relocation, they usually fail, [and] they lose their credibility. If they're for the relocation, they lose their credibility because inevitably the majority of the people don't want to move. So at the very time your population moves, you end up with no good leaders. So there's a whole bunch of socio-cultural stresses. You put these all together [and] there's a synergism. The multi-dimensional stress is very significant.[15]

The first responsibility for this state of affairs almost always lies with the borrowing governments. Governments are often reluctant to borrow for the cost of resettlement and rehabilitation, and many seem to view their poorer and socially marginal populations as expendable in the pursuit of national economic power and grandeur. Too often, government agencies actively tried to conceal the full extent of resettlement from Bank appraisal missions, or continually misrepresented their progress in preparing and carrying out resettlement plans. And they often found pliant accomplices in ambitious Bank staff eager to push through projects.

In other cases, in which governments agreed to resettlement plans and borrowed the money, the sheer incompetence and corruption of local agencies prevailed. The Brazil Itaparica dam resettlement loans of the late 1980s provide an illuminating example.

This was an instance in which the dam itself was nearly completed, we recall, when the World Bank lent $500 million in 1986 to the national Brazilian electric utility, Eletrobrás, to finance the finishing touches on Itaparica and a number of other projects in Eletrobrás's long-term power investment plan, the Plan 2010.* Several World Bank executive directors

* See discussion on the Brazil Power Sector loan in Chapter 5. Much of the power of the 2,500-megawatt Itaparica dam was destined to go to energy-intensive, export-oriented industries such as aluminum, pig iron, caustic soda, cement, and petrochemicals. Most of

had insisted that the Bank include an explicit condition in the terms of the loan to ensure the equitable rehabilitation of 40,000 people it would displace. The Bank subsequently approved two additional loans of $132 million and $100 million (in 1987 and 1990, respectively) to finance the resettlement and rehabilitation of the Itaparica relocatees. As a confidential 1990 Bank evaluation of Itaparica noted, "For the first time in any comparable Brazilian project, therefore, displacees were offered a comprehensive range of resettlement options which did not automatically spell disaster for a large proportion of those affected."[16]* (This was not due to the initial vigilance or commitment of Bank staff or Brazilian authorities to carry out the 1980 resettlement policy, but was the consequence of vociferous and well-organized protests led by the local population, beginning in 1979 and culminating in sit-ins of thousands of men, women, and children at the dam site in 1986 and 1987.)

The physical relocation proceeded in an orderly fashion in 1987–88, but most of the 40,000 were relocated to desertlike lands that were completely uninhabitable without irrigation services from the dam—which the Bank loans were supposed to finance. But the money the Bank had lent for economic rehabilitation simply disappeared, even though total World Bank support for the resettlement amounted to $63,000 per family after cost overruns of 350 percent. The relocatees subsisted on minimal monthly welfare payments provided by the regional Eletrobrás subsidiary, CHESF (the São Francisco Hydroelectric Company). Protests grew, as did social problems—alcoholism, child abuse, divorce.[17] In desperation, a number of families returned to the dam site in June 1991 and staged a sit-

---

these industries benefited from massive tax holidays and artificially low power rates subsidized by the Brazilian government. (See Tarcian Portella, "Itaparica: A Dor de um Povo Gerando Energia," [Petrolândia, Brazil: Centro de Defesa dos Direitos Humanos do Sub-Médio São Francisco Petrolândia-Pernambuco, 1992], 10–12.)

* Obviously, this is a lamentable comment on the Brazilian government's and the World Bank's records up to that time. The same report, prepared by the Operations Evaluation Department, indicts the Bank's record in three 1970s projects—the Paulo Afonson IV (Sobradinho) Hydropower Project and the Lower São Francisco Polders and Second São Francisco Irrigation Projects—which uprooted and destroyed the livelihoods of 130,000 poor without adequate restitution. The projects caused massive problems of downstream destruction of floodplain agriculture and upstream pollution from uncontrolled use of pesticides and fertilizers, as well as the poisoning of domestic water supplies, fish, and crops. Poor irrigation management promoted spreading soil salinization. These projects were leading examples of the McNamara poverty strategy in Brazil, and even on these terms they failed: the OED evaluation concludes that the projects benefited not the poor, but a relatively small number of landowners, concentrating large holdings, promoting a capital-intensive, export-oriented irrigated agriculture that "may have an adverse impact on local poverty levels and food security, while also contributing to the rapid growth of urban squatter settlements" (OED, São Francisco Valley Draft Report [see endnote 16], v, ix, x).

in to protest the situation. But most of the money was gone, and the Bank suspended further disbursements. The only measure that might have prompted the Brazilian authorities to behave in a more responsible fashion would have been the threat of suspending other ongoing World Bank loans to Brazil—something the Bank has never done.

The saddest fate of all was endured by 190 families of Tuxá Indians, whose livelihood had depended for centuries on the cultivation of a very fertile 108-hectare island in the middle of the São Francisco River, which was flooded by the Itaparica reservoir.* The island, called the Ilha de Viúva, was, according to a Bank confidential evaluation report, "irrigated by a combination of aqueducts and diesel pumps to produce bountiful crops of onions, rice, beans and manioc, as well as a range of fruits, thereby providing for the group's subsistence needs and generating a commercial surplus."[18] The resettlement of the Tuxá embodies Thayer Scudder's description of relocation-induced social breakdown. The resettlement exacerbated an existing political dispute among the Tuxá, dividing the group between two separate resettlement projects in different locations. In the words of the World Bank's Operations Evaluation Department,

Although acculturated, their ancient, but still strong mythical-religious belief systems created an important bond between the people and their land. Once broken, a process of increasing social disintegration appears to have been set in motion. . . . Internecine family quarrels and alcohol abuse, previously rare among the Tuxa, have reportedly become commonplace.[19]

The Bank's Brazil country staff responded to this in-house criticism by asserting that

if anything the Tuxa have received considerably more attention, resources and services than other affected groups. Their problem is basically the same as [that] of the other rural resettlers plus the general difficulties they experience as Indians under the jurisdiction of FUNAI [the Brazilian Indian agency].[20]

Itaparica illustrates what many argue is the hopelessness of bureaucratically engineered large-scale resettlement and rehabilitation. The botched

* The fate of the Tuxá is a case study in the failed implementation of two Bank environmental and social policies—resettlement and "Tribal People in Bank-Financed Projects" (World Bank Operational Manual Statement No. 2.34, February 1982, revised in September 1991 as Operational Directive 4.20). The 1982 policy (which was binding during the preparation and carrying out of the Itaparica resettlement project) declares that "the objective at the center of this directive is to ensure that indigenous peoples do not suffer adverse effects during the development process, particularly from Bank-financed projects, and that they receive culturally compatible social and economic benefits" (World Bank Operational Directive 4.20, pp. 1–2).

resettlement left the affected population much worse off than before in almost every respect—at a cost per family that for northeast Brazil was a small fortune. Moreover, because of the intense international scrutiny, Itaparica received more World Bank staff attention and resources than almost any other resettlement effort; the 1990 Bank appraisal report for the $100-million Itaparica Supplemental Resettlement loan argued that this extraordinary attention was necessary because the very credibility of the Bank's resettlement policy was at stake.[21]

Despite the enormous cost, the Bank's Operations Evaluation Department concluded that the Itaparica resettlement plan was

still considered to be the least-cost solution for carrying out a comprehensive resettlement program of this nature and indicate[s] the financial repercussions that are likely when executing and funding agencies are required to meet full relocation obligations to the affected populations.[22]

This last observation is perhaps the key to the failure of the Bank's resettlement policy: most Bank projects involving forced relocation would be economically nonviable if the full cost of resettlement and economic rehabilitation of the displaced were included. Governments would not borrow for such projects, exacerbating the Bank's ever-looming quandary of lack of bankable projects and increasing net negative transfers from its borrowers back to Washington.*

Saving the Forests

All forestry projects now contain a strong environmental orientation.[23]
—World Bank, first annual environment report,
September 1990.

We have mobilized the best brains in the world on this.[24]
—World Bank Africa region staffer, March 1990.

When Conable promised in May 1987 that the World Bank would become an active environmental lender, he announced that the

---

* Bank staff continue to assert that the Bank can achieve success in managing resettlement by insisting that its stated policy be respected. For the Zimapan and Aquamilpa dam projects in northwestern Mexico, the Bank claims that 4,000 people have a good chance of being rehabilitated thanks to extensive local consultation and participation in the elaboration of the resettlement plan. (See Scott Guggenheim, "Salvaging the Dammed," *The Bank's World*, vol. 10, no. 2 [February 1991], 14–15.)

most important focus of the Bank's new green loans would be "a global program to support tropical forest conservation"—the Tropical Forest Action Plan.[25] To that end, Conable committed the Bank to increase its forestry lending 150 percent by 1989, and, in a speech he delivered in Tokyo in September of 1989, he announced a further tripling of forestry lending through the early 1990s.[26]

It was an urgently needed priority and a politically astute one. By the late 1980s, tropical deforestation had become, in the view of many environmentalists and scientists in the industrialized world, the most visible and urgent environmental crisis in the developing world. And the disastrous rainforest destruction unleashed by Polonoroeste and Indonesia Transmigration had aroused more international outrage than any other Bank activity.*

The Tropical Forest Action Plan (TFAP) was conceived in the mid-1980s by the Bank, the Food and Agriculture Organization of the United Nations (FAO), the United Nations Development Program (UNDP), and the World Resources Institute (WRI), a Washington-based environmental think tank. The TFAP sought to alleviate the pressures causing deforestation in developing countries by proposing to mobilize $8 billion from multilateral and bilateral aid agencies over a five-year period for a variety of forestry and agricultural activities. These included the strengthening of forestry and environmental institutions, supply of fuelwood needs, conservation of protected areas and vulnerable watershed regions, and support of forest management for industrial uses.

But the plan had been prepared largely behind closed doors in Washington, New York, and Rome (FAO headquarters), with little input from nongovernmental groups in tropical forest countries.** The World Resources Institute played a highly ambiguous role; it presented itself as an independent nongovernmental group and research organization, but financed part of the preparation of the plan with money from the very aid agencies, including the World Bank, that might receive billions in additional funds if the Tropical Forest Action Plan could be sold to the taxpayers of industrialized nations. In preparing the TFAP, WRI worked closely

* It is interesting to note the parallel between Conable's focus on tropical forests and George Bush's announcement (at the Earth Summit in Rio de Janeiro) in June 1992 of increased U.S. bilateral aid to conserve rainforests as a means of diverting attention from the U.S. refusal to sign strong international conventions on protection of biodiversity and climate change; in each case, the World Bank and a U.S. president announced environmental half-measures that deflected international criticism of the overall environmental records of the bureaucracies they headed.
** Once the TFAP was a virtual *fait accompli* in its basic approach, the sponsors actively sought the endorsement of nongovernmental groups to give it more credibility and persuade governments to fund it.

with the Bank's head forestry advisor, John Spears, who was anxiously seeking stratagems to increase the Bank's forestry lending portfolio.

WRI justified its approach by claiming that it was seeking to change the Bank by influencing it from the inside. The premise was a familiar one among Washington think tanks—that sound, apolitical policy research could convince large bureaucracies like the World Bank of the error of their ways. But environmental advocates felt the approach, however well intentioned, reflected a combination of more than a little hubris and naiveté. Institutions like the Bank often already had more information on how they should change than they could digest, much of it generated by their own staffs. The problem was not lack of information, but the absence of institutional incentive to use it and act accordingly.

Many of the internal memoranda and reports circulated by Bank staff and consultants had been aggressively critical of the Bank's environmental record for years—sadly, much more critical than many of the diluted assessments of outside independent research organizations that were anxious not to give offense. A very real and perverse effect of the efforts of some environmental groups and development think tanks to appear "balanced" and "reasonable" no matter what environmental disaster the Bank might be financing was the undermining of the efforts of those inside the Bank who had fought for years to make the institution more responsible.

By 1986, a number of Third World NGOs such as Friends of the Earth, Brazil, and the Malaysia-based Asia-Pacific Peoples' Environmental Network (APPEN) had published urgent protests maintaining that the Tropical Forest Action Plan was a fraud. It had been prepared, they alleged, without the significant consultation or involvement of NGOs and local communities in tropical forest countries. Worse, it appeared to be mainly a plan to promote traditional export-oriented timber industry investments, camouflaged by small components for environmental purposes such as conservation and watershed management. The Third World NGOs were particularly outraged because the plan, they alleged, blamed an amorphous mass called "the poor" for the destruction of tropical forests, while promoting investments in export-oriented forest exploitation rebaptized as "sustainable forestry."

WRI attempted belatedly to address many of the criticisms, and finally dissociated itself from the plan altogether. It was too late. Following the World Bank's 1987 endorsement, the Tropical Forest Action Plan, under FAO's coordination, gathered seemingly unstoppable momentum to become the most ambitious environmental aid program ever conceived. By the end of 1989, sixty-two developing nations had requested forestry sector aid under the plan. By 1990, twenty-one nations had completed forestry sector reviews under the aegis of the TFAP, with the World Bank as the leader or a major participant in eight. The plan appeared to be on track to mobilize billions for forestry projects in every country in the world with remaining tropical forests.

The national forest action plan for Cameroon, prepared by the FAO, was as revealing an example as any of the ecological bankruptcy of the TFAP. The plan's principal stated goal was to make Cameroon the biggest forest product exporter in Africa by the twenty-first century. To accomplish this would require opening up nearly 14 million hectares (an area the size of Florida) of pristine tropical forest in the southeastern part of the country. The FAO-TFAP document observed that getting the timber out would require the construction of a major penetration road to the sea. All of this would cost hundreds of millions of dollars. But the TFAP document provided for only $4.4 million to address what it admitted was the major domestic pressure on tropical forests in the country—fuelwood demand. Even more startling, it suggested that given stiff international competition for wood exports, especially from Indonesia, the government would have to grant special tax incentives and subsidies to stimulate timber production.[27]

Environmentalists around the world feared an ecological Frankenstein's monster had been unleashed. The World Rainforest Movement (another Malaysia-based coalition of mainly Third World NGOs) prepared a critique in 1990 of nine completed national TFAP plans—for Peru, Guyana, Cameroon, Ghana, Tanzania, Papua New Guinea, Nepal, Colombia, and the Philippines. The study concluded that in the first four cases the forestry investments proposed would dramatically accelerate the rate of deforestation through increased logging; in no instance was it found that the investments would actually reduce deforestation.[28] Prince Charles publicly criticized British support for the TFAP, which he said amounted to little more than a plan for chopping down trees. The Tropical Forest Action Plan seemed to embody every error of the top-down, socially oblivious, resource destructive approach that had been a major factor in the poor results of development assistance over the past twenty years.

Environmental groups around the world intensified their criticism of the plan in an increasingly coordinated campaign. In 1989, seventy-eight West German nongovernmental groups, including every major environmental organization in the country, endorsed a "Rainforest Memorandum" to the German government that condemned German support for the TFAP as well as the effect of World Bank policies and projects on tropical forests.[29] Australian groups, inspired by the German example, prepared a similar statement, "The Australian Rainforest Memorandum," in 1991.[30] The governments that were to foot the bill for the TFAP became skittish; they refused to commit funding unless the overall plan and the national plans were reformed so that there would be a chance of actually promoting the TFAP's stated goals of forest conservation and greater involvement of local populations in the identification and carrying out of projects.

The donors, WRI, and the World Bank saw FAO's domination as the most immediate obstacle to reformulating the TFAP, but it proved difficult to wrest power from the Rome-based U.N. bureaucracy; it was also difficult to maintain interest in funding an effort that had so blatantly traduced the goals it purported to advance. By 1991, the TFAP was for all practical purposes dead.

But as the Tropical Forest Action Plan collapsed in ignominy, the World Bank continued at full throttle to prepare the forestry loans Conable had promised. The Bank astutely distanced itself from the TFAP, taking the tack that its forestry projects were not necessarily related, and Bank staff criticized some national TFAP plans.

In early 1990, the new loans that were to show how the Bank could help save tropical forests were unveiled to the world. The first project to come under scrutiny was a $23-million forestry and fisheries scheme for the West African country of Guinea. A few days before the project was to be approved by the World Bank's Executive Board, the World Wide Fund for Nature (WWF) received several project documents that allowed it to conduct an independent appraisal. The heart of the project was what Bank staff called a "forest management and protection" component; the WWF analysis suggested it amounted to a deforestation scheme. The Bank's money would help support the construction of seventy-five kilometers of roads in and around two forest reserves totaling 150,000 hectares, of which some 106,000 hectares were still pristine rainforest. Worse, hidden in the fine print of the "management and protection" section of the Bank's project document was its real thrust: two-thirds of the remaining 106,000 hectares of rainforest were to be opened for timber production.

WWF sent its critique of the loan to the Bank board, where it sparked considerable but somewhat bewildered discussion. If the project was as environmentally beneficial as Bank management claimed, why were mainstream environmental organizations trying to stop or modify it? Bank staff argued that without the project, logging would proceed at a much greater rate, that the Bank project would manage logging within "sustainable" limits by increasing the time period (and also the area) of logging concessions; it was the only hope, the sole alternative to total deforestation, they maintained. It was an argument that would be repeated again and again, and which, in one form or another, Bank staff had used to justify numerous disastrous schemes in the past. The board unanimously approved the project.

In reality, it was often the large infusions of foreign exchange, rapid construction of infrastructure such as roads, and an international stamp of approval provided by the Bank that had ensured that a government's environmentally destructive plans become physical reality within the shortest time possible.

On the heels of the Guinea project an even bigger forestry scheme was ready to be presented to the Board for approval—an $80-million forestry sector loan to the Côte d'Ivoire, another West African country whose forests are rapidly disappearing. Groups like the Environmental Defense Fund and WWF were horrified when in January 1990 they obtained confidential World Bank documents on the Côte d'Ivoire loan; its main thrust was to finance and promote timber production in a half-million-hectare rainforest under the management of private logging companies—the same companies that had been leading protagonists in the rape of the Côte d'Ivoire forests over the previous two decades. Worse, over 200,000 people inhabited or were dependent on the area where the forest concessions were to be extended; most of them would have to be forcibly relocated. In flagrant contradiction of Bank policy, Bank staff and the Côte d'Ivoire government had not prepared or negotiated a resettlement and rehabilitation plan. U.S. groups alerted the U.S. executive director of the Bank, E. Patrick Coady, who in January 1990 requested from Bank staff a copy of the draft project appraisal report for the Côte d'Ivoire loan. It was scheduled to be presented for approval within a few weeks.

The Bank's Africa region staff refused Coady's request; he was told he would receive documents on the project two weeks before the board meeting on the project, the standard Bank practice. The decision was backed by the Bank's senior vice-president for operations at the time, Moeen Qureshi, and was a trenchant reminder of the Bank's lack of fundamental accountability.

The Executive Board discussion that took place on April 3, 1990, to review the project was heated; the U.S. director refused to approve the loan on environmental grounds, citing both the lack of a convincing forest conservation strategy and the lack of resettlement provisions for as many as 200,000 people. The other board members approved the project, but had increasing doubts about the competency of the Bank's forestry strategy. In a rare effort to exercise some accountability, the U.S. executive director led an effort of the board to request that management halt all forestry lending while the Bank prepared a new, ecologically more focused policy on forests.*

---

* The new forest policy was completed in July 1991. It was a major step forward, for it was prepared with input from NGOs and pledged that the Bank would finance no logging in intact primary forests. But skeptics were all too aware of the Bank's penchant for proliferat-

It was a sobering humiliation. Six months after Barber Conable had pledged in Tokyo to triple its forestry lending, the normally pliant Executive Board—under growing international pressure from NGOs—told the Bank that the keystone of its new environmental lending was an ecological menace.

"An Ecological Tone— Which Has Been Very Fashionable Lately"

In early 1990, still another example of Bank efforts to fund environmental projects became a subject of international controversy. The Bank had been preparing since 1988 $317 million in new loans to Brazil for "agro-ecological zoning" in the Polonoroeste project area in Rondônia and Mato Grosso. The Bank claimed it had learned its lessons, and that it had a responsibility not to abandon northwest Brazil to the destructive forces it had helped to unleash. More cynically, some observed that the disaster created by the first half-billion dollars of loans now presented the World Bank with an opportunity to lend nearly a third of a billion more to try to clean up the mess.

The Rondônia and Mato Grosso Natural Resources Management projects were appraised with no projected economic rate of return; the loans were to be justified by their unquantified ecological and social benefits. To give greater weight to gains not amenable to conventional economic calculation was in one sense a step forward, but the criteria to monitor performance in the projects were fewer, more ambiguous, and less specific than in more conventional Bank loans. The approach created new opportunities for government bureaucracies to divert funds to classic pork-barrel, political patronage uses.

The Bank touted the loans as a model approach for addressing the management of tropical forest ecosystems, suggesting that it might be

---

ing lofty general policies that staff ignored with impunity in preparing and carrying out projects. Indeed, in the autumn of 1991 Bank sociologists continued to protest in internal memos that the Côte d'Ivoire project could result in the "largest forced resettlement ever carried out under a bank-financed project in Africa . . . possibly including several hundred thousand people [who] may be driven from their forests, and no resources are available for their resettlement in agricultural areas" (Keith Bradsher, "Rain Forest Project in Africa Stirs Debate at World Bank," *New York Times,* 14 October 1991). On January 7, 1992, the U.S. executive director complained before the Bank's board that "despite the fact that there is still little data on the resettlement, the provision of logging contracts [to private companies] is proceeding faster than expected" and raised the possibility of "a mad rush to get as much valuable timber out as possible" (statement by E. Patrick Coady, U.S. Executive Director to the Executive Board, 7 January 1992 [U.S. Treasury Department, typewritten]).

replicated elsewhere.[31] The projects were to promote the zoning of Rondônia and northern Mato Grosso according to strict, scientifically based land-use criteria, and finance the setting aside of extractive reserves for the rubber tappers and the protection of Indian reserves, as well as national parks, forest reserves, and other protected forest areas. The first loan, for Rondônia, was to be presented to the World Bank's Executive Board for approval in early 1990.

What the Bank did not mention in its public relations claims for the new Rondônia project was that on October 13, 1988—nine weeks before his murder—Chico Mendes had written World Bank President Barber Conable to express the opposition of rubber tapper groups who were its alleged beneficiaries. Mendes asserted that the "Polonoroeste II" plans were prepared by the World Bank and Brazilian authorities with little con-sultation or involvement of the people affected by the project. In fact, he warned, it was a fraud:

We think that the extractive reserves included in Polonoroeste II only serve to lend the Government's project proposal to the World Bank an ecological tone— which has been very fashionable lately—in order to secure this huge loan. . . . What will be created will not be extractive reserves, but colonization settlements with the same mistakes that have led to the present disaster of Polonoroeste. In other words, a lot of money will be spent on infrastructures [*sic*] which do not mean anything to the peoples of the forest and the maintenance of which will not be sustainable.[32]

The Bank never responded to Mendes's plea, nor did Bank officials respond to several similar queries by Mendes's colleagues over the next two years calling upon Bank staff to address problems in the project first identified by the murdered *seringueiro*.

Mendes's fears were more than justified. For example, the project was supposed to finance, for the second time around, four protected areas and eight Indian reserves that were never fully demarcated and protected as required under the original 1981 Polonoroeste loan conditions. But the new project was actually weaker in its implementation and monitoring provisions than that of 1981; the Bank had learned nothing. And the risk of fraud was literal: rumors abounded that the corrupt governor of Rondônia, Jerónimo Santana, was anxious to obtain the loan to finance pork-barrel political payoffs in preparation for an October 1990 election.

On January 9, 1990, thirty-five environmental and human rights groups from Brazil, the United States, and ten other countries sent a let-ter and a research dossier to the Bank's executive directors urging them to delay consideration of the project until it was strengthened in its imple-mentation and monitoring provisions.[33] Rather than deal substantively with the issues the letter addressed, the World Bank Brazil country department launched a probe that required numerous Bank staff to appear before the Bank's "ethics officer,"* who attempted to ferret out who had leaked project documents—an ironic commentary on the accuracy of the NGO criticisms. In February, some members of the Bank's Executive Board, already concerned by the questions the NGOs had raised, called for a temporary delay of the loan. They had just learned that Brazil's president Sarney, in response to a request by the Rondônia governor, had issued a decree abolishing the largest Indian reserve in Rondônia on January 30, 1990, at the very moment negotiations were concluding for the new Rondônia loan. The establishment of this reserve for the Uru-Eu-Wau-Wau Indians had been one of the most important conditions of the Bank's earlier Polonoroeste loans.[34]

But the World Bank's manager for the Rondônia loan argued that the project should be approved as quickly as possible because the Rondônia state government was strongly committed to environmental protection. In March 1990, officials sent by Governor Santana of Rondônia traveled to Brasília to lobby the Brazilian environment secretary, José Lutzenberger; they urged him not only to push for immediate approval of the loan, but to back their suggestion that the Brazilian government make the unprecedented request that the Bank disburse the entire $167 million in one lump sum, up front, before the October 1990 election.[35] Lutzenberger was outraged; he sent a letter to the president of the Bank requesting that the project be delayed until more extensive consultations could be held with local NGOs later in the year, effectively killing the loan for 1990.[36] Jerónimo Santana was subsequently condemned by the Rondônia state legislature for malfeasance, ending his tenure in disgrace.[37]

The Bank's Brazil country department, however, persisted with the project, without resolving its serious flaws. The World Bank Executive Board approved the Rondônia Natural Resources Management Project in the spring of 1992, over the protest of numerous local NGOs and of Oxfam, which was now also working on the ground in Rondônia. Among other things, the Brazilian groups and Oxfam pointed out in letters to the Bank's Brazil staff and the Bank's executive directors that at the very moment the Bank was presenting the loan to the board for approval, the Brazilian land agency, INCRA, was proceeding with plans to settle some

* The Bank's ethics officer is part of its Personnel Management Department; one of his or her functions is to grill staff suspected of leaking documents. The Bank's conception of ethics is remarkably self-centered, relating to compliance with internal rules affecting staff and the institution (petty corruption and harassment of other staff are typical issues). At the same time, negligent disregard of Bank environmental and social policies with disastrous consequences for whole ecosystems and hundreds of thousands of developing-country poor is not a matter of concern for the ethics officer.

50,000 new colonists a year in areas that were supposed to be set aside as protected forests and extractive reserves for rubber tappers under the Bank project. All of this was in total contravention of the Bank loan agreement, as well as a flagrant violation of Brazilian law, which requires environmental impact assessments for land settlement activities.[38] As the project proceeded these abuses continued, and in April 1993 twelve non-governmental organizations from Rondônia wrote the Bank imploring it to halt all disbursements on the loan.[39]

Power for the Poor— at the Greatest Possible Cost

Energy efficiency is another area where the Bank, in Barber Conable's words, promised to "play a leadership role."[40] Of all economic sectors, energy is arguably the most important environmentally and economically for the future of the world. It has also been the Bank's largest or second largest lending area in recent years—accounting for between 14.3 and 18.6 percent of annual lending in the period 1990–1993.[41]

We have seen that current patterns of energy development in developing countries entail profound local and global environmental problems. Large hydroelectric dams are the main causes of forced resettlement of rural populations in many countries, and are a major factor in the destruction of forests and riverain farmlands. The growing use of coal for power production by China and India will make these countries the largest emitters of CO_2 and other gases contributing to global warming in the next century if alternatives are not found.

The cost of large-scale energy projects keeps mounting; in many developing countries one-quarter to one-third of all public investment is now going for electric power, diverting desperately scarce capital from other investments such as health, education, and conservation. Moreover, this proportion is growing and is still insufficient to meet energy demand. With considerable help from the World Bank, India's investments for energy infrastructure grew from 20 percent to 31 percent of its national budget over the 1980s.[42]

The answer to this environmental and economic quandary has been known for years. According to internationally respected Third World energy specialists*—as well as, ironically, World Bank studies dating back

---

* See, for example, Amulua K. N. Reddy and José Goldemberg, "Energy for the Developing World," *Scientific American,* September 1990, 111–18. Reddy is vice-chairman of the Karnataka State Council for Science and Technology in India; the president of Brazil appointed Goldemberg as that country's secretary of the environment in April 1992.

to the mid-1980s*—Brazil, India, China, Costa Rica, and many other developing countries can cut the need for growth in power-generating capacity by as much as 50 percent through investments in state-of-the-art industrial equipment, lighting systems, air conditioners, and other energy-saving improvements and appliances.** The cost of such end-use efficiency investments is often a third or a quarter of the cost of the new power plants and dams that would be necessary to generate the equivalent amount of power. Many of these measures have already been proven in practice in pilot programs in developing nations as well as in larger scale end-use conservation programs in some industrialized countries—including the United States.***

Yet through the early 1990s the Bank consistently refused to shift its focus from lending almost exclusively for giant dams and thermal power plants (as well as transmission lines) to promoting end-use efficiency and conservation. This was despite an avalanche of studies showing the environmental and economic folly of such a course.[43] In late 1991, a comprehensive EPA-financed review of the Bank's energy lending by the Washington-based International Institute for Energy Conservation concluded that the Bank was devoting less than one percent of its energy lending to end-use efficiency and conservation investments, and that the proportion actually decreased slightly in the late 1980s.[44] This was not only in spite of the pledge of Barber Conable, but also in disregard of the Bank's major financial contributors, who in the 1990 Donors' Agreement that accompanied the ninth replenishment of the International Development Association explicitly called upon the Bank to "expand its efforts in end-use energy efficiencies and renewable energy programs and to encourage least-cost

* The Bank's Energy Department published an excellent study in 1986 outlining specific measures for end-use electricity efficiency investments, whose conclusions it has systematically ignored in its lending operations. (Howard Geller, "End-Use Electricity Conservation: Options for Developing Countries," World Bank Energy Department Paper No. 32 [Washington, D.C.: World Bank Energy Department, October 1986].)

** To cite one example—and there are many—in 1988, Howard Geller and other Brazilian researchers concluded that technically and economically feasible energy efficiency measures would eliminate the need to construct 19,000 megawatts of power capacity, *two-thirds* of the 28,000-megawatt additional generating capacity that Brazil's national power utility, Eletrobrás, estimated needed to be constructed in the period from 1985 to 2000. (Howard Geller et al., "Electricity Conservation in Brazil: Potential and Progress," *Energy* 13, no. 6 [1988], 469–83, cited in Julie Van Domelen, *Power to Spare: The World Bank and Electricity Conservation* [Washington, D.C.: Osborn Center, A Joint Program of World Wildlife Fund and the Conservation Foundation, 1988], 14–18.)

*** Some U.S. electric utilities, such as Pacific Gas and Electric, the largest power supplier in California, have freed up additional power to meet increasing demand for more than a decade by financing investments in conservation and efficient use by consumers and corporations. These investments have provided power at a fraction of the cost of the huge sums that utilities would otherwise have to borrow to construct new power plants.

planning in borrower countries."[45] The U.S. Congress has included instructions every year since 1985 to the U.S. World Bank executive director to promote end-use efficiency and conservation—with virtually nothing to show for its efforts.*

On the energy question let us leave the last word to the Bank, whose staff in a 1990 energy study proposal succinctly summarized the enormous *economic* implications for developing countries of continuing to neglect the end-use efficiency energy investment scenario:

Estimates suggest that if 20 percent of commercial energy in developing countries were saved, total gross savings for developing countries would amount to about U.S. $30 billion per annum or about 7.5 percent of the total value of merchandise imports. This is about 60 percent of the net flow of resources out of developing countries for debt service in 1988, and about two-thirds of the official development assistance from OECD and OPEC countries in 1987.[46]

OED

As the World Bank pushed forward to project the image of environmental lender, it learned little from earlier mistakes. The Bank would always be "learning-by-doing," as Conable and other officials put it, since it seemed to be incapable of remembering. At first sight this was perplexing because since the early 1970s the Bank has had an internal Operations Evaluation Department (OED), whose express function is to carry out independent audits of completed projects and to prepare recommendations to ensure that errors are not repeated. The OED reports directly to the Bank's Executive Board and in recent years has reviewed more than 40 percent of completed projects.** Many of the most damning indictments of Bank performance can be found in OED studies, yet OED is one of the most marginalized and impotent parts of the Bank; it is viewed by many Bank staff as a professional purgatory, a dumping ground for those who cannot be fired or who are exiled from operations, where the real action of moving money takes place.

* The Bank claims it is already promoting efficiency through its supply-side investments in transmission, distribution, and generation, as well as through its adjustment policies to promote higher pricing of electricity. These measures are important and necessary, but beg the fundamental issue, reiterated by numerous independent studies, of the need for true least-cost energy planning—which would examine demand-side investment options alongside proposed new generating infrastructure. Such an approach would immediately reveal the Bank's gross negligence in virtually ignoring investments in end-use efficiency and conservation.
** This proportion of Bank projects reviewed by OED has continually declined since the 1970s, when it originally conducted independent audits on all completed Bank projects.

There are several reasons for OED's ineffectiveness. First, rhetoric to the contrary, quality control and learning from experience have never been priorities in the Bank's institutional culture. The OED owes its existence in large part to pressure by the U.S. Congress, which enacted legislation in the late 1960s and early 1970s urging its representatives in international organizations to push for internal audit divisions, at a time when the United States vote in the World Bank was more predominant than today. The first head of the OED, according to one former Bank professional, "had to threaten to resign almost once every week to ward off pressure to undermine his autonomy in the evaluations."[47]

In theory, the Bank's executive directors could invest the OED with much more power—but historically they have declined to do so, keeping in character with their relatively ineffectual role in monitoring the Bank operations they must approve. Moreover, intense attention to quality control in project lending would go against the official interests of borrowing governments as well as those of industrialized nations. Large borrowers like India are interested in obtaining the maximum amount of money with the least conditionality, and, along with other developing countries, have consistently lobbied for this position in international gatherings of all kinds, not just on the board of the Bank. With the entry of the Bank into adjustment lending in the 1980s, Bank management viewed fast disbursements of project loans as an important adjunct in infusing adequate foreign exchange into nations with drastic balance of payment problems and crises in servicing their foreign debt.* Following the OED's recommendations on improving project quality would only throw a monkey wrench into the efforts of country departments to keep the money flowing.

And indeed, in both the pre- and post-1987 Bank, country departments operated with virtual autonomy, accountable neither to the new environmental staff nor to the OED. One of the rare documented examples of this can be found in a special review of the Bank's environmental record in Brazil, which the OED carried out in cooperation with the Brazilian planning ministry in 1989 through 1991.[48] The studies reviewed a number of projects in Brazil in the 1980s, including Polonoroeste and Carajás.** The conclusions vindicated many of the most strident criticisms of nongovernmental critics over the past decade.

Among other things, the OED report on Polonoroeste accuses Bank staff of never having properly appraised the project to begin with. Accurate soil surveys that would be requisite for land settlement do not exist to

---

* For example, the "Special Action Program" of President Clausen, which accelerated disbursements to Polonoroeste and other projects to alleviate the Brazilian debt crisis.

** The OED's review of several environmentally and socially disastrous projects in the São Francisco River Valley is discussed above.

this day, nor does much other basic knowledge; a leading scientist in a Bank-financed assessment described in 1989 the protected areas in the project area as "a farce"; and the main source of economic growth in the region has been the creation of a huge government bureaucracy fueled by international funding, and predatory logging and gold mining, as well as a bubble of land speculation linked to a highly inflationary economy. Most damning of all, the OED report accuses the proponents of the project, both within the Bank and in Brazil, of actively—and successfully—hindering their more critical colleagues from completely appraising the project, and concludes that if the Bank had refused to fund Polonoroeste it would have bought time for the rainforest and its people, and reduced the legitimacy of unsustainable frontier agricultural colonization schemes.[49]

A similar story emerges for Carajás. Bank operations staff and management prevented the Bank's environmental staff from appraising the broader adverse regional environmental and social consequences of the scheme.* But faced with financial criticisms of the project's riskiness and an unsatisfactory projected economic rate of return, senior management suggested fudging the appraisal with references to the project's indirect, "unquantified" regional economic multiplier benefits.** As it was, the appraisal substantially—and conveniently—overestimated future prices for iron ore to come up with a projected financial rate of return of 11.7 percent. Prices fell for iron ore, and the Bank project was an economic white elephant, with an after-tax financial rate of return of 1.7 percent.[50] While official Bank literature continually emphasized that the Bank-financed mine, railroad, and port should not be directly associated with or held responsible for the environmental and social problems in the greater Carajás area, OED concluded that the raison d'être and justification for the

---

* "Despite [the] stated concern with the project's likely environmental effects, the February, 1981 preparation mission for the Carajas operation did not include an environmental specialist, nor were environmental questions listed among the issues mentioned by the mission team in its Back-to-Office report or the accompanying Project Brief. . . . A Bank environmental officer did participate in the project preappraisal mission" (OED, Carajás Draft Report [see endnote 50], 60–61). OED notes, "The terms of reference of the environmental officer for this mission . . . however, curiously restricted his analysis to the environmental consequences of the project . . . excluding the so-called Greater Carajas Program" (ibid., note 24, p. 61).

** "One senior advisor express[ed] strong reservations about the operation because it was 'an extremely risky project of only marginal or little value costing $U.S. 4.5 billion.' In response to this observation it was suggested that, although the riskiness of the operation should be made clearly evident in the appraisal report, the document should also justify why these risks were worth taking, while greater emphasis should be given to 'the unquantified benefits and impact of the project on future regional development'" (OED, Carajás Draft Report [see endnote 50], 66). The latter suggestion and quotation are taken, according to OED, from a memorandum dated June 10, 1982, "transmitting comments of senior Bank management on the green cover appraisal report" (ibid., note 38, p. 66).

Bank project was its role as infrastructure for broader regional economic transformation, a context that was explicitly cited in the appraisal report and in the project files.

The Operations Evaluation Department further concluded that the Bank's project, besides catalyzing accelerated deforestation on a vast scale, played an important role in contributing to increased land concentration and poverty,* extensive public health problems, increased rural violence, and—incredibly, given the billions invested—to increased malnutrition and reduced food security for large numbers of poor:

Possibly significant impacts on the health and nutritional status of the rural population in the area of influence of the Carajas Project may occur as the result of a loss of food security arising from longer term trends such as the shift from stable food production to livestock and cash crops for export, the monopolization of land in largely unproductive estates, increasing landlessness among small farmers and the rise in temporary wage labor. Within the larger Carajas region, there is already evidence of a growing food deficit. . . . Health data at the municipal level reveal a substantial increase in disease levels in key areas affected by Carajas developments. In the municipalities of Maraba, Parauapebas and Tucurui, for example, the most common recorded diseases are malaria, leprosy, tuberculosis, venereal diseases and leishmaniaisis, together with gastro-intestinal problems due to parasitic infections.[51]

Finally, beyond all considerations of project quality, the OED reports confirm that an overriding factor pushing Bank lending for huge projects such as Polonoroeste and Carajás was

the Bank's desire to step up its lending to Brazil at a time when it was facing increasing balance of payments difficulties and when the continued flow of Bank resources was considered essential to maintain the confidence of other international lenders in the country's medium and long-run development prospects.[52]

One would have hoped that the Bank would sort out the implications of the analysis of its own quality control department. Alas, a 1991 booklet prepared by the Bank's Brazil country department, "Brazil and the World Bank: Into the Fifth Decade," tells the world a tale at odds with the incriminating paper trail in that department's own files:

The Bank-supported Polonoroeste program and the 1982 Carajas Iron Ore Project included environmental protection measures at their inception. For both proj-

* "In the municipalities bordering on the Carajas railway, two-thirds of the region's 100,000 or so farming families do not own the land they work, but are increasingly hired . . . as wageworkers, sharecroppers or tenants. Furthermore, many of these farm workers are no longer allowed to live on the land they cultivate, but [now] reside in poor squatter neighborhoods in burgeoning towns such as Acailandia and Maraba. . . . [Remaining i]ndependent smallholders tend to be concentrated in relatively reduced areas" (OED Carajás Draft Report [see endnote 50], 169).

ects the environmental covenants were met. But the projects' unanticipated spillovers and the inability to control spontaneous unrelated activity have had a serious social and environmental impact.[53]

In a 1992 booklet entitled "Environment and Development in Latin America: The Role of the World Bank," the Bank's Latin American regional staff concludes, with unconsciously murderous irony, "The Carajas experience shows how countries of the region and the Bank are still learning-by-doing in environmental assessment."[54]

The Global Environment Facility

While systemic problems in whole sectors of Bank lending and policy continued to fester, and operations staff continued to ignore OED reports, the Bank pressed ahead in the early 1990s to secure over a billion dollars in additional funding for the newly formed Global Environment Facility (GEF). By late 1992, the GEF was well under way to becoming the main international funding mechanism through which the international community is attempting to address global environmental problems such as climate change and destruction of biodiversity. The genesis of the GEF is particularly revealing, since it was an initiative driven by the Bank's financial department, led by Ernest Stern, rather than by its environmental staff, which had little input into the GEF's original formulation. There are signs that one of the GEF's unstated functions for the Bank is sweetening the financial terms of larger Bank loan packages—a matter of key concern for an institution with the chronic problem of a lack of bankable projects and an ever-looming threat of net negative transfers with many of its developing members.* (We shall return to the latter issue in Chapter 7.)

At the same World Bank annual meeting in autumn 1989 where NGOs from around the world denounced new ecological and human rights abuses in Bank projects, France and Germany expressed a willingness to contribute hundreds of millions of francs and marks for a new "green fund" in the World Bank to finance environmental projects. Together with several other nations, they asked Bank management to review possible "green" funding mechanisms.[55] The Bank's finance department responded with impressive alacrity. By February 1990—a matter of weeks—the Bank developed and presented its proposal for the Global

---

* Additional concessional funds or grants administered by the Bank are one way to help stanch the net negative transfer problem with its borrowers. In fact, Mason and Asher, writing in 1973, emphasized the "need to increase IDA to avoid net negative transfers" with a number of the Bank's developing members later in the 1970s. (Mason and Asher, *Since Bretton Woods* [see endnote 15, Chap. 1], 418.)

Environment Facility to major industrialized nations, in the hope of securing funding commitments in March and starting operations in the beginning of the Bank's 1991 fiscal year, which began on July 1, 1990. On this schedule, a new, potentially multibillion-dollar arm of the World Bank would be created practically *ex nihilo* and be operating in less than nine months.

The February 1990 GEF proposal already contained the major elements of its initial form. In theory, it would be jointly sponsored by the Bank, the United Nations Environment Program (UNEP), and the United Nations Development Program (UNDP), and disburse grants to developing nations for projects in four areas of global environmental importance— conserving biodiversity, reduction of CO_2 emissions and other gases contributing to global warming, protecting the ozone layer, and cleaning up international waterways. Implicit in the proposal, but not clearly explained, were a number of other matters: all GEF investment projects would be prepared and carried out by the Bank,* and Bank GEF projects of more than $10 million would be linked to, indeed often subsumed as, components of larger World Bank loan packages in areas where the Bank's environmental record was notoriously poor, forestry and energy, for example.

The Global Environment Facility proposal had been prepared covertly, almost secretly. NGOs, the U.S. Congress, and other national parliaments were kept in the dark; even the Bank's environmental staff initially had little information about the proposal. The Bank officially presented the GEF to the leading industrialized nations for approval at a March 1990 meeting in Paris. But even the government delegations were poorly informed and prepared; they had so little time to coordinate a position on the GEF proposal that officials from the finance, environmental, and foreign ministries of the same nation took in some cases inconsistent or contradictory positions. The GEF start-up would have to be delayed a little, while the Bank "educated" its major donor governments a bit more coherently about what they were being asked to contribute hundreds of millions of dollars to support. In November 1990, the donor governments gave the go-ahead, and committed some $1.3 billion for a three-year GEF pilot program; at the end of the pilot phase, its successes and failures were to be evaluated to see if the effort was worth continuing, halting, or expanding.

The formulation of the Global Environment Facility was a model of the Bank's preferred way of doing business: top-down, secretive, with a basic contempt for public participation, access to information, involvement of democratically elected legislatures, and informed discussion of

---

* UNDP would be the executing agency for a small number of technical assistance projects, mainly research and feasibility studies.

alternatives.* Worse, it was a regression; it made the standard Bank loan appraisal process appear like an exercise in grass-roots democracy. The identification and choice of individual GEF projects was no better. Member countries of the GEF would meet twice a year to review a "work program," but the whole project cycle from identification to approval was mainly in the hands of the Bank; senior Bank management would have virtually total discretion in approving Bank GEF projects entailing less than $10 million, and the others would be presented to the World Bank Executive Board—which in the Bank's forty-six-year history had never turned down a single project. UNEP formed a scientific and technical advisory panel whose task was to formulate scientific guidelines to guide the selection of projects. But the panel had no say over the original choice of the four main project areas, nor over the design of individual projects. The virtual irrelevancy of the panel became apparent when the first round, or "tranche," of GEF projects—totaling $193 million—was prepared by the Bank and rubber-stamped by GEF member states before the panel had even developed project selection guidelines.

In the 1980s, global green movements from Russia to Brazil, from India to the United States, had linked the themes of public participation, access to information, and democratic consideration of alternatives as essential elements of environmental decision making. Environmental assessment laws in many countries (starting with the United States) embodied these principles, even if in developing nations the laws were new and weakly enforced. The European governments had expressed a willingness to contribute additional funds for global green projects mainly in response to growing popular pressure spearheaded by domestic environmental movements. What the world got in return was a travesty and a betrayal: a billion-plus dollars of potentially good money thrown after a $24-billion World Bank annual lending portfolio largely lacking environmental credibility.

Once the GEF proposal was a *fait accompli*, the growing criticisms of nongovernmental groups in several countries pressured the Bank to set up meetings with NGOs. These meetings, which the Bank subsequently touted as examples of consultation and information-sharing, were one-

* In a letter sent to Barber Conable on March 9, 1990, several major U.S. environmental organizations as well as the Woods Hole Research Institute and the Union of Concerned Scientists stated, "We are shocked and dismayed that, despite the special interest and knowledge of NGOs and other members of the public on issues of environment and development, the Bank has refused participation to the public in the formulation and discussion of its proposal. The Bank has refused repeated requests of NGOs to review the proposal, to participate formally in the discussion process, and even to meet with Bank staff on this issue" (Natural Resources Defense Council et al., letter to Barber B. Conable, President, World Bank, 9 March 1990).

sided affairs where groups were informed of decisions already taken behind closed doors. Bank staff studiously circumvented criticisms of governance and lack of "transparency," that is, openness. But the Bank was hardly the only culprit, since it could rightly point out that several participant nations themselves (particularly France) insisted that NGOs not be admitted to any of the official GEF meetings, something that the Bank claimed it had no objection to.

The data the Bank made available on proposed GEF projects were limited to short, generally one-page "project description briefs," insufficient for any informed evaluation. NGOs and participating governments did not have access to other internal Bank documents and memoranda on the GEF projects, nor to any detailed information on the larger Bank loans to which many GEF projects were to be linked. Officials of the two other U.N. agencies supporting the GEF, UNDP and UNEP, bitterly complained in private that the Bank cut them off, too, from access to many of the same documents.

The consequences of the Bank's approach to environmental management can best be seen in what has been hailed as a model*—the $10-million GEF Congo Wildlands Protection and Management Project, which became a subject of intense controversy in early 1992. On its face, from reading the one-page project brief the Bank made available to NGOs and donor nations in 1991, the plan would appear to be exemplary: it was described as a "free-standing" project to protect biodiversity in the rich, untouched Nouabele rainforest in the north of the Republic of the Congo.

But at the same time the Bank was preparing the GEF project, it had been preparing a large forestry loan for the Congo. Although the scandal over the Guinea and Côte d'Ivoire loans in early 1990 had prompted a moratorium on presenting forestry projects to the Executive Board until the Bank prepared a new forest policy, ongoing preparation of forestry projects was not halted. The Bank's Congo loan proceeded, but, in keeping with the Bank's new green image, it was baptized the "Congo Natural Resources Management Project." Unbeknownst to the GEF donor governments (like any other member of the public, they had no access to most Bank project documents), the Congo Natural Resources Management Project's main purpose—to cite World Bank project preparation documents—was to "bring forestry exploitation back to life" so that it would "regain its former place as the most stable foreign exchange earner for the Congo." The proposed loan would fund infrastructure, roads, and

---

* It was even the subject of a highly favorable cover story in *Time* (Eugene Linden, "The Last Eden," *Time*, 13 July 1992, 62).

technical support to remove transportation bottlenecks, with the goal of increasing logging exports.

The Congo, however, has a problem in borrowing more money from international agencies—one of the highest per capita foreign debt ratios in the world. Indeed, a highly critical UNDP report on the GEF project asserts that the World Bank was concerned by the reluctance of the Congo government to borrow for a new forestry project.[56] Thus, Bank memoranda describing the Congo Natural Resources Management Project suggest that its loan conditions require the Congo to agree to the GEF project,* and state that the larger Bank project is designed to mobilize grant funds "to make the package sufficiently concessional."[57] The Bank's intention was to use the GEF project to financially jump-start a much larger scheme to increase logging exports.

All of this might have been secret, had not the Environmental Defense Fund and other groups obtained internal World Bank documents in the autumn of 1991. The Bank's supposed partner in the GEF was bitterly critical of the GEF project: UNDP condemned the Bank proposal as one that would open up a hitherto intact, isolated rainforest area to logging and encroachment pressures, under the pretense of protecting it.[58] According to UNDP, the GEF project itself had dubious elements not described in the one-page project brief made available to governments: it would finance a twenty-five-kilometer road in the Nouabele forest area, bring at least 250 people to the area in addition to numerous construction workers, and attempt to set up organized safaris in one part of the reserve, while another part would actually be opened up to logging concessions. UNDP's recommendation was to leave the Congo's isolated northern rainforests alone and commit GEF funds to protect more immediately endangered areas in the southern, more populated part of the country. According to UNDP, the major threat to the Nouabele Reserve and surrounding area in the near future is, ironically, the GEF project itself, with its proposed road building, tourist safaris, and logging concessions.[59]

One of the more bizarre and revealing aspects of the GEF Congo proj-

---

* Ironically, the World Bank's wildlands policy, promulgated in 1986, requires the Bank to finance the protection of equivalent areas of forests or other woodlands when a Bank loan—such as that for the Congo Natural Resources Management Project—results in the conversion of a given area of an intact ecosystem. The GEF is theoretically forbidden from funding activities that would otherwise be financed from other sources. But the wildlands policy has been difficult to carry out, since Bank staff have viewed it as a further obstacle in pushing through projects and getting governments to borrow for them. In effect, the GEF has opened up another potential loophole through which Bank staff can avoid carrying out Bank environmental policies by artfully devising packages combining Bank loans with GEF projects in which the GEF will foot the bill for environmental actions the Bank loan otherwise would have been required to finance.

ect was the environmental assessment the Bank commissioned for it. The hapless U.S. Fish and Wildlife Service consultant who was charged with conducting the study wrote it in his office in Nebraska because the Bank refused to pay for a site visit (at the same time it financed trips to the area for a New York-based NGO that the Bank was considering hiring to execute the GEF scheme). The Bank refused him all access to documents on the Congo Natural Resources Management Project, as well as copies of memoranda and correspondence critical of the GEF proposal sent to the Bank by UNDP and the World Conservation Union (he finally obtained these from the Environmental Defense Fund). The consultant subsequently wrote Bank staff with a modest proposal: in the future environmental assessments might be more "useful" if the preparers were allowed to visit the project sites, allowed access to more information in Bank files, and if the assessment itself were made available to the public.[60]*

The Congo GEF project is a startling example of the Bank's negative environmental alchemy—its uncanny ability to present proposals whose underlying thrust is the conversion and partial destruction of ecosystems as unadulterated exercises in environmental protection. Once again, the roots of the problem lie in the Bank's strict control and rationing of information, the lack of open public discussion of alternatives, and the perverse dynamics behind the all-pervasive pressure to lend.

One of the final ironies of the Global Environment Facility is that the more bureaucratically realistic environmental advocates within the Bank (their number, still few, had grown following Conable's 1987 reforms) saw the GEF as the last hope for reforming Bank lending, for pushing country directors to take Bank environmental policies more seriously. Their argument, reduced to its bare elements, started with the acknowledgement that the place was basically driven by moving money: country directors and project officers (known as "task managers") didn't carry out Bank environmental and social policies because there were few career incentives or rewards for the effort. If operations people were given the lure of more money, particularly in highly desirable grants that could be combined with Bank loans to make a more attractive financial package, they could be seduced into seeing things from a greener perspective. Bank country departments would be rewarded for the extra time and effort that would go into carrying out Bank environmental policies with chunks of green, GEF bait that would grease the skids for easier borrowing by their

---

* The Bank's position was that while it "urges" governments to make environmental assessments public, they are the property of the borrowing government, and that it would not release these assessments to the public without the express permission of the government in question.

often recalcitrant country clients. The leap of faith that this line of reasoning presumed was enormous: skeptics asked Bank staff whether they ever had encountered a dog wagged by its tail.

In reality, the controversy over the Global Environment Facility revealed contradictions in the international political system that militated against an ecologically consistent, politically open and democratic approach in dealing with global environmental problems. Like the World Bank itself, the GEF was an affair of nation-states, most of which were suspicious of freedom of information and public participation in any international decision making, including matters of global environmental significance. Like the Bank itself—which in most cases was careful to heed the predilections of its major donors—major industrialized and developing countries were happy to view the global environmental crisis as a matter of more money for foreign assistance projects, this time ones with a green hue.

There was a great silence about the much greater need to reform not only the World Bank's lending, but the entire $55–60-billion annual flow of development aid from the North to the South, much of which was environmentally unsound and unsustainable. And foreign aid was only a small (but highly visible and influential) component of international economic activity. No country, North or South, wanted to face the financial and social implications of restructuring its own economy to promote the conservation of biodiversity, reduction of greenhouse gases, and other global environmental goals,* nor were the finance and foreign ministries of the world's nation-states disposed to heed the call of green groups for a more open and participatory approach to international environmental decision making.

* Only an immediate threat to life itself seemed to be sufficient to mobilize effective international environmental agreement and action. It required alarming scientific evidence of the direct menace to human welfare caused by the disintegrating ozone layer—including the prospect of millions of new cases of skin cancer in future years in the industrialized nations—to spur nations to create an internationally binding agreement on reducing ozone-depleting chlorofluorocarbons (CFCs) in 1988, the Montreal Protocol. Even here, leading developing countries such as India and China refused to sign unless the North agreed to transfer financial and technical resources to developing countries to ease the economic burden of switching to alternatives.

······· ··········· ········ ·········· ·········· ··········

7

The Castle of Contradictions

Where do the pressures come from, pressing down on
the World Bank to degrade its own procedures and to
bring its own integrity into question?[1]
      —Representative James Scheuer

The Bank's attempts to respond to international pressures
for environmental reform exposed a whole series of paradoxes that up
through the early 1980s had been unarticulated. The crystal palace of
global economic development, whose mission seemed so certain in earlier
years, had become a castle of contradictions by the early 1990s.

Internally, the Bank was at war with itself, showing signs of acute
bureaucratic schizophrenia. Conable's 1987 environmental reforms had
taken place as part of a larger reorganization of the Bank, one the Bank
had initiated in response to U.S. Treasury pressures to reduce personnel.
Most Bank staff members were put on a kind of probation, left uncertain
of the future existence of their jobs until the two-year reorganization was
completed. Survival often depended on finding a godfather in senior management, rather than on any indicator of merit. The effect on morale was
devastating.

Worse, the main effect of the reorganization was to exacerbate a longstanding split between the institution's operations staff, who identify and
prepare loans, and its policy, planning, and research divisions. The reorganization gave operations staff, particularly country directors, increased
power and virtual autonomy; policy, research, and external relations functions were concentrated in a single complex which was more isolated than
ever from daily input into projects. The reorganizers—a New York consulting firm—had performed a clumsy frontal lobotomy, cutting most
remaining connections between the Bank's operations and policy hemi-
spheres. Half of the Bank's sixty-plus environmental staffers were to be
found in the central Environment Department, which was now part of the

policy, research, and external affairs (formerly policy, planning, and research) complex; the other half were placed in four newly created environmental divisions for the Bank's four operations regions—Africa, Asia, Latin America and the Caribbean, and Europe and the Middle East. The regional environmental staffs were supposed to exercise closer scrutiny over projects, but, hampered by both limited budgets and limited authority, were all but powerless to stop ambitious country directors from riding roughshod over Bank policies. The Environment Department itself inhabited a world of paper, publishing upbeat accounts of strengthened internal directives and producing volumes of environmental issues papers and action plans, while the lending juggernaut lumbered ahead on a separate planet called Operations.

Operations was the part of the Bank where the action was, where careers proceeded on the fast track. Many Bank staff viewed policy, research, and external affairs as a bit of a dead end, and the Operations Evaluation Department as a humiliating exile. Those in operations proper who were responsible for pushing through debacles like Polonoroeste, Indonesia Transmigration, and Narmada Sardar Sarovar suffered no consequences to their careers. On the other hand, Bank operations staff who opposed or delayed proposed projects on policy and even ethical grounds have suffered the wrath of irate country department directors; the typical fate has been forced exile to the Environment Department.

Operations was driven by the pressure to lend, but where did this lending pressure come from? It is the proclivity of most large bureaucracies to measure success in terms of their own growth and expansion, but the pressure to lend was also inherent in the peculiar nature of the World Bank. For one thing, as we have seen (in chapters 3 and 4, above), the lack of acceptable, "bankable" projects—and the Bank's charter required it to lend mainly for projects—was a dilemma even in the 1950s, creating pressures on staff to aggressively hunt for whatever might pass muster. McNamara initiated annual lending targets, a practice that further exacerbated lending pressures and mitigated against scrupulous observance of Bank environmental and social guidelines—indeed, against project quality in general. The net negative transfer problem also had been a source of lending pressure for years, since, as the landmark Mason and Asher history of the Bank observed in 1973, it could hardly call itself a development institution if it was collecting more money from poor, economically floundering countries than it was lending to them.* The tremendous capital and

* Already by the mid 1960s (1965–67), 87 percent of all new lending, private and public, to Latin America was flowing back to the North for debt service and amortization, and 73 percent for Africa. (Report of the Commission on International Development, Lester B.

lending increases of the McNamara era only postponed the net negative transfer problem for another decade, when it would loom even greater.*

Indeed, in the late 1980s a number of developing countries were paying more back to the Bank in principal and interest than they were receiving, and by the early 1990s the problem in a number of key nations was acute. The Côte d'Ivoire had a net negative transfer of $618 million to the Bank for the period 1989–93, of which $209 million was for 1989–90 (explaining in part the urgency with which Bank staff pressed for the approval of the disastrously appraised 1990 $80-million forestry sector loan); in 1993, Nigeria contributed $328 million more to Bank coffers than it received, Egypt $92 million more ($890 million more for 1989–93), and Indonesia $428 million more.[2] In some of the most heavily indebted Latin American countries, the net negative transfers to the Bank ballooned enormously: for Brazil, $1.312 billion in 1993 ($5.3 billion for 1989–93); for Mexico, $714 million that same year; for the whole Latin American region, $7.985 billion over the years 1989–93.[3]

The Bank's own projections for the first half of the 1990s were alarming: net negative transfers from its developing members would run at a rate of nearly $3 billion per year, totaling some $13.7 billion for the period 1990–94. At the 1991 Bangkok Bank/Fund annual meeting, a number of the Bank's borrowers clamored for speeding up loan disbursements, for new ideas for projects, and for increases in funding from IDA (the virtually zero–interest concessional lending branch of the Bank)—anything that would stanch the perverse flow of money from the Third World back to the world's leading development institution.[4]

Contributing further to the pressure to lend is the fact that the World Bank never has to answer directly for the disastrous financial consequences of emphasizing quantity over quality in lending, the way a private institution would. Repayment of its loans has no connection whatsoever with the economic performance of projects, since borrowing governments (or more precisely, their hapless taxpayers) are the debtors and guarantors for most Bank loans; moreover, for developing nations the Bank and the IMF

Pearson, chairman, *Partners in Development* [New York and London: Praeger, 1969], 74, cited in Cheryl Payer, *Lent and Lost: Foreign Credit and Third World Development* [London and New Jersey: Zed Books, 1991], 57.)

* "The pressure to lend," according to one recent study of the Bank in the 1980s, "is both general, to return the Bank toward being a positive net lender to developing countries, and particular, to give special assistance to highly indebted Latin American borrowers where U.S. commercial banks had dangerously high exposures. The Bank's top management does not admit that its decisions are influenced by net negative transfers, but that is only to be expected in the circumstances" (Mosley, Harrigan, and Toye, *Analysis and Policy Proposals* [see endnote 5], 47).

have first priority for repayment, since these countries know that access to all private international credit is contingent on staying on good terms with the Bank and the Fund.

Although the Bank's preferred-creditor status has protected it from major defaults up to now, the threat of defaults by important borrowers has become more real in recent years.[5] The desire to stave off this threat has further encouraged increased lending, as well as a reluctance to halt disbursements because of violations of Bank policies.* At the end of the Bank's 1993 fiscal year, some $2.5 billion in loans from four smaller countries (Congo, Liberia, Iraq, and Syria) and the former Yugoslavia were in non-accrual status—that is, overdue. This is 2.39 percent of outstanding Bank loans. The non-performance of these loans reduced by nearly 18 percent the Bank's net income for fiscal year 1993, which was $1.13 billion.[6]

If one of the Bank's major borrowers—such as India, Brazil, or Indonesia—were to default, this would put between 11 percent and 13.5 percent of the entire portfolio in non-accrual status,** and leave the Bank with its first annual loss. In this event the Bank probably would have to tap its callable capital, causing consternation in the U.S. Congress and other national parliaments of its donor countries. (The callable capital guarantees for the World Bank are like the guarantees of the U.S. federal government for the savings and loans institutions—they are not included in the budget until the crisis breaks.) The Bank's credit rating on international capital markets would be lowered, and its financial credibility permanently undermined. In the early 1990s, both Brazil and India are faced with enormous financial crises—uncontrolled inflation in Brazil, and a balance of payments and adjustment crisis in India—which make default a real possibility.

Finally, there are two additional factors that complete the inventory of the external pressures on the Bank to lend and to ignore project quality. Representatives of the Bank's biggest borrowing nations—such as India, Brazil, and Indonesia—strongly resist additional loan conditions, particularly those required by the Bank's strengthened environmental and resettlement policies. And, we recall, the industrialized countries, led by the United States, pressured the Bank to deal with the Third World debt crisis

* According to Mosley et al., "Formally, its [the Bank's] policy is not to allow fresh loans to countries in arrears on past loans. To permit this to happen, an elaborate ritual can be performed involving borrowing from a third party to pay off the Bank's arrears, in the knowledge that forthcoming Bank lending will allow the third party to be promptly repaid" (Mosley, Harrigan, and Toye, *Analysis and Policy Proposals,* 48).
** An IBRD loan or an IDA credit is classified by the World Bank as non-performing if payments on interest or principal are more than six months overdue. If a single loan or credit for a given nation is non-performing, the Bank is obliged to declare the entire country loan portfolio in non-accrual status.

through huge, quick disbursing structural adjustment loans and accelerated project disbursements. The debt crisis was a global macroeconomic
problem whose solution was far beyond the Bank's capacity to influence,
but the creditor nations ruled out the most sensible and equitable solution—massive debt forgiveness.

In fact, a clear contradiction emerged between the Bank's efforts to
deal with the macroeconomic crises of debt and adjustment and its purported goals of poverty alleviation and increased attention to environmental concerns. Adjustment as promoted by the Bank* and the IMF resulted
in government domestic austerity programs on the part of borrowing
countries and intensive efforts to increase export earnings; too often such
measures resulted in reduced education, health, and environmental protection expenditures, and reductions in real wages for working populations already on the edge of poverty (in Mexico, often cited as a model,
real wages plummeted by 50 percent in the 1980s). Countries already
burdened with net negative transfers to the Bank, such as Côte d'Ivoire,
were encouraged to borrow still larger sums in exchange for agreeing to
squeeze more money out of their domestic economies and environments
to repay their foreign debt.

In a world with growing disequilibria in financial flows between South
and North,** the richer countries essentially were using the Bank and the
Fund as a front to increase the burden of economic adjustment on those
who could least bear it. Numerous case studies documented an appalling
drop in education and public health services for the poorest populations
of the poorest countries, particularly in Africa.*** The United Nations
Children's Fund (UNICEF) and the United Nations Economic Commission for Africa published reports in the late 1980s that bitterly indicted
the Bank's approach.[7] The UNICEF report reached the conclusion that
World Bank and IMF adjustment programs bore a substantial responsibility
for lowered health, nutritional, and educational levels for tens of millions
of Third World children.[8]

By the early 1990s, the evidence was more and more alarming. In a

---

* In the late 1980s and early 1990s about a quarter of World Bank loans were for adjust-
ment.
** The Bank's net negative transfer problem was only a window on an upside-down world
where the poor increasingly bankrolled the rich: net capital flows from the South to the
North were running at a rate of $50 billion a year in the late 1980s.
*** See, for example, A. Peter Ruderman, "Economic Adjustment and the Future of
Health Services in the Third World," *Journal of Public Health Policy,* Winter 1990, 481–89;
Judith Marshall, "Structural Adjustment and Social Policy in Mozambique," *Review of
African Political Economy* 47 (Spring 1990), 28–41; Howard Stein and E. Wayne Nafziger,
"Structural Adjustment, Human Needs, and the World Bank Agenda, *Journal of Modern
African Studies* 29, no. 1 (1990), 173–89.

1993 report, the international aid and relief organization Oxfam condemned World Bank adjustment programs for "dramatically worsen[ing] the plight of the poor" in sub-Saharan Africa. Oxfam recounts that under Bank/Fund adjustment programs, consumer prices for low-income families in Zambia doubled in an eighteen month period, and that over the past decade the number of Zambian children "suffering from malnutrition has risen from 1 in 20 to 1 in 5." Bank adjustment policies during the 1980s, the Oxfam report continues, bear responsibility for many African countries spending less in 1990 on public health per capita than they did in the 1970s, and contributed to a drop in primary school enrollment in the region from 78 percent at the beginning of the decade to 68 percent at its end.[9]

The environmental effects of adjustment were also considerable.* For example, adjustment in Mexico during the 1980s resulted in the budgets of the Department of National Parks and the Bureau of Urban Development and Ecology falling faster, according to a World Wide Fund for Nature study, "than government spending in general."[10] Reductions in agricultural extension services in several countries pushed more small-scale farmers into unsustainable practices, such as depleting lands they owned or expanding into tropical forests and other marginal areas.[11] Increased social disparities and poverty precipitated by adjustment were a major cause of environmental degradation in themselves. A case study of World Bank–IMF adjustment policies in the Philippines prepared by Robert Repetto and Wilfredo Cruz concluded that

real wages fell more than 20 percent between 1983 and 1985. As vastly increase[d] numbers of workers migrated to the open access resources of the uplands and coastal areas, deforestation, soil erosion, the destruction of coastal habitats, and the depletion of fisheries increased.[12]

In the Philippine case as in many other countries, adjustment did not succeed in launching export-led growth as intended. Many argued that given the weakness of many developing-country economies, without massive debt forgiveness adjustment was a cruel hoax. In addition, terms of trade worsened for many of the agricultural and mineral commodities on which poorer nations depended for export revenue. The industrialized

* Adjustment is in theory mixed in its environmental implications: one important environmental benefit could be the reduction of government subsidies that encourage profligate energy and water consumption, and the overuse of agricultural chemicals. Overall, however, Bank and Fund adjustment conditions seemed to be more vigorous and successful in reducing government funding for "soft" social and environmental services, in lowering real wages, and in promoting cash crops for export, than in cutting energy and water subsidies for powerful vested industrial and agricultural interests—a hardly unexpected outcome, given the political bargaining power of those affected.

countries that pushed the Bank and the Fund to promote adjustment demanded open markets in developing countries, but increased protection of their domestic markets against the light industry exports—for example, textiles and shoes—of the Third World nations that attempted to diversify.*

The Bank's approach worsened this crisis rather than alleviating it. In Africa, it led to what Oxfam calls "export-led collapse." The Bank encouraged numerous countries around the world to convert agricultural land and tropical forests to increased production of commodities such as coffee, cacao, and cotton—and prices for these commodities plummeted, as could have been expected. In West Africa between 1986 and 1989, Oxfam notes, "cocoa exporters increased their output by a quarter, only to see foreign-exchange receipts fall by a third as prices collapsed." In some cases adjustment-promoted cuts in domestic spending further crippled the export capacity that adjustment was supposed to increase: in one district in rural Tanzania in 1992 farmers were unable to market most of their cotton crop because of the collapse of road maintenance prompted by adjustment-sponsored cuts in government expenditures.[13]

The World Bank contends the failures of adjustment are a consequence of poor government compliance with Bank prescriptions as well as the result of a global economic slump. In the Philippine case, Repetto and Cruz conclude that if the Bank adjustment program had achieved its goals, unsustainable exports of natural resources and environmentally negligent production would have been the consequence; in their simulation, "both logging and mining expand dramatically, by 7.3 percent and 29.4 percent, respectively. Energy use grows by 3.0 percent, and erosion-prone agriculture by 2.5 percent."[14]

Repetto and Cruz are right on the money, to use in this case what is a particularly apt metaphor. In Ghana, the star student of the Bank-style adjustment in Africa and a recipient of huge amounts of aid, annual economic growth of 3.8 percent in the 1980s stands out as an apparent success story**—but it was achieved through, among other things, expanding mineral production and logging at a rate that could be characterized as pillage. Timber exports from Ghana increased from $16 million in 1983 to $99 million in 1988. The country's tropical forest has been reduced to 25 percent of its original size, and, according to *Time* Nairobi bureau chief and Council on Foreign Relations fellow Marguerite Michaels, "since 75 percent of Ghanians depend on wild game to supple-

---

* The Philippines in the late 1970s and early 1980s provides an enlightening case study. See Robin Broad, *Unequal Alliance: The World Bank, the International Monetary Fund, and the Philippines* (Berkeley, Los Angeles, London: University of California Press, 1988).
** But population grew 3.1 percent annually, negating most of these gains.

ment their diet, its stark depletion has led to sharp increases in malnutrition and disease."[15]

The Bank's response to evidence of the deteriorating situation in borrowing countries was to concede there were some short-term adverse effects on the poor, but that its adjustment policies were necessary to ensure "long-term sustainable growth," which, it claimed, would benefit all. To attempt to alleviate the supposedly short-term adverse social effects of its adjustment lending, the Bank responded with still more loans for "social impacts of adjustment." Their objective was to soften the effects of increased food prices and reduced wages for particularly vulnerable poor populations. Oxfam studied two such "social impacts of adjustment" programs of the World Bank in Zambia and Ghana, and concluded that they "probably have served more of a political purpose in giving adjustment the appearance of a human face, rather than a genuine compensatory purpose."[16] The one certain impact of this approach was to further increase the immense debt burden of many developing countries—a principal cause of their having to submit to adjustment in the first place.

The failures and paradoxes of adjustment are not exceptions to the Bank's culture. On the contrary they reflect an institution increasingly driven by external and internal pressures to use self-defeating, contradictory approaches in attempting to achieve goals which themselves may be irreconcilable. For example, the all-pervasive pressure to lend has had eminently predictable, but totally deleterious consequences for the quality of individual projects. Bank management and staff have tended to judge internal efficiency by the number of staff hours put into shepherding a project proposal through the project cycle.* Small projects, and projects requiring greater attention to environmental and social concerns, involve much more staff time for the amount lent, even though they might be economically and ecologically more desirable for the borrowing nation.

The internal incentives to move money at all costs are so great that every June, in the waning days of the Bank's fiscal year, there is a phenomenon known as the "bunching season," a time when it is difficult to reach many operations staff as well as the executive directors. With the bunching season comes a final rush to push before the Executive Board for approval as many loans as possible before the beginning of a new annual lending cycle. In a few final, frenetic weeks the board approves as much as a full quarter of the Bank's annual lending, some five to six billion dollars.

---

* This is one of the reasons why Global Environment Facility projects are unpopular among Bank country departments: they take an inordinate amount of staff time for the amount of money they move. The main mitigating factor is the more attractive financial package for borrowers the GEF grants create when blended with larger Bank loans.

Bureaucrats heading government ministries and agencies in developing countries often faced analogous concerns, and had considerable incentive to secure large loans for big projects that provided enticing opportunities for patronage and political pay-offs—not to speak of outright corruption. The energy sector provides the preeminent example of this dynamic. Despite the overwhelming economic and environmental advantages of end-use efficiency and conservation investments, Bank staff and developing-country energy bureaucrats have strong incentives to promote much larger, inefficient mega-projects such as large dams and power plants. A politically rational energy minister who wishes to become prime minister would be foolish to sponsor a plan to install energy-efficient lightbulbs and irrigation pumps, when three or four times as big a loan can be secured from the World Bank for a gigantic dam to produce the same amount of power, with immensely more attractive opportunities for building political patronage. A World Bank country director would have to be masochistic to promote an energy efficiency loan that would alienate the developing country energy ministry he or she is trying to cultivate, and at the same time move only one-quarter the amount of money for a greater amount of staff work.

Thus the schizophrenia between Bank environmental and social guidelines and internal and external pressures to lend often put Bank operations staff in an impossible double bind: the more time and effort they put into tailoring a project to respond to both local ecological and social conditions and to Bank guidelines, the less attractive it became for developing-country bureaucrats eager to build influence in their ministries, or for Bank country directors anxious to build a loan portfolio, and the more detrimental for their own careers.

Projects that moved quickly through the pipeline and that were suited to facile theoretical quantification tended to resemble one another. The very reasons contributing to the ease of a project's preparation and approval were the ones that ensured developmental failure. We have seen that many of these factors were already characteristic of Bank poverty projects in the 1970s: most projects lacked participation and input from local populations and even local government officials, they used inappropriate but easily replicable technology, and they were designed and analyzed in obliviousness to the local social, cultural, and ecological context.[17]

It could only be expected that the Bank's much-vaunted environmental reforms often degenerated in practice into elaborate charades. To keep the money flowing, developing-country bureaucrats and some Bank operations staff have a strong interest in what Amazon ecologist Philip Fearnside characterizes as "symbolic actions," public gestures that are confused with concrete measures that could reasonably be expected to achieve their stated objectives. Symbolic actions include announcements of grandiose plans that are never to be executed, and undertaking visible environmental measures that are either inherently ineffective . . . or are carried out on a merely token scale. . . . The strength of the phenomenon in Brazil is reflected by the hundreds of environmental protection laws that have been enacted but never enforced. . . . Symbolic actions play an important role in diminishing public concern over environmental impacts during the key time period when a development project is not yet a fait accompli. . . . The failures of previous projects are frequently acknowledged, with the corollary that these known mistakes will be avoided. The new projects then proceed without fundamental changes.[18]

So, Fearnside concludes, we see a "continued pattern of [governments] decreeing economic development projects before studies are made." Increased funding for environmental add-ons, he observed, cannot "substitute for qualitative changes in the structure of decision making."[19]

One could also conclude that member nations were asking the Bank to carry out too many objectives simultaneously: maximizing economic growth, increasing attention to ecological sustainability, social equity, and poverty alleviation, all while helping to solve the debt and adjustment crisis and promoting the opening up of developing-country markets for investment and trade. It would be impossible to optimize all of these variables even if they were complementary, and many inside and outside the Bank thought they were contradictory.

The Bank's official response to this global mire of economic, ecological, and social contradictions is that greater economic growth can pay to solve all problems. This pandered to the natural proclivity of governments to avoid thinking about difficult political choices. The Bank projected in its *World Development Report 1992* that world economic output will increase 3.5 times in real terms by 2030, but that environmental problems will be dealt with through the "substitution, technical progress and structural change" that the growth will finance "if sound policies and strong institutional arrangements are put in place."[20]

The Crisis of Multilateralism and Accountability

Bureaucratic administration always tends to be an administration of "secret sessions": in so far as it can, it hides its knowledge and action from criticism. . . .

The pure interest of the bureaucracy in power, however, is efficacious far beyond those areas where purely

functional interests make for secrecy. The concept of
"official secret" is the specific invention of bureaucracy,
and nothing is so fanatically defended by the bureaucracy as this attitude, which cannot be substantially justified beyond these specifically qualified areas. . . .
Bureaucracy naturally welcomes a poorly informed and
hence powerless parliament.[21]
—Max Weber, "Bureaucracy"

Multilateral organizations like the World Bank are, since the
fall of the Soviet Empire, among the purest, most insular bureaucracies on
earth. The Bank is a microcosm of a larger global political and environmental crisis, a crisis of accountability and sustainability. What are the
roots of this crisis? For one thing, economic and social modernization,
Max Weber noted, spurs two trends that are at best in tension with one
another and are often opposed—bureaucratization and democratization.
National bureaucracies are held accountable in varying degrees (mostly
insufficiently) to the political institutions of the nation-state; international
bureaucracies answer only to nation-states in theory, and more often only
to themselves in practice. Global ecological, social, and economic problems are intensifying, as are links and networks among nongovernmental
actors of all kinds. As a result, there is a growing loss of legitimacy for the
nation-state as the sole or even privileged actor in addressing global problems, the solutions to which often must be locally devised and carried out.

The problem of achieving an ecologically sustainable economic order is
an outstanding example, perhaps *the* outstanding example of this political
dilemma. It has become a challenge of global and national urgency, but if
this goal is to be reached, all experience points to the need for development efforts that are finely attuned to local ecological and social conditions, for initiatives that have the support of and respond to the needs of
local people. And this kind of development can only be based on a participatory, open planning process premised on early consideration of alternatives and full public access to information, as well as on the economic and
political empowerment of those communities and economic actors on
whose efforts a given project depends.

One response of governments has been, we have seen, to devolve critical aspects of global environmental management into the hands of the
World Bank; but the manifest weakness of governments in holding the
Bank and other international bureaucracies accountable simply underscores the incapacity of a system built on nation-states to deal with global
problems. We have seen that the Bank, like other multilateral institutions,
is not directly accountable to the public and civil society within borrower

and donor nations, nor to the elected representatives of its democratic members, nor, for that matter, to other multilateral agencies of the United Nations. By its charter, the Bank only answers to and lends to governments of nation-states, represented by their executive directors on the board; indeed, the charter states further, "Each [nation-state] member shall deal with the Bank only through its treasury, central bank, stabilization fund or other similar fiscal agency, and the Bank shall deal with members only by or through the same agencies."[22]

The Bank has cited the need to respect the sovereignty of its member states as the rationale for withholding nearly all written documents prepared in the planning of projects from the public and elected parliaments in both donor and borrowing countries,* despite an increasing volume of Bank literature that pays lip service to the importance of involving NGOs and community groups in its development activities.** Within the Bank, too, the free flow of information is heavily restricted within various levels of the hierarchy: we have seen how much of the critical information in the files never circulates very widely and is sometimes actively suppressed. But these external and internal imperatives of bureaucratic power and hierarchy—so aptly described by Max Weber—restrict the flow of information necessary for sound decision making; there are few feedback loops for corrective action and institutional learning, and the ones that exist—like OED—are rendered impotent.

A prerequisite for beginning to make economic development more sustainable is a free, open market in information, with decentralization of decision making. The World Bank is the embodiment of the contrary.

Even the Bank's appeal to respect sovereignty rings hollow on closer examination, since Bank management withholds even from the executive

---

* There are at least two partial exceptions. In the late 1970s, the appropriations committees of the U.S. Congress enacted legislation requiring that they be given the same information available to the U.S. World Bank executive director, or all appropriations would be halted. The commercial and trade ministries of several major donors (including the United States, the U.K., and Germany) maintain libraries of some documents available to the executive directors—appraisal reports and some country economic studies—for consultation by businesses interested in obtaining Bank procurement contracts. In the United States, after protest, NGOs now have access to the Department of Commerce library set up for this purpose.

** To cite one of numerous examples: "The Bank's role in the environmental area is [to] work with member governments toward better understanding of the problems, to assess the chain of causality, and to assist in formulating appropriate policies and financing investments. This should be done with the full participation of those people most affected by the activities" (Joint Ministerial Committee of the Boards of Governors of the World Bank and the International Monetary Fund on the Transfer of Real Resources to Developing Countries [Development Committee], *World Bank Support for the Environment: A Progress Report* [Washington, D.C.: World Bank, 1989], 36).

directors (representing the member countries) most of the documents produced by Bank staff and consultants in the identification and preparation of projects. Although a project may take over two years to prepare, the directors receive appraisal reports only two weeks before they are asked to approve the loan. This means that the directors' principal recourse for detailed information on projects are oral briefings and, occasionally, special, sanitized memos prepared by Bank staff. However, such briefings often present a distorted picture of project risks and problems, which is possible because Bank staff know the directors lack access to the original project paper trail. The briefings often turn out to be little more than confidence-building exercises in which the directors nervously seek reassurances that controversial projects are under control—which Bank staff gladly provide them.

In reality, then, the Bank uses national sovereignty as a smokescreen for withholding information not only from the public, but from its sovereign members. And, ironically, in its attempts to address international, macroeconomic imbalances, the Bank has undermined sovereignty: the whole thrust of adjustment lending is that debt-strapped nations agree to broad, sweeping economic and social conditions that were once matters determined by sovereign domestic politics.

Even if the Bank dealt more openly and candidly with member governments, the more fundamental problem remains of the political and social legitimacy of the way in which development is defined and carried out. Hollis Chenery, the Bank's lead economist in the late 1960s and 1970s, defined "[e]conomic development [a]s the set of structural changes required to sustain the growth of output and to respond to the preferences of society."[23] This statement raises two issues that are more critical and urgent than ever. The first concerns the assumption that organizing society for the growth of material output is the *sine qua non* of development. The second issue is how social preferences are determined, and whether the nation-state and its agencies can continue as the sole legitimate interlocutors in reflecting them in the international political system. "If the essential element of development is an increasing ability by society to respond to social preferences," Mason and Asher asked in 1973, "what is the 'society,' and how does its preference function get expressed? Who are 'the people,' and how do we know what they want?"[24]

Addressing the global ecological crisis will require new ways of dealing with these two issues. As never before, alarming evidence of global and regional environmental limits to economic activity has called into question the viability of pursuing development defined as an increase in output. The rise of grass-roots green movements around the world, often coupled with pro-democracy, human rights, and social equity movements in developing countries, directly challenges the notion that environmental problems can be solved by governments alone or by passing the buck to multilateral institutions like the World Bank.

The Elusive Grail

The pressures the Bank had to deal with in the 1980s and early 1990s highlight what is perhaps the most intriguing contradiction of all: through its entire history the World Bank, the Vatican of international development, has never been able to put forth a coherent or convincing theory of what it was doing. If growth was the means to achieve a socially desired goal called development, Mason and Asher had already observed in 1973 that the emperor called development economics was at best scantily clad, noting "the lack of an adequate growth theory or set of testable hypotheses relating the behavior of relevant variables to an acceptable concept of what development means."[25] An argument can be made that Bank lending—and most foreign aid—was perverse in its effects, whatever the intentions. Already in the 1970s, prominent economists produced evidence that foreign lending did not add to net investment in a country, or to growth in economic output, but reduced incentives for, and the actual amount of, domestic savings.[26] By the 1980s, two of the leading pioneers of international development theory, Lord Bauer and Gunnar Myrdal, were so disillusioned with aid in general, and Bank lending for large capital-intensive projects in particular, that they advocated the halt of most foreign assistance, except for disaster relief and, in the case of Myrdal, for health care, sanitation, and food production for the poor.*

Others have pointed out over the years the tremendous constraints posed by the unreliability or absence of economic statistics and other information in developing countries, as well as the hubris of attempting to build economic models with little concern for the insights of other sciences, such as anthropology and ecology. Most astounding of all is the propensity of economists and planners to draw conclusions based on assumptions that have little empirical or historical basis.[27] One of the most

---

* "Foreign aid," wrote Lord Bauer, ". . . often serve[s] to underwrite and prolong extremely damaging policies commonly pursued in the name of comprehensive planning" (P. T. Bauer, "Remembrance of Studies Past: Retracing First Steps," in Meier and Seers, *Pioneers in Development* [see endnote 30], 42). "I am of the opinion that we should discontinue aid for industrial projects, particularly large-scale ones," wrote Gunnar Myrdal at the same time (Gunnar Myrdal, "International Equality and Foreign Aid," Meier and Seers, op. cit., 161). Myrdal and Bauer made these statements in a series of lectures delivered at the World Bank in the early 1980s.

famous examples was the argument of numerous distinguished econo-mists (including Nobel laureate Paul Samuelson, author of the most widely used college textbook on economics) that lighthouses were a pub-lic good of such a nature that it was economically infeasible for them to have been built and administered privately. In 1974, Ronald Coase, a law school professor who was awarded the Nobel Prize in economics in 1991, published an essay that examined the history of nineteenth-century British lighthouses. Coase discovered the highly embarrassing fact that the theo-retically impossible was simple historical reality: from Elizabethan times until well into the nineteenth century, most lighthouses in Britain had been privately financed and managed.[28]

The deeper questions raised by the ecological crisis of the 1980s and early 1990s, together with political and macroeconomic pressures on the Bank to lend, have left the emperor of development nude. At the same time, Bank economists, keeping in step with the fashions of their profes-sion, developed increasingly sophisticated mathematical appraisal tech-niques that resembled nothing so much as the epicycles of the proponents of the Ptolemaic view of the solar system in the sixteenth century, attempting to explain a world that many suspected was moved by other forces—natural and social—than those of either neoclassical or Keynsian economics.*

Sustainable Development: An Oxymoron?

The attempt of many governments and international insti-tutions like the Bank to address—or paper over—these contradictions is called "sustainable development." The term was popularized by a Switzer-land-based international NGO, the World Conservation Union (IUCN) in the early 1980s** and multilaterally canonized in the 1987 Brundtland Commission report, entitled *Our Common Future,* a widely cited study prepared by a special United Nations World Commission on Environment and Development headed by the prime minister of Norway, Gro Brundt-land.

Sustainable development is a mother-and-apple-pie formulation that everyone can agree on; there are no reports of any politician or interna-

---

* Lord Bauer is worth citing on this topic: "Economic development is but one facet of the history of a society, and attempts to formulate general theories of history have so far been conspicuously unsuccessful. . . . In the more narrowly economic context, I have found the approach embodied in the conventional growth models to be unhelpful and even mislead-ing. . . . The models take as given such decisive factors as the political situation, peoples' atti-tudes, and the state of knowledge" (Bauer, "Remembrance of Studies Past," 34).

** In *World Conservation Strategy,* released by IUCN in 1980.

tional bureaucrat proclaiming his or her support for unsustainable development. The Brundtland Commission defines it as "meet[ing] the needs of the present without compromising the ability of future generations to meet their own needs."[29] The Brundtland Commission shied away from hard choices and uncomfortable thoughts, arguing that sustainable development has to be achieved by increasing economic growth in both the developing and the industrialized worlds. Growth, it maintained, is essential to the alleviation of poverty, which intensifies pressures on the environment and as such is a major cause of environmental degradation in many developing countries. The report does mention the need to conserve and enhance the natural resource base, the necessity for participation of local people in development, and the need to change the quality of growth to one that is less materials and energy intensive—but there is little discussion of how all this might come about. In the end, the Brundtland report is an endorsement of business as usual, papered over with pious expressions of good intentions; at best, it is an unintentional exposition of the very contradictions it purports to transcend in the notion of sustainable development.

For one thing, global economic growth—at least if expanding material production is an input and indicator of growth—cannot continue ad infinitum, even with increasing efficiency in energy use and an agriculture that would be much more conservation oriented (trends that are already occurring in some countries). Walt W. Rostow,* of all people, observed in 1983 that "trees do not grow to the sky. It is wholly possible, even certain, that, with the passage of time, man's perceptions of affluence will change—or the change will be forced upon him."[30] Rostow's hope—and the premise of the existing global economy and political order—was that there would be enough time to permit the North and the South "to level off in population, and later, in real income per capita when we are so minded, not when faced by bitter Malthusian or other resource-related issues."[31]

Profound structural changes will be required in the societies and economies of all countries to begin to cope effectively with the unsustainable use of natural resources that threatens many of the world's regions, as well as menacing global ecological stability. Highly unequal land-tenure systems in many tropical countries, particularly in Latin America, have been a major factor in deforestation, both by forcing populations with smaller holdings to overwork the land, and by pushing millions of others into marginal tropical forest ecosystems, often with government and

* Who introduced generations of college freshmen to international development in *The Stages of Economic Growth: A Non-Communist Manifesto* (Cambridge, England: Cambridge University Press, 1960).

World Bank support. Similarly, as a first step, the industrialized nations—particularly the United States and Canada—as well as the developing world, must shift to production technologies that are less energy and materials intensive. The political and social barriers to such changes are huge, and change will only take place with the widespread mobilization, support, participation, and free access to information of the public and of local communities in both the North and the South.

The World Bank is clearly an important political obstacle to finding and carrying out such solutions. Real change is inhibited not only by the Bank's centralization and secrecy, but by the logic of its bureaucratic raison d'être: Bank officers and staff are obliged by the charter to base their decisions and actions exclusively on economic considerations;* moreover, the charter states that they owe their allegiance entirely and exclusively to the Bank. Thus, though Bank policies can formally recognize the importance of public participation, for example, the underlying rationale is that this is a means to the end of an elusively defined goal of economic development. Even in cases where Bank staff succeed in convincing reluctant governments to involve local populations in development decisions, the participation and consultation is pro forma: typically public meetings are held to inform local groups of decisions that have already been reached. The people (not to speak of natural ecosystems) are not involved as actors, they are objects acted upon, or instruments for the realization of the project.** The terminology of development-speak expresses the underlying relation of technocratic dominance: people living in a project area are either "beneficiaries" or, if their livelihoods and culture will be harmed or destroyed, "project-affected populations," PAPs.

Max Weber identified the domination of this kind of instrumental reason as the inevitable adjunct of modernization, of the pursuit of economic development allied with technological progress, and as a special characteristic of modern bureaucracies. In a world dominated by instrumental rationality no one can question ultimate ends or goals, nor is anyone responsible for the ultimate consequences of his or her actions—which are typically mediated through others. Everyone is just doing a job. The Great Chain of Being is replaced by the chain of command. The twentieth century has shown the full potential for destruction of human populations and of nature itself when institutions and societies view and treat other

* A criterion that in practice serves to exclude more diverse social and public input, rather than to make loans more "economical."
** This is not to say that in practice individual Bank staffers cannot succeed in promoting participation that involves more genuine empowerment; but to do so is to fight against a heavy institutional bias and the modus operandi of the Bank.

human groups and whole ecosystems as means or instruments to achieving a "greater" end.* The ineluctable modernization that Weber dissected, and Dostoyevsky feared, produced a culture that became global by the mid-twentieth century: modernity. The World Bank is one of the main institutions that this culture produced, and its crisis is part of the broader crisis of modernity, which is in transition—political, economic, social, and cultural—to something else.**

What lies, then, at the heart of "modernity"? For one thing, a belief, or rather a collective revelation (perhaps a collective planetary hallucination) of the world as it presents itself: "A . . . basic truth is that development cannot be halted, only directed," spoke Bank President Conable in May 1987. In other words, development appears as a force so powerful that it is beyond the ability of any single human institution—be it bank or government—to stop or fundamentally change. The only question is whether to be a part of it or not: "The Bank cannot influence progress from the sidelines. It must be part of the action."[32]

Where did this belief in development as a global, impersonal, irresistible force come from? It was not so for most of human history, and for many human societies well into the twentieth century, and may not be so in the near future.

* See Zygmunt Bauman, *Modernity and the Holocaust* (Ithaca, New York: Cornell University Press, 1989).
** See, for example, David Harvey, *The Condition of Postmodernity: An Enquiry into the Origins of Cultural Change* (Cambridge, Massachusetts and Oxford, U.K.: Blackwell, 1989); and Zygmunt Bauman, *Intimations of Postmodernity* (London and New York: Routledge, 1992).

From Descartes to Chico Mendes: A Brief History of Modernity as Development

> Instead of the speculative philosophy taught in the Schools, a practical philosophy can be found by which, knowing the power and effects of fire, water, air, the stars, the heavens and all the other bodies which surround us, as distinctly as we know the various trades of our craftsmen, we might put them in the same way to all the uses for which they are appropriate, and thereby make ourselves, as it were, masters and possessors of nature.[1]   —René Descartes, *Discourse on Method*

> We treat the fatal consequences of technology as though they were a technical defect that could be remedied by technology alone. We are looking for an objective way out of the crisis of objectivity.[2]   —Václav Havel

That economic development cannot be halted, or, to cite the World Bank once again, that its "desirability . . . is universally recognized"[3] would seem to be a basic truth as the twentieth century draws to its end. Respectable debate centers on what kind of development—whether it is environmentally sustainable or socially equitable. The specific term *development* is a post–World War II phenomenon, but what it refers to—progress, modernization, technology, growth—has been going on in the West since the seventeenth century.* The core phenomenon is in one

---

* The literature on the subject of the origins of economic development in the modern era is of course enormous; for an introduction, see H. W. Arndt, *Economic Development: The History of an Idea* (Chicago: University of Chicago Press, 1987); Walt W. Rostow, *How It All Began: Origins of the Modern Economy* (New York: McGraw-Hill Book Company, 1975); J. B. Bury, *The Idea of Progress: An Inquiry into its Origin and Growth* (New York: Dover Publications, 1932).

sense, as Walt Rostow put it, "simple and obvious: What distinguishes the world since the industrial revolution from the world before is the systematic, regular, and progressive application of science and technology to the production of goods and services."[4] Technology, in the sense of toolmaking and action upon nature to satisfy human needs, has always existed; indeed, recent studies indicate that other primates have similar proclivities. The critical juncture in human history came with the Enlightenment, when several societies in Western Europe began to organize themselves in a feedback loop of continuous technical innovation and transformation, a new social dynamic that joined the production of economic surpluses to the method of modern science and the expansion of markets.

The whole complex of social values and objectives associated with development, what Gunnar Myrdal calls "the modernization ideals," became by the 1960s the "official creed, almost a national religion" in most developing countries.[5] As Myrdal points out in his monumental study of development in South Asia, *Asian Drama,* these values are rooted in the Western Enlightenment, and include an eagerness to apply scientific, technological methods to increase material production as well as a desire for institutions and cultural transformation that embody values right out of Max Weber—efficiency, frugality, orderliness, diligence, punctuality, and above all, rationality in decision making liberated from tradition, custom, and group allegiances.[6] The political unit of the nation-state, another seed of the Enlightenment nurtured to fruition by the twentieth century, would be the favored vehicle for these goals and values.* The postcolonial era paradoxically heralded the triumph of Western, Enlightenment social goals and cultural values in most non-Western parts of the world, at least as a project of developing-country elites. Driving this project is the allure of technology, the midwife of salvation through economic growth; growth in turn would be the foundation of national power and prestige.** Nehru summed it up neatly in 1961:

* Rostow notes that through the eighteenth century, modernization was largely a "top-down" affair: technical research and the creation of manufactures and markets were assiduously and painstakingly promoted by national governments that were gradually establishing a sense of nationhood. "With respect to the future," he optimistically proclaimed, "the economic tasks undertaken by governments in early modern Europe approximate those of the least industrialized parts of the post-1945 developing world" (Rostow, *How It All Began,* 20, 103).

** Arndt points out that the poverty, basic needs, and alternative technology goals that entered international development discourse in the late 1960s and 1970s were viewed skeptically by most developing-country elites and governments as diversions from the central project of increased national power through economic modernization. These concerns seemed to reflect growing Western doubts about the virtues of ceaseless economic growth and continued social inequality rather than any demand from the developing-country governments. (Arndt, *Economic Development,* 108–11.)

"The test of a country's advance is how far it is utilizing modern techniques."[7]

It is all the more remarkable and thought-provoking—and a sign of the arrogance of our epoch—that for almost all of human history, and for most societies that have existed on this planet, this concept and practice of development did not exist. Obvious examples come to mind: the European High Middle Ages, when social surplus was invested in monuments to God—cathedrals and crusades—or traditional Asian civilizations like that of China, in which sophisticated bureaucracies and highly developed trade and technology did not result in the ceaseless technical innovation and economic growth that we think of as characterizing modern development.

Even more intriguing is the situation of some tribal and indigenous societies before they go down the road of cultural disintegration and economic dependency. In a famous essay published over two decades ago, "The Original Affluent Society," anthropologist Marshall Sahlins pointed out the ultimate paradox of modern development: the most "primitive" hunting and gathering societies on earth, Australian aborigines and African bushmen, enjoy material and social plenty, working at most an average of three to five hours per day at a leisurely pace to satisfy all of their material needs. They "keep banker's hours, notably less than modern industrial workers (unionized) who would surely settle for a 21–35 hour week."[8] The considerable leisure time at their disposal—enough to make the average American two-job household jealous or depressed—is spent socializing, sleeping, and in surprisingly sophisticated cultural activities.

Claude Lévi-Strauss's description of the cultural life of Australian aborigines, spent in endless elaboration and discussion of fine totemistic classifications and distinctions, focuses on aboriginal culture's extraordinary social complexity and—there is no other word—development, the product of long isolation:

Moreover, this development was not undergone passively. It was desired and conceptualized, for few civilizations seem to equal the Australians in their taste for erudition and speculation and what sometimes looks like intellectual dandyism, odd as this expression may seem when applied to people with so rudimentary a level of material life. But lest there be any mistake about it: these shaggy and corpulent savages whose physical resemblance to adipose bureaucrats . . . makes their nudity yet more incongruous . . . were, in various respects, real snobs. . . . Theorizing and discussion was all the rage in this closed world and the influence of fashion often paramount.[9]

In his appraisal of hunter-gatherer and agricultural subsistence societies, Sahlins reaches a startling conclusion: that paleolithic and neolithic cultures knew less real hunger, both proportionally and absolutely, than the world does today:

In the Old Stone Age the fraction [of hungry in the world population] must have been much smaller. *This* is the era of hunger unprecedented. Now, in the time of the greatest technological power, is hunger an institution.[10]

For Sahlins, not only hunger but especially poverty is socially produced, ironically, through the process of economic development itself. Poverty, he observes, is above all a relation of relative status among people; although "the world's most primitive people have few possessions . . . *they are not poor.*" The evolution of social structures and technologies we call development is "like the mythical road where for every step the traveller advances his destination recedes by two."[11]*

How did this conception of social organization, which most of the humans who have ever existed did not know and lived well enough (and sometimes better) without, become, in less than four centuries, not just universally desirable but something perceived as an unstoppable, almost supra-human force of planetary organization and domination? What is at the heart of this evolution that distinguishes modern society from all others? For Rostow, the deciding factor was the triumph of the scientific revolution of the seventeenth and eighteenth centuries, which taught that the natural world could be systematically and continuously transformed for human benefit.[12] Max Weber's thesis on the importance of Protestantism in the rise of capitalism is somewhat discredited, but his fundamental insight on the changed nature of reason and rationality in modern society remains valid: "Confucian rationalism meant rational adjustment to the world, Puritan rationalism meant rational mastery of the world."[13] French anthropologist Louis Dumont describes the foundation of what he calls "modern ideology" as the triumph of societies in which the relations between people and things are paramount, as opposed to the primacy of relations among people.[14]

The ultimate answer to the question of how we got to here, however, takes us back to 1619, the year the first slaves were brought to Virginia, while the English Puritans, exiled in Holland, prepared for their imminent voyage to the New World. In April 1619, another foreign exile in the low

* It is clearly a mistake, however, to think of all traditional societies as necessarily better adapted to their environments, less violent, or otherwise "happier" than our own. UCLA anthropologist Robert B. Edgerton, for example, criticizes the belief "that small-scale societies are better adapted to their ecological circumstances than our own. . . . Some may be, but others decidedly are not. In a number of small societies, people are chronically hungry and care little about one another's welfare" (Robert B. Edgerton, *Sick Societies: Challenging the Myth of Primitive Harmony* [New York: Free Press, 1992], 12).

countries, a twenty-three-year-old French mercenary in the pay of the Prince of Nassau, left on a six-month trip through central Europe as troops mobilized at the outbreak of the Thirty Years War. On the tenth of November, 1619, in a garret room in the small Bavarian town of Ulm, he had a series of waking visions and dreams.[15]

The Metaphysics of Modernity

> Only now do we arrive at the philosophy of the modern world, and we begin it with Descartes. . . . Here, like the sailor at the end of his long voyage on the stormy seas, we may cry "Land."[16]
> —Hegel

For the young René Descartes, the dreams were intensely disturbing as well as mysterious: someone gave him a strange, exotic melon from a faraway land; he was surrounded by lightning and thunderbolts; he tried to find a verse for a stranger in a book before him which vanished and reappeared.[17] The soldier was also a mathematician and philosopher, and he had been struggling with a program to revise nothing less than the way human knowledge was generated and used. Eighteen years later, in the *Discourse on Method*, he set down the ultimate object of his visions: "I spent the whole day shut up in a room heated by an enclosed stove,"[18] he recalled of that day in Ulm; his aim was "to seek the true method of arriving at knowledge of everything my mind was capable of grasping."[19]

Descartes's method was the essence of simplicity: doubt everything except what presents itself to the mind directly and distinctly, dissect the problem into as many parts as possible, reconstruct the whole through a step-by-step, inductive process, and enumerate and record everything.[20] One could paraphrase the four steps as abstraction, analysis, synthesis, and control.[21]

The goal, Descartes wrote, was not just knowledge, but power and welfare—"a practical philosophy [science]" that would make humankind the "masters and possessors of nature" through "the invention of an infinity of devices by which we might enjoy, without any effort, the fruits of the earth and all its commodities" as well as "the preservation of health, which is undoubtedly the first good."[22]

The familiarity of this famous passage should not dim its astounding audacity: Descartes is promising us not only an infinity of new inventions and devices to master and possess nature, but literally the entire earth—without any effort.

It was this vision above all that captured the imagination of his contemporaries, and of subsequent commentators to this day. Along with his contemporary, Sir Francis Bacon, Descartes articulated a new program for human society, a new organizing principle for social relations, which Bacon called the "Empire of Man Over Things." Bacon explored the social and political implications in more detail, but Descartes founded the epistemology and metaphysics of what has come to be known as the modern project.[23]

Descartes's first step, that of systematic doubt, extended even to his perceptions of his own body, and ended with only one certainty, that something was thinking and therefore existed: "I think, therefore I am." From this given, he proves the existence of God and reconstructs the world. In his "Second Meditation" he concludes that the fundamental, certain, irreducible characteristic of the world is "extension." He takes a lump of wax as an example, which can be molded, melted, formed again, but which always occupies a three-dimensionally defined extension in space.[24] In this world of extended space, objects are presented and represented for a self-certain subject, a thinker and actor who applies the rules of abstraction, analysis, synthesis, and control.

The key to the mastery of extension, as well as to Descartes's method, is a certain vision of mathematics; he invented, we remember, analytic geometry, the representation of algebraic functions through geometric methods.* Truth is not only certainty, rooted in the subject, truth is also correctness: "A child who has been taught arithmetic, having added up according to the rules, can be sure that he has found out, as far as the sum he was examining is concerned, all that the human mind is capable of finding out."[25] Descartes's vision was unitary, universal, and absolutist: "I shall not perhaps appear to you too vain, if you consider that, as there is only one truth of each thing, whoever finds it knows as much about the thing as there is to be known."[26] There is only one answer to any problem.

The Cartesian approach was an almost totally novel, alien vision of the world in 1637. Its promise of unimagined power entailed a Faustian bargain—the progressive "devalorization of being," a world reduced to a geometric extension occupied by objects for a rationating, calculating subject.[27] Nowhere was the hubris of this new attitude to nature more pithily encapsuled than in the epigraph "Donnez-moi de la matière et du

---

* "These long chains of reasonings, quite simple and easy, which geometers are accustomed to using to teach their most difficult demonstrations," he writes in the *Discourse on Method,* "had given me cause to imagine that everything which can be encompassed by man's knowledge is linked in the same way" (*Discourse on Method and the Meditations* [see endnote 1], 41).

mouvement, je ferai un monde" (Give me matter and motion, and I shall make a world) that prefaced one of Descartes's treatises on physics;[28] but, unwisely pursued, this was also a formula for the destruction of the earth.

By the mid-twentieth century many of the elements of the Cartesian vision were embedded at the deepest, most unconscious level as fundamental assumptions of a global culture of modern institutions and bureaucratic decision making. In this global bureaucratic culture, the world appears as reified extension, and the earth's myriad ecosystems and human societies are abstracted expanses of space awaiting planning, inputs, and infrastructure, to be rearranged at will according to the circumstances and calculation. It is a culture that tends to assume there is only one answer to any problem. Above all, our age has transformed almost every society in the world into a system with one overarching goal—the possession of nature, the setting upon the earth with an infinity of inventions to transform it into a source of commodities for human use.

The ghost of Descartes haunts in particular the world of large international development bureaucracies like the World Bank. Nothing symbolizes this better than an image from the British television film on the fate of the Amazon, *The Decade of Destruction*. At one point in the film, Brazilian scientist and environmental activist José Lutzenberger is discussing maps with an employee of the Brazilian federal land colonization agency, INCRA. The INCRA maps, prepared with the assistance of the Bank in the mid-1980s, divide huge areas of the Amazon rainforest state of Rondônia (the size of Oregon or Great Britain) into perfect, geometric grids, symmetrical small rectangles connected by perfectly parallel straight lines, feeder roads from the main Bank-financed highway. Each tiny rectangle is a plot of land to which prospective colonists are to be granted title.

Lutzenberger is enraged. Can't they see that this is an insane way to divide land—that the perfect geometric, Cartesian symmetry of the land grants ignores topography, soils, and access to water? It was indeed a plan that looked like it had been drawn by someone sitting alone in a room in Brasília* or Washington, or even by a French mathematician in Holland in the seventeenth century.** NASA satellite photos of the vast deforesta-

---

* A city whose creation and physical design embodies a very Cartesian project of domination of space, both as an urban center and as a planned new national capital to open up and control the Brazilian interior.

** The image is a caricature, but unfortunately true, and revealing of a mind-set that views large parts of the earth's surface with little more discrimination than that with which Descartes viewed his ball of wax, which, the great philosopher concluded, was nothing "except something extended, flexible and malleable." The Bank claims it is promoting now the approach it should have had in the 1980s—so-called "agro-ecological zoning," which in theory starts with topography, soil quality, existing land uses, etc., in land use planning for the Amazon. But in practice less has changed than meets the eye (see Chapter 6).

tion that ensued show an eerie, gridlike pattern of environmental devastation, spreading and increasing annually from perpendicular and parallel axes like the computer-generated geometric projection of a strange new mathematical function.

The Empire of Man Over Things

As Francis Bacon so aptly stated, ". . . in this theatre of man's life it is reserved only for God and angels to be lookers on." We at the World Bank are determined not to be onlookers.[29]   —Barber Conable, 1988

In one probably unintended sense it was uncannily appropriate for Barber Conable to quote Sir Francis Bacon, for if Descartes was the metaphysician of modernity, Bacon was the prophet of technocracy. In 1620, a year after Descartes had his vision in Ulm, Bacon published *The Great Instauration;* it was nothing less than a grand program to reform human knowledge, "to lay the foundation of human utility and power,"[30] an undertaking he already had begun in *The Advancement of Learning*, published fifteen years earlier. Bacon's project bore much in common with Descartes's—a desire to reevaluate all previous learning, an emphasis on method and induction, and a grand vision of the domination of nature, as well as of human affairs, through the application of this "new philosophy."

One finds embedded in Bacon's writings many of the sociological implications of modernity that would become manifest centuries later. For one thing, he envisages the critical role of instrumental reason in a world rationally redirected towards the conquest and utilization of nature: "Neither the naked hand nor the understanding left to itself can effect much. It is by instruments and helps that the work is done, which are as much wanted for the understanding as for the hand."[31] But, Bacon complains, these instruments are lacking for the understanding because of the prevalence of deductive, Scholastic reason, which has had "scanty success" in studying nature and inventing new works.[32]

In the second part of *The Great Instauration, Novum Organum* (New instrument), he sets forth in "progressive stages of certainty"[33] a "doctrine concerning the better and more perfect use of human reason in the inquisition of things, and the true helps of the understanding."[34]* The new

* Commentators have noted that the use of the word *inquisition* here is of critical importance; Bacon's method envisages an active program of experimentation and manipulation of nature as the key to knowledge and power: "The secrets of nature reveal themselves more readily under the vexations of art than when they go their own way" (*Novum Organum* [see

method "shall analyze experience and take it to pieces, and by a due process of exclusion and rejection lead to an inevitable conclusion."[35] The goal is not to win arguments with academicians, but "to command nature in action."[36]* He suggests that only with the division of labor and specialization "will men begin to know their strength, when instead of great numbers doing all the same things, one shall take charge of one thing and another of another."[37] His most revealing metaphor for the new, instrumental role of reason and knowledge can found in book 2 of *The Advancement of Learning*: he compares his age's lack of logical and scientific method to a lack of "ready money." "For," he tells us, "as money will fetch all other commodities, so this knowledge is that which should purchase all the rest."[38]

Thus, in Bacon's new, modern age "human knowledge and human power meet in one,"[39] and, since nature to be conquered must be obeyed, "[t]ruth therefore and utility are here the very same things."[40]

Some critics of contemporary development, like India's Jatinder K. Bajaj, have emphasized that Bacon's vision of modernity was from the beginning one of domination over others as well as over nature.[41] Near the end of the *Novum Organum*, Bacon declares that his method can "embrace everything. For I form a history and tables of discovery for anger, fear, shame and the like; for matters political; and again for mental operations of memory . . . judgment and the rest; not less than for heat and cold, or light, or vegetation, or the like."[42] Explicit in Bacon's plan, Bajaj asserts, is the conquest and domination of the non-Western world.[43] And indeed, the last aphorism of the *Novum Organum* exhorts the reader to "only consider what a difference there is between the life of men in the most civilised province of Europe, and in the wildest and most barbarous districts of the New India; he will feel it be great enough to justify the saying that 'man is a god to man.'" This difference which is already beginning to make some humans gods over others, Bacon concludes, comes only from the arts of invention, that is, technology.[44]

Finally, in Bacon's utopian vision of the future, technology and full access to information are in the hands of a few, who are accountable only

endnote 31], aphorism 98). See Jatinder K. Bajaj, "Francis Bacon, the First Philosopher of Modern Science," in Ashis Nandy, ed., *Science, Hegemony and Violence: A Requiem for Modernity* (Delhi: Oxford University Press, 1990), 47. Shiv Vivanathan calls this "the vivisectional mandate, where the other becomes the object of experiment which is in essence violence and in which pain is inflicted in the name of science" (Vivanathan, "On the Annals of the Laboratory State," in Nandy, op. cit., 259).
* Weinberger notes that Bacon's Latin version uses the word *vinvitur,* literally "conquer," rather than "command." (*New Atlantis and The Great Instauration* [see endnote 30], p. 21, note 40.)

to the state, if at all.[45] In the *New Atlantis* he portrays an imaginary kingdom ruled by benevolent but despotic philosopher kings. Almost all of the kingdom's inhabitants are forbidden access to the outside world. Only a few members of a secretive technocratic elite, called the "Fellows or Brethren of Solomon's House," make intermittent voyages to foreign countries to procure "knowledge of the affairs and state of those countries . . . and especially of the sciences, arts, manufactures and inventions of all the world," as well as to bring back "books, instruments and patterns in every kind."[46]

The declared purpose of the House of Solomon is, besides knowledge, "the enlarging of the bounds of the Human Empire, to the effecting of all things possible."[47] Above all it is a strict hierarchy, and its guiding ethos is secrecy, even with respect to the state it is supposed to serve:

We have novices and apprentices . . . besides a great number of servants and attendants, men and women. And this we do also: we have consultations, which of the inventions and experiences which we have discovered shall be published, and which not; and take all an oath of secrecy, for the concealing of those which we think fit to keep secret: though some of those we do reveal sometimes to the state, and some not.[48]

Perhaps the speechwriters for the World Bank president should have thought twice before citing Bacon as a guiding spirit in Barber Conable's annual speech on the Bank's institutional progress quoted above. In 1618, Bacon was appointed to the highest legal office in England, Lord Chancellor, from which he personally supervised the torture of prisoners (when the practice was illegal and had been universally condemned in England for a generation), issued monopolies to curry favor with the court, accepted bribes and favors from prospective litigants, and tampered with trials and judges.[49] In 1621 he was indicted by the House of Lords for corruption, pleaded guilty, and was banished from London, as well as permanently disbarred from public office and fined 40,000 pounds, a huge sum for the times.

Thus, one need look no further than Bacon's life to see that his new philosophy, equating knowledge with utility and power, had tremendous potential for political evil, as well as improvement. In the words of the great nineteenth-century historian Thomas Macaulay,

Intellectually, he was better fitted than any man that England has ever produced for the work of improving her institutions. But, unhappily, we see that he did not scruple to exert great powers for the purpose of introducing into those institutions new corruptions of the foulest kind.[50]

Modernity, Development, Technology

> Chronologically speaking, modern physical science be-
> gins in the seventeenth century. In contrast, machine-
> power technology develops only in the second half of
> the eighteenth century. But modern technology, which
> for chronological reckoning is the later, is, from the
> point of view of the essence holding sway within it, the
> historically earlier.[51]
> —Heidegger, "The Question Concerning Technology"

A common view of the origins of modern economic development (most convincingly set forth by Walt Rostow in *How It All
Began: Origins of the Modern Economy*) identifies the scientific revolution
of the seventeenth and eighteenth centuries as the defining, originating
event that made possible the increasingly rapid evolution of technology
and economic development. Indeed, the latter half of the seventeenth
century was a period of unprecedented scientific discovery, culminating in
the work of Isaac Newton, which defined the parameters of Western science for the next two centuries. As the number of scholars interested in
natural science grew, they began to meet and correspond in a regular
fashion; in the 1660s both the British Royal Society and the French Academy of Sciences were established. State-sponsored institutions to promote
economic development also flourished: the first national central bank, the
Bank of England, was founded in 1694.

A strong argument can be made, however, that technology and
economic development are not the children (sometimes perceived as
errant) of modern science, but precisely the contrary*—that accelerating

---

* Several more recent studies (than Rostow's) by economic historians emphasize the role of
new, economically more efficient social, legal, and property arrangements which, coupled
with technological innovation, created self-reinforcing incentives for individual economic
effort and therefore the "key to growth." (Douglas C. North and Robert Paul Thomas, *The
Rise of the Western World: A New Economic History* [Cambridge, England: Cambridge University Press, 1973], 1; see also Nathan Rosenberg and L. E. Birdzell, Jr., *How the West
Grew Rich: The Economic Transformation of the Industrial World* [New York: Basic Books,
1986].) These arrangements include, in Britain in the latter half of the seventeenth century,
"the creation of the first patent law to encourage innovation, the elimination of many of the
remnants of feudal servitude . . . the joint stock company . . . the coffee house, which was a
precursor of organized insurance; the creation of securities and commodities markets; the
development of the goldsmith into a deposit banker issuing bank notes, discounting bills
and providing interest on deposits" (North and Thomas, 155); and, of course, the founding
of the Bank of England in 1694. Clearly, this is *what* happened; but *why* did it happen, and
what was (and is) the essence of the whole process? These are essentially philosophical questions, whose answers depend on what one is looking for. See Martin Heidegger's essay "The
Question Concerning Technology" (see endnote 51).

advances in practical, economically oriented technology directly spurred the evolution of Western science. Science is a by-product of technology, or, otherwise put, the original and dominant historical project was not knowledge, but power over nature and humankind. Early seventeenth-century Holland, where Descartes spent many years in exile, is a case in point. The landscape that Descartes encountered was being transformed before his eyes by ambitious drainage and land reclamation projects; everywhere one could find dikes, sluices, polders, and windmills. By 1640, twenty-seven former lakes had been pumped and reclaimed in the penin-sula north of Amsterdam alone.[52] Even today the Dutch landscape—an extended, perfectly flat expanse, largely modified and created by human intervention—is the perfect inspiration for the Cartesian vision of nature. In the words of Clarence Glacken,* "One could write an illuminating essay on the influence of Dutch hydraulic engineering on optimistic inter-pretations of modification of the land by human agency."[53]

Bacon states that the inspiration for his program to reform human knowledge and inquiry is the tremendous practical, technological progress of his age:

It is well to observe the force and virtue and consequences of discoveries; and these are to be seen nowhere more conspicuously than in those three which were unknown to the ancients . . . printing, gunpowder and the magnet. . . . No empire, no star seems to have exerted greater power and influence in human affairs than these mechanical discoveries.[54]

But the most critical indicator of the will to power that underlay the birth of modernity is the remarkable growth of interest in the occult sci-ences in the seventeenth century—alchemy, black magic, and witchcraft. C. S. Lewis, in a marvelous essay on the social and political risks of tech-nocracy called *The Abolition of Man*, advances the thesis that the birth of science and the modern age is often misinterpreted, especially by those who claim that magic and the occult were medieval remnants to be swept away by the Enlightenment:

Those who have studied the period know better. There was very little magic in the Middle Ages: the sixteenth and seventeenth centuries are the high noon of magic. The serious magical endeavor and the serious scientific endeavor are twins: one was sickly and died, the other strong and throve. But both were twins. They were born of the same impulse. . . . For magic and applied science alike the problem is how to subdue reality to the wishes of men: the solution is technique.[55]

In no life is the strange relationship between science, magic, and modernity more evident than in that of Sir Isaac Newton.

* His *Traces on the Rhodian Shore* (see endnote 52) is still the definitive study of concep-tions of nature in Western history through the end of the eighteenth century.

"Not to Be Communicated Without Immense Dammage to Ye World"

It is July 14, 1936; the place, Sotheby's, London. An unusual auction is going on. For sale are thousands of pages of recently rediscovered manuscripts of Sir Isaac Newton, the product of more than a quarter-century of research and thought by Newton in the late seventeenth century. There are only three buyers; the most enthusiastic is none other than John Maynard Keynes.[56] Keynes ultimately acquired nearly half of the papers, which he left on his death to Kings College, Cambridge. When he read the manuscripts he and many others were shocked: the apotheosis of Enlightenment science had spent much of his life obsessed with black magic and the occult.[57] Newton left behind more than 650,000 words on alchemy and related subjects, citing more than a hundred hermetic treatises.[58] Keynes, after poring over these papers, reached the startling conclusion that Newton was not "a rationalist, one who taught to think on the lines of cold and untinctured reason," but rather an alchemist and magician. It was false, Keynes argued, to consider Newton as the first great modern scientist, since Newton thought of himself as heir to an "esoteric brotherhood" connected to the "papers and traditions handed down by the brethren in an unbroken chain back to the original cryptic revelation in Babylonia." "As many hundreds of pages of unpublished manuscript survive to testify," Keynes insisted,

Newton was seeking the philosopher's stone, the Elixir of Life, and the transmutation of base metals into gold. He was, indeed, a magician who believed that by intense concentration of mind on traditional hermetics and revealed books he could discover the secrets of nature and the course of future events, just as by the pure play of mind on a few facts of observation he had unveiled the secrets of the heavens.[59]

But Newton was no exception to his time. He corresponded extensively on alchemy with an enthusiastic elder mentor on the subject— Robert Boyle, whom most people remember as one of the founders of modern chemistry and the formulator of a famous law concerning the behavior of gases. Boyle published numerous alchemical and occult tracts, including a 1676 treatise* in which he claimed to have found the fabled philosophers' stone, the goal of the hermetic quest, which enables the transmutation of lead into gold.[60] Newton was so concerned by the implications of Boyle's apparent discovery that he warned in a letter to a mutual acquaintance that the magic knowledge was "not to be communi-

* "Of the Incalescence of Quicksilver into Gold," which appeared in the *Philosophical Transactions of the Royal Society.*

cated without immense dammage to ye world."[61] John Locke also had a strong interest in the occult and alchemy, and part of Newton's fourteen-year correspondence with Locke from (1690 to 1704) reveals a mutual obsession with the subjects. In fact, Boyle had shared alchemical recipes and formulas with both Newton and Locke, and following Boyle's death in 1691 they exchanged with one another the different incantations and procedures the old alchemist had left them, in the hope of piecing together the ultimate secrets.[62]

Most revealing of all is the progression of Newton's long journey into the occult. It was not, as one might think, that he investigated alchemy in the spirit of scientific inquiry, proceeding by trial and error to the more rational, empirically rooted beginnings of modern chemistry. Rather, as one of his principal biographers notes, "he started with sober chemistry, and gave it up rather quickly for what he took to be the greater profundity of alchemy."[63]

None of these revelations are incongruous if one accepts the thesis of C. S. Lewis, and many others, that what was at work in the seventeenth century in Western societies was the emergence of a historically unprecedented will to power, a will to control and dominate all aspects of being. The late seventeenth century revival of alchemy helps illuminate the cultural and social currents that gave birth to its twin, modern natural science. The hermetic quest involved several levels: a search for spiritual truth and insight into the nature of matter, the pursuit of occult power over nature, and technical investigations to find the key to transforming matter for human ends. The crowning achievement, in which the spiritual and the technical would unite, is the manufacture of the philosophers' stone; the successful formula was thought to involve an elaborate process of purification and combination of mercury and sulfur, which in turn were believed to be the fundamental constituents of all metals. Once found, the philosophers' stone would enable the transmutation of base metals into gold. In alchemy, knowledge of nature unleashed the power to transform it, and, most importantly, to create the ultimate embodiment of, and means to, economic wealth—gold.

In fact, one could say that alchemy and the process of modern economic growth have much in common in their goals.*

---

* This is the view of Swiss ecological economist Hans Binswanger (whose namesake and relation, ironically, is a leading agricultural economist in the World Bank), who, in a fascinating interpretation of the second part of Goethe's *Faust,* describes the foundation of the modern economy as an alchemical process. (Hans Christoph Binswanger, "Die Moderne Wirtschaft als alchemistischer Prozess: Eine oekonomische Deutung von Goethe's 'Faust,'" [The modern economy as alchemistic process: an economic interpretation of Goethe's "Faust."] *Neuen Rundschau,* Nr. 2, 1982, reprinted in *Leviathan, Zeitschrift fuer Sozialwissenschaft,* 1986, Heft 1.)

In this light, the last stage of Newton's career is most intriguing, since his interests turned from alchemy to finance: he became Warden of the Mint in 1696. His experience in alchemy served him well in analyzing and assaying the proper proportions of gold and silver in the coinage of the realm.* At the Mint, Newton wrote a number of treatises on money. More than anyone else, he was responsible for the creation of the gold standard, which, biographer Frank Manuel points out, "lasted just about as long as his universal [scientific] system."[64]

The Perfection of the "Universal Idea"

> The change in the universal idea which the human mind is now striving to perfect was begun by Bacon, in whose works it has a purely philosophic character. Descartes began to give it scientific form. Locke and Newton found the means to give it permanent scientific form. Circumstances are favorable for the organization of the new system.[65]
> —Claude-Henri Saint-Simon, 1808

In an elegant mansion near downtown Washington, D.C., less than a mile from the World Bank, is located one of the most unusual and exclusive clubs on earth: the Society of the Cincinnati. The Society of the Cincinnati was formed after the Revolutionary War, and is the only institution in the United States based on primogeniture: its members (deceased and present) are limited to officers who fought in the American War of Independence, and their eldest male descendants of each generation. Employees of the World Bank and other international development agencies might think that the Society of the Cincinnati is among the institutions on earth with the least connection to their work—after all, the society's quirky museum is filled with eighteenth-century battle flags, musty antiques, and rare, expensive collections of toy soldiers acquired by members, some of whom seem to have cultivated a lifelong predilection for a hobby normally associated with small boys. But in one important sense they would be wrong, for one of the most celebrated members of the Society of the Cincinnati was also the intellectual and spiritual godfa-

---

* A fascinating aspect of Newton's tenure at the Mint was the energy with which he hunted down counterfeiters, setting up networks of informers and spies all over England, visiting, incognito, taverns and quarters infested by thieves to ferret out information. In a single nineteen-month period (June 1698 to Christmas 1699) Newton appeared in 123 separate days at the Mint to interrogate some 200 informers and suspects, many of whom were subsequently executed. (Manuel, *Portrait of Isaac Newton* [see endnote 58], 230.)

ther of modern development, in particular of modern finance capitalism as well as of socialism.[66]

In a life filled with surrealistic escapades, the French count Claude-Henri de Saint-Simon fought as a nineteen-year-old adventurer in the American War of Independence and years later was interred in the same insane asylum as the Marquis de Sade.[67] Henri Saint-Simon's early experience in America inspired his life's mission—to work for the improvement of humankind.[68] Material, industrial production, and technology would be the means to accomplish this improvement, and indeed, in the system of Saint-Simon these things became synonymous with it. But the precondition for unleashing technological and productive forces for human betterment was the total reorganization of society.

Saint-Simon saw himself as the transitional figure between the seventeenth-century Enlightenment founders of the modern project, and what he hoped would be its concrete social realization in the nineteenth century. For Saint-Simon, the irradicable will to power in human nature was the key problem of society, the root of war, violence, crime, and discord. But "from this time onward," he declared, "the desire to dominate which is innate in all men has ceased to be pernicious, or at least we can foresee an epoch when it will not be harmful any longer, but will become useful."[69] Descartes and Bacon pointed the way to the solution, and "the development of action against nature has changed the direction of this sentiment by leveling it against objects. The desire to command man has slowly transformed itself into the desire to make and remake nature in accordance with our will."[70]

Saint-Simon and his followers envisaged a society reorganized to channel human aggression into massive development projects and incessant industrial growth. "Tout pour l'industrie, tout par elle" was their motto; this might be (very loosely) translated into 1990s terms as "Everything should be devoted to growth, and everything will be obtained through growth." They envisaged government as applied economics; politics would be replaced by technocratic, instrumental reason, by the "science of production."[71] According to his followers,* the key to this transformation would be the organization of all material activity in society through a "unitary and directing bank" that would be the ultimate planning and economic authority, "represent . . . the government in the material order," and "be the depository of all the riches, of the total fund of production, and of all the instruments of work."** The unitary bank would

* Who set out the Saint-Simonian system in a series of lectures between 1828 and 1830, published as *The Doctrine of Saint-Simon: An Exposition* (see endnote 72).
** According to Manuel, the "unitary bank" would be supplied with credit equal to what

oversee a "general system of banks" and credit institutions which would ascertain and be responsive to localized production needs in the economy.[72] Historian Frank Manuel characterized the new society as the "utopia of finance capital."[73]

Saint-Simon was arguably the first international development planner. Following the conclusion of the American Revolutionary War in 1783, the young count traveled to Mexico, where he tried unsuccessfully to convince the Spanish vice roy to invest in a plan for the construction of a canal across the Isthmus of Panama. In 1787 he surfaced in Spain, attracted by rumors that the Spanish government was committed to building a gigantic (for the times) canal to link Madrid to the sea. He landed a job consulting with the Spanish king's financial advisor and chief architect for the project, and prepared a plan for the mobilization of a work force of 6,000 men—under Saint-Simon's direction. But the French Revolution broke out, and the plan was abandoned.[74] He survived the Terror and prospered during the Directorate, promoted a project for a stagecoach service from Paris to Calais, earned a fortune in real estate speculation, lost it, married, divorced, and ended up in Switzerland in 1802 and 1803.

In 1803 Saint-Simon published *Letters from an Inhabitant of Geneva to His Contemporaries,* which was really addressed to Napoleon, to whom he sent a copy. (Napoleon ignored it.) He suggested that the papacy be replaced by a "Supreme Council of Newton" in which twenty-one eminent men of science and artists would govern the world and assume the moral authority that hitherto rested in the church; society would be "one workshop" whose efforts would be directed by the council.[75]

In this and later works Saint-Simon promoted European unification; he espoused the creation of a "Baconian Society" to further the cause of Anglo-French union, which would be the first stage of the proposed unification and a global industrial system.[76] As a consequence of his thesis on the prevalence of the will to power in human nature, the social equilibrium of the new society would be guaranteed through gigantic internal and international economic development programs:

Without external activity there can be no internal tranquility. The surest method of maintaining peace in the [European] confederation will be ceaselessly to direct its efforts outside of itself and to occupy it without a let-up on great internal pub-

---

the Saint-Simonians called the total annual product of industry, something like today's GNP. Numerous local credit institutions and specialized industrial banks would determine the debit side. "In this bankers' dream world," Manuel concludes, "the [financial] demands of centralized supervision and of local special institutions were delicately balanced—in a way, the contemporary practice, though not the theory, of all highly organized economies" (Manuel, *The Prophets of Paris* [see endnote 73], 177).

lic works. To people the globe with the European race, which is superior to all other races, to open the whole world to travel and to render it as habitable as Europe, that is the enterprise . . . which . . . should continually engage the activity of Europe and always keep up the momentum.[77]

"The fate of the Africans and Asiatics under the religion of Newton," biographer Frank Manuel observes, "would not have been an enviable one."[78]

Later, Saint-Simon replaced Newton with Descartes as the patron saint of his brave new industrial world, perhaps as a reflex of Gallic patriotism during the Napoleonic Wars with Britain. In his *Letters to the Bureau of Longitudes* (another attempt to woo Napoleon), he proposed the erection in Paris of a colossal statue of Descartes with the inscription "Au Fondateur du Systeme du Monde"—To the Founder of the System of the World.[79]

Saint-Simon died in 1825, but by the early 1830s his writings had attracted a large following, and had spawned a journal that was read all over Europe—*Le Globe*. The editors of *Le Globe* extolled huge development schemes such as canals across Panama and Suez, and a political and economic union of Europe and the Near East, linked together by a system of railroads and canals that would be financed by new industrial development banks. (One of the most avid readers of such articles, we recall, was none other than Goethe.)[80] Although Saint-Simon was a proponent of the economic theories of classical liberal political economists like Say and Adam Smith, an important number of his followers concluded that the principal obstacle to the unleashing of his technocratic utopia was the existence of private property and inheritance laws. Thus it was that *Le Globe* invented in February 1832 one of the most fateful neologisms of the modern age—*socialisme*.[81]

The followers of Saint-Simon were no idle theorizers; most fascinating of all is the saga of how they attempted to put their ideas into practice—in some cases, successfully. Barthélemy-Prosper Enfantin is perhaps the most interesting. He coedited *Le Globe* with Saint-Amand Bazard, and in 1833, after a year's imprisonment (French authorities feared the subversive effect of the new "socialist" turn of *Le Globe* on restive urban workers), traveled to Egypt.* With two of his followers who were engineers, he tried to con-

---

* Other aspects of Enfantin's career would make an interesting subject for an historical novel. He tried to convert the Saint-Simonian movement into something resembling what today would be called a New Age cult; he promoted a kind of utopian, pantheistic religion (based on Saint-Simon's vision of the new epoch that would arrive when his ideas were put into practice); he advocated free love and the abolition of marriage; he established himself as the "Father" of the cult of "apostle" followers, and contemplated the publication of a Saint-Simonian bible of texts from the master, as well as the construction of a Saint-Simonian temple to be built of iron. (Markham, introduction to Saint-Simon, *Selected Writings* [see endnote 65], xxxvii–xxxix.)

vince the sultan, Mehemet Ali, to undertake several gargantuan projects—a dam on the Nile, a railroad from Cairo to Suez, and, of course, the Suez canal. The sultan liked the idea of the dam, and Enfantin and his associates worked on it through 1836. Enfantin's approach was more like that of an idealistic Peace Corps worker than that of a World Bank consultant: he refused to work for money, and he and his colleagues insisted on living and eating with the native workers. "We are not like the British engineers who ask for millions of pounds," he wrote, "we live like workers. This great enterprise, of a truly universal nature, must be the work of enthusiasm and devotion."[82]

Outbreaks of fever and disease plagued the work camp, and the Nile dam had to be abandoned. But the ill-fated mission left its mark in an area that today would be called "institution building": several of the Saint-Simonians stayed in Egypt to engineer highways, found the Polytechnique (engineering) School in Cairo, head the Artillery School, and direct the School of Medicine.[83]

Indeed, many of the Saint-Simonians were engineers, graduates of the École Polytechnique in Paris, as well as chemists, geologists, and financiers. In the history of European development their influence was immense, particularly with respect to railroads and banking. The Saint-Simonians Émile and Isaac Pereire founded the first railway in France (from Paris to Saint-Germain in 1835) and, with other Saint-Simonian bankers and engineers, promoted and financed the construction of railroads during the Second Empire in Switzerland, Italy, Spain, Hungary, Austria, and Russia. The Pereire brothers founded the first modern industrial development bank, the Crédit Mobilier, in 1852, which, according to economist Frederick Hayek, was the catalyst and the model for modern Continental capitalism.

The goal of the Pereire brothers, Hayek maintains, was to create an institution along the lines of the "unitary bank" the Saint-Simonians first proposed in 1832. It would be not just a financial institution, but also a center for development planning and control, "a center of administration . . . which was to direct according to a coherent program the railway systems, the town planning activities and the various public utilities and other industries," industries the Pereires attempted to manage and dominate through mergers linked to the bank.[84] In Germany, Holland, Austria, Switzerland, Italy, and Spain, similar development banks, modeled after the Crédit Mobilier, were founded either by the Pereires and their financial allies, or by bankers inspired by their example.[85]

Enfantin went on to promote business undertakings in the new French colony of Algeria, tried unsuccessfully to revive the idea of a Suez canal, and played a key role in organizing and managing the French railway system until his death in 1864. At the end of his life he reflected that the disciples of Saint-Simon had "covered the earth with a network of railways, gold, silver, and electricity."[86] Even the proposed Suez Canal was eventually crowned with success; the project was completed in 1869 by Ferdinand de Lesseps, who was the French vice-consul in Alexandria during Enfantin's stay. It had been Enfantin's dream that at the ceremonies opening the canal a monument would be dedicated with the inscription "To Humanity, the sons of Saint-Simon."[87]

The Saint-Simonians preceded the "development crusaders" of the 1950s and 1960s (to use Walt Rostow's term) by more than a century. But more than one historian has observed that even in the latter half of the twentieth century, Saint-Simon and his followers were the spiritual forebears of the "technocratic faith" (or, if one prefers, "modernization ideals") of many of the leaders and governments of developing countries.[88]* In the nineteenth century they had an enormous influence on the leaders of new nationalisms—on Alexander Herzen and many other of the Russian intelligentsia in the 1860s and 1870s, for example, and on Garibaldi and the Young Italian movement.[89] After all, the allure of the Saint-Simonians for many nationalist politicians and intellectuals was the promise of power and faith in the future. In the newly independent countries of South America, the Saint-Simonians exerted a strong attraction, providing an apparently rational faith in scientific and material progress as an alternative to Catholicism.

The influence in Latin America of Auguste Comte, Saint-Simon's personal secretary between 1818 and 1823, was particularly strong. Comte embodied the right wing of the evolution of Saint-Simonism, holding private property sacrosanct. He elaborated a systematic (and authoritarian) philosophy of history, society, and politics, in which humanity evolved in three stages, the final, modern phase being the "positivist" epoch, in which empirical science and rationally organized labor are the goal and content of human existence. The new, scientifically organized society would require a new religion—the "religion of humanity," whose object of worship was the "Great Being," the abstract embodiment of reason in history, in some respects a Gallicized version of Hegelian *Geist*.[90] The motto of the religion of humanity, and of the positivist epoch of history would be "Order and Progress."

* The Saint-Simonian flavor of their technocratic faith was particularly unbounded in the first generation. Nassar proclaimed that after the construction of the Aswan dam, Egypt "would be a paradise"; for Nehru, India's gigantic dams were its "modern temples"; and Nkrumah, the first leader of independent Ghana in 1958, declared that the giant Volta River dam (financed by the World Bank) would herald a new era in which "Ghanians would cease being hewers of wood and drawers of water for the west" (Vivanathan, "On the Annals of the Laboratory State," in Nandy, ed., *Science, Hegemony and Violence* [see endnote 41], 279).

In the center of the Brazilian flag is a blue sphere with the stars of the Southern Hemisphere; circling it is a white banner, with the Portuguese words *Ordem e Progresso*—Order and Progress. Comte's philosophy became in the 1860s the official ideology of the newly independent Brazilian state.[91]

Before we leave Saint-Simon and his disciples, we might reflect that they personified—and consciously saw themselves as carrying out—the realization of modernity as development, a project that began with Descartes and Bacon, and which continues. Arguably, Saint-Simon, through his writings and above all through his followers, played as pivotal a role as any single individual in the early evolution of both modern capitalism and socialism. There was a more troubled side to his vision, however, since all through his life he suffered from recurrent symptoms of paranoia and megalomania. Following his release from the asylum at Charenton (the Marquis de Sade remained), he wrote his nephew that "insanity . . . is nothing but an extreme exaltation, and this extreme exaltation is necessary for the achievement of great things."[92]

The Paradoxes of Modernity Triumphant

> This order is now bound to the technical and economic
> conditions of machine production which today deter-
> mine the lives of all the individuals who are born into
> this mechanism, not only those directly concerned with
> economic acquisition, with irresistible force. Perhaps it
> will so determine them until the last ton of fossilized
> coal is burnt.[93]   —Max Weber, *The Protestant Ethic*
> *and the Spirit of Capitalism*

Although modernity had its origins in the seventeenth century, the practical, worldwide social and economic transformations it entailed only began to be fully realized two centuries later.* Its nineteenth-century embodiments were not only Saint-Simonian exuberance and the expansion of railroads, canals, and banks, but the first truly global world fairs, beginning with the Great London Exhibition of 1851, held in the Crystal Palace. The most vigorous proponent of the exhibition was Prince Albert, Queen Victoria's husband. In a speech shortly before its opening, he explained,

* Development is, as one Dutch sociologist put it, "after all nothing but the Enlightenment applied or modernization operationalized" (Jan Nederveen Pieterse, "Emancipations, Modern and Postmodern," *Development and Change*, vol. 23, no. 3 [July 1992], 5, 23).

We are living at a period of most wonderful transition, which tends rapidly to accomplish that great end to which indeed all history points—*the realization of the unity of mankind. . . .* On the other hand, *the great principle of the division of labor,* which may be called the moving power of civilization, is being extended to all branches of science, industry and art. . . . Gentlemen, the Exhibition of 1851 is to give us a living picture of the point of development at which the whole of mankind has arrived in this great task, and a new starting-point from which all nations will be able to direct their further exertions. [Emphasis is in text.][94]

Before, human evolution and history had consisted of many parallel, differing "narratives," with different origins based on different ways of conceiving and ordering the world—indeed, different worlds coexisting on one earth. The plurality of human societies, communities, and worlds mirrored and were in part based on the diversity and autonomy of the myriad ecosystems of the earth. There were as many "natures" and "futures" as there were different human societies with different pasts rooted in different local ecological contexts. The Crystal Palace was a particularly timely and symbolic embodiment of the global triumph of one narrative, one history, and one future from that time onward. From the mid-nineteenth century, various versions of capitalism and socialism were competing global programs to realize the same modern project.

A fundamental paradox of the modern project was already apparent in the contradiction between the noble goals of Bacon's writings and the sordid betrayals and subversion of freedom that characterized his political career. The empire of man over things was from the beginning rooted in a will to power and domination, and in historical fact entailed the empire of some men over other men—and women—and of Western societies over all others. A collective will to power was not a new thing in history, but societies in past ages had been limited by the absence of the will and the method to transform all of nature for their ends.

The liberation of the individual and society from previous constraints left the world and society as empty fields for new, more total forms of control through instrumental reason. As C. S. Lewis observed, "We reduce things to mere Nature *in order that* we may 'conquer' them. We are always conquering nature because 'Nature' is the name for what we have, to some extent, conquered." [Emphasis in original.][95] If humans choose to view and act on the world and themselves as raw material, as something else to be transformed, administered and/or exchanged—they eventually become raw material.[96] Ultimately, not only the freedom of individuals, groups, and whole societies may be threatened, but their physical survival, not to speak of the ecological foundations of life.

And so it was that when Dostoyevsky visited the Crystal Palace in

222 • MORTGAGING THE EARTH

1862* he wrote of his amazement and dread at what the Exhibition portended:

You feel the terrible force which has brought these innumerable people, who have come from all ends of the earth, all together in one fold; you realize the grandeur of the idea . . . and you feel nervous. However great your independence of mind, a feeling of fear somehow creeps over you. . . . You feel that a rich and ancient tradition of denial and protest is needed in order not to yield . . . not to bow down in worship of fact, and not to idolize Baal. . . . If you had seen how proud the mighty spirit is which created that colossal decor and how convinced it is of its victory and its triumph, you would have shuddered at its pride, its obstinacy, its blindness, and you would have shuddered, too, at the thought of those over whom that proud spirit hovers and reigns supreme.[97]

Forty years after Dostoyevsky, Max Weber analyzed what was at work in this proud, blind spirit. For Weber, we recall, pervasive rationalization and bureaucratization characterized the evolution of modern development in both the private and public sectors. "Bureaucratic administration," Weber wrote, "means fundamentally domination through knowledge. This is the feature of it which makes it specifically rational."[98]

Weber saw that formal rationality within an organization—its thrust toward greater calculability, effectiveness, and control—becomes more important than the variety of substantive values and ends the organization can serve. It replaces traditional ethics with instrumental calculation, with technical competence in performing a limited function in the organization's chain of command. Indeed, formal rationality tends to become a value in itself—though one that is fundamentally nihilistic, since it lacks any fixed content. The last step is the subordination of substantive values to formal rationality—bureaucracy choosing and subverting the values and ends it might serve in light of the functional efficiency that they further in the organization.[99]

All of this we have come to think of as classic, though disquieting, characteristics in the behavior of large bureaucracies. One might recall, for example, that the World Bank calls in its ethics officer to deal with (among other things) the consequences for the organization of staff leaking documents, rather than to hold them accountable for the horrendous, often foreseeable, environmental and social consequences of specific projects. One might also note how the Bank over its nearly five decades of existence quickly proved unsuited for the ends of European reconstruction and proceeded to serve radically different notions of the word "development," adeptly redefining its mission to tack with the blowing political winds—from poverty alleviation under McNamara, to an about face to

---

* After 1851 the Crystal Palace was taken down and reassembled in another part of London, and the exhibition continued on a semi-permanent basis for years.

squeeze the poor to pay their debts in adjustment lending under his successor Clausen, to global environmental management or "sustainable development" in the 1990s.

One might argue that the global environment is an attractive new area for the Bank because it conveniently fits into the formal logic of its institutional needs. Global environmental management is an untapped theme for new projects, and thus can help the Bank deal with its perennial lack of quality project proposals. It is also an area for which industrialized nations are willing to contribute funds for grants, and thus provides an opportunity for the Bank to help reduce the threat of growing net negative transfers to its developing members.

For Weber, the rationalization of the world that made possible this "tremendous cosmos of the modern economic order" was also "an iron cage" that threatened human liberty.* "Material goods," he wrote in 1901, "have gained an increasing and finally an inexorable power over the lives of men as at no previous period in history."[100] However, he also offered an analysis of how bureaucratic threats to freedom might be forestalled. For one thing, he believed that the existence of rival bureaucracies and the divergence of interests between organizations in the private and public sectors meant that they checked and limited one another, creating some space for freedom. The true nightmare would occur, he wrote in 1906, with "the abolition of private capitalism," which "would simply mean that also the *top management* of the nationalized or socialized enterprises would become bureaucrats . . . merged in a single hierarchy."[101]

Weber noted that since bureaucracy's power is rooted in knowledge and information, the most critical safeguard of all lay in the liberation of information. Without freedom of access to information no supervision or control of a bureaucratic organization would be possible. This could best be accomplished through systematic, far-reaching powers of parliamentary investigation. The "mere existence" of the "parliamentary whip of inquiry," he hoped, "will force the administrative chiefs to account for their actions in such a way as to make its use unnecessary. . . . Only the committees of a powerful parliament can be the vehicle for exercising this wholesome pedagogic influence. Ultimately, the bureaucracy can only gain by such a development."[102]

The power of bureaucratic information, Weber elaborated, has two aspects to it: first, technical, specialized expertise and know-how; second, the organization of critical knowledge as "official information" held confi-

* "How will democracy even in [a] . . . limited sense be *at all possible*?" "How," he asked, "can one possibly save *any remnants* of 'individualist' freedom in any sense?" (Weber, *Economy and Society* [see endnote 98], vol. 2, 1403).

dentially with the organization, "only available through administrative channels and which provides him [the bureaucrat] with the facts on which he can base his actions." The way to challenge the misuse of technical knowledge, or the misuse of administrative power under the guise of a technical decision, is through "systematic cross-examination (under oath) of experts before a parliamentary commission in the presence of the respective departmental officials." Weber noted that the German Reichstag did not have this power, and therefore was condemned to "amateurish ignorance."[103] Most critical of all to the supervision of bureaucracy, Weber noted, is the abolition of the "official secret" or "confidential information," the freeing of access to administrative information "independently of the officials' good will."[104]

Obviously, the implications of Weber's analysis extend to many other modern bureaucracies. One cannot help but reflect that in practice the World Bank's Board of Executive Directors has hardly shown more capacity and will to supervise the bureaucracy for which it is responsible than Max Weber's impotent and ignorant German Reichstag of nearly a century ago.

However, when developing countries started borrowing from the World Bank for huge projects to realize the "ideals of modernization," their leaders and their lenders were certainly not thinking of Max Weber's gloomy warnings. Rather, many of them dreamt of replicating the Tennessee Valley Authority, the Bonneville Power Administration, the great highways and public works of American cities, and other great public projects of the world's most powerful and economically successful nation.

The Politics of Technocracy

If the end doesn't justify the means, what does?[105]
—Robert Moses

It is December 4, 1952, the beginning of winter in one of the larger cities of the world. One thousand five hundred thirty households—perhaps five or six thousand people—receive letters telling them they have ninety days to move before the government proceeds with demolition of their apartment buildings to make room for a giant highway. They are terrified, they think they have no recourse, they do not know where they will go.[106]

Their fear is all too well founded: they soon learn that nearby are thousands of displaced people who have already been ousted from their homes, long since demolished, for the same highway. The government agencies had promised them they would be relocated into comfortable, equivalent housing, that they would receive cash compensation for their losses and moving expenses. But for six years no housing has been found for many of them. Living literally out of suitcases, whole families have been shunted from one temporary dwelling to another, to apartments that also were in the path of the great highway, and which in turn had to be demolished. Some have been forcibly resettled five or six times in as many years, with no final home in sight.

Those who have already been relocated describe some of the apartments the government provided as "hovels," "not fit for rats," with no heat, and broken windows, half abandoned; the lobbies of the buildings are littered with trash and excrement, animal and human; outside are rubble, clouds of dust, and the ceaseless racket of bulldozers, demolition workers, and construction teams. Sometimes the displaced families had spent only weeks in such an apartment before the government moved them to another. Worst of all, each time they moved the rent went up 15 percent, and many of them were paying more for tiny, dilapidated slum lodgings than what they had once paid for decent, two-bedroom apartments. Old people had refused to move and had been forcibly evicted.[107]

Woe to those who resisted, believing that the country's laws or municipal agency policies entitled them to better treatment. The families that had refused to move—not willing to be dispossessed, or hoping for more equitable compensation—had been notified that if they did not leave by a given deadline, the amount of funds for moving expenses would be halved; if they still remained after the next deadline, the moving indemnification would be reduced again.[108]

On this winter day in 1952, the five or six thousand people who are about to be resettled lack critical information: they do not know, and will never find out from the authorities who are trying to remove them, that the government has not yet acquired the land, nor obtained the money to build the stretch of highway in question. If everything goes without a hitch, it will take at least a year and a half before demolition can begin. The letter is in part a bluff, a shameless effort, as one official explained, "[to] shake 'em up a little and get 'em moving."[109]

The five or six thousand are among 60,000 who will be forcibly removed for the construction of a seven-mile highway; they are among an estimated 320,000 people who were to be involuntarily displaced for gigantic development schemes, many, if not most, without adequate notice or compensation, between 1946 and 1956. Perhaps half a million since the 1930s. The hardship is particularly great because the resettlement takes place within a city, and most of the displaced are either poor or of very modest means, and are members of ethnic minorities in a larger national society.[110]

Was this city perchance in northern India—Delhi perhaps, with its chilly winter days? Was the developer a Third World bureaucracy in a country with an authoritarian government and a nontropical climate— maybe Buenos Aires? Or the Soviet Union?

No, it was New York, and the developer Robert Moses. The highway was the Cross-Bronx Expressway, finally completed in the 1960s.

The career of Robert Moses, and the autonomous public works empire he created in the state and city of New York from the 1930s through the 1960s, is a case study in the politics of twentieth-century technocracy. Robert Moses, his Pulitzer Prize biographer Robert Caro wrote, "was America's greatest builder. He was the shaper of the greatest city in the world."[111] Indeed, according to Lewis Mumford, "in the twentieth century, the influence of Robert Moses on the cities of America was greater than of any other person."[112]

There are some uncanny analogies and parallels between Robert Moses's empire and that of the World Bank. The foundations of Moses's power were lack of political and financial accountability, and the control and withholding of information. In particular, the Moses empire was based on the establishment of numerous independent "public authorities"—autonomous development agencies that generated their own revenues. Thanks to ingenious and deceptively inconspicuous legal innovations pushed through by Moses, these public authorities became, in Robert Caro's words, a virtual "fourth branch" of government, unaccountable to elected officials.[113] They included the Triborough Bridge and Tunnel Authority, the Henry Hudson Parkway Authority, several park commissions, and the New York State Power Authority, which collected and administered revenues from hydroelectric dams on the Niagara and Saint Lawrence rivers.

Before Moses, a "public authority" had a limited duration and powers: generally it was established to issue bonds, construct a specific project such as a bridge or tunnel, and then would go out of existence once the bonds were paid off with revenue from the project (say, bridge or tunnel tolls over a limited period). The legal innovations that Moses achieved created public agencies under his control with indefinite lifespans, and permitted him to use their continuous flows of revenue for activities other than simply retiring the bonds; he was freed from the need to go to the city or the state for appropriations. Moreover, the powers of a public agency were established in its bond covenants, which courts had ruled were private contracts, untouchable and unalterable by any government or legislature in the land.

Most important of all, Robert Caro observed, "the official records of most public agencies are public records, but not those of public authorities, since courts have held that they may be regarded as the records of private corporations, closed to scrutiny by the interested citizen or reporter."[114] Such public authorities achieved the powers of a "sovereign state," with their own, unappealable governing rules and laws, as well as the power of eminent domain.[115] At the peak of the Moses empire, in 1960, the lands administered by Moses-dominated public authorities totaled 161 square miles (equivalent to half the area of New York City), and controlled $213 million annually, over a billion 1993 dollars.[116]

One cannot help but see uncanny analogies with the World Bank's crucial role in promoting the creation of numerous independent, autonomous project authorities in the developing world—the Electrical Generating Authority of Thailand (EGAT), and the National Thermal Power Corporation (NTPC) of India, for example. Through the decades, as we have seen, the creation of these agencies has been one of the World Bank's most important strategies. These agencies often were not subject to the normal legislative and judicial scrutiny of their countries, operated according to their own charters and rules (frequently drafted in response to Bank suggestions), and were often staffed with rising technocrats sympathetic, even beholden, to the Bank. In New York, the Moses-controlled public authorities provided him with a steady stream of independent revenues as well as with the means to physically develop and transform the city without the bothersome procedures of democratic review and discussion of alternatives. He staffed the public authorities with his own, handpicked protégés, bright engineers and lawyers often grateful for the opportunity he gave them to exercise power and advance their careers at a young age. For the Bank, the worldwide promotion of independent project and development agencies served similar goals: it created a steady, reliable source of what the Bank needed most—bankable loan proposals—as well as critical power bases within nations to transform and influence the direction of their economic and social development. Last, but not least, hundreds of thousands of people—mostly poor and disadvantaged—were in the way of Moses and the Bank, and were forcibly resettled.

One should not forget either that the ostensible goal of the Moses empire, as of the Bank's, was the public welfare, to be realized through major development projects in an economically efficient, technically proficient way, insulated from the corrupting influence of politics. According to Robert Caro, the public—including journalists and academics—believed this myth about the Moses project authorities for decades, and even those skeptics who were disposed to test its truth had no facts with which to make the case, because the records of the Triborough [the public authority from which Moses ruled his empire] were so effectively sealed. If, however, they had been able to see the records . . . they would have learned that the legend was a gigantic hoax.

Prudent, efficient, economical? So incredibly wasteful was Moses of the money he tolled from the public in quarters and dimes that on a single bridge alone he paid $40,000,000 more in interest than he had to. . . . Covert "loans" made to [the Moses public] authorities by the state—loans designed never to be repaid—ran into the hundreds of millions of dollars. . . . The cost of taxpayer-financed toll roads leading to [public] authority facilities ran into the billions.[117]

Caro declares that the final big lie of the Moses technocratic empire was its purported separation from politics. "Had the records of the [public authorities] been open," he concludes, it would have been clear that above all they were a giant—if unconventional and, compared with their predecessors, more refined—political machine, "oiled by the lubricant of political machines: money."[118]

To get what they wanted from Robert Moses, Bronx politicians of the 1950s had considerably less to bargain with (and more limited ambitions) than many a developing country's politicians, generals, and ministers. If one considers the World Bank–financed economic and environmental debacles of the 1980s, and the nature of the regimes it was negotiating with, one can only imagine what kinds of discreet, unwritten understandings could have helped to determine the alternatives considered and choices made.

The Moses approach to development was no exception for the time—on the contrary, it was a kind of apotheosis. On a national scale, similar tactics and myths characterized the massive hydroelectric, irrigation, and flood-control dams of the Federal Bureau of Reclamation and the Army Corps of Engineers.* The Bureau of Reclamation was created by the Reclamation Act of 1902, its principal mandate being the construction of irrigation dams and canals to promote agricultural development in the arid Western states. But already by the 1930s, according to Michael Robinson, the Bureau's "semi-official historian,"[119]

the high cost of projects made it increasingly difficult for Reclamation engineers to meet economic feasibility requirements. In the early 1940s, the Bureau devised the plan of considering an entire river basin as an integrated project. It enabled the agency to derive income from various revenue producing subfeatures (notably power facilities) to fund other works not economically feasible under Reclamation law.[120]

* The whole epic tale of the economic profligacy and environmental waste propagated by these two agencies is set out in Marc Reisner's *Cadillac Desert* (see endnote 119).

So it was, according to environmental researcher and writer Marc Reisner, that "river basin accounting" gave the Reclamation Bureau a license to build uneconomic schemes. In fact, it also gave the Bureau an actual incentive to find "bad," economically profligate projects so long as a site for a hydroelectric dam could be found on the same river.[121] One can see in such creative economic accounting the ancestor of World Bank project appraisal techniques, which in the hands of Bank staff under pressure to lend miraculously produced the required double-digit annual rates of projected economic return for one economic debacle after the other. Indeed, a somewhat analogous approach to the Reclamation Bureau's was used by the Bank in its appraisal of the India Sardar Sarovar dam in 1985: for the Indian government the chief purpose of the dam was irrigation and water supply, but the Bank could not justify the scheme economically on the basis of its estimated irrigation benefits alone, and came up with a 12 percent "estimated rate of return" in the project appraisal based mainly on the dam's power benefits.[122]

The Bureau's main rival was the Army Corps of Engineers, whose turf in the dam building area was supposedly projects concerning flood control and navigation. But these proved to be artificial distinctions, since it can be argued that many irrigation dams enhance flood control and vice versa. Here, Reisner notes, the Corps had a powerful economic advantage in peddling some of its projects: "If the Corps of Engineers builds the dam, and calls it a flood-control dam, the [irrigation] water is free."[123] Thus the Corps beat out the Bureau of Reclamation in building two major irrigation schemes on the Kings and Kern rivers in California in the 1940s, projects that provided free water to land belonging to some of richest private farmers not only in the United States, but in the entire world.[124] Not to be outdone, the Bureau succeeded in pushing through the Garrison Diversion project on the upper Missouri River in the mid-1980s; it irrigated 130,000 acres of mainly; surplus, government-subsidized crops at a cost of $1.65 million per farm.[125]

In some cases, North American Indians hardly fared better under the Corps of Engineers than Amazonian tribes ravaged by World Bank–financed roads and dams. The Garrison dam (which provided the water for the Bureau's reclamation scheme, mentioned above) is a case in point. Since the time of Lewis and Clark, Reisner recounts, the Mandan, the Hidatsa, and the Arikara had lived on the rich bottomlands along the upper Missouri in North Dakota. They raised cattle, and even the Bureau of Reclamation recommended that no dam should ever flood this territory, since it was the best place for winter grazing in the entire state.[126] In the mid-1940s the three tribes passed a resolution that was a desperate plea:

We have kept our side of all treaties. We have been, and now are, as nearly self-suf-ficient as the average white community. . . . But we cannot agree that we should be destroyed, drowned out, removed, and divided for the public benefit while all other white communities are protected and safe-guarded by the same River development plan.[127]

They tried to compromise; when they saw that the dam probably would be built they asked for equitable compensation—an equivalent amount of land, electricity to run irrigation pumps to improve the land, rights to graze their cattle on the edge of the reservoir, and mineral and timber rights. Their requests would have fitted admirably within the World Bank's resettlement policy—they simply wanted enough resources to give them a chance of being no worse off than before. But the U.S. Congress followed the recommendations of a particularly vindictive Colonel Pick of the Corps, condemning the three tribes to slow social disintegration and economic destitution. They were not permitted to have access to the reservoir for grazing or fishing, they were not allowed to purchase electricity at cost to improve any new land, they were not allowed to harvest the trees that would be drowned by the reservoir, and they received cash compensation for their land ($33 an acre) with a special congressional proviso that none of the money could be used to hire lawyers to appeal the settlement.[128]

Altogether the Corps built six dams along the Missouri from the late 1940s on, at a cost of $1.2 billion, which would probably total at least 6 billion 1993 dollars. The main economic justification was flood control and navigation; according to Reisner, the flood-control benefits are limited, and the navigation increases projected by the Corps never materialized. On the other hand, in addition to the shameful mistreatment of the three tribes, some of the best winter grazing land and waterfowl habitat in North America vanished forever.[129] One can sympathize with former U.S. Secretary of the Interior Harold Ickes, when he excoriated the Army Corps of Engineers in 1951 as "a willful and expensive . . . self-serving clique . . . in contempt of the public welfare" that "wantonly wasted money on worthless projects" that served "land monopolies," in short, a "lawless and irresponsible group. . . . It is truly beyond imagination."[130]

The classic pork-barrel politics behind big water projects has similarities all over the world, whether it be the United States or Brazil or India. Though such projects are economically inefficient, as well as environmentally and socially destructive (for powerless minorities who are in the way), some local interests gain huge windfalls. These include the construction contractors, some farmers (most often the already more influential and prosperous ones) who receive free or inexpensive water, and local businessmen and merchants who enjoy a temporary boom during the construction period. To cement it all together, the interests and influence of the local, national (and international) bureaucrats and politicians involved are reciprocally enhanced.[131]

In more recent years, both the Army Corps of Engineers and the Bureau of Reclamation have shifted their dam-building expertise outside the United States as technical advisors to the United States Agency for International Development (U.S.A.I.D.)—and to the World Bank. In fact, Bureau of Reclamation engineers participated in the appraisal of the Narmada Sardar Sarovar dam, as well as in studies and technical assistance for irrigation projects in Brazil's São Francisco River Valley, and for other water projects in a half dozen other countries, from Egypt to China.

While continuing to promote big projects outside the United States, the Bureau claims that its role has shifted from developing big projects to "resource management,"[132] and the Corps asserts it has embraced the concepts of "sustainable development" and "green engineering,"[133] including trying to undo, at great expense, some of the ecological harm of earlier interventions.* Needless to say, these belated affirmations of environmental values may be rooted in something else besides conviction, or even politics: there are simply very few rivers left in the United States with attractive sites for big dams where the Reclamation Bureau or the Corps have not already been at work.

Of all the great development models of twentieth-century America, none was as influential in the developing countries as the Tennessee Valley Authority (TVA). Established in 1933 as one of the top priorities of the incoming Roosevelt administration, TVA was nothing less than the first modern, large-scale effort in the world to plan and finance integrated regional development. Visiting TVA in 1946, journalist John Gunther called it "the greatest development in large scale social planning ever undertaken," as well as "quite possibly . . . the greatest single American invention of this century, the biggest contribution the United States has . . . made to society in the modern world."[134]

TVA was the culmination of decades of efforts by American progressives and conservationists.** They sought to promote economic growth and conservation of natural resources by taking management of water and electric power out of the hands of monopolistic private utilities and

---

* In the words of Lt. Gen. Henry J. Hatch, commander of the Army Corps of Engineers, the proposed, enormously costly "unstraightening" of the Kissimmee River in Florida to save Lake Okeechobee and the entire water table of South Florida from the ecological threats caused by earlier Corps projects that straightened and canalized the same river is "a terrific case study" of the Corp's new approach. (Lt. Gen. Henry J. Hatch, in "Green Engineering and National Security" [see endnote 133], 43.)
** According to Tennessean William Chandler, author of *The Myth of TVA* (see endnote 135), on which I rely heavily in this discussion.

putting it in the hands of government agencies that would serve the people. The fact that conservation and reforestation were part of TVA's mandate, along with power generation, flood control, navigation, and agricultural extension and development, makes it appear in some respects uncannily ahead of its times.

TVA at first sight had many of the virtues (and dangers) of the public authorities promoted by Moses, but without the corrupting influences of big-city political patronage. The TVA area of influence covers the watershed and basin of the Tennessee River—nearly all of Tennessee, plus parts of six adjacent states. Almost all administrative power is concentrated in three directors appointed by the U.S. president for nine-year terms. This power was unprecedented: the TVA directors chose all projects, set electric rates, and made all other decisions without effective oversight or review on the part of Congress or the federal government. Congress, which at least in theory had to authorize and appropriate funds for each of the individual projects of the Bureau of Reclamation and the Army Corps of Engineers, gave up this power for TVA. Remaining congressional control, through annual lump-sum appropriations for the Authority, was mostly phased out in 1959 when the TVA Act was amended to make the system self-financing. From then on the Authority was to use its revenues from power generation to cover operating costs, and it was authorized to raise new capital by issuing bonds, which would not be guaranteed, however, by the U.S. Treasury.[135] It was truly a law unto itself.

The physical impact of TVA was immense: it constructed twenty-one dams, promoted rural electrification, created an inland navigation system, and introduced modern, fertilizer- and pesticide-intensive agriculture as well as soil conservation and reforestation measures into what had been one of the most backward rural regions of the United States. Power from TVA fueled secret government laboratories at Oak Ridge in the early 1940s, helping to build the atom bomb. In the 1950s and 1960s, it continued its electric power expansion through the construction of coal-fired plants, and embarked on an ambitious program to build seventeen nuclear generating facilities.

The received wisdom on TVA appeared to be unchallengeable when journalist John Gunther visited it shortly after World War II. The TVA region had grown economically more rapidly than the rest of the United States,* and even the opponents of TVA estimated that supporters outnumbered critics twenty to one.[136] TVA was such a success, its many pro-

---

* Gunther notes that per capita income was up 75 percent from 1933 to 1946, as opposed to 56 percent in the rest of the country; wages up 57 percent, as opposed to 47 percent; and value of manufactured products up 68 percent in contrast to 54 percent elsewhere. (Gunther, *Inside U.S.A.* [see endnote 134], 738.)

ponents proclaimed, because it took economic development out of the hands of politicians and let it be guided by autonomous, highly trained, dedicated technocrats and civil servants whose ethos was emblazoned on a tablet conspicuously visible on every one of its projects: "Built for the People of the United States."[137]

The Authority's international influence was also immense: by the 1960s thousands of engineers, politicians, and planners from around the world had visited it, and TVA directly inspired gigantic river-basin development schemes from Brazil to India,* not a few of them partly financed by the World Bank and other international aid agencies.[138] David Lilienthal, one of TVA's most able directors, was prescient: writing in the 1940s, he saw international economic development as "the dominant political fact of the generation that lies ahead" and "the central fact with which statesmanship tomorrow must contend."[139]

But by the late 1970s there were second thoughts. The same autonomous, technocratic power that TVA enthusiasts assumed would automatically realize the goals of economic efficiency, environmental conservation, and enhancement of public welfare seemed instead to be the power to waste huge capital investments in inefficient schemes without market controls or discipline, to displace poor farmers for projects that benefited the already prosperous, to become the single biggest violator of the Clean Air Act, and to despoil huge areas through strip mining to provide coal for thermal power plants that were not needed.

Much of the initial information and statistics trumpeting TVA's successes was generated by its own management and public affairs department.[140] TVA scholar William Chandler demolishes the myth piece by piece. While it is true that the TVA region grew considerably more rapidly economically than the average for the United States from TVA's founding through the 1950s, other adjacent non-TVA areas in the South starting at the same below-average economic level in the early 1930s grew more rapidly. Indeed, improvements in various other social welfare indicators in adjacent areas also exceeded those of the TVA region. Not only per capita income, but manufacturing employment, rural electrification, installation of running water and of electric home appliances all advanced at a superior rate in surrounding, non-TVA counties and states.[141] Chandler analyzes the twenty-one dams that TVA built, and concludes that twelve were economically unjustified even without looking at the demand-side, energy conservation alternatives—"low-sulfur, coal fired power would have been much cheaper."[142] Chandler's hypothesis for the better economic record of similar, non-TVA areas appears plausible: TVA channeled huge amounts of the

* These include the Damodar Valley Corporation in India, the São Francisco Valley Commission in Brazil, and the Cauca Valley Corporation in Columbia.

region's financial and human capital into sub-optimal investments, and as a result the Tennessee Valley region incurred large opportunity costs.[143]*

To supply the coal-fired plants TVA did operate, it promoted environmental devastation through the strip mining of coal in the 1950s and 1960s. In the early 1970s, TVA fought federal attempts to enact environmental controls on strip mining, such as banning mining on slopes of greater than 20 degrees. TVA's New Deal optimism degenerated in practice to statements like the following one made by Aubrey Wagner, TVA's chairman for nearly twenty-five years: "Strip mining looks like the devil, but . . . if you look at what these mountains were doing before this stripping, they were just growing trees that were not even being harvested."[144]

Finally, although TVA started during the Great Depression with a progressive bias towards helping the poor in one of the poorest regions of the United States, critics contended that the economic benefits of TVA tended to accrue to better-off farmers and commercial interests** rather than to sharecroppers and small landholders.[145] Forced resettlement was another aspect of TVA's fondness for dams: some 50,000 people were either displaced or had their livelihoods disrupted because of TVA projects, and most of them were poor. In just one area, the Norris River basin, upstream of Chattanooga, a total of 3,000 families, or 15,000 people, were flooded out. Ninety-six of these families physically resisted attempts to move them and had to be forcibly evicted.[146] The single most important justification for the entire TVA dam system was flood control, but the dams themselves permanently inundated an area the size of Rhode Island—considerably larger than the area that would be affected by the worst conceivable, once-in-500-years flood disaster calculated by the Army Corps of Engineers.[147]

Although TVA attempted to reform itself in the late 1970s and early 1980s, instituting environmental assessment procedures and putting a greater emphasis on energy conservation, Chandler notes that big, inefficient projects continued to go foreward. The Tellico dam, for example, completed in 1980, was not only economically dubious, it dispossessed hundreds of farm families for a reservoir the main benefits of which are "recreation and second-home development."[148] Or, as Chandler puts it, "when resources are allocated by persons who answer neither to the marketplace nor to the electorate, they are not allocated efficiently."[149]

The history of TVA illustrates well a fatal flaw of technocracy: without

---

* That is, economic costs incurred through choosing investments less productive than feasible alternatives.

** Chandler observes that this criticism should be tempered by a recognition that there is probably little TVA could have done in any case "to offset the nationwide trends toward rger farms and mechanized agriculture" (Chandler, The Myth of the TVA, 98).

external, democratic mechanisms to review decisions and ensure public discussion of alternatives, the fundamental, internal logic of self-preservation
for bureaucracies—in Weberian terms, their formal rationality—eventually
subverts and subsumes the values and goals they are supposed to serve.

The Danger

The important thing is to get things done.[150]
—Robert Moses

The seemingly unstoppable, inevitable face of development
is in part rooted in the proliferation of bureaucracy and the instrumental
reason that rules it if it is not subject to countravailing forces or outside
accountability. Typically, too, the instrumental reason of bureaucratic
undertakings is characterized by long sequences of mediated actions
which lose sight of their "original act of definition" as well as of their ultimate consequences.[151]

In fact, an original bureaucratic decision may appear with hindsight
erroneous, harmful, pernicious, and irrational in terms of the organization's substantive values and goals, not to speak of reasonable ethical
norms. But once a sequence of actions is launched, the formal rationality
of the organization takes over, and each intermediate decision appears
eminently rational in terms of the situation that immediately preceded it.
With each incremental action, the original decision is ratified; even if only
a single individual is involved in the whole process, notes sociologist Zygmunt Bauman, "the actor becomes a slave of his past actions. . . . Smooth
and imperceptible passages between steps lure the actor into a trap; the
trap is the impossibility of quitting without revising and rejecting the evaluation of one's own deeds as right or at least innocent."[152]

In a large organization, different individuals are charged with taking
different actions in a long sequence of administrative and managerial decisions dealing with the same matter, and the sense of individual responsibility for the original decision or the ultimate consequences beyond one's
"time-slice" of action and decision is further attenuated. If at any moment
broader considerations are raised concerning a specific action—for example, the irreversible impacts on nature or social groups, or objections
rooted simply in basic ethics or fundamental human reason—the self-referential, formal rationality of the institution is invoked. Only those objections that are phrased in terms of the organization's rules and that are limited to the immediate task and "time-slice" at hand pass the threshold of
"legitimate" discourse.

This "social production of distance" between human actions and their consequences is a ubiquitous characteristic of modernity. It creates an increasingly organized world where "the effects of human action reach far beyond the 'vanishing point' of moral visibility."[153] This gives us a deeper insight, perhaps, into the impressive, impervious, machinery through which disastrous World Bank development projects have continued for years and have been repeated. Beyond the particular internal and external political constituencies for a specific project, the simple momentum of sequential, discrete bureaucratic actions makes it extraordinarily difficult for Bank staff to reconsider the premises and consequences of an entire scheme.

This dynamic casts light on another apparent paradox: Many bureaucratic institutions that attempt to administer, order, and transform the world as raw material invoke scientific principles and economic efficiency, but their activities are often irrational from a broader economic and scientific perspective. What is at work here is frequently not mere incompetence or oversight; rather, the mass of sequential bureaucratic decisions accumulates, and principles such as economic efficiency, if applied to whole chains of bureaucratic actions, increasingly contradict the formal rationality of the organization, its effectiveness in continuing to do whatever it has been doing.

Thus, in a given case the continued technological transformation of nature and society may appear nihilistic and irrational to those affected, but it is eminently rational in terms of the organization. Indeed, in a given undertaking—say, continued World Bank financing of the Narmada dam or the "second stage" of Indonesia Transmigration—the original goals or principles justifying the project often become dysfunctional for further action of the organization or system, so a new end or justification is chosen. The merits of the original "defining act" and the ultimate consequences have long vanished from the horizon of institutional perception and decision making.

Through such mechanisms, technology and technocracy as organizing principles of human society appear to take on an autonomous dynamic of their own. Scientific and economic principles serve as means and tools for this dynamic, but are ignored or discarded when they challenge it.*

Another element in this seemingly unstoppable, impersonal dynamic of modern development is what Langdon Winner calls the "technological

---

* There is no contradiction here: the fact that massive technological interventions on the earth may be unreasonable or unsound from a broader scientific or economic perspective (e.g., the agricultural colonization of tropical rainforests, the construction of gigantic dams) does not mean they cannot be carried out, and indeed science and economics provide the technological and administrative means to carry out such projects effectively.

imperative"—the fact that modern technological interventions often entail further interventions and changes that restructure the entire natural and social environment where they take place. "One must provide," Winner states, "not only the means but also *the entire set of means to the means*."[154] The choice, for example, among alternatives for producing electric power—between a coal-fired plant, nuclear power, a hydroelectric dam, or investments in end-use efficiency and conservation—has tremendous social, political, and environmental consequences which, once the choice is made, acquire a certain inevitability. Many other consequences are also unintended, calling for still more technological intervention and social engineering. This is particularly true in less developed societies, where elements of traditional social structures remain; "whole cultures must be literally ripped apart and reassembled before the 'take-off' of the great airship 'modernity' can begin."[155] Modernization in this sense is nothing less than the final practical application of Cartesian method to whole societies and ecosystems—abstraction, analysis, reconstruction (or synthesis), and control.

The fundamental problem of modernity may be that development pursued as an absolute goal is nihilistic. This has been a somber theme of some of the twentieth century's leading philosophers. Writing in exile in New York shortly after the end of the Second World War, the German-Jewish philosopher Max Horkheimer revisited the themes of modernity and development in the light of the catastrophe of two world wars and the threat of nuclear holocaust. The nihilism of modernity, Horkheimer argued, is rooted in Cartesian epistemology, because it leaves on one side an "abstract ego emptied of all substance except its attempt to transform everything in heaven and on earth into means for its preservation, and on the other hand mere stuff to be dominated, without any other purpose than that of this very domination."[156]

Reason surrenders its autonomy and becomes an instrument, "completely harnessed to the social process. Its operational value, its role in the domination of men and nature, has been made the sole criterion."[157] The transformation of every realm of existence into a "field of means" creates conditions that can lead to the destruction of the subject who is to use them, to what C. S. Lewis called the abolition of man.[158] This entails not just the abolition of a certain social idea of human freedom and individuality, but in extreme cases the preconditions for the mass physical destruction of human beings. The intellectual tour de force embodied in the totalization of instrumental reason, Horkheimer wrote, "lays the ground for the rule of force in the domain of the political."[159]

From a different philosophical perspective, Heidegger makes a similar analysis. His very language is disorienting and opaque because he is striving to convey a notion of our relation to the world that would begin to transcend the nihilism of anthropocentric Cartesian dualism; it is language that tries to make us think of the world as not grounded in the perceptions and actions of human subjectivity. Technology, Heidegger writes, is the way in which Being reveals itself in the modern era, a "challenging setting-upon through which what we call the real is revealed as standing-reserve (Bestand)."[160] Although "man drives technology forward, he takes part in ordering as a way of revealing"; "the unconcealment itself, within which ordering unfolds, is never a human handiwork, any more than is the realm through which man is already passing every time he as a subject relates to an object."[161] Rather, this unconcealment in which ordering takes place is Being, which, as a "challenging claim which gathers man thither to order the self-revealing as standing reserve," Heidegger calls *"Ge-stell"* (Enframing).[162] The "Enframing" is the continual setting up, ordering, transformation, and revealing of everything in the world as "standing reserve"—as something ready to be used, and to be transformed and used again. The Enlightenment project, which establishes an epistemology based on the Cartesian subject and its objects, entails the ontological justification and reduction of the world as raw material to be known, ordered, transformed, controlled, used, again and again.

Heidegger's concept of "Enframing" has its historical counterpart in the interpretation* of Western economic development as a process of enclosure. One definition of enclosure is, according to the *Oxford English Dictionary,* to "insert in a frame or setting."[163] As a historical process, enclosure means much more than the fencing in and expropriation of English common pastures that took place in the eighteenth century. Enclosure is the social and economic dynamic of modernity itself, tearing "people and their lands, forests, crafts, technologies, and cosmologies out of the cultural framework in which they are embedded,"[164] and reordering them into a new framework for rationalized use and development. It is the very process of ripping apart former social contexts and patterns of resource use and reembedding the fragments in a framework in which eventually all of nature and humankind becomes the open arena for the exercise of instrumental reason. But "any pieces which will not fit into the new framework are devalued and discarded."[165] The "useless" pieces include almost all of the other species on earth, except to the extent their continued existence can be justified, not as an end itself, but as a func-

---

* See, for example, "Development as Enclosure," and "The Encompassing Web," in *Whose Common Future?* special issue of *Ecologist,* vol. 22, no. 4 (July/August 1992), 131–57; for a popular account, see Jeremy Rifkin, *Biosphere Politics: A Cultural Odyssey from the Middle Ages to the New Age,* part 1, "Enclosing the Global Commons" (New York: Harper Collins, 1991), 11–94.

tional element in an instrumental rationale—as reservoirs of biodiversity for future economic use, for example, or as sinks to absorb industrially produced carbon dioxide. Enclosure has also meant the increasing marginalization of huge numbers of humans, forcibly expelled and relocated from the local communities and natural commons where they dwelled.

Ironically, Heidegger observes, in such a world, perceived and ordered as standing-reserve, "man everywhere and always encounters only himself."[166] There is a tendency to view almost everything as makable, doable, replaceable, exchangeable.[167] The "supreme danger," Heidegger notes, is that at the very moment when humankind "exalts [itself] to the posture of Lord of the earth," humanity itself becomes "standing reserve," raw material whose ultimate and only justification for being is that it can be organized and ordered to be used for something else.[168]

The Revolt of Nature
and the Crisis of Modernity

The World Bank was founded on the ruins of a world war and the Holocaust, both made possible by technology and modern bureaucratic organization. A fundamental political challenge at the end of the twentieth century remains our inability to master politically the gigantic technological and social apparatus forged to develop the planet. Indeed, it is precisely the frightening and potent combination of rationalized bureaucratic, economic, and technological organization in the service of politically unaccountable ends that has resulted in the worst horrors of this century. Now, nature itself appears in revolt against this empire of man over things, as do local communities and indigenous societies dependent on threatened ecosystems. Nature's revolt has globalized the political crisis of modern, technological society.

We have seen that the World Bank is the quintessential institution of high mid-twentieth-century modernity, a practical embodiment of the philosophical and historical project of the modern era that began with the Enlightenment. At the very moment of its global triumph, the project of modernity is increasingly beset by unintended, uncontrollable natural consequences and social pathologies. The notion of a unitary, universal future of progress based on technology, development, and the continuous transformation of nature and human society as raw material for material growth and output appears problematic—even to a minority within the Bank.

Václav Havel has written that "the end of Communism . . . is a message we have not fully deciphered and comprehended," since it portends "an end not just to the 19th and 20th centuries, but to the modern age as a whole." The modern era, Havel continues, has been dominated by the belief

that the world—and Being as such—is a wholly knowable system governed by a finite number of universal laws that man can grasp and rationally direct for his own benefit. . . . [It] gave rise to the proud belief that man . . . was capable of objectively describing, explaining and controlling everything that exists, and of possessing the one and only truth about the world. It was an era in which there was a cult of depersonalized objectivity . . . an era of belief in automatic progress brokered by the scientific method. It was an era of systems, institutions, mechanisms and statistical averages. It was an era of ideologies, doctrines, interpretations of reality, an era in which the goal was to find a universal theory of the world, and thus a universal key to unlock its prosperity.

Communism was the perverse extreme of this trend . . . an attempt, on the basis of a few propositions masquerading as the only scientific truth, to organize all of life according to a single model, and to subject it to central planning and control regardless of whether or not that was what life wanted.

The fall of Communism can be regarded as a sign that modern thought—based on the premise that the world is objectively knowable, and that the knowledge so obtained can be absolutely generalized—has come to a final crisis. This era has created the first global, or planetary, technical civilization, but it has reached the point beyond which the abyss begins.[169]

One can venture that initial efforts to respond to this crisis will require actions on two levels. First, it is necessary to create effective mechanisms of political accountability and transparency for institutions like the World Bank that have an important role in global resource planning and management. Indeed, it will be necessary to reinvent these institutions, and to shift resources from them to less centralized, more flexible and responsive alternatives. But such efforts in themselves will be of little avail without a reevaluation and transformation of the relation of human societies to nature and the world. Otherwise, we shall finally become "masters and possessors of nature" at the moment when both humankind and nature are destroyed. Different futures must not only be imagined, but liberated and allowed to happen.

The managers of billions of dollars of loans, with unparalleled access to technology and political leverage through these loans, declare the impossibility of different futures and struggle with the difficulties of halting even a single one of their own projects. Meanwhile some of the poorest, most powerless people on earth, from Chico Mendes and the Brazilian rubber tappers to the tribal peoples of the Narmada Valley, have physically interposed themselves to assert that not only can development be directed, it can be redirected and rethought by the people affected by it, and, greatest sacrilege of all, it can and should be halted, at least in the form it is currently practiced. These revolts of local knowledges, of many discourses and possible futures against a single, totalizing global juggernaut have risen from the "rich and ancient tradition of denial and protest" of which Dostoyevsky spoke, at the very moment when the need is greatest.

Who Shall Rule the World— and How?

In the spring of 1992, only six months after the Bangkok World Bank/IMF gathering, another developing-country government was completing feverish preparations for a gigantic international conference. The "Earth Summit" in Rio de Janeiro was to be the largest diplomatic gathering in history. Thirty thousand people attended the summit, officially known as the United Nations Conference on Environment and Development (UNCED), in June; 9,000 journalists and 118 heads of state flew to Rio for the global eco-event. Once again, no expense was spared. The government spent $33 million to refurbish a huge convention hall, Rio-Centro, where the official meetings were to take place.[1] It built a special seven-kilometer highway at a cost of $130 million, to whisk heads of state from the airport to their luxury hotels. Brazil's national environmental laws, which would have required the preparation of an environmental impact study, were suspended to permit construction in record time.[2]

In an attempt to reduce the risk of crime from the city's hundreds of thousands of slum dwellers, thousands of soldiers were put on alert during the two weeks of the Earth Summit, guarding every hotel entrance, bridge, and street corner in the prosperous downtown areas where the delegates congregated. On June 11 and 12, 1992, when most of the heads of state were in town, fifty kilometers of city streets were barred to all but VIPs. Just as in Bangkok in 1991, all government employees were given a two-day special holiday to reduce traffic congestion. On a more sinister note, journalists reported that special police death squads intensified the systematic murder of homeless street children* (a source of much petty crime) in the weeks preceding the summit, as part of the cleanup campaign to present Rio's best face to politicians and environmentalists from around the planet.[3]

UNCED was held on the twentieth anniversary of the United Nations Stockholm Conference on the Human Environment, the first international gathering in which nations attempted to address global environmental issues. Apart from focusing international public opinion on the global environment, the Stockholm Conference resulted in the founding of the United Nations Environment Program (UNEP) and catalyzed the negotiation of a number of international conventions to protect the marine environment. But at Stockholm the developed nations, led by the United States, ensured that UNEP would not be given the mandate or the funds to accomplish very much on its own. Operating out of Nairobi, Kenya, its exclusive role was to cajole and "catalyze" other U.N.-affiliated agencies—including the World Bank—and the nations of the world to undertake environmental commitments and actions. Up to 1990, its budget never amounted to much more than $40 million a year—a smaller amount than the cost of most individual World Bank projects.

Twenty years of steady worldwide environmental deterioration and increasing public alarm had raised the stakes immensely. Climate change, the depletion of the earth's ozone layer, and the biological holocaust unleashed by tropical deforestation had become unprecedented global problems. Since 1988, an international convention, the Montreal Protocol, had been in effect to phase out worldwide emissions of CFCs (chlorofluorocarbons), the chemicals that destroy the ozone layer. It was hoped that the centerpiece of the Earth Summit would be the signing of three new conventions—a global climate treaty in which nations would pledge to reduce emissions of carbon dioxide, methane, and other gases responsible for global warming, a treaty to protect biodiversity through commitments to conservation of endangered habitats and species, and a convention to conserve the world's forests. Brazil agreed to host the global environmental summit as part of a diplomatic initiative to clean up its tarnished international environmental image, still suffering from the aftereffects of the murder of Chico Mendes and a decade of accelerating Amazon deforestation.

But much more than the signing of new environmental treaties was at stake at the Earth Summit. Developing governments were clamoring for money from the North as never before. After thirty years of large-scale

* The murder of homeless street children, almost all of them black or of mixed race, by police death squads, had been going on for years in Brazil's cities and has been condemned by numerous Brazilian and international human rights organizations.

244 • MORTGAGING THE EARTH

international development assistance, the gap between rich and poor countries had doubled: in 1960 the 20 percent of the world's population living in the poorest countries had incomes that were one-thirtieth of those of the planet's richest 20 percent; in 1990 the world's poorest 20 percent had incomes of one-sixtieth of those of the richest 20 percent.[4] For many countries, the 1980s had been a lost decade in which national income, and especially the real wages of the poorest, fell dramatically: in Latin America, the lowest nonagricultural wages were down 41 percent in 1981–87; in Mexico, manufacturing wages fell by over 50 percent in real terms.[5] Indicators of social welfare such as nutrition and access to doctors were lower in a number of African countries than they had been in colonial days. Even India, one of the World Bank's star pupils for three decades, entered the 1990s with a gigantic balance of payments crisis, and submitted to a major structural adjustment program formulated by the Bank and the IMF.

The South's governments argued that global environmental issues could hardly be isolated from the economic and social woes that plagued their nations, where 90 percent of the earth's population lived. Twenty years earlier, at Stockholm, Indira Gandhi had declared that "poverty is the greatest polluter," and this was if anything more true than ever. But the sad record of failed mega-projects that benefited vested interests and powerful elites (aptly characterized by Brazilian journalists as "pharaonic" in their pretensions and futility) and of pervasive corruption made many Southern governments as much a part of the problem of poverty as the solution. The North's foreign aid to the South had amounted to $55 billion annually in recent years; this was approximately the same sum that poorer countries were paying the North as interest and principal on their outstanding loans. Moreover, the lion's share of this aid went back to the North in the form of procurement contracts and purchases. In 1992 the World Bank's borrowers paid $198 million more to the rich, developed countries for procurement of goods and services on IBRD and IDA loans than they received in net disbusements.* It was by no means a frivolous or cynical observation that the poor in developing nations might be better off if all foreign assistance were abolished and the South's foreign debt written off.

* In the Bank's fiscal year 1992, borrowing countries paid $6.751 billion for procurement of services and goods for IBRD loans, in addition to $2.347 billion in procurement contracts associated with IDA credits. About 71 percent of the total procurement of $9.098 billion, $6.457 billion, was paid to the inductrialized OCED countroes. Net disbursements of the IBRD in FY 1992 (gross disbursements minus repayment of interest and principal) were only $1.818 billion, and for IDA $4.441 billion, totalling $6.259 billion. (World Bank, *Annual Report, 1992* [Washington, D.C.: World Bank, 1992], 17, 81–83, 87.)

Now, at last, the developing nations' governments had a bargaining chip: without their cooperation there could be no "global bargain" to reduce carbon dioxide emissions or preserve biodiversity and the earth's forests. The price of that cooperation was to be money—lots of it—and not just for the environment, but for development—"sustainable development," of course.

In response to these concerns diplomats had hammered out a plan for UNCED that purported to set out principles and programs needed to develop, sustainably, the entire planet—Agenda 21, so called because it purported to be a global agenda for the beginning of the twenty-first century. The 800-page draft that was sent to Rio for final negotiation was full of grandiose exhortations that would be difficult to disagree with and even more difficult to carry out. The bottom line, however, was a heavy one: Agenda 21 calls upon the industrialized countries to support huge investments in developing countries in a multitude of areas related to the environment in the broadest sense, including health, sanitation, conservation, education, technical assistance, etc. The cost: $600 billion a year, of which the North is supposed to supply $125 billion annually. Industrialized countries would have to more than double current levels of development assistance, while Southern countries somehow would come up with an extra $475 billion annually in matching funds. Some uncritically saw Agenda 21 as a program to save the planet; others, having seen other U.N. action plans blaze and vanish like shooting stars, saw it as a uniquely cynical charade, even by U.N. standards, given the full awareness of almost all of the national governments involved that they would not and could not carry out most of their commitments.

As the preparations for UNCED advanced, it appeared likely that most of the real money that would flow out of the Earth Summit would be managed by the World Bank, despite objections of the South, since the Bank was controlled by the industrialized Northern donors. And the World Bank had been preparing: in little more than a year of existence the Bank-dominated Global Environment Facility (GEF) had committed hundreds of millions of dollars for global environmental projects, and Bank management was already declaring it a success and suggesting that its capital be tripled or quadrupled. Indeed, at the last preparatory meeting for UNCED, in April 1992, Maurice Strong, the Canadian secretary general of the conference, not only called for a $3-billion replenishment of the GEF, but also urged the industrialized nations to add on a special five $5-billion bonus to the upcoming replenishment of the World Bank's low-interest lending facility, the International Development Association (IDA). Strong called the proposed extra $5 billion an "earth increment" to be added to the

$18 billion the Bank was already requesting, since it could be used to fund items on the Agenda 21 laundry list.[6]

As the World Bank geared up for the Earth Summit and its aftermath, three events—the leak of a memo authored by the Bank's chief economist, the release of the report of the independent commission on the Narmada River Sardar Sarovar dam in India, and the completion of a high-level internal study of the Bank's deteriorating project quality—raised serious questions about the Bank's integrity and competence to manage any funds for environmental purposes. Strangely enough, although the Bank's president and Executive Board were apprised of each event, the three incidents nevertheless seemed to unfold in separate, compartmentalized worlds, as if they were occurring in three separate institutions while a fourth one went to Rio to ask for more money.

"Perfectly Logical But Totally Insane"

It was almost a pleasant surprise to me to read reports in our papers and then receive [a] copy of your memorandum supporting the export of pollution to Third World Countries and the arguments you present for justifying it. Your reasoning is perfectly logical but totally insane. It underlines what I just wrote in a chapter on the absurdity of much of what goes for "economic thinking" today as part of a book that will be presented at the RIO-92 Conference. Your thoughts will be quoted in full . . . as a concrete example of the unbelievable alienation, reductionist thinking, social ruthlessness and the arrogant ignorance of many conventional "economists" concerning the nature of the world we live in.[7]   —José Lutzenberger, letter to Lawrence Summers, February 1992

In early 1992, Larry Summers—young star of the Harvard economics department, economic advisor to the presidential campaign of Michael Dukakis in 1988, and now World Bank chief economist—was leading the Bank's efforts to shape the intellectual and ideological framework in which environmental issues would be considered at Rio. He was directing the writing of the *World Development Report*, the Bank's most prestigious and widely read annual publication. The 1992 theme was to be "Development and the Environment," and Summers and a team of Bank economists and writers were hard at work to finish the report so that it could be distributed around the world weeks before the Earth Summit.

(The report was a labored attempt to prove that world economic output could increase three-and-a-half-fold in less than forty years without environmental deterioration.)[8]

There was no question that Summers was a brilliant economist, Nobel Prize material in the opinion of some of his colleagues; the incisiveness of his thought regrettably was lost in a bureaucratic document like the *World Development Report*. The world was able to see the real implications of a rigorous, purely instrumental analysis of markets and the environment in a December 12, 1991, memorandum by Summers, which, once leaked, was faxed to dozens of countries by the Washington, D.C., office of Greenpeace. Soon the World Bank's chief economist received publicity unequalled by any of his predecessors, which upstaged any possible media attention the 1992 *World Development Report* would receive.

The infamous memorandum consisted of a series of editorial comments on the draft of another report Bank economists were writing (entitled "Global Economic Prospects"). In the middle of the memo was a section entitled "Dirty Industries" that Summers subsequently claimed was ironic and by no means a serious policy recommendation, a thought exercise to prompt some Bank staff to think in an economically more rigorous manner. "Just between you and me," he queried his colleagues in the memo, "shouldn't the World Bank be encouraging *more* migration of the dirty industries to the LDCs [lesser developed countries]?"

He cited three reasons. First, the conventional economic measurement of the costs of pollution to public health is calculated on the basis of lost earned income caused by the premature death and illness of wage earners. Obviously, the income and GNP lost through the death of a Mexican, let alone an Ethiopian, is much lower per unit of pollution than that lost through the death of a worker in the United States or Switzerland. Thus, "the economic logic behind dumping a load of toxic waste in the lowest wage country is impeccable and we should face up to it."[9]

There was a second reason, Summers continued with the same implacable logic: environmentally uncontaminated countries were logical places to dump pollution and waste since the marginal, incremental costs of pollution in heavily polluted places were higher. "I've always thought that underpopulated countries in Africa are vastly *under*-polluted, their air quality is probably vastly inefficiently low [*sic*—he meant to say "high"] compared to Los Angeles or Mexico City," the chief economist lamented. Alas, it was only the laws of physics that prevented "world welfare enhancing trade in air pollution and waste"—that is, shipping dirty air from Los Angeles to the Zaire in a classic, "welfare-enhancing" market transaction. Finally, Summers noted, "the demand for a clean environment for aes-

thetic and health reasons is likely to have very high income elasticity"—
that is, the poor of the world will endure a filthy, toxic environment
because they die sooner ("[T]he concern over an agent that causes a one
in million chance in the odds of prostrate [*sic*] cancer is obviously going
to be much higher in a country where people survive [longer]"). Another
argument for shipping pollution to the poor, Summers implied, is that
clean air is a luxury that they can do without, a matter of "aesthetics"
("Much of the concern over industrial atmospheric discharge is about visibility. . . . These discharges may have very little direct health impact").[10]
In fact, one need only consult statistics on bronchial infections, asthma
and pneumonia for children of the poor in heavily polluted neighborhoods of Mexico City and São Paulo to realize that while a tourist's concern over atmospheric discharges may be "aesthetic," for the most vulnerable this is a question of a threat to their very survival.

His words were quoted in headlines around the world, and often on
the front page, as in Brazil's leading newspapers, something that was particularly unfortunate for the Bank given Brazil's sensitivities as the host
nation for UNCED. The entire memo was reproduced in *The Economist,*
and the normally reserved London *Financial Times* ran a prominent piece
with the headline "Save Planet Earth from Economists."[11] For the World
Bank it was a public relations disaster of unique proportions. At the very
moment the leaked memo was hitting the world's headlines, President
Lewis Preston was flying across the Atlantic on his first official visit to
Africa. Arriving in the Harare, Zimbabwe, airport, the hapless Preston was
bombarded by questions on whether the Bank's new environmental policies envisaged shipping toxic wastes to Africa. Brazil's secretary of the
environment, José Lutzenberger, was enraged. His letter to Summers,
quoted in part above, called Summers's views "an insult to thinking people all over the World." If the World Bank kept Summers as vice-
president, Lutzenberger fumed, "it would confirm what I often said as an
environmentalist, years ago, fighting ecologically devastating and socially
disruptive World Bank 'development projects,' namely that the best thing
that could happen would be for the World Bank to disappear."[12]

But the intense moral outrage directed personally at Summers by
Lutzenberger and environmental groups around the world, as well as by
several of Summers's own Bank colleagues, missed the point. His great
error was to write ingenuously and rigorously on the implications of neoclassical economic thinking unadulterated by any extraneous concerns or
values. It would be hard to find a purer, more instructive example of the
dangers of untrammeled instrumental reason, of the grave perils of
"enframing" humankind and nature as "standing reserve," as raw material
for augmenting material output. The Bank's chief economist was merely

an all too exemplary pupil and beneficiary of the worldwide proclivity of bureaucracies and of governments to embrace technocratic rationales to justify their actions.

The most revealing and thought-provoking part of the Summers memo was overlooked by many of his critics:

The problem with the arguments against all of these proposals for more pollution in LDCs (intrinsic rights to certain goods, moral reasons, social concerns, lack of adequate markets, etc.) [is that they] *could be turned around and used more or less effectively against every Bank proposal for [economic] liberalization.* [Emphasis added.][13]

Ironically, Summers achieved beyond his wildest dreams his purported goal in writing the memo, to clarify thinking on international environmental and economic issues. Unintentionally, he demonstrated the implacable urgency of creating and re-creating a political and social space at the local, national, and global levels where values such as "intrinsic rights to certain goods, moral reasons, [and] social concerns" will define the parameters of institutions making decisions that affect human development.

"Gross Delinquency"

The Bank, in crafting our terms of Reference, invited specific recommendations. . . . If essential data were available, if impacts were known, if basic steps had been taken, it would be possible to know what recommendations to make. But we cannot put together a list of recommendations to improve resettlement and rehabilitation or to ameliorate environmental impacts, when in so many areas no adequate measures are taken on the ground or are even under consideration.[14]
—Bradford Morse and Thomas R. Berger, June 1992

In late May 1992, only days before the opening of the Earth Summit, the Bank's India country department was in a panic. The independent review of the Sardar Sarovar dam was going to the printers, and the news was all bad. The first outside, independent assessment of a World Bank project documented nearly a decade of bureaucratic malfeasance, willful withholding of information from the Bank's management and Board of Executive Directors, and sheer, brazen incompetence. The independent review was authored by the first group of outside experts that had been allowed full access to the secret files of the World Bank—files not available even to the Bank's own Executive Board.

The creation of the independent review was a consequence of growing international protest and pressure on the World Bank to cease funding the project. After the October 1989 hearing in the U.S. Congress on Sardar Sarovar, over a dozen U.S. congressmen and senators wrote the Bank to ask it to reconsider its support; hundreds of legislators in the Japanese Diet and the Finnish and Swedish parliaments signed letters asking the same, and the European Parliament passed a resolution urging the Bank to withdraw. Barber Conable increasingly came to mistrust the Bank's India country department staff, who gave him optimistic progress reports on the environmental and resettlement problems in the project. Finally, in the waning months of his tenure in 1991, he asked his old friend Bradford Morse, who in turn had been a U.S. congressman, the U.N. Undersecretary General, and the director of the United Nations Development Program, to undertake a unique independent investigation of the environmental and resettlement aspects of the project. The World Bank India country department objected, in vain.

The members of the independent review—or the Morse Commission, as it came to be called—were appalled by what they found. Their report, released at a press conference in Washington on June 18, 1992, not only confirmed virtually all of the criticisms made by NGOs in India and abroad, it revealed a pattern of gross negligence and delinquency on the part of the World Bank and the Indian government that was much worse than anyone had imagined.

To begin with, the report uncovered the fact that the Sardar Sarovar dam had never been properly appraised, not only with respect to environmental and resettlement matters, but even concerning its engineering viability. The Morse Commission hired its own hydrologist to examine the likely water flows for the dam's irrigation and power components, and concluded that "there is good reason to believe that the projects will not perform as planned."[15] The report estimates that the dam and its associated canals probably would make 240,000 people homeless, not the 90,000 or 100,000 originally envisaged: in addition to the 100,000 people the Sardar Sarovar reservoir would displace, the enormous water-channeling systems in the command area of the dam would forcibly resettle some 140,000 others—a fact never even discussed in the original World Bank appraisals for the dam and the command area canals. The independent review concluded that humane resettlement for most of the people affected was a simple impossibility.

"There appears to have been an institutional numbness," the report continued, "at the Bank and in India to environmental matters," "a history of omissions, unmet deadlines, and *ex post facto* revisions," all of which the Morse Commission concluded amounted to "gross delinquency."[16]

Quoting a Bank consultant's study—which would never have seen the light of day without the commission's access to Bank files—the independent review concluded that the entire Narmada scheme "appear[s] to have been planned, designed and executed without incorporation of Health Safeguards. He [the consultant] describes various parts of the Projects as 'death traps' and as 'taking Malaria to the doorsteps of the villagers.'"[17] "People have died. Yet the Bank's status reports simply say that the preventive measures [for health] required by the formal [loan] agreements seven years ago are 'not yet due.'"[18]

In fact, the Bank and the Indian government had been so negligent in gathering the basic information necessary to evaluate the project that the Morse Commission refused to give any recommendations for improving its implementation, as the Bank had requested. Instead, it urged the Bank and the Indian government to undertake the fundamental environmental and human impact assessment studies that should have been completed before the project began nearly a decade before. The independent review warned that the hostility of tens of thousands of people in the Narmada Valley to the project would make further "progress . . . impossible, except as a result of unacceptable means."[19]

Moreover, the commission revealed a bureaucracy that was not only negligent, but rife with what could only be characterized as intellectual corruption and dishonesty. It describes how certain Bank staff and the Indian government wilfully ignored—and on several occasions between 1983 and 1989 tried to prevent the gathering of information on—the resettlement impacts of the projects.[20] The Morse Commission similarly accuses the Bank's India country department of "obscuring" and distorting the observations and conclusions of a Bank legal expert in an April 1987 mission to ascertain what proportion of the people to be resettled by Sardar Sarovar were tribal and thus subject to special treatment under the Bank's operational policy on tribal peoples. It was "a striking example," the report warns, but apparently hardly an isolated one, "of how important findings on the ground fail to reach management."[21]

The pattern of coverup and deception went still deeper. Sardar Sarovar was neither planned nor ultimately feasible as a single stand-alone project; its engineering and economic viability were significantly dependent on the construction of still another huge dam upstream, Narmada Sagar (which would regulate water flows), as well as on two medium-size dams associated with Narmada Sagar, Omkareshwar and Maheshwar.* The commis-

* "Thus" a 1990 World Bank office memorandum states, "the three dams of the NSC [Narmada Sagar Complex], together with the two SSP [Sardar Sarovar Project] projects [for the dam and the canals] and the related R & R [Resettlement and Rehabilitation of forcibly displaced populations] and area development aspects for all four reservoirs and their catchment

sion cites a World Bank internal memorandum dated January 1992, in which Bank staff estimate that without the Narmada Sagar dams, power production of Sardar Sarovar would be reduced by 25 percent and the irrigated area by 30 percent.[22] For that very reason the Narmada Water Disputes Tribunal Award of 1979—the legal agreement that settled the question of water rights among the three Indian states to be affected by the dams—provided that the Narmada Sagar dam be completed prior to or, at latest, concurrently with Sardar Sarovar.[23]

But Narmada Sagar would be as costly or more so than Sardar Sarovar, which was already, according to the Bank, "one of the most ambitious water resource development projects ever attempted."[24] It would also require the forced resettlement of over 100,000 more rural poor, and flood a large area of intact tropical forest. So the Bank appraised Sardar Sarovar as a separate, discrete project, with virtually no mention of its inextricable and broader ecological, economic, and engineering links to future projects. The Bank's executive directors, when they approved $450 million in loans and credits for Sardar Sarovar in 1985, had no awareness that its viability was in large part contingent on future funding of at least three other dams that would cost billions of dollars, nor that its construction prior to the Narmada Sagar dam was contrary to the Narmada Water Disputes Tribunal Award.

This pattern of deception continued right into 1992, as World Bank India country department staff prepared a new, $90-million Narmada River Basin Development Project. The Morse Commission charged Bank staff were deceitfully trying to keep Narmada Sagar alive by proposing a "stand-alone environmental project" that in reality was a scheme to covertly finance resettlement and environmental mitigation measures that would only make sense if Narmada Sagar were completed.[25]*

Finally, the Morse Commission charged that the abuses in Sardar Sarovar were not an isolated exception, particularly with respect to the mistreatment of hundreds of thousands of forcibly resettled rural poor: "The problems besetting the Sardar Sarovar Projects are more the rule than the exception to resettlement operations supported by the Bank in India."[26] In India alone, over a twelve year period from 1978 to 1990 the Bank financed thirty-two separate projects entailing the forced displacement of over 600,000 poor.

---

areas, should be viewed as a technically and economically interdependent development complex" (World Bank office memorandum, 14 March 1990, p. 2, cited in *Sardar Sarovar: Report of the Independent Review* [see endnote 14], 238).

* "As with Sardar Sarovar," the Morse Commission notes, "almost all [the project's problems] are well documented in the Bank's files but are not reflected in the Staff Appraisal Report" (*Sardar Sarovar: Report of the Independent Review*, 336).

The report confirmed again the most extreme charges of Indian NGOs:

Upper Krishna I Project . . . closed in 1986 with a backlog of 100,000 people still to be resettled. . . . Upper Krishna II, a project with 250,000 oustees, was not supervised during a critical phase of implementation. . . . The Gujarat Medium II Irrigation Project, which affects tribals similar to those who will be displaced by the Sardar Sarovar Projects, was approved in 1984 without project-specific resettlement plans and despite documented resettlement failures during the first Gujarat Medium Irrigation Project. Subsequent supervision reported the predictable widespread failure to rehabilitate the nearly 90,000 people displaced by these dams.[27]

When the Bank became aware of resettlement problems in its India projects, "it . . . failed firmly to address them. Violations of legal covenants are flagged, and then forgotten; conditions are imposed and when the borrower fails to meet them, the conditions are relaxed or their deadlines postponed."[28]

Why did this happen and why was it continuing? The Morse Commission states that its comprehensive review of Bank files and numerous discussions with Indian government officials all point to the same conclusion, that "the Bank is more concerned to accommodate the pressures emanating from its borrowers than to guarantee implementation of its policies."[29]

This pattern of abuse, deception, and misinformation served an all too familiar dynamic, that of keeping the money flowing, whatever the cost, to the Bank's single biggest borrower, accounting for more than 15 percent of its total portfolio.* In fact, the decade-long sequence of hundreds of bureaucratic decisions involved in the debacle of the Narmada projects is an outstanding example of the production of moral indifference and engineered cruelty through the formal, instrumental rationality of modern bureaucratic organizations, discussed in the previous chapter. The key, we remember, is that with each incremental bureaucratic act, the originating or defining decision both is further ratified (and harder to challenge) and quickly recedes beyond the horizon of ethical responsibility. Similarly, the ultimate impact of the decision chain on human beings also disappears beyond a moral vanishing point.**

And so it was that on June 23, 1992, five days after the release of the Morse Commission report, the World Bank in an official response

---

* Total outstanding IBRD Loans and IDA credits amounted to $152,662 billion in the Bank's fiscal year 1992, of which $23,649 billion was owed by India. (World Bank, *Annual Report 1992*, 202–3, 222–23.)

** From an institutional standpoint (i.e., of formal rationality) the reasonable decision appears to be the one that does not contradict all the decisions that have come before or create unpredictability by breaking out of this iron cage of bureaucratic *faits accomplis*.

announced its intention to continue financial support for the Sardar
Sarovar dam. The Bank claimed it concurred with most of the criticisms in
the report, but disagreed with its main recommendation to "step back."
Instead, Bank management advocated continued funding coupled with
the "incremental approach"—further conditions and deadlines—that the
Morse Commission charged had been an abject failure. To support its
contentions, the Bank claimed that "since 1987, the Sardar Sarovar projects have received more Bank supervision attention than any other project in [the] India Department's portfolio." Indeed, "supervision inputs in
the SSP projects have been about 10 times the Bank average." Although
there were implementation difficulties, the Bank argued that it was better
to be involved and not to restrict its lending to situations where "the borrower had already established an exemplary track record," since

this would in practice mean forgoing opportunities for potentially important
change. A decision by the Bank not to get involved could well mean that the project in question will still proceed but under much less favorable circumstances.[30]

Inside the World Bank, rumors circulated that there was another reason why management persisted with the project. As the Bank's biggest
borrower, the Indian government was playing financial brinkmanship:
already staggering under the burden of an acute balance of payments crisis, and criticized domestically for a highly unpopular adjustment program
designed by the Bank and the Fund, it was threatening default on its
World Bank loans if the Bank ceased its support for Sardar Sarovar.[31]

"There Is Reason to Be Concerned!"

In the spring of 1992—while chief economist Summers
became the first World Bank official to be featured in *People* magazine (in
its Earth Day issue, as one of the top eight "enemies of the earth"),[32] and
the Morse Commission drafted its final report—a high-ranking World
Bank official was preparing another indictment of the Bank. In February
1992, Bank president Lewis Preston had asked his special adviser and vice-
president, Willi Wapenhans, to oversee a study on the Bank's project quality, an issue that deeply concerned Preston. Preston was reported to have
stated, just prior to assuming his tenure at the Bank, that he wondered
whether the Bank could find at its current lending rates enough well-
prepared quality projects to finance.[33]

What Wapenhans and his special team, called the Portfolio Management Task Force, discovered showed that the findings of the Morse Commission report were only the tip of the iceberg. Judging by standard indi-

cators such as meeting appraised economic rates of return and compliance with loan conditions, the quality of the Bank's entire loan portfolio—which amounted to $140 billion in loans and credits to help finance projects and programs whose total cost approached a third of a trillion dollars—was deteriorating at an alarming rate.[34] Moreover, the deterioration had been "steady and pervasive,"[35] worsening every year for more than a decade, with no action to reverse the trend by the Bank's management or Board of Executive Directors.

"There is reason to be concerned!" Wapenhans concluded in a June 1992 presentation before members of the Bank's board.[36] It was an understatement. Statistics spoke for themselves. The annual review of completed projects conducted by the Bank's Operations Evaluation Department showed a steady increase in unsatisfactory projects from 15 percent in 1981, to 30.5 percent in 1989, to 37.5 percent in 1991.[37] In some sectors, like water supply and agriculture, 42 percent of ongoing projects were encountering serious problems in the later years of their implementation.[38] This was alarming news indeed, especially because many of the projects the Bank claimed to be successes were failures from both a poverty alleviation and an environmental standpoint.

But there was even worse news. "Borrowers' compliance with legal covenants—especially financial ones" was "startlingly low."[39] According to one internal Bank study, Wapenhans discovered, "only 22 percent of the financial covenants in loan/credit agreements were in compliance."[40] In one of the Bank's four major operations regions* "a review of compliance with financial covenants for revenue earning entities . . . shows only 15 percent of the projects in full compliance."[41]

The credibility of the Bank's appraisal process, according to the Wapenhans task force, "is under pressure"[42]—another felicitous understatement. More bluntly the report adds, "Many Bank staff perceive appraisals as marketing devices for securing loan approval (and achieving personal recognition). [Other] funding agencies perceive an 'approval culture' in which appraisal becomes advocacy."[43] The picture of the project cycle that emerges from the report verges on travesty. After Bank country staff market the appraisal, come the loan negotiations: "The Negotiations stage of the project cycle is seen by many Borrowers as a largely *coercive* exercise designed to 'impose' the Bank's philosophy and to validate the findings of its promotional approach to Appraisal."[44] Confidential surveys of Bank staff revealed that the pressure to move money quickly and meet lending targets overwhelms all other considerations: "Only 17 percent of

* The report did not examine recently commenced lending for Eastern Europe, or for the former republics of the Soviet Union that were joining the Bank as the report was being written.

staff interviewed felt that analytical work done during project preparation was compatible with the achievement of project quality"; most believe that "timely delivery is given preference over project quality."[45]

Thus, environmental performance is not the sloppiest, most mismanaged area in Bank operations—it may even be one of the best, because of the outside scrutiny and constant pressure from advocacy groups. The Wapenhans report indicates that the Bank continues to disburse money freely despite indications that nearly four-fifths of its financial loan conditions are worthless. The really bad problems may be in financial management and economic appraisal.

But doesn't the Bank have a top-notch reputation as a financial institution, and aren't over 97 percent of its loans promptly repaid? And what about its highly qualified professional staff, which includes more Ph.D. economists from top universities than any other institution on earth? Recall the Bank's unique situation in the international system: its loans and credits are backed by the direct contributions and guarantees of the taxpayers of the industrialized world, and the borrowers are governments that pay the Bank back with general revenues extracted from their people and taxpayers. Moreover, the borrowing governments always try to repay the World Bank first, since their access to private international credit depends on promptly repaying their obligations to the Bank. With such a setup, it makes no difference whether the projects the Bank lends for are well managed or mismanaged, or whether some or all of the money disappears. The $24 billion a year of World Bank loans and credits could be buried in a hole, or burnt, and governments would continue to repay promptly and the Bank would continue to lend. In fact, for more than a few projects, many would argue that the people, the ecologies and the economies of borrowing nations would have been better off if the Bank's money *had* been buried in a hole or burnt.*

Blame It on Rio

Lewis Preston was only one of numerous world celebrities at Rio, and one of the less publicized ones. Shirley Maclaine, the Dalai Lama, John Denver, Ted Turner, Jane Fonda, George Bush, Fidel Castro,

---

* The economies too? Recall the huge recurring costs, year after year, that developing countries have been saddled with after borrowing for ill-advised and inappropriate megaprojects such as huge dams and irrigation systems (e.g., India), recall the hundreds of millions that Brazil and Indonesia are borrowing for environmental rehabilitation in the wake of Polonoroeste and Transmigration—all of which divert future capital and more foreign loans to salvage and maintain "sunk investments," money that could be otherwise channeled into more productive and sustainable uses.

Olivia Newton-John, Bella Abzug, and Al Gore would all make their appearance—to name only a few. José Lutzenberger would not welcome the world as Brazil's environment secretary. Lutzenberger was prone to disabling attacks of undiplomatic candor and honesty; three months before UNCED he delivered a speech at the United Nations in which he urged industrialized nations not to give more money to developing nations for environmental purposes, because most of it would probably disappear in corruption.[46] For the Brazilian government, anticipating a unique opportunity to solicit more funds, this was the last straw, and the irascible scientist was immediately sacked.

Preston visited the Earth Summit in its very first days; he had an important speech to make. It was his mission to convince richer nations to support the IDA "earth increment" and to increase the replenishment of the Global Environment Facility. Before the delegates of more than a hundred nations he made an assertion which continued the Bank tradition of dubious environmental claims: "The GEF has already demonstrated its ability . . . to implement well-designed programs and projects in an effective manner."[47] Yet not a single GEF project was anywhere near conclusion when Preston spoke. (The first series, or tranche, of projects had been reviewed by member nations only fourteen months before; in only a handful at most had any actual activities even begun to be implemented, let alone completed, let alone subjected to any kind of independent evaluation.) The GEF's one indubitable success had been to commit hundreds of millions of dollars in record time to projects that scientists and NGOs thought in many cases were too hastily designed, railroaded through by Bank staff under pressure from senior management. Just four days after Preston's speech, the World Bank administrator of the GEF admitted in a briefing before NGOs that indeed the projects "could not yet be evaluated," given that "the GEF is very young."[48]

The United States played a spoiler's role in Rio. Although it weakened the climate change treaty and refused to sign the biodiversity treaty,* most of the earth's nations signed both. The climate change convention sets no legally binding targets or timetables for reducing emissions of CO_2 or other gases responsible for global warming, and the biodiversity treaty is so vague (countries commit themselves generally to conduct biological inventories, establish protected areas, and conduct environmental assessments for development projects) that there are no legal criteria through which compliance or noncompliance can be determined. The two conventions provide for separate international funds to compensate developing nations for the costs of reducing emissions of carbon dioxide and other

---

* In 1993, the Clinton administration signed the biodiversity convention, reversing the United States' position.

gases causing the greenhouse effect, and to cover the costs of beginning to inventory and protect habitats rich in biological diversity.

From the World Bank's perspective, the agreements were an important breakthrough in strengthening the Bank's role as money manager for the global environment. Over the objections of some Southern nations such as Malaysia, the GEF was selected as the interim funding mechanism for both conventions. The "interim" designation hardly reassured skeptics; the Malaysian delegates remarked that the World Bank was the kind of guest that, once let into one's house, was very hard to kick out. The same debate over funding instruments occurred in the final discussions over Agenda 21. As a concession to the South, the financing section of Agenda 21 allowed for numerous mechanisms, bilateral and multilateral, to fund its gigantic laundry list of projects. But again, the whole document is legally nonbinding; and the nations that have the money to give prefer it to be channeled via the World Bank, which they control, at least in theory.

A few days later, on June 11 and 12, fifty-four heads of state flew from around the world to join the more than fifty others already in Rio to attend the concluding plenary session of UNCED. The special airplanes of world leaders landed at the Rio Airport, one after the other, hour after hour, at intervals only minutes apart. "Rio Under Siege" screamed the headlines, as scores of tanks, armored vehicles mounted with machine guns, and thousands of armed troops patrolled the city in the largest security operation in history.[49]

The extraordinary display of naked military force was a disquieting backdrop to a world conference meant to usher in a new era of global environmental management. Was the state of siege an anomaly, or did it reveal and symbolize something about the whole approach of UNCED? It was an approach that was based on the nation-state as the principal legitimate interlocutor in the international system, an approach that attempted to deal with the global environmental crisis through a top-down, centralized, global project of agreed-upon administration and control among national governments and international organizations, with the World Bank in the lead.

Many at UNCED viewed the enormous security measures as not only completely normal (witness the precautions typically taken for the appearance of a single major head of state), but so banal as to be hardly worthy of thought. But perhaps we need to reconsider what we have come to accept as everyday and normal. That a military state of siege was required to hold such a meeting can also be seen as a forceful commentary on the degree of trust and transparency that existed at the end of the twentieth century between most of the world's national rulers and international bureaucrats, and the citizens of the planet. If the answers to global envi-

ronmental problems are to start with, and must be based on the local participation and trust of communities around the world, the Earth Summit
embodied in more ways than one the social and political approaches that
have gotten the planet into such a mess.

And yet citizens' groups and NGOs from several countries had attempted to influence the preparatory meetings for the Earth Summit held at the
United Nations over the preceding year. They had even succeeded in seeing a few vague but favorable phrases concerning nongovernmental organizations and indigenous peoples inserted into the nonbinding Rio Declaration and Agenda 21. However, for these two documents words were
cheap since in reality they committed no one to do anything. For the
most part the NGOs were relegated to a colorful ghetto, an eco-Wood-
stock called the Global Forum, in Rio's Flamengo Park, thirty miles from
the official conference center outside the city, Rio-Centro, a modernistic
structure built of asbestos cement. The Global Forum could boast its own
impressive statistics: 5,000 NGOs from around the world were represented,
more than 600 had a stand or booth at the Global Forum grounds, and
over a two-week period more than 400 meetings and events took place.[50]

And there were protests. The first was on June 9 in front of Rio-Centro; about a hundred NGO activists from several countries arranged themselves in the form of a human heart outside the main entrance, carrying
placards with messages such as "No Dams, No Eucalyptus, No Forced
Resettlement," "No Environment Without Democracy," and "Thailand
NGOs and People: Voice of the Voiceless." Police and military soon outnumbered the protesters, and helicopters circled. When a Venezuelan NGO
representative began a speech, stating, "We are here to get a voice that
inside has been denied," a soldier quickly forced him to stop.[51] The next
day 50,000 people marched through the streets of Rio in a demonstration
organized by Brazilian labor unions and supported by the Catholic
church, chanting slogans to samba tunes against the government, the
United States, and the International Monetary Fund. One of the most
popular chants was aimed at UNCED: "What is the use of all this ecology if
our people are oppressed and massacred?"[52]

The ugly face of UNCED was revealed in full force the following day. A
young Kenyan woman, Wagaki Mwangi, representing a Canadian youth
organization, was giving one of the few NGO speeches allowed in the plenary session at Rio-Centro. She criticized the summit, declaring that
"UNCED has ensured increased domination by those who already have the
power," and began to cite issues that the conference had completely
ignored, such as the disproportionate consumption of natural resources by
the North and the environmental destruction caused by the military. For
the only time during the entire two-week conference, the speaker's micro-

phone went dead, the translation of her speech halted, and the closed-circuit television broadcast to delegates in other parts of the conference center ceased. About ten NGO representatives from several countries gathered in a large open area inside the conference center to protest; they hoisted a banner reading, "UNCED Is a Farce." U.N. security police, who had been flown in from New York to guard the conference building proper, quickly intervened and forcibly dragged the protesters away, stripping them of their credentials. Delegates and journalists gawked, and a glass door shattered as U.N. police tried to force it shut against a television crew that was trying to come closer. The protesters denounced the "total disregard by the U.N., for the right to freedom of speech and assembly" at the UNCED sessions; a spokeswoman for the United Nations declared that "protests and demonstrations are prohibited on U.N. territory."[53]

The absurdity of the whole spectacle became apparent when time constraints allowed each national leader only five minutes for his or her main speech; the speeches were intoned in succession in the cavernous conference hall, hour after hour over two long days. Several leaders of the industrialized world—Helmut Kohl and John Major among them—endorsed a tripling or quadrupling of GEF resources, just as the Bank had hoped, but the "earth increment" received less support. George Bush proclaimed that he "had not come to Rio to apologize," and Fidel Castro gave the shortest speech of his entire life, four and a half minutes. It was an eloquent swan song for the aging Cuban despot, who, gray-bearded in his medal-bedecked uniform, evoked nothing so much as a lost extra from a Marx Brothers film. Quixotic costume aside, Castro's address was one of the most eloquent: "The ecological debt should be paid, not the foreign debt," he declared. "May hunger disappear, not man."[54]

Thanks to the maladroit diplomacy of George Bush, the United States was cast by the press as the villain of the Earth Summit. In reality, Bush rendered an enormous public relations service to many other national delegations, who were equally hypocritical and cynical on less publicized issues than the climate and biodiversity conventions. When the Malaysians and Indians, for example, criticized the GEF and the World Bank as "undemocratic," they meant that they preferred funding mechanisms where one country would have one vote, and where money would be disbursed with less oversight and fewer conditions. As leading developing nations called for "democracy" in the international system, they fought attempts to promote greater participation and access to information for their own people in the development process. That same summer of 1992, the Indian executive director of the World Bank led a lobbying campaign with other executive directors to ensure that the Bank's much-touted environmental assessments would not be made available to the public. The Indians, supported by other developing nations and by many European directors representing nations presumed to be progressive, trounced a token proposal of the U.S. executive director that the completed assessments at least be made available for consultation in a small room for scholars and NGOs, whose access to the Bank could be screened.*

The Malaysians and Indians also sabotaged proposals for a third convention that, it was hoped, would be signed at Rio, one protecting the earth's forests. Thanks to their opposition, all that emerged was a totally vacuous, nonbinding statement of "forest principles," which the negotiators officially designated as a "non-paper." There was a certain Alice-in-Wonderland quality to long hours of meetings among international diplomats and experts from over 150 nations debating the wording of what they agreed would be a "legally non-binding non-paper." But even here, as with most other issues, the hypocrisy and bad faith were hardly limited to one side.

The South rightly pointed out that Northern proponents of the proposed forest convention valued preservation of tropical forests as a "carbon sink" to offset the global warming caused by their own emissions of CO_2. Why should developing nations bear the cost of setting aside large areas of forest to help alleviate global warming when the biggest greenhouse glutton of all, the United States, responsible for nearly a quarter of all CO_2 emissions, arrogantly refused to undertake any measures to reduce them? Indeed, the Brazilians pointed out that the United States was subsidizing the destruction of its remaining old-growth forests in the Pacific Northwest while it sanctimoniously promoted the forest treaty. In the plenary meeting, the Emir of Kuwait announced that oil-producing nations "should not suffer further depletion of their resources" because of efforts to pursue sustainable development in the rest of the world. An epiphany of bad faith occurred when Saudi Arabia and Kuwait joined the United States in calling for the forest convention, but led other oil-producing nations in a fight that lasted until 3:00 A.M. on the last night of the conference to exclude any reference to renewable energy in Agenda 21.[55] (They lost.)

UNCED, from beginning to end, hinged on the question of money, and when all was said (a strong argument can be made that little was done in Rio), it was clear that the industrialized nations were going to commit much less than the developing nations had hoped, and most of it was to be channeled through the World Bank. The $125-billion annual amount cited in Agenda 21 was pure fantasy. In Agenda 21, the industrialized

* But a "Public Information Center" was finally set up in 1993 under a new Bank information policy.

nations "reaffirmed" the pledge they made in Stockholm in 1972 to contribute 0.7 percent of their GNP for foreign aid—a pledge that only five countries, all in Europe, had honored over the past twenty years. The United States was happy to sign on to this provision, since it maintained that it had never made any pledge in 1972 to reaffirm.

This was not the only step backward at UNCED. The Rio Declaration, which most of the world's nations signed at UNCED's conclusion, originally was intended to be a bold statement of principles and intentions of the world's nations concerning the environment and the next century. Unfortunately, it is in some respects weaker and a step backward in environmental commitment from the 1972 Stockholm Declaration.[56]

The Earth Summit, the leading German newsmagazine *Der Spiegel* proclaimed, was "The Festival of Hypocrisy."[57]

Unsaid at UNCED

Perhaps the most astounding accomplishment of UNCED was its success in removing from the official international agenda the very issues that many felt were the most fundamental for the ecological fate of the planet. Population, to begin with, was a non-issue at the official meetings, because of pressures from the Vatican and developing nations, as well as from the United States. Poor and rich nations alike had an interest in skirting the issue, because it concerns not only the consequences of demographic growth in developing countries, but also the much greater impact of population growth in the North on the earth's resources. Every new inhabitant of the United States makes a sixtyfold greater contribution to global warming than does an additional Mexican; a single Canadian's contribution is the equivalent of that of 190 Indonesians.[58] The environmental legacy of the world's military establishments was a non-issue, and complicated questions associated with the environmental impacts of transnational corporations received short shrift. Although UNCED deliberations focused heavily on the issue of more foreign assistance, little was said and nothing decided on the need to improve the ecological and economic quality of existing aid, totaling some $55 billion annually.* The tens of billions of dollars lost annually for developing countries because of trade barriers on the part of the industrialized nations was not on the agenda. Nor was the need for forgiveness of developing-country debt discussed,

---

* In such a convocation of governments, this was perhaps to be expected: Northern governments have never given much priority to assuring their funds are well used, and Southern governments resist as a matter of principal all efforts to attach more strings, conditions, and oversight to the funds they receive.

although by 1990 developing nations were paying over $50 billion a year to their creditors in net debt-related transfers (interest plus repayments of principal).

Most important of all, the official participants at UNCED based their deliberations, such as they were, on three premises that many nongovernmental organizations and critics—including an embattled minority within the World Bank itself—considered to be fatally flawed. David Korten, a longtime consultant to several international development agencies, former Ford Foundation professional, and grass-roots worker with Philippine nongovernmental groups, summarized these assumptions most succinctly: growth is the solution (or, there can be no solutions without growth); global economic integration will contribute to solving global ecological problems; foreign assistance and investment will make things better.[59]

Needless to say, these three premises are cornerstones of the World Bank's view of the world, and its message to the Earth Summit, embodied in the Larry Summers–dominated *World Development Report 1992* on "Development and Environment." The report provides the official rationalization of the issues. As such, it is worth examining a bit more closely, particularly with respect to the first premise on the ecological need for increased global economic production, since the implications of greater trade and more foreign aid are largely linked to how one interprets the impacts of growth.

The report assumes that economic growth in the North and South must continue, and indeed accelerate, with world GNP increasing 3.5 times by the year 2030. Although "if environmental pollution and degradation were to rise in step with such a rise in output, the result would be appalling environmental pollution and damage," and "tens of millions more people would become sick or die each year from environmental causes," the report declares that there is no need to worry "if sound policies and strong institutional arrangements are put in place."[60] Additional economic growth coupled with a market approach will buy or help develop whatever technological and policy fixes and cleanup measures are needed to manage the environment. The fundamental premise amounts to a reckless, blind gamble: with enough money, humans can buy whatever they need in the future to deal with whatever problems arise.

The report extrapolates dangerously from certain well-known facts. It is true that the most advanced economies have become less energy- and materials-intensive over the past sixty years, per unit of gross domestic product. Worldwide, this has meant a steady long-term decline in prices for most basic commodities, with disastrous consequences for developing countries dependent on the export of such raw materials (which doesn't seem to affect the World Bank's strategy of aggressive promotion of increased production of such commodities in many poor nations).* Projections popularized by the Club of Rome twenty years ago that there would be drastic shortages of metals and petroleum in the 1990s have been largely contradicted by trends towards lower prices and increased supplies. Thus, the report concludes, the problem with the ongoing destruction of the world's forests, water resources, and atmosphere is that unlike with minerals and energy, the scarcity of these resources is not reflected in market prices which would unleash "the forces of substitution, technical progress, and structural change."[61]

But major phenomena of global environmental deterioration—the destruction of the earth's ozone layer, global warming, and the destruction of biological diversity—are neither linear nor reversible, nor are their causes amenable to substitution. It is astounding that at the end of the twentieth century, the complex ecological interactions and biological phenomena which sustain planetary life should be viewed as so many "sinks" to absorb pollution, as "resources" whose being is defined by human economic demand and for which, once markets are created and prices are set, substitutes will be found. At the heart of the report's analysis is the extraordinarily risky wager that as-yet-undreamed-of technological fixes will magically make the world right. Here is the last gasp of a view of the world as pure, caricatural Cartesian "extension," as a homogenous "standing reserve" which can always be transformed into something else with the application of the correct method.

Let us examine one of the outstanding success stories in the twentieth century of how economic growth created demand and a market, which unleashed technical innovations leading to substitution of an older technology with a less materials- and capital-intensive alternative, structurally transforming the industrialized economies of the planet. It is nothing less than a paradigm of the economic and technological trends of modern economic growth, an outstanding example of the process in which the Bank's *World Development Report 1992* puts so much faith. And indeed, for decades, this story appeared to be a model of a "win-win" solution to an ecological and economic problem that fostered economic growth, increased human welfare, and virtually eliminated environmental risk.

* According to a study of the Organization for Economic Cooperation and Development (OECD), more than 60 percent of Africa's export earnings come from basic commodities (e.g., cocoa, palm oil, coffee, minerals, etc.) for which prices fall so rapidly with increased production and supply (i.e., for which the price elasticity of demand is such) that increases in export volume actually result in a decrease in earnings. (M. Godfrey, in T. Rose, ed., *Crisis and Recovery in Sub-Saharan Africa* [Paris: OECD, 1985], 178, quoted in Redclift, *Sustainable Development* [see endnote 89], 59.)

In the first quarter of the twentieth century mechanical refrigeration became widespread in North America and Europe, replacing the inefficient and unreliable use of ice. Refrigeration technology at that time relied on the cooling effect of the rapid expansion of compressed gases, mainly ammonia, but also sulfur dioxide and methyl chloride. It was a capital- and materials-intensive technology, using large, cumbersome compressors that had to attain high pressures. Accidents and explosions were a constant risk, and the gases were poisonous for humans. Thus, according to a U.S. National Academy of Sciences study, "toxicity and the need for large expensive compressors kept mechanical refrigeration from making headway with retail customers, who represented an immense potential demand."[62] The General Motors Frigidaire Division saw the potential, and one of its scientists, Thomas Midgely, Jr., achieved a technological breakthrough in 1931, when he invented Freon 12.

Nonflammable, nonexplosive, noncorrosive, and nontoxic, the various forms of Freon gas seemed the perfect technical solution to a host of environmental and safety problems. They also required less pressure to produce the desired cooling effect, so compressors could be smaller and less expensive. Freon soon came to dominate the market for refrigeration and opened up new retail markets because of its diminished capital requirements.[63]

The economic and social structural transformations catalyzed by the invention of Freon went far beyond what anyone could have imagined in 1931. Not only did it make the home refrigerator possible, but also air conditioning and the tremendous shift of economic growth to the American "Sunbelt."

Only after fifty-four years, in 1985, did the catastrophic global ecological consequences of the use of Freon gases, otherwise known as chlorofluorocarbons (CFCs), become apparent: scientists discovered the growing ozone hole over Antarctica. Ironically, the National Academy of Sciences concludes, "We now understand that the very quality that made them seem so safe—their stability—means they will continue to destroy ozone molecules far into the future even if we were to end their production and use at this instant."[64]

Is this example an unhappy fluke—or a paradigm of the danger of putting too much confidence in the technological fix? One thing is clear: humanity and the other forms of life on the planet cannot afford too many more global ecological surprises of this ilk, surprises delivered by blind faith in the forces of technological innovation and substitution. We might recall Václav Havel's warning against treating "the fatal consequences of technology as though they were a technical defect that could be remedied by technology alone."

The World Bank's message to the Earth Summit, welcomed by all governments and politicians, was the triumphant proclamation that "the environmental debate has rightly shifted from concern about *physical limits* to growth toward concern about incentives for *human behavior* and policies that can overcome *market and policy failures*." [Emphasis in original.][65] Yet in recent years a growing literature of "ecological economics," has increasingly focused the debate on precisely the issue the Bank claims is moot—the physical limits to economic growth. A number of studies have pointed out that neoclassical economic analysis has grossly overestimated the overall amount of energy saved through substitution (the use of energy-saving production processes by firms in industrialized economies).* According to Nobel Prize–winning economist Jan Tinbergen,** "Environmental degradation is a consequence of production and its growth . . . [and] it follows that saving the environment will certainly check production growth and probably lead to lower levels of national income."[66] Simple logic and common sense, along the lines of 1950s "development crusader" Walt Rostow's second thoughts that "trees do not grow to the sky," would seem to point to an hour of reckoning between human societies and the biosphere if they continue their present course.

Extraordinarily sanguine assumptions about the continued ability of market-driven technology and substitution to deliver more and more material wealth with less and less material impact do not appear to hold up very well. British researcher Paul Ekins points out that the most optimistic demographers estimate that world population will increase to at least 10 or 12 billion over the next fifty years before it begins to level out. Just to keep pace, world economic output would have to more than double, and technological improvements and efficiency would have to reduce by half the physically destructive impacts on the environment in order for the ecological stress of human economic activities not to increase. But the 1987 Brundtland report, the World Bank, and almost all politicians assume that a 3 percent annual growth or more in global economic output is needed to alleviate poverty in poorer countries. At 3 percent growth, production and consumption double every twenty-three years. Thus, Ekins points out, simply to stand still in terms of ecological impact

---

* "The increase in energy used indirectly to support labor and produce capital offsets some fraction of the direct energy savings and reduces the amount of energy saved by price-induced microeconomic substitution. As a result, *the macroeconomic energy savings associated with substitution are less, perhaps much less, than the sum of the energy savings at the microeconomic level* [emphasis added]" (Robert K. Kaufman, "A Biophysical Analysis of the Energy/Real GDP Ration: Implications for Substitution and Technical Change," *Ecological Economics*, vol. 6, no. 1 [July 1992], 49).

** Tinbergen was also the first chairman of the United Nations Committee on Development Planning.

over the next forty-six years, "technology must have reduced the environmental impact of each unit of consumption to one sixteenth of its present level . . . [a] more than 93% reduction." If population stabilizes in the middle of the next century and "green growth" continues to 2100, "every unit of consumption would [have to] be making only 1.6 percent of its current environmental impact."[67]

Worse, Ekins notes, in key sectors such as energy there are disturbing signs that efficiency is not increasing: the Organization for Economic Cooperation and Development (OECD), which gathers economic statistics on industrialized nations, forecasts a 1- to 2-percent yearly increase in fossil fuel use for its member nations through the beginning of the next century.[68] The world fleet of cars, trucks, and buses is growing at a rate of about 5 percent a year, mainly in developing countries, where the pent-up demand is enormous. Ekins notes that at this rate fuel efficiency will have to double every sixteen years simply to keep global vehicle emissions at their current level.[69]

The most definitive attack on the religion of ecological salvation through continued economic growth was published by none other than the World Bank. After bitter battles with Bank operations staff over the years, many of its most creative, innovative thinkers had been exiled to the Environment Department, where they would have less opportunity to raise objections to specific projects and loans. They had more time, however, to write. In the summer of 1991, economist Herman Daly and ecologist Robert Goodland edited and published a Bank "environment working paper" entitled *Environmentally Sustainable Economic Development: Building on Brundtland*.[70] This collection of essays argued that human societies had entered a critical historical transition from "empty-world" to "full-world" economics. Two Nobel Prize laureates in economics—Jan Tinbergen (1969) and Trygve Haavelmo (1989)—contributed pieces, and the environment ministers of Indonesia and Brazil (Emil Salim and José Lutzenberger) "warmly endorse[d] the clear thinking expressed" in the book.[71]

The conclusion of *Building on Brundtland* is a truly unpleasant one for politicians and governments, particularly in the North—in the words of Tinbergen and his coauthor, Roefie Hueting, "no further production growth in rich countries."[72] The theoretical underpinning of this viewpoint is that increased global economic growth necessarily entails greater total use, or "throughput,"* of natural resources and energy, even if resource use becomes more efficient, as has been the global trend. Good-

---

* "Throughput is the entropic physical flow of matter-energy from nature's sources, through the human economy, and back to nature's sinks" (Herman Daly, *Steady-State Economics,* 2nd ed. [Washington, D.C., and Covelo, Calif.: Island Press, 1991], 36).

land and many others argue that global ecosystems show worrying signs of having reached critical thresholds of unsustainable ecological stress and potential collapse—with the deteriorating ozone layer, global warming, and mass species extinctions as lead indicators.[73]

To maintain the quality of life and habitability of the planet in the future, the argument continues, the North must forgo its wasteful consumer values and embrace a changed notion of social development not linked to material growth. The material growth that does occur must be redistributed to the South to raise the minimum living standards of the poor. A strong push to accelerate environmentally friendly and economically more efficient technologies, and to transfer them to the South, will play a key role in the transition to a global "steady-state" economy,* with a steady-state population. Natural resources accounting—changing the calculation of national economic accounting to reflect and internalize the cost of the depletion of forests, fisheries, and other resources as capital losses (instead of as pure economic gain)—should also play a critical role in economic planning.**

If further growth along current trends is problematic, there are also

* A steady-state economy is one in which there is no growth of population or physical capital, with a constant (not increasing), sustainable "throughput," or flow-through, of matter and energy. It is "an economy with constant stocks of people and artifacts [physical capital], maintained at some desired, sufficient levels by . . . the lowest feasible flows of matter and energy [throughput] from the first state of production (depletion of low-entropy materials from the environment) to the last stage of consumption (pollution of the environment with high-entropy wastes and exotic materials)" (Daly, *Steady-State Economics,* 17).

** See Salah El Serafy, "Sustainability, Income Measurement and Growth," in Goodland et al., *Building on Brundtland* [see endnote 66], 54. Economist Robert Repetto of the World Resources Institute has published several studies on Indonesia and Costa Rica that demonstrate how conventional calculations of economic growth for these nations have grossly overestimated their real progress. For example, official statistics cite Indonesia's gross domestic product as having grown at a rate of 7.1 percent between 1970 and 1984; according to Repetto, if one attempts to internalize as a loss of capital (as one should, instead of treating conversion of natural resources as pure gain) the cost of the depletion of petroleum, timber, and soils during that period, real GDP growth is only 4 percent. Similarly, factoring in this loss of natural capital reduces the annual growth of investment from 11.4 percent to 1.3 percent. On the island of Java, an apparently vigorous upward trend in agricultural production was in reality totally offset by roughly equivalent losses, which Repetto quantifies, in soil productivity. (Robert Repetto, "Balance Sheet Erosion," *International Environmental Affairs,* vol. 1, no. 2 [Spring 1989], 131–35.) The example of Costa Rica–often viewed as an economic and ecological model—is equally sobering. Again, Repetto looks at the depletion of only three resources—forest, soils, and fishing stocks—and concludes that over the 1970s and 1980s the loss of natural capital in Costa Rica amounted to over 5 percent of the gross domestic product most years, rising to around 10 percent in the late 1980s. Conventional economic accounting, by ignoring these losses, overstated capital formation in Costa Rica by 41 percent over the same period. (Robert Repetto, "Earth in the Balance Sheet: Incorporating Natural Resources in National Income Accounts," *Environment,* vol. 34, no. 7 [September 1992], 19, 43.)

serious doubts concerning the two other questions—international trade and aid. According to Trygve Haavelmo and Stein Hansen, the worldwide trend towards freer trade and global economic integration—a key purpose behind the founding of the World Bank at Bretton Woods—"as we know it at present, is a curse from the perspective of sustainable development;" this is because "in a regime of free trade," countries that try to internalize the national, not to speak of the global, ecological costs of production lose out to countries that do not.[74] Finally, in light of the foregoing, it goes without saying that more foreign aid, World Bank–style, is part of the problem rather than a solution to global ecological problems.

Even if only part of what economists such as Tinbergen and Haavelmo are saying is valid, the political and social implications are enormous. It is astounding that the Bank's official message for the Earth Summit simply ignored these alternative views. If much of the official discourse of the Rio Summit was a "festival of hypocrisy," it was also a carnival of denial.

Although the "steady-state" view of the world espoused by Daly, Goodland, Tinbergen, Haavelmo, and others is more receptive in theory to local ecological and social concerns,* it also entails, like more conventional models, a vision of global, centralized environmental management. The World Bank, reformed according to the tenets of "steady-state economics," would play a key role in redistributing material growth from the North to the South, and in transferring environmentally friendly technologies. Herman Daly suggests that

in the new era the World Bank's official name, The International Bank for Reconstruction and Development, should emphasize the word reconstruction and redefine it to refer to reconstruction of natural capital devastated by rapacious 'development.'[75]

The Global Environment Facility, of course, is the prototype, however imperfect, for this "reconstruction of natural capital."

Who Shall Rule the World—and How?

Rio has been about governments, not about the planet.[76]
—Comment of the Malaysian ambassador to UNCED

* Haavelmo and Hansen, for example, condemn most current foreign assistance because it reinforces a pattern that transfers rents from resource-endowed developing nations to rich countries, which in turn supply "the South with machinery for speedier resource extraction . . . keeping down their prices of natural resources." But aid that assists "development of location specific technologies and patterns of consumption adapted to local, cultural, and habitual patterns . . . should be encouraged" (Haavelmo and Hansen, in Goodland et al., *Building on Brundtland*, 32).

On the penultimate day of the Earth Summit, an open debate on what it all meant took place among NGOs in a packed ballroom of the Gloria Hotel, the somewhat faded, turn-of-the-century edifice that served as headquarters for the nongovernmental Global Forum. The topic of the day summed up better than any other the stakes at and after UNCED: "Who will rule the world after Rio—the Bretton Woods Institutions, the United Nations, or the people?"[77]

It was hard to disagree with those who argued that the Bank would have a still more influential role in ruling the world. The accession in 1992 of the republics of the former Soviet Union to Bank membership had realized the Bretton Woods dream of a truly universal institution. And the Earth Summit confirmed the emergence of the World Bank as the preferred institution to assume the project of global environmental management. Through the Global Environment Facility, it would manage funds for the two conventions signed at the conference, and it appeared to be a main beneficiary of whatever additional funds the industrialized nations might contribute for the enormous Agenda 21.

Less publicized than the Earth Summit or the creation of the GEF, but equally significant, was the proposal put forth by Chancellor Helmut Kohl of Germany at the annual economic summit of the Group of Seven (G7) that had taken place in Houston, Texas, in 1990.* The conservative Kohl, hardly known before for his intense interest in biological diversity or rainforests, proposed at Houston that the Seven finance a "pilot program" to conserve the Brazilian rainforest. It was a calculated political response to defuse growing German popular pressure that Kohl's government do something about tropical deforestation. The Group of Seven entrusted the $250-million pilot program's formulation and implementation mainly to the World Bank. Initially, the Bank suggested incorporating these funds into the GEF, an attempted—and typical—bureaucratic sleight of hand that in this instance exceeded the habitual indulgence of the Group of Seven donors, who made it clear that the pilot program was to be a separate undertaking.

But the Bank's growing power was directly linked to the fact that the rich nations liked it that way—they controlled it. They were quite content to funnel more and more funds into the Bank on the assumption that somehow, somewhere, there were experts who, if given enough money, could come up with projects and solutions to deal with any problem. Helmut Kohl and the German government didn't know what to do about Amazon deforestation (the German aid ministry, like others in countries

* The Group of Seven consists of the seven countries with the largest industrialized economies: the United States, Japan, Germany, France, Italy, Britain, and Canada.

with big aid programs, was understaffed and overworked) but surely, with enough money, someone in the World Bank could devise a plan. Or so it appeared in Bonn.

The global economic playing rules are largely set by the Group of Seven, and these are the rules the Bank has to take as a given. These seven nations control 63.4 percent of world economic production and well over three-quarters of all world trade. Germany would certainly not lower interest rates, nor would the U.S. Treasury urge New York banks to forgive their Third World debt, simply to make the gross contradictions in the Bank's dealings with poorer nations less egregious. In the Gloria Hotel debate, a Brazilian NGO representative concluded that "the G7 practically control all our lives."[78]

Few put much hope in the capacity of the United Nations to deal with global environmental challenges. For one thing, the U.N. and its affiliated agencies are even less accountable than the Bank. Institutions like the U.N. Food and Agriculture Organization and the United Nations Development Program operate as virtually autonomous fiefdoms, the only practical occasion for oversight occurring at the annual or biennial meetings at which member states approve their budgets and work plans.* These gatherings of governing councils are, in the words of a high-ranking Rome-based U.N. official quoted in the *Washington Post*, "basically rubber stamp bodies." "There is no supervision of any agency on a weekly or monthly basis as you have in government."[79]

In recent years tremendous abuses and corruption have been uncovered at some U.N. agencies—with little or no ameliorating action taken. An internal review circulating within the United Nations Development Program—one of the three executing agencies of the GEF—describes "a deplorable vacuum of basic ethics," and "operational inefficiency and . . . gross mismanagement of financial and personnel resources."[80] According to the *Washington Post*, the same report cites a number of cases of corruption involving UNDP "that totaled millions of dollars in pilfered funds."[81] And according to Bo Jerlstron, the deputy director of a study team financed by Scandinavian governments (the Nordic U.N. Project), corruption and mismanagement "is a systemic problem to a very great extent.

* In September 1992, the *Washington Post* published a devastating four-part exposé of U.N. abuses. "Despite broad agreement on the need for reform," the *Post* concluded, "abuses within the [U.N.] organization persist and often go unpunished. The chiefs of some autonomous U.N. agencies rule their fiefdoms like autocrats, answering to no one. Regional mafias of U.N. bureaucrats have taken root, consolidating their power through favoritism in hiring and promotions. Recipient governments also routinely plunder U.N. programs, diverting aid from intended beneficiaries, with little remonstration from U.N. agencies" (William Branigin, "As U.N. Expands, So Do Its Problems," *Washington Post*, 20 September 1992, A1).

We have a governmental system in the U.N. that is not geared to get accountability."[82] The truly bad news is that in the public international system, the World Bank is possibly the *most* accountable and transparent institution.

That being said, Agenda 21 calls for the creation of a new U.N. "Commission on Sustainable Development." It would monitor governments and international agencies like the World Bank to oversee their fulfilling the conventions and agreements of UNCED, and their compliance with the principles of sustainable development in general, however the U.N. decides to define these terms. But at the opening sessions of the U.N. General Assembly in September and October 1992, a contentious debate was already brewing over the functions of the proposed commission: Southern countries were objecting to Northern proposals allowing a vigorous role for nongovernmental organizations, which in turn were hoping to use the commission as a forum to pressure governments. Since the World Bank has ignored the United Nations when it so pleased, it is difficult to imagine how one more U.N. commission could exercise even a smidgen of genuine accountability. One need only recall the 1947 agreement between the Bank and the U.N., in which the Bank reserved the right to withhold any information it chose, and the vain entreaties of U.N. Secretary-General U Thant to the Bank in the mid-1960s to cease lending to South Africa and Portugal, lending which violated a General Assembly resolution as well as the U.N. Charter itself.

The great paradox of the Earth Summit is that it occurred in large part because of growing popular discontent all over the world with the ecological deterioration of the planet. The money that richer governments were committing to the World Bank for the GEF was a reaction to growing popular and political pressures to do something. UNCED was monstrously unwieldy, and illustrated the inadequacies of attempting to address the ecological crisis of what was now a global industrial civilization through a convocation of representatives of 172 nation-states. Worse, it marginalized representatives of thousands of citizens' groups from around the world as a folkloric sideshow. But for those who criticized UNCED, what alternative could they propose? It was the only show on the planet, or so it seemed.

Near the end of the session in the Gloria Hotel on "who will rule the world," an elderly, distinguished gentleman from India rose to the microphone. To loud applause, in a vigorous voice he declared that "the question should not be who will rule, the question should be how will the people rule. It was the people who brought the governments to this forum."

Global Environmental Management

> Modernity's failure is the failure of a global techno-
> economic short-term project, locked into itself because
> it has become 'unhinged' from natural and social reali-
> ties. It works against the local and concrete interest of
> every human society (even if it serves immense private
> interests) and also against the general, long-term inter-
> ests of the planet as a whole and its inhabitants.[83]
> —Jean Chesneaux

The premise of the Earth Summit was that global environmental management can work. The project as it emerged out of Rio has
two principal approaches—a growing body of international environmental
treaties among nation-states, and increased foreign aid for environmental
protection and management, as well as purported poverty alleviation,
channeled and managed mainly through the GEF and other financing arms
of the World Bank. The vision is a quintessentially late-modern one, based
on assumptions with shaky underpinnings and contradictions more visible
than ever before. It assumes a world where investigators and officials can
efficiently gather information, starting with countless local ecosystems and
communities, and devise plans, programs, and rules at the local, national,
and international level to administer and manage the biosphere. The
nation-state is the basic unit in such a system of global environmental
management, though key powers at the global level are devolved to
bureaucracies with planetary responsibilities, such as the World Bank. In
short, global environmental management assumes—to summarize an
analysis published in the British journal *The Ecologist*—universally applica-
ble knowledge, effective global enforcement, and a world political culture
in which such knowledge and enforcement would be grounded.[84] Let us
examine these assumptions in turn.

The first question is epistemological, and cannot be neatly separated
from the structures of politics and governance in which it is embedded;
the growing revolt of local knowledges against the generalized, universal
development schemes of the World Bank that has been a theme of this
book is a leading example. Surely, if decades of failed international development efforts have taught anything, it is the folly of induced, uniform,
top-down projects. Such schemes ignore and often destroy the local
knowledge and social organization on which sound stewardship of ecosystems as well as equitable economic development depend. The most
important elements of local knowledge are lost when attempts are made

to abstract and generalize them to a national or global level—if the attempt is made at all. This knowledge cannot be separated from the place in which it is used and continually evolving; nor can local people's customs, methods, and skills be artificially reconstructed through top-down, administrative efforts.

A typical example, we might recall, is *muang phai,* the watershed conservation measures and water-channel maintenance practices of village groups in Thailand. Foreign aid assisted the government irrigation authority to build new, more expensive dams and channels, with little attention to local knowledge and practices. Control of the modernized infrastructure was vested in the government irrigation authority. Not unexpectedly, the new systems encountered unforeseen ecological and maintenance problems, since the alleged beneficiaries, local farmers, had been effectively dispossessed by the enclosure of the natural resources over which they once had real control. Attempts by the government irrigation authority, on the recommendation of foreign development experts, to set up new water users' associations among the farmers failed. There is ample documentation of analogous problems in many other areas of resource management, such as afforestation; and, once again, the World Bank's forestry projects are a paradigm of failure.* The conclusions of an Indian forestry official, describing the ruin of a World Bank reforestation project in the Himalayas which depended on the involvement of local villages, are worth repeating: "These solutions do not require much money, but they require attention to details, commitment. That is what is lacking. What we have learned is that you cannot throw money at these problems."[85]

The whole mode of "global policy discourse" that has become fashionable over the past decade is so general and jejune as to be irrelevant to many real political and social challenges. The key insight that such discourse misses is the extraordinary and irreducible heterogeneity of the biosphere at all levels. The diversity of local and regional ecosystems is the direct evolutionary and historical underpinning of the remarkable social and cultural diversity of human communities and societies. Effective social and political action has to be based at the appropriate level in the specific elements and constraints of this heterogeneity.

This profound heterogeneity of ecosystems and societies has other implications concerning attempts to know, predict, plan, and manage

* See, for example, Steve Coll, "A Plan to Save the Globe Dies in a Village," *Washington Post,* 24 May 1992, A1. In an article written in anticipation of the Earth Summit, Coll describes the collapse of a World Bank reforestation project in a small Indian village, Chopta. He views it as a troubling portent for the Earth Summit, which will call for more funding of similar projects. He cites interviews with villagers who contend that Indian government officials and World Bank staff never even visited the village, let alone tried to ascertain their needs.

global environmental crises and changes. There is increasing speculation that the behavior of regional and global ecologies, economies, and societies conforms more to the rules of new mathematical theories about chaos and complexity, or to the patterns of evolutionary biology, than to a predictable Newtonian-Cartesian model. Management authority Peter Drucker and French mathematician David Ruelle have advanced this view concerning the global economic system and national economies.[86]

At the Santa Fe Institute in New Mexico, an eclectic gathering of scientists and thinkers have formulated a whole new concept of economies and ecologies as "complex adaptive systems" whose units and structures are "self-organizing" entities in constant coevolution and coadaptation. One can think of such systems as immense networks of agents—whether they be cells, neurons, species, or households—operating in parallel, acting and reacting to what other agents are doing. Evolution and change continually originate from the bottom up, and neoclassical economic concepts of equilibrium and optimization are meaningless since the whole system is in a state of flux, delicately poised between order and "the edge of chaos."[87]

The behavior of these complex systems cannot be predicted or controlled, since they may be altered unexpectedly by factors which, statistically speaking, are insignificant. Thus, Drucker points out, "no complex system can exclude anything as 'external.'"[88] This phenomenon, known as "sensitive dependence on initial conditions," and popularized as "the butterfly effect,"* may make ambitious, centralized attempts to formulate and carry out global policies based on the gathering of statistically significant data problematic. Such information is essential for appraising what has already happened, but may be only as useful for ecological, economic, and social "management" as is information on last week's weather for knowing whether to carry rain gear for next weekend's outing. Ambitious attempts at national and international regulation may be inherently unreliable or ineffectual with respect to global ecological and economic change.** The flexibility and responsiveness needed to deal with such

---

* So called because of the now widely accepted hypothesis that global weather changes of great impact may result from minute changes in apparently trivial initial circumstances; for example, a butterfly flapping its wings and flying in one direction in the Amazon rather than another may initiate a sequence of events that results in a blizzard in Chicago several weeks later. (See James Gleick, *Chaos: Making a New Science* [New York: Viking, 1987], 8, 20–23.)

** For example, Peter Drucker notes that "the Chicago economist George J. Stigler (winner of the 1982 Nobel Prize in Economics) has shown in years of painstaking research that not one of the regulations through which the U.S. government has tried over the years to control, direct, or regulate the economy has worked. They were either ineffectual or they produced the opposite of the intended results. Stigler had no explanation; we now know that this is precisely how the 'butterfly effect' works—and will work again" (Drucker, *The New Realities* [see endnote 86], 166).

unpredictability can perhaps be exercised only in a more decentralized, local fashion.

A corollary of the butterfly effect is that events that have great global environmental and social repercussions may start from local incidents which at the time are indistinguishable from others. Over the late 1970s and 1980s, more than a thousand social activists were murdered in obscurity in the Brazilian Amazon, a number of them rubber tappers fighting for the protection of the rainforest. The assassination of one more in December 1988—Chico Mendes—and the immediate, intensive efforts of a handful of environmental activists in Brazil and the United States to ensure that the lifework of Mendes would not be forgotten, catalyzed an unprecedented outpouring of international concern and made the social and ecological crisis in the Brazilian Amazon an issue the Brazilian government could no longer ignore. Mendes became the first global ecological martyr. The uproar over his death was also a factor leading to the Brazilian government's subsequent lobbying to host the United Nations Conference on Environment and Development. And so an obscure Brazilian union activist in one of the most remote corners of the Amazon did more through his life and death to catalyze global environmental consciousness than most of the international conferences and environmental education programs ever undertaken.

The example of Mendes and the Brazilian rubber tappers aptly confirms the thesis of British researcher Michael Redclift that successful environmental management has to operate through the very "social groups which are being marginalized by the development process." "Attempts to 'manage' the environment internationally," he concludes, "through designated 'biosphere reserves' in vulnerable areas and international agreements to restrict access to 'the commons,' have proved largely unsuccessful."[89]

The impotence of many existing international environmental treaties further confirms Redclift's observations, and gives little ground for confidence in the effectiveness of many future conventions if nothing else changes. Most environmental treaties have no effective provisions for enforcement, and few data are collected on compliance.[90] Norway is a country that ranks near or at the top for its domestic and international environmental commitment. And yet a survey conducted by a Norwegian NGO, Bellona, concludes that Norway is probably failing to comply with twelve of twenty-seven international environmental agreements it has signed.[91] The long history of attempts to regulate whaling under the International Whaling Commission (IWC), for example, has been a sad tale of the exploitation of many species to the point of extinction by the very nations that one would think would have an interest in at least conserving resources for future harvests. Through the years, the commission consis-

tently agreed on quotas only after over-hunted stocks of a given species were already collapsing—some, it seems, irreversibly. In 1992 and 1993 Iceland withdrew from the IWC and Norway recommenced whaling despite international protests.[92]

One of the main functions of the United Nations Environment Program (UNEP) since its founding in 1972 has been to catalyze and promote international environmental agreements. Prior to the signing of the Montreal Protocol (1987) to regulate emissions of ozone-destroying CFCs, UNEP's crowning achievement was its Mediterranean Action Plan (1975), the most successful by far of ten action plans to clean up the world's seas by region. The highlight of the plan is the Barcelona Convention (1978), in which all eighteen Mediterranean states agreed to take drastic actions to reduce and purify sewage and chemical waste effluents in coastal areas.

Although the Mediterranean Action Plan was a great diplomatic success—it brought Albania, Libya, and Israel to the same negotiating table to agree on environmental collaboration—it is an environmental failure. The Mediterranean is becoming a dead sea. After huge expenditures, only 30 percent of the Mediterranean's sewage receives any treatment whatsoever.[93] In flagrant violation of other international conventions supposed to regulate discharge of petroleum at sea (the MARPOL Protocol), vessels release 650,000 tons of oil and other hydrocarbons annually in the Mediterranean, the equivalent of seventeen Exxon *Valdez* oil spills every twelve months.[94] The main sources of pollution—huge volumes of agricultural runoff and chemical waste flowing from the watersheds into every river and stream that debouches in the Mediterranean—do not come from so-called point sources on the coast, and are not adequately addressed by the "Land-Based Sources Protocol" (1980) to the Barcelona Convention. Fertilizer- and pesticide-intensive "green revolution" agricultural techniques, grossly subsidized through the European Community's agricultural policies, have drastically increased this "non–point source" pollution over the past twenty years.

The most optimistic assessments of the environmental effectiveness of the Mediterranean Action Plan claim that overall water quality has not gotten any worse since its inception in 1975, something of an accomplishment since population and production have increased in the Mediterranean region during the same period. This is a bit like a physician boasting that his or her treatment of a dying cancer patient has at least not hastened the patient's demise. According to political scientist Peter M. Haas, even these modest claims are anecdotal since "no synoptic data are available on Mediterranean water quality, nor are there time series data."[95]

Optimists concerning the effectiveness of international environmental treaties cite the Montreal Protocol mentioned above. Signed in 1987, it is

an almost unqualified diplomatic and technical success; in 1990, the industrialized and developing countries revised it and agreed on the total phase-out of production of ozone-destroying CFCs by 2000.* Unfortunately, to come to terms with many global environmental problems, diplomatic successes and technical breakthroughs alone may be largely irrelevant by the time they occur. Alas, the balance of the biosphere does not always respond on command even when, in rare cases such as the phasing out of CFCs, the world's nations become sufficiently concerned to agree on something and carry it out in good faith. The very thing that prompted unprecedented international action—the long-term persistence of ozone-destroying CFCs in the atmosphere once they are released— means that the ozone hole may continue to grow for years and perhaps decades after production and use of CFCs ceases. Moreover, as a National Academy of Sciences study on global environmental change warns,

> there is no guarantee that the chemicals developed as substitutes for CFCs will prove benign in the long run (CFCs themselves were thought to have ideal properties when they were introduced in the 1930s). Hydrochlorofluorocarbons (HCFCs) and hydrohalocarbons (HFCs), prominent among the candidates to be used as substitutes for CFCs, have already provoked opposition from those concerned about their potential contribution to the greenhouse effect.[96]

The same study warns against taking the Montreal Protocol as a precedent for dealing with global environmental change. The Montreal Protocol requires no real changes in national and global economic and social behavior; it phases out one technical fix and replaces it with another,** which, it is hoped, will prove environmentally more benign (an all too familiar story). Truly addressing other global environmental problems— tropical deforestation and climate change, for example—may require changes of historical dimensions, involving millions or even hundreds of millions of responsible actors, and poses thorny questions of equity within nations and among them.[97]

Centralized, legalistic environmental management fails at the national level, too, in most developing countries. Costa Rica is a particularly illuminating example since it has often been cited as a model—a developing nation that has set aside and protected a larger proportion of its forests and other natural areas than the United States. Costa Rica has benefited from a more intense level of international environmental assistance than almost any other country, through project-oriented NGOs like the World

---

* Other ozone unfriendly chemicals such as halons, methyl chloroform, and carbon tetrachloride are also to be phased out.

** The study points out that there are only two dozen CFC manufacturers worldwide, and leading companies such as Dupont had already developed substitutes by the time the Montreal agreement was in place and saw economic opportunities in promoting them.

Wildlife Fund and other bilateral and multilateral agencies, and it is the beneficiary of one of the largest "debt-for-nature" swaps.* Indeed, partially because of this international attention, an oversized environmental bureaucracy has proliferated in Costa Rica over the past fifteen years. A 1988 study identified twenty-seven "sections, divisions, units, juntas, institutes, councils and oficinas, often working at cross purposes and almost never acting in cooperation with each other, charged with implementing one or another aspect of environmental policy."[98] The country has over 1,500 different environmental laws and decrees in force, many of them incompatible with one another,[99] something that is not the problem it appears, since few laws are enforced.

But in recent years, Costa Rica has also had one of the highest rates of deforestation of any nation on earth, averaging 4 percent annually for much of the 1980s.[100] By 1985, 25 percent of the area of the country's legally protected forest reserves had been cleared, and many of the country's famed national parks were threatened or already partly deforested.[101] Most of the deforestation has proceeded through a cycle that starts with logging, followed by occupation for three to five years by landless farmers, and ends with final conversion into cattle pastures. The deeper causes are structural ones that post-UNCED solutions of global environmental management, such as the biodiversity convention and more aid for environmental projects, could hardly begin to address—highly unequal land tenure coupled with a population growth of 2.7 percent a year, and a sadly typical macroeconomic crisis linked to the country's declining earnings from commodity exports and the increasing burden of its foreign debt.

By the mid-1980s, Costa Rica had the highest per capita foreign debt in the developing world, $1,500 for every inhabitant of the country. Forty percent of Costa Rica's foreign exchange earnings was going to service this debt, and three-quarters of all the new foreign loans the country received simply went to help pay it back.[102] The country was obliged to follow the conditions of a typical World Bank–IMF adjustment program, resulting in disproportionate budget cuts for the National Parks Service and the Forestry Directorate, as well increased economic pressures on the poorer, landless members of the population to migrate into still unoccupied forest lands and protected areas.[103] A plausible case can be made that the adverse environmental effects of the World Bank–sponsored adjustment program far exceed in scale and magnitude whatever marginal envi-

* A debt-for-nature swap involves the writing down or reduction by creditors (which can be industrialized-country governments or private international banks) of a specific amount of a developing nation's foreign debt with the condition that a portion of the forgiven debt be used in domestic investments in nature conservation.

ronmental benefits the country might obtain from a few million dollars for discrete environmental projects it might receive from an expanded GEF.

Thus, the project of global environmental management alone is unlikely to succeed, based as it is on the existing international political system of nation-states and multilateral organizations.* "In circumstances of accelerating globalization," sociologist Anthony Giddens observes, "the na-tion-state has become 'too small for the big problems of life, and too big for the small problems of life.' "[104] International organizations reflect at best a lowest common denominator among nation-states, and all too often, as we have seen, a Weberian nightmare of unaccountable bureaucratic self-perpetration. Public international environmental law is in large part unenforced and unenforceable. Nation-states and international organizations seem increasingly unable to deal with the unpredictability of larger, complex ecological and economic systems, whose behavior can be radically altered by statistically invisible events; most often they lack the capacity and the flexibility to deal with the heterogeneity and unpredictability of local ecosystems, local knowledges, and local communities—in other words, to address reality.

Finally, the state and multilateral organizations, when they do act effectively, tend to pursue technical solutions for problems that have been caused by the relentless pursuit of technical solutions, an approach that exacerbates, in Havel's words, "the crisis of contemporary technological society as a whole, the crisis that Heidegger describes as the ineptitude of humanity face to face with the power of technology."[105]

* There are numerous proposals for such management: Vice President Al Gore has outlined a "Global Marshall Plan" in *Earth in the Balance,* and in May 1989, a total of forty nations, including most European states (but not the United States), called for the creation of a new, supranational United Nations environmental authority to regulate the global environment. Their appeal subsequently became known as the Hague Declaration.

What on Earth Is to Be Done?

We know now that social situations, social behavior, social problems are much too complex to admit a simple "right answer." If they can be solved at all, they have several solutions—and none is quite right. . . . We thus find ourselves at the end of two centuries of Western history.[1]
—Peter Drucker

Virtually everywhere in the world, pockets of resistance against modernity's misdeeds are growing.[2]
—Jean Chesneaux

The year 1994 marks the fiftieth anniversary of the Bretton Woods Conference. The ideals of Bretton Woods were, above all, worldwide freedom and peace. The World Bank was founded as a means to these ends. But for nearly half a century it has often been a prime accomplice in a quiet war against the diversity of human cultures and our planet's biological inheritance, the social and biological underpinnings of humankind's future. It was not a conscious war, at least for the first decades, and it is important to emphasize the word "accomplice"—since the Bank was often only a helpmate for the modernizing, initially well-intentioned megalomania of a thousand government bureaucracies around the world. But it became, more and more, an agent itself, establishing new bureaucracies and setting the agenda for many more.

Some may ask how an institution such as the World Bank, engendered of such noble goals, could become so intellectually corrupt and institutionally debased. But given the premises the Bank was founded on, it was inevitable. From the seventeenth century on, the project of development has been one of unprecedented power and control, over nature and other humans. To centralize such power leads to disaster. In surveying the ruins of the twentieth century's totalitarian nightmares, we realize that few misapprehensions have led to more human misery than to entrust the means to affect the lives of hundreds of millions into the hands of a few who not only are unaccountable, but claim that their decisions are dictated by objective systems of reason that are beyond appeal. These systems are ideologies. Development, too, is an ideology, the last modern ideology. We must cease seeking objective solutions to the crisis of objectivity. When we pretend that politics is banished from institutions with tremendous power to affect other humans, politics eventually reigns pervasive, camouflaged, corrupt, and unchecked.

In the World Bank we see the foundering dream of modernity, the failure of a universal institution that would attempt to predict, induce, and administer global development. The Bank's disarray may be only one sign among others of the twilight of the modern era: the collapse or weakening of multinational states such as the U.S.S.R., Yugoslavia, India, and Canada; the growth of ethnic and regional nationalisms, many of them alarmingly atavistic; the increasing appeal of religious fundamentalism not only in the Muslim world, where for the most part the promise of development has simply failed to materialize, but also in industrial countries.

In many countries there is a growing distrust of the power of multilateral institutions, which many now view as a historical regression in terms of political accountability and transparency, values embodied, however imperfectly, in the democratic procedures arduously won in Western nations through hundreds of years of social and political struggle. The attempts of European Community bureaucrats to proceed with the devolution of democratic powers to a centralized bureaucracy in Brussels have rightfully encountered resistance across the Continent.

Commentators refer to these contradictory social and political phenomena as harbingers of "postmodernity," as consequences of the very culmination of modernity in a global market and communications culture that paradoxically unleashes pluralistic forces and movements of unexpected intensity.[3] The growing perception that neither local nor global economic and ecological systems are predictable from the standpoint of the state, means that the world cannot be managed through conventional centralized projects of administration and control. Peter Drucker calls this realization "no more salvation through society,"[4] and David Korten calls it "the end of the dominant state."[5]

The postmodern world appears to be one of global interdependency rife with indeterminacy, at times at the mercy of random events that can unleash abrupt, discontinuous change. We are faced with the end of what have been characterized as grand, universal narratives (international development World Bank–style is one of the grander), with the impossibility of totalizing knowledge, and with the demise of administered society, all of which began with Descartes and Bacon. As Drucker and others have observed, there is no longer one right answer to a given social problem, but often several, each one a function of a specific, local situation. In the place of the universal, modern project, we confront the irreducible, and somewhat menacing, because uncontrollable, heterogeneity of post-modernity.[6]

The danger and the political crisis of modern technological society are now global. The danger, we have seen, lies in the continued pursuit of self-referential, autonomous technology, and in the enclosure of the entire surface of the planet as a field for the unrestrained exercise of instrumental reason. Continuing in this direction leads not to economic equity and social equilibrium, but to increasing disorder, ecological instability, and violence. The political crisis is above all a question of the lack of account-ability, responsiveness, and openness of the institutions and bureaucracies, public and private, that are the vessels and administrators of this uncanny planetary technological nihilism. The more these institutions with univer-sal agendas try to predict, administer, and control the world, the more it evades them in increasing turbulence and chaos.

When the nation-state and the international system fail, as they increas-ingly do, we are left with a Somalia, a Bosnia, a Haiti, a Kashmir. We shall see many more if a way cannot be found to reinvent national and interna-tional institutions, and to find diverse alternatives to deal with the world-wide economic, political, and environmental challenges of the postmod-ern era.

The global environmental predicament embodies these dilemmas of postmodernity, but it may also point to a path that leads beyond them. It poses a conundrum that existing international institutions cannot unravel: the threats are increasingly worldwide, cumulative, and total, but solu-tions must take place at the local level everywhere on the planet. Indeed, if the proponents of limits to growth and the need for a steady-state econ-omy are even partially right, the economic and social behavior of most of the world's inhabitants must change radically.

What on earth is to be done?

Global Civil Society

For many years, out in the forests, we have been putting our bodies between the chainsaw gangs sent by the ranchers and the trees that provide our way of life. Now, we are doing the same thing here in the city, at this hearing, with the law on our side.[7]

—Julio Barbosa, 1990

It is therefore intended that the Climate Alliance of European cities with the Amazonian peoples would make possible direct contacts between local authorities in Europe and in the Amazon region. . . . They [the inhabitants of the Amazon rainforest] are right to fear that large-scale and centrally planned environmental protection projects will . . . brush them aside and disregard their . . . requirements. There is already experience to show that nature reserves or reservations usually only drive them away or rob them of their autonomy, while the destruction of the forest often continues unabated. The Climate Alliance . . . wants to create a cooperative relationship in which the partners respect other forms of knowledge and ways of learning, i.e. of social existence.[8]   —The Climate Alliance of European Cities, working paper, 1990

We might begin by looking back once more at the Earth Summit. For all its disappointments and hypocrisies, its real significance may be the simple fact of its taking place. It took place because nation-states and international organizations were forced to respond, albeit clumsily and ineffectually, to the growing worldwide pressures of an emerging global civil society. The summit will fade into history, perhaps much more quickly than the heads of state who were present would like to think. But the deeper worldwide social and political currents that made it inevitable will continue—and intensify. These currents, and the nongovernmental movements to which they are giving birth, can be a source for the rejuvenation and restructuring of national and international institutions, and for the creation of new institutional structures. The Indian gentleman at the last debate in the Gloria Hotel was right: it was the people, after all, who had brought the governments and leaders of the world to Rio.

We have seen how over the past decade and more, around the world but with particular vehemence in developing countries, local populations long marginalized from the grand narrative of modern history are mobilizing to defend ecological balance and fight against the destruction of resources upon which their survival depends. Altogether, in the developing nations there are hundreds of thousands of NGOs with more than 100 million members.[9] In this book we have only been able to mention the activities of a few in countries such as Thailand, Brazil, Indonesia, and India. In a country we have not examined, the Philippines, over 5 million people belong to some 16,000 NGOs, of which probably 4,000 are concerned with development and environment issues.[10] Many of these developing-country NGOs are in turn members of broader-based national coalitions, and these coalitions have become increasingly vocal and effective. Environmental, social justice, and human rights groups around the world are forming dense, flexible, information-rich networks with one another, self-organizing systems that have their own evolutionary dynamic.

These grass-roots movements, with all their limitations, have emerged as cultural and political antidotes to the dangers of technological nihilism and unaccountable bureaucracy. They embody a saving power in a time of great danger—a sense of planetary responsibility rooted in and arising from very specific local concerns. This concrete political capacity to link the local with the global is the cornerstone of emerging global civil society. It is a new phenomenon in history. Let us examine several more examples to identify other characteristics of global civil society.

First of all, at the local level the phenomenon is not as new as it may appear. Many social movements in developing nations embody in new forms long traditions of popular protest against injustice and exploitation. The Chipko movement in India started in 1973 with spontaneous interventions by women in Himalayan villages to protect local forests from logging contractors, who had been granted permits to deforest by state forestry agencies.* Although commonly thought of as an ecology movement, or even as a feminist one, Chipko is in reality a continuation of more than a century of rural revolts and peasant movements by Indian villagers against the enclosure and logging of common forest areas by state forestry agencies, first under the British, and after 1947 by the national and state governments of independent India.[11] Indeed, some authors have suggested that the popular origins of Chipko can be traced to a famous protest that occurred in 1763 in Rajasthan, when members of a Hindu sect sacrificed their lives to prevent tree felling ordered by the Maharajah of Jodhpur.[12]

Chipko and the rubber tappers' movement in Brazil are among the best known cases of local forest peoples organizing to protect resources held in common; there are many others. In the pine forests of Honduras

---

* The women literally encircled trees with their bodies, embracing them in an ultimate gesture of protection and care—thus "Chipko," which comes form the Hindi verb meaning "to hug." The Chipko protests spread through the Himalayas and to forested hill regions in the South of India such as the Western Ghats. As a result, in 1981 India's Prime Minister Indira Gandhi declared a fifteen-year ban on tree felling in the Garwahl Himalayas, the region where the Chipko protests originated. But the movement continued to spread; Ghandian activist Sunderlal Bahuguna led a 5,000-kilometer foot-march from Kashmir to Bhutan to spread the Chipko message between 1981 and 1983. In Bahuguna's words, "Ecology is permanent economy" (Bahuguna, cited in Paul Ekins, *A New World Order: Grassroots Movements for Global Change* [London and New York: Routledge, 1992], 143). (See Guha, *The Unquiet Woods* [see endnote 11], especially pp. 152–84.)

more than 6,000 families depend on resin tapping. In the early 1970s, these villagers launched logging blockades and organized cooperatives to obtain forestry concessions for extractive resin harvesting to conserve the pine trees on which their livelihood depends. Today, the villagers physically patrol the forest and limit access to loggers and agricultural encroachers; on two occasions they went to meet with the head of the national forestry agency to demand that outside logging and encroachment be halted. Ironically, the greatest threat to the pine forests of Honduras now may be proposals to transfer the forests to private timber companies, on the theory that common property resources cannot be protected.[13]

A similar tale occurred in the heavily forested Sierra de Juarez mountains of southern Mexico in 1980, when thirteen communities formed the Organization for the Defense of the Natural Resources and Social Development of the Sierra de Juarez.* In 1981, they organized the first national meeting of forest community organizations in Mexico. After a bitter fight, the communities won a major legal precedent in 1982 and established their right to community control of adjacent forests in their mountain homeland.[14] Halfway around the world, on the large southern island of Mindanao in the Philippines, a comparable grass-roots movement began in the late 1980s: logging blockades by local villagers spread to protests at the regional and national level, finally leading the government to acquiesce to a logging ban for the entire Mindanao province of Bukidnon.[15]

A key characteristic of many of these movements is the attempt to regain local management and control of common resources that are threatened by unsustainable harvesting and exploitation. Much of the literature on such common property resources reveals a prejudice on the part of some development planners and economists that private, individual property rights are the only means to protect "the commons," for example, forests and water resources.[16] Without private ownership, the thesis goes, resources held in common will simply be ravaged on a first-come-first-serve basis, since no one has a long-term interest in conserving a resource he or she does not own. The social and economic reality in many poorer countries, however, is often the contrary: private ownership and/or government management frequently has resulted in over-exploitation, while many local communities have evolved sustainable management

---

* They were fighting the renewal of a forestry concession to a large paper and logging enterprise, Fabricas de Papel Tuxtepec (FAPATUX). They launched their own newspaper and declared in its first edition, "We will no longer permit our natural resources to be wasted, since they are the patrimony of our children. The forest resources should be in the hands of our communities" (David Barton Bray, "The Struggle for the Forest: Conservation and Development in the Sierra Juarez," *Grassroots Development*, vol. 15, no. 3 [1991], 15).

systems for natural resources to which they have access and upon which they depend, even if they do not legally own them.*

Indeed, the proportion of national land area administered by government agencies in many developing nations is startlingly high. In India, nearly a third of the country's land is owned by the government, 22 percent of it by state forest departments. The Thai Royal Forestry Department's 7,000 employees attempt to administer 40 percent of Thailand's land, occupied by millions of farmers who are technically squatters. Fifty-five percent of the Philippine land area (occupied by more than 18 million people) is administered by the government forest agency, and 74 percent of Indonesia, occupied by between 30 and 40 million people, is the domain of that country's forest department. Many of the locally based environmental movements in developing nations are in essence movements to reverse enclosure, to regain the huge commons that have become the property of the state.

Many community-based systems of environmental knowledge and management embody a historical coevolution between particular local ecosystems and distinct human cultures. Some researchers suggest that since human societies have evolved until recently as subsystems of ecosystems, human communities all over the world have inherent self-organizing capabilities to manage local ecosystems in a sustainable fashion, provided they are not dominated or destroyed by subsequently imposed top-down control and management:

Examples include communal land tenure in high mountain meadows and forests in Torbel, Switzerland; common land management in Hirano and area villages in Japan; and the *huerta* irrigation system in the Valencia area and elsewhere in Spain. . . .

These common property institutions are found with all resource types, many of them non-traditional, covering a large range of regions and cultures throughout the world. Specific institutions can arise in less than ten years, and may endure over centuries (but evolve constantly).[17]

These examples illustrate a concept of critical importance: local human communities and economies, while embedded in larger social and ecological systems, can be thought of as complex adaptive systems in their own right, evolving and creating their own conditions, within their environments, of order, feedback, and adaptation.** Moreover, the widespread

* A critical need for the long term success of common property systems is the legal securing of land tenure or usufruct rights for local communities. See Stanley, "Demystifying the Tragedy of the Commons" (see endnote 13), 35.
** It is equally important to bear in mind the numerous examples of environmentally and economically *maladaptive* human societies, a good many of them "traditional" or "primi-

existence of such self-organizing capacities in human societies (at different, interconnected levels from the local to the regional, national, and international) implies the possibility of an alternative global order—or rather, set of orders—to the one based exclusively on centralized nation-states, multilateral organizations like the World Bank, and transnational corporations.

The internationalization of ecological and social conflicts in Brazil during the 1980s is a good case in point for examining the relationship between an evolving national civil society and the state. It may also illustrate the emerging qualities of a nascent global civil society. As with the Chipko movement, the protests of the Amazon rubber tappers and Indian populations have deep historical roots. The rubber tappers' resistance dates back nearly a century, and that of the Indians to the dawn of the modern age—which for indigenous populations began as a still continuing nightmare of enclosure, dispossession, and death. For Brazilian anthropologist Eduardo Viveiros de Castro, the unexpected emergence of local, national, and international environmental activism transformed not just politics in the Amazon, but the whole nature and space of international social and economic policy.

In the 1980s NGOs began to articulate local social and environmental interests on a worldwide scale, becoming an unexpected counterweight to the unchecked exercise of transnational economic interests and the geopolitical machinations of nation-states. "Establishing a new context between the local and the global, the regional and the planetary, questioning abuses of political representation at the national and international level," these groups form nothing less than a global "antibureaucracy."[18]

The idea of the extractive reserve itself—the most innovative solution to the dilemma of rainforest conservation—came, in the words of leading Amazon researcher Marianne Schmink, "like many other initiatives proposed by peasants, rubber tappers, and Indian groups . . . not from a planning office but from more than a decade of struggle in a changing political environment."[19] The pressures of Brazilian NGOs led to the adoption in 1988 in the new Brazilian constitution of several critical provisions establishing the rights of Indians to their lands and the rights of all Brazilians to a sound and healthy environment. Brazil's leading environmental journalist, Ricardo Arnt, cites some fifteen examples in the 1980s where inter-

---

tive." (See Robert B. Edgerton, *Sick Societies: Challenging the Myth of Primitive Harmony* [New York: Free Press, 1992].) The point is not that a technologically advanced society is necessarily maladaptive, and a rural or traditional community necessarily in balance with its environment (both can be either adaptive or maladaptive), but that the consequences of maladaption in a single, global culture may entail disaster on a scale unprecedented in human history.

nationally organized pressures by Brazilian and foreign NGOs not only influenced lending decisions of the World Bank and the Inter-America Development Bank, but led to specific changes in Brazilian government policy.[20] These changes include environmental impact procedures that provide for public participation and access to information, and (a more mixed blessing) the establishment of numerous governmental agencies concerned with environmental conservation.[21] The expanding alliances and campaigns involving local organizations of forest inhabitants in the Amazon, national Brazilian groups, and NGOs abroad empowered local groups with resources and political credibility they had never before possessed.[22]

Armed with lap-top computers, faxes, and modems, NGOs in the Amazon have formed powerful, responsive networks with national groups in São Paulo and Rio, and international NGOs in Washington, Berlin, and Tokyo. They influenced—and are continuing to influence—not only Brazilian government policy, but also the flow of public international finance, through a kind of global electronic *polis*.[23] And they were only one example of how the spread of affordable information technologies has contributed to the growing empowerment and proliferating networks of grass-roots organizations all over the developing world.[24] Nation-states and international organizations must wake up to a rude surprise, one they still have trouble digesting: international politics and policy must now deal not just with the negotiations and conflicts between governments, but also with those of nongovernmental organizations vis-à-vis the state and organizations of states.

Many of the achievements of the Brazilian NGO movement over the 1980s—the demarcation of new kinds of protected areas, the creation of environmental impact assessment laws and new governmental agencies—can and will fail if they are carried out in the spirit of global environmental management, treating people and localities as inputs or fields for the exercise of instrumental reason and centralized power. The effectiveness of such governmental and legalistic reforms depends on their responsiveness to the needs of civil society, and on civil society's full involvement and participation. Indeed, environmental assessments can be counterproductive if carried out without real public consultation and timely consideration of alternatives because they can merely ratify ill-considered and unsound projects.

Brazil's relatively new environmental assessment law (1986) is a case in point.[25] Brazil's law does not only call for environmental assessments for certain kinds of projects, it recommends that the assessments be written in publicly understandable language and requires public hearings to review the studies. For the first four years it was largely ignored, not only by the

Brazilian government, but by the World Bank and the Inter-American Development Bank. It was just one of tens of thousands of unenforced and unenforceable environmental laws and regulations enacted and quickly forgotten—and not just in developing nations.

But in the Brazilian state of Acre, at least, public awareness and mobilization made the law enforceable, indeed, required that it be enforced. On May 11, 1990, 450 people gathered in the municipal auditorium of Rio Branco, Acre, for the first public hearing ever held in the Amazon on proposed forest clearing. A consortium of cattle ranchers had applied to the Acre state environmental agency for a license to clear 14,300 acres of rainforest for pasture expansion. The National Council of Rubber Tappers, with the help of sympathetic lawyers and scientists, prepared a detailed rebuttal of the environmental assessment presented by the ranchers. The ranchers argued that deforestation and pasture expansion would bring more economic progress to all of Acre—implying that the fundamental issue was a "trade-off" between "growth" and "protection."[26] The public hearing went on for over three hours, and cheers resounded when activist Gumercindo Rodriguis proclaimed,

We want a moratorium on forest clearing because we know that for us, the local people, the sustained use of forest resources is better than cattle ranching. This is our political proposal for all of Amazonia.[27]

A few days later, the state environmental agency ruled against the deforestation proposal.

Fourteen months later, an even larger public hearing, attended by nearly a thousand people, took place in the town of Laranjal do Jari, Amapá state, in the northeastern Amazon basin. Here the state government wanted to construct a road 125 kilometers long through a forest area that had been designated as an extractive reserve for rubber tappers; the town of Laranjal was accessible only by riverboat, and the road would link it to the state capital. The rubber tappers were not against the road, but they thought it essential that the forest areas where they lived be legally demarcated and protected as extractive reserves before construction commenced; conflicting land claims with ranchers also needed to be settled. After the hearing, the governor of the state set up a special commission that included local communities and NGOs to demarcate four extractive reserves. The state halted illegal gold mining, which was causing mercury pollution, in the demarcated areas. It also agreed to support a Brazil-nut processing plant run by the rubber tappers; Brazil nuts are one of the most valuable export products of the rainforest.[28]

Both cases were examples of organized groups regaining control of local resources for sustainable use and ensuring the enforcement of a new national environmental policy. Both show that there was a way out of what for two decades had been a virtual pandemic of armed conflict over land rights in the Amazon; the public hearings and debates allowed land disputes with cattle ranchers to be resolved peacefully. In the case of the highway in Amapá, road building in the rainforest did not have to unleash deforestation and violence, provided the rights and interests of local populations who had an interest in conserving the forest were recognized and guaranteed *first*.

Emerging global civil society is also giving rise to new forms of international assistance which circumvent the nation-state and the cumbersome multilateral organizations based on it. Some of these initiatives link the local and the global by channeling growing international public awareness and civic activism into concrete actions that simultaneously reduce consumption in the rich localities of the world and assist environmental conservation in the poor. For example, the German state of Hessen, in response to growing public pressure and NGO activism, has banned the use of tropical timber in public projects it finances.[29] It is one of thousands of municipalities and provinces all over Europe that have taken this step (more than 1,200 in Germany alone). Hessen has also granted $250,000 to a local NGO in Rondônia, the Instituto de Pré-História, Antropologia, e Ecologia (IPHAE), to rehabilitate degraded forest lands. According to veteran journalist Juan de Onis, IPHAE has successfully launched three tree nurseries growing local species, which are helping hundreds of farmers to raise tree crops on deforested land. The program is fast on its way to becoming a statewide system. "The state forestry institute spent millions of dollars provided by the World Bank's Polonoroeste Project," de Onis records, "and put 800 people on its payroll, but it was never able to organize a state-wide nursery system."[30]

The Hessen example is not an isolated one. In fact, combining local and international action to protect the biosphere in a network that circumvents existing national and international institutions could provide a new model for the evolution of global civic action and foreign assistance in the future. The most ambitious initiative along these lines is the Climate Alliance of European Cities with Indigenous People of the Rainforests for the Preservation of the Earth's Atmosphere, founded in 1990.

Already 217 municipalities in Germany, Holland, Austria, Italy, and Switzerland have pledged to reduce CO_2 and other greenhouse gas emissions below national norms, ban the use of tropical timber, and simultaneously provide community-to-community support for tropical forest regions in developing nations. The Climate Alliance has formed a partnership with the regional umbrella organization for the various Indian groups in the Amazon basin, the Coordination of the Indian Organizations of the Amazon Basin (COICA). COICA, founded in 1984, includes the Brazil-ian Union of Indigenous Peoples (UNI), which represents Brazil's 300,000 Indians, belonging to more than 150 distinct tribes; the Peru-vian national Indian organization, the Inter-Ethnic Unification towards Development of Peruvian Forests (AIDESEP), with 300,000 members in more than 60 ethnic groups; and national Indian organizations for Columbia, Ecuador, and eastern Bolivia. The Climate Alliance is consider-ing financing a number of COICA project proposals to support demarca-tion of Indian areas, reforestation of degraded lands, and education and community services.[31]

The Climate Alliance was formed by activists in Germany as a specific response to the global political conundrum posed by the worldwide envi-ronmental crisis—how to think locally and globally, and act locally and globally. The Alliance's founders explain that

as a result of the breakdown of existing institutions (it's true—they were not creat-ed for such large-scale problems) . . . it is important to fall back on a tradition that gave modern Europe distinctive political and cultural impulses—the city democracy. Although the public can act as a sounding board that secures the nec-essary practical decisions involved with climate protection, the societal and cultural dimensions of the necessary reorientation are still far removed from the conscious-ness of this society. Changes that affect the everyday life of every citizen don't need only large political majorities. . . . They [must] also allow for comprehensive opportunities for participation by the public.[32]

The partnership of the Climate Alliance and COICA illustrates one of the aforementioned aspects of evolving global civil society: the explosive growth of worldwide networks among local communities and NGOs. These networks are nothing less than a "global scale learning process"[33] in which international social and political evolution is put into fast forward. Unlike the World Bank's "learning by doing," this process works toward finding new forms of social, political, and economic organization, and new combinations of old forms (like a rejuvenation of European city democracy) that will create not one common future, but many sustainable futures. It is an ongoing global evolution to conserve a plurality of cul-tures, social values, and narratives, and many separate human destinies, in the face of the totalizing juggernaut of modernity.

Evolving global civil society is based above all on the free generation and exchange of information, with openness and participation as prerequi-sites. It is the recognition that decentralized, flexible, locally rooted responses are indispensable if world civilization can hope to deal with the global environmental crisis. Global environmental management alone fails, because there are no global solutions, only local ones with a global understanding and perspective.* Such understanding and perspective is best communicated through networks, not through centralized efforts of prediction and control. In the words of Thomas Hines, a Philadelphia writer who has written eloquently on these issues,

thinking on a global scale may make it more urgent to solve problems in a particular geographic region or a particular community, but it probably won't suggest how to solve them. Answers will more likely come from an understanding of differences and the complexity of their interaction than from any glib globalism.[34]

The proliferating movements and networks of global civil society also embody another principle forgotten in the global technocracies—that there are limits to the exercise of instrumental reason, that human societies and communities if they are worthy of the name embody distinct cultural values and principles not subject to "trade-offs" or to eradication because they are pockets of "market failure." In practice, this means reaffirming the primacy of the political in the root sense of the word—reaffirming the values of the community, of the *polis,* rather than surrendering them to technocratic decision-makers outside the democratic process. Only in open, participatory, democratic hearings and debates can the legitimate place of these values and these choices be worked out. Global civil society of necessity demands accountability head-on from all political and economic institutions, something that has put it on a collision course with the World Bank and similar organizations. In the face of governments and international organizations that to solve our current predicament invoke more of what has caused it, global civil society calls not just for caution, but for care. The evolution of global civil society may be the best chance for the goals of global environmental management—conservation of biodiversity and the arrest of global warming, for example—to be supported and realized, as they must be, place by place, community by community.

Whither the State?

This is not to say that we should, or could, live in a world without large national and international institutions; the whole point is that many of these institutions are failing and need to be reinvented or

* In the words of Indian activist Vandana Shiva, "The global must bend to the local, since the local exists within nature, while the 'global' exists only in offices of the World Bank and IMF and the headquarters of multinational corporations. The local is everywhere. The ecological space of global ecology is the integration of all locals" (Vandana Shiva, "The Greening of Global Reach," *The Ecologist,* vol. 22, no. 6 [November/December 1992], 258–59).

replaced with alternatives. The nation-state, for example, is faltering in many parts of the developing world. Many governments are corrupt, inefficient, and incompetent, but we have seen how in countries such as Brazil, India, Thailand, and the Philippines vigorous, dense networks of self-organizing NGOs and community movements have proliferated. In case after case we can see the growing potential of NGOs and local communities to change laws and policies, to invent new, better-adapted political institutions and processes, and even more important, to ensure their effectiveness. In the end, the viability of the state and the vigor of civil society are interdependent. Well-intentioned laws, policies, and institutions are ineffectual without participation, equity, accountability, and transparency. With the encouragement of the state, the organizations of civil society can evolve and flourish, or with its intolerance or indifference, they can wither. The key is to maintain and encourage the delicate but necessary tension, which at times is an adversarial relationship, between the state and civil society. This dynamic tension opens a space between order and chaos, allowing human communities to evolve, learn, and develop.

Summarizing discussions on the study of complex adaptive systems with physicist Doyne Farmer and computer theorist Chris Langton, science writer M. Mitchell Waldrop speculates on these political implications:

The mysterious "something" that makes life and mind possible is a certain kind of balance between the forces of order and the forces of disorder. . . . Right in between the two extremes . . . at a kind of abstract phase transition called the "edge of chaos," you also find *complexity:* a class of behaviors in which the components of the system never quite lock into place, yet never quite dissolve into turbulence, either. These are the systems that are both stable enough to store information, and yet evanescent enough to transmit it.

Common sense, not to mention recent political experience, suggests that healthy economies and healthy societies alike have to keep order and chaos in balance—and not just a wishy-washy, average, middle-of-the road kind of balance either. Like a living cell, they have to regulate themselves with a dense web of feedbacks and regulation, at the same time that they leave plenty of room for creativity, change and response to new conditions. "Evolution thrives in systems with a bottom-up organization, which gives rise to flexibility," says Farmer. "But at the same time, evolution has to channel the bottom-up approach in a way that doesn't destroy the organization."[35]

Indeed, Sheldon Annis of Boston University has observed that the competence and efficiency of the state is often stronger where the nongovernmental sector is more prolific and vigorous. Countries like Costa Rica and Mexico, with all their problems, have both governments and grass-roots social movements that are better organized, more democratic and more effective than those in Benin or Paraguay. The more developed the country, the greater its organizational density and complexity at all levels. While NGOs try to change the policies and institutions of a given state to make it more responsive to local and national needs, the successful state will seek to adapt and respond through more finely tuned, more flexible and efficient systems of information gathering and governance.[36] If the notion of development has any meaning, it must start with the fostering of an appropriate social, economic, and political order, one which allows the organizational density and complexity of a society to evolve with the greatest freedom and robustness.

There are specific policies that states and international development organizations can promote which encourage rather than stifle the evolution of grass-roots organizations and the strengthening of communities. Participation and access to information concerning development plans and decisions come at the top of the list. Legal frameworks that legitimize NGOs, labor unions, and grass-roots groups follow, along with land reform and titling; community-based systems in health, family planning, and nutrition; education for women; agricultural and commercial credit that would truly reach the landless and the poor—the list, which can be gleaned from much existing development literature, goes on and on. Carrying out such measures requires an active partnership between civil society and the state in order to create a "virtuous circle" which would strengthen society and government in poorer countries.[37] It is important to promote these policies in poorer nations, and Annis believes this should be the role of the World Bank.

The World Bank should be encouraged, but alas, rhetoric notwithstanding, it has been largely incompetent and often a major obstacle to the realization of measures that foster the development of civil society. Even when governments and aid agencies succeed in carrying out such policies on a piecemeal basis, their longer-term effectiveness is often undermined by the enormous economic pressures of global integration and the seemingly irresistible technological imperatives of modernity gone awry. For example, in many poorer regions, including China, India, Africa, and the Islamic world, increased global economic integration over the past decade has resulted in an alarming decline in the relative status, freedom, and welfare of women—despite the attempts of some aid agencies to give a special emphasis to assisting women.[38]

We are faced again with the classic quandary of an interconnected global system: for anything to change anywhere, everything must begin to change everywhere. It is not simply an affirmation of faith or hope, but an empirical observation that the phenomena we have identified in global civil society are signs that this change is starting to emerge in response to, and almost as a function of, the ever more imminent dangers posed by the current world system.

At the heart of this change is an evolution in the way in which humankind and its institutions, small and large, think about and relate to the world. It is a transition towards overcoming Cartesian dualism and the concurrent adulation of instrumental reason that still reigns over our world. This is a transition that began in the physical sciences earlier in this century, but which still has to run its full cultural course.

Once again, let us take a specific example of how some thinkers perceive this change. In a seminar held at the Santa Fe Institute in 1989, Stanford economist Brian Arthur outlined three levels of analysis that policy makers in governments and institutions might use to think about the environmental and economic fate of the Amazon rainforest. The first level is traditional cost-benefit calculations, although, according to Arthur (as paraphrased by Waldrop), "all too often, the apparent objectivity of cost-benefit analysis is the result of slapping arbitrary numbers on subjective judgments, and then assigning the value of zero to the things nobody knows how to evaluate."[39] A second level of analysis is political and institutional, looking at the social and political players as elements of a system. This is the approach of anthropologists, sociologists, and historians. The third level of analysis, according to Arthur, is that of new ideas about complexity, which reject the Cartesian, Enlightenment duality between an actor and that actor's environment:

There's no division between doers and done because we are all part of this interlocking network. If we, as humans, try to take action in our favor without knowing how the overall system will adapt—like chopping down the rain forest—we set in motion a train of events that will likely come back and form a different pattern for us to adjust to, like global climate change.[40]

We have seen that the complex systems of which we are a part are constantly in flux, and in some sense may be fundamentally unknowable: we have developed methods and techniques for understanding and explaining them, but prediction and control do not work very well. It is meaningless, Arthur says, to talk of "optimizing benefits or options" if the system or network is the unit; it would be like parents talking about optimizing their benefits and options vis-à-vis their children. This makes no sense at all if the idea is to think and act for the good of the family. Accommodation, coadaptation, responsiveness, and flexibility are the key goals, not predicting and controlling events to maximize benefits for a single actor or group of actors.[41] "So the question is," Arthur concludes, how do you maneuver in a world like that. And the answer is that you want to keep as many options open as possible. You go for viability, something that's workable, rather than what's "optimal." A lot of people say to that, "Aren't you then accepting second best?" No, you're not, because optimalization isn't well-defined anymore. What you're trying to do is maximize robustness, or survivability, in the face of an ill-defined future.[42]

The end of Cartesian duality means, then, the abandonment of "optimalization" as an overarching value—in other words, the end of a world in which totalizing instrumental reason can reign supreme. We are in the midst of a momentous historical transition in which the world we have created through three centuries of modernity is now so changed that it is forcing us to abandon its epistemological, cultural, and political assumptions. In such a period of change and uncertainty, values such as preserving future options and diversity, and conserving the robustness of ecosystems, local communities, and institutions assume extraordinary importance. These are the very approaches and values, we have seen, that are emerging out of global civil society, in the struggles and proposals of the growing networks of NGOs and grass-roots groups all over the earth. The societies that will succeed will be the ones where the state and civil society recognize their interdependence and their mutual roles as evolving, learning, coadapting processes in a larger system, one in which human society and nature are inextricably intertwined in an embrace of life—or death.

Whither Large Institutions?

Cartesian universalism was realized economically in the giant corporations . . . all but taming the future through planning and capital resources. But the gigantic markets that once provided fertile fields for mass production are disappearing. . . . [To survive] their rigid hierarchical structures are giving way to flatter hierarchies and more flexible and decentralized forms of organization.[43]
—Albert Borgman

The network is the paradigm, not the Catholic Church or the military.[44]
—John Sculley, CEO of Apple Computer

The emergence of global civil society over the past decade is connected with other long-term economic and social changes to which all large institutions must adapt. These changes are elements of what could be characterized as an evolving global postmodern political economy.

Some of them we have already mentioned: the failure of hyper-centralized management and planning; the abandonment of "salvation through society"; the recognition that there are many different paths to resolve social problems, rather than a single, universal approach; and the suspicion that economies and societies may behave like complex systems in mathematics, statistically unpredictable and discontinuous. All of this means we dwell in a world that no longer is, and never really was, amenable to totalizing, Cartesian visions of knowledge, prediction, and control. This postmodern planet of "new realities"* could almost be in a different galaxy, separated by millions of light years from the one Robert McNamara thought he inhabited when he ran the World Bank.

One of these new realities is an ongoing global economic metamorphosis that has been characterized as a transition from "Fordism" to "Flexible Accumulation,"[45] or "flexible specialization."[46] In this evolution, capital is becoming truly transnational, and economic transactions are undergoing increasing compression of time and space through global communications technologies. International money flows, with a new dynamic of their own, have replaced the exchange of goods and services as the dominant, integrating factor in the global economic system.[47] Subnational and supranational regions rival nation-states as prime economic units. Flexibility, adaptability, and rapidity of response become key factors for the success of large companies, and the centrally managed and planned firm is faced with its competitive demise if it cannot restructure and decentralize to meet these demands.[48]

The implications of these trends for large economic and political institutions have already been momentous. The collapse of the Soviet Union and the crises of IBM, General Motors, Sears, and even that of the New York City school system** may not be unrelated. According to John Scul-

---

* The term in this context is Peter Drucker's, from the book with the same title.
** The following lament of the former head of the New York public school system reads as an elaborate metaphor for the World Bank. Replace chancellor with president, schools and classrooms with programs and projects, district superintendents with country directors and task managers.

> The chancellor is chief executive of a byzantine central bureaucracy. . . . Questions of quality and individuality are lost in the quagmire. The central bureaucracy cannot think creatively. It adapts very slowly and tries to control and manage rather than lead and support. At the same time the chancellor has no direct authority over elementary and junior high schools. District superintendents do not report to the chancellor and the chancellor has few tools available to change what happens in individual schools and classrooms. . . . Minor changes like increasing the size of the central board . . . or creating more local districts will not accomplish real reform. We need to learn from corporate restructuring efforts that less is more and that monolithic entities are not responsive to customers or successful in the marketplace. . . . We need to decentralize. (Anthony J. Alvarado, "No One Person Can Save New York City's Schools," *New York Times,* 20 February 1993, 19.)

ley of Apple Computer, "The command and control model of running a large organization no longer works." Successful companies are decentralized and close to the customer, with locally attuned feedback systems.[49] Michael Rothchild, writing in *Forbes*, notes that "successful information age companies such as Johnson & Johnson and Dow Corning, are flattened networks of smaller, independent organizations that share little more than a bank account and a corporate logo."[50] The key, once again, is the nature of self-organizing learning and evolution in complex systems. As Rothchild notes, intelligence, whether in humans, machines, or organizations "emerges from communication among processors arranged in massive parallel networks," whether the processors are neurons, microcomputers, or small groups and communities.[51] In this rapidly evolving global ecology of information and institutions, the World Bank resembles nothing so much as a bulky, rusting mainframe computer conceived in the age of vacuum tubes.

Successful economies are becoming "knowledge societies,"[52] and thus increasingly less materials- and energy-intensive. These factors are being replaced with information and skills custom-tailored to specific local situations and problems. These trends are encouraging, since they point to the need to humanize and naturalize technology, rather than to technologize humankind and the earth. Such an approach renders technology adaptive, local, and particularized, depending more on organizing information in response to specific human and environmental needs than on the proliferation of massive ecological interventions and gigantic, standardized hardware.*

Many of the alternative approaches advocated by critics of conventional development embody such characteristics, for example, the "soft" energy paths of end-use efficiency and conservation,[53] and new approaches of alternative agriculture and (not so new) integrated pest management. According to a U.S. National Academy of Sciences study on alternative agriculture, these approaches are not a single system, but combinations of systems and practices finely tuned to local ecological circumstances, replacing capital and energy inputs with "more information, trained labor, time, and management skills per unit of production than conventional farming."[54]

Integrated pest management (IPM), for example, replaces intensive pesticide applications with continual monitoring of the specific ecological conditions that encourage pest proliferation in a given farm. Flexibility

* Thomas Hines has coined the phrase "subtle progress" to characterize this approach. "Subtlety would depend on immense technological sophistication, but that would probably be the easy part. The tough, but crucial task would be to take the vast machinery of modern society off automatic pilot" (Hines, *Facing Tomorrow* [see endnote 34], 240; see also pp. 207–41).

and timing are critical. Careful soil preparation practices, encouragement of natural pest predators, and judicious application of smaller quantities of pesticide at critical stages of the pest cycle are key elements. IPM is more knowledge- and labor-intensive, but when successfully applied drastically reduces pesticide use (and costs) and increases production. Paradoxically, though many of these approaches have evolved in the North, and particularly in the United States, they would seem to be suited for developing countries, rich in human resources, time, and existing or potential local knowledge, and short on money.*

Governments and large agencies have an indispensable role in diffusing these new technologies, but to do so they must learn a new flexibility and responsiveness. The World Bank, with its centralized, uniform approach, dominated by overwhelming pressure to lend, has shown that for the most part it is a singularly inappropriate institution to promote and transfer such approaches.**

Some observers of official international development institutions are beginning to reach the same conclusions that the private sector and some NGOs are acquiring in practice. Stephen B. Cox, who leads Acceso, an NGO working in Central America, and is director of planning for the Central American Institute for Business Administration in San José, Costa Rica, declares that "it is time to adopt a humbler epistemology of development. The complex challenge of promoting effective development requires more complete knowledge of a wider array of variables than any organization can hope to command." Development institutions need to emphasize "feedback, incentives, participation," and "accountability links," all of which Cox characterizes as a need to shift from "rigor in design" to "rigor in process."[55]

In the private sector, the evolution of economic institutions proceeds in a freer setting than that of the international leviathans of government-subsidized development assistance. The successful behemoths of only a decade ago are faced with extinction if they cannot reinvent themselves, and more fail than succeed in the longer term. Meanwhile, a diversity of alternatives emerge and flourish; the once lilliputian Microsoft now has a larger market capitalization, and many think a brighter future, than IBM.

* In Indonesia, a national IPM program supported by bilateral aid agencies and FAO has reduced pesticide use 50 percent between 1986 and 1992, while raising rice production 14 percent. The Ministry of Agriculture's $130-million annual insecticide subsidy was eliminated (Peter Kenmore, U.N. Food and Agriculture Organization, Manila, personal communication, 23 February 1993). Only in 1993 did the Bank begin to support the program.
** Even in the case of the Indonesian IPM program described in the previous footnote the Bank has been reluctant to abandon support for its traditional clientele in the Indonesian agriculture ministry, who have been incapable of delivering IPM training and consultation with the farmers they are supposed to serve.

What Is to Be Done with the World Bank?

The urgency of reinventing the World Bank—or stopping it—became apparent as never before with its obstinate insistence through early 1993 to continue financing the Sardar Sarovar dam in India. The last months of the Bank's involvement in Sardar Sarovar reveal a total crisis of accountability and credibility at the highest levels.

Bank management, we recall, recommended continuing disbursements despite the urgings of the Morse Commission that the Bank step back. On October 13, 1992, Morse wrote president Lewis Preston, with copies to all of the executive directors, charging that Bank management "ignore[d] and misrepresent[ed] the main findings of our review." Preston wrote back with an angry, blanket denial that did not deign to respond to any of the specific examples of misrepresentation Morse had enumerated. Morse, in failing health, at the end of a distinguished career that spanned decades in the U.S. Congress and in high-ranking posts in the United Nations, flew to Washington to plead with the executive directors not to rubber-stamp the Bank management's proposal to pour more money into the project.[56]

On the afternoon of October 23, 1992, in the Bank's august wood-paneled boardroom, the directors met to vote on the fate of the project, with Preston, the India country department staff, and numerous other high-ranking Bank officials attending. The Dutch executive director acidly reminded all present that the Executive Board had called for the creation of an independent commission because they could not trust Bank staff.* The representative of Austria lambasted Bank management for its strong-arm lobbying of the directors in preceding days to keep the project going, also expressing his own doubts about management's trustworthiness. Then U.S. Executive Director E. Patrick Coady rose and accused management of a "coverup," noting that "what is at stake is the credibility of the Bank." He observed that if the Executive Board allowed Bank management to continue with the project "it will signal that no matter how egregious the situation, no matter how flawed the project, no matter how many policies have been violated, and no matter how clear the remedies prescribed, the Bank will go forward on its own terms." Although the representatives of Canada, Australia, Germany, Japan, and the Nordic countries joined with Coady to oppose continued disbursements, they

* Although she condemned the Bank's mismanagement of the project, she endorsed continued funding, arguing that the recently elected Indian government should be given one more chance. The fate of the nearly one-quarter of a million people the dam and canal system would displace did not seem to weigh very heavily in her calculations.

represented less than a majority of voting shares, some 42 percent. The Bank would continue to fund Sardar Sarovar for at least another six months. Back in India, among tens of thousands of tribal people in the Narmada Valley, the news spread shock waves of despair.[57]

At the end of March 1993, the Board was to meet again to consider Sardar Sarovar. Now it appeared more likely that directors holding a majority of votes would call for the Bank to halt funding. As a face-saving device for both the Bank and the Indian government, Indian officials announced a few days before the meeting that they would not ask the Bank for any more disbursements. At a press conference to explain the Bank's withdrawal, officials of its India country department continued to tout the virtues of the dam.

What to do with the World Bank is first of all a question of how to better address the needs of the people, particularly the poor, in developing countries. These nations now include much of the former Soviet bloc as well as what used to be thought of as the Third World. Part of this task may require large-scale international institutions, but the ones that will be successful will acquire more and more of the characteristics of decentralized networks. Clearly, if the World Bank were to be "reformed," the reforms would have to be so far-reaching that it would be in effect a new institution. Such changes would require a critical mass of mobilized public opinion and pressure in the Bank's major donor countries. Large private corporations, faced with the brutal competitive imperative to change or perish, sometimes achieve such a transformation, but often they are replaced by new, more agile competitors. One of the problems is that the World Bank does not feel the spur of competition (the regional development banks are more clones and junior accomplices than competitors). The Bank's quasi-monopoly is an artificial one, conferred upon it by its major donors, most recently at Rio with the role they have assigned to the Global Environment Facility.

The first step is to halt the source of the problem—money, which after all is the ultimate source of the pressure to lend. If the Bank is not reformable (we shall return to the specific elements of some reforms a bit later), reducing its finances will limit its influence; if it is, experience shows that credible threats to funding are the last recourse, and the most effective one, to force recalcitrant bureaucracies to reinvent themselves. But even more important, the public should pressure the Bank's member governments to encourage and support a diversity of alternative institutions and channels for foreign assistance, ones that would have a better chance of helping people and the environment. Greater diversity and competition are desperately needed to generate alternative structures and networks, to create a flexible, effective, and responsive international system, one that can deal with global problems at the local level.

For example, the novel model for community-based action of the European Climate Alliance is worth developing on a broader scale. To address the problem of global warming, the Climate Alliance recognizes the need for simultaneous change in the North and South, and tries to put this into practice in a decentralized fashion by linking local actions to change economic behavior in the North to aid for communities in the South. The classic approach of centralized, supranational aid agencies is to throw money at governments in the South while failing to address the need for change in the North. The links and exchanges between European municipalities and Southern NGOs that characterize the Climate Alliance are much closer to the management model we discussed earlier of a network of micro-processors (or other organized systems of information and intelligence, be they neurons or social groups) operating in parallel, as opposed to a single, central operating system or mainframe computer. If the goals of global environmental management are to be achieved, and if foreign assistance is to be truly reinvented, one could start with supporting and creating networks, like the Climate Alliance, that embody common interests and shared responsibilities of real communities in the North and South.

There are also international development agencies that take an alternative approach to that of the Bank, one that is better attuned to civil society and local circumstances. Their approach focuses on providing technical assistance and small grants and loans (typically less than $500,000) to local communities, small businesses, farmers, entrepreneurs, nongovernmental groups, and cooperatives in the developing world. This is a strategy that has a demonstrated capacity for promoting economic development that is much more likely to be environmentally sustainable and culturally appropriate, and to help the poor.[58] Three such organizations based in the United States are the Inter-American and African Development foundations, and Appropriate Technology International, established by acts of Congress in 1969, 1980, and 1976, respectively. These institutions are almost a reverse image of the World Bank: they were conceived to circumvent large government ministries and support small projects at the local level.

The Inter-American Foundation (IAF) and the African Development Foundation (ADF) have a high proportion of anthropologists and sociologists on staff, as well as economists. A typical project involves a small grant to a women's or farmers' cooperative to promote small business enterprises, or to a local community organization for afforestation. As their names indicate, IAF and ADF support projects in Latin America and the

Caribbean, and in Africa. IAF has directly supported rubber tappers' organizations in northwest Brazil, and has played a key role in financing and supporting the resin tappers' cooperatives in Honduras and the community forestry organizations in Mexico discussed earlier. Appropriate Technology International (ATI) has a mandate to provide small-scale enterprises and farmers in developing countries with environmentally benign technologies, access to capital, and marketing assistance.

Another prototype is the British private voluntary organization Oxfam, which now has operations all over the world. In Africa, for example, Oxfam works in twenty-five countries, and in most of these nations it has offices. In 1992, hundreds of Oxfam staff were at work all over Africa managing $36 million in grants to support some 1,200 community-based projects.[59]

The annual budgets of such institutions are small, less than those of many single World Bank projects: about $30 million annually for the Inter-American Foundation, $10 million for the ADF, and less than $5 million a year for ATI. Their funding and operations should be expanded, and the creation of similar organizations encouraged. Both the Netherlands and Norway have established comparable public foundations for community-oriented foreign assistance.

It is true that even with substantial funding increases, the amounts of money that can be transferred from North to South through such community-oriented foreign assistance is only a small fraction of what the World Bank and its sister institutions are capable of lending. But if our examination of the Bank reveals anything, it is that foreign aid, particularly in the form of big projects, is a highly perverse and counterproductive way to move money to alleviate the very real and urgent macroeconomic pressures on developing nations. These pressures should be alleviated through debt relief and relaxation of trade discrimination against the poorer nations of the world, an alternative we shall discuss more a bit later.

The chances for reforming the Bank are in large part linked to making its member governments more accountable and responsive. The international campaign of NGOs for environmental reform of the past decade has shown that mobilized nongovernmental activism can make a difference in influencing governments and, in some respects, the multilateral development banks, but we have seen that most of the changes that have occurred so far have been more bureaucratic than substantive. The Bank's major shareholding governments have been willing to challenge individual projects and policies, but not more deeply rooted institutional problems. But we should also remember that some of the changes that the campaign has prompted are of great environmental and social significance: for one thing, the Bank has gotten out of the business of funding agricultural colonization schemes in pristine rainforests. We shall see no more World Bank–financed Polonoroestes and Transmigrations.

When all is said and done, it is clear that the Bank's member governments find that it serves important, if dubious and disingenuous political purposes, purposes more important than the consequences of individual projects. Indeed, most of them have tacitly endorsed a situation where Bank management and staff have operated semi-autonomously over the years, withholding information from the Executive Board and on occasion misleading and deceiving the directors. For the countries of the North, we have seen that the Bank is a convenient political and financial tool in the attempt to plaster over the contradictions of inequitable North-South economic relations and provides an excuse to avoid dealing substantially with debt relief. Most recently, the Bank has been useful in bolstering cosmetic responses to public pressures to deal with the global ecological crisis. As an institution, the Bank is not suited to address these issues or to resolve them, but it serves governments as a dangerously deceptive alibi and furthers the illusion that something is being done while the problems fester.

Ministers and officials of Southern governments, while they protest against the Northern-dominated voting structure of the Bank and its arrogant negotiating tactics, have become addicted to its loans. The Bank's $24-billion annual lending is nothing less than a global political patronage machine without precedent in world history, one that greases the gears of finance, planning, energy, and agriculture bureaucracies—and the ambitions of their cadres—around the developing world.

In the near future, the World Bank will continue to occupy a unique international political space, a kind of Archimedes' point from which powerful leverage can be exercised on certain points of the globe at a given time. Over the long term, its attraction for governments has nothing to do with what it is doing or promoting at a given moment, and everything to do with the political point in space where it is located. The leverage that can be exercised from this point, when ill used, has infused life into countless disastrous schemes which might have otherwise died natural deaths through insufficient financing and divided domestic support. Could the same leverage be used to help open up the terrain for global civil society vis-à-vis governments, to promote a necessary coevolution and coadaptation between governments and social and environmental movements? Could the Bank itself be radically restructured to reflect the values of global civil society—accountability, flexibility, transparency, freedom, care?

Although there are countless grounds for pessimism, restructuring the Bank is not an impossibility, but a question of international political will. Let us summarize some of the prerequisites for such a transformation.

The accountability question is the most important one, on which all other changes depend. There can be no accountability without transparency. We might recall Max Weber's analysis of bureaucratic power, which he saw as based above all on control of information, on the "official secret." Full freedom of information is a prerequisite for any international public institution worthy of the name. This means public access to Bank documents, particularly in the earlier stages of project preparation. The Bank's standard response to this challenge has been to invoke the national sovereignty of its borrowers—ironically, perhaps the only instance where in practice the Bank has consistently respected this principle. National sovereignty, too, is an Enlightenment concept, one that waxed in strength for 500 years, through the mid-twentieth century, but which is increasingly challenged by the new global economic, social, and ecological realities.[60] And, sovereignty is not absolute, but derives its legitimacy from the informed consent and participation of the governed.[61]

According to the United Nations Declaration of Human Rights, "[T]he will of the people shall be the basis of the authority of governments."[62] The myriad movements of global civil society have shown that it is no longer viable for governments to withhold information on development projects from the people who will be affected, and, in the case of the World Bank, from the taxpaying citizens of the countries that fund and guarantee Bank projects. The essence of the environmental assessment process involves public access to information and participation in meaningful open hearings to consider alternatives before development decisions proceed.[63] The Bank belatedly instituted an environmental assessment procedure in the early 1990s, and now urges governments to make these assessments public.

But even if all environmental assessments are made public, most of the essential information on Bank projects remains secret. Renewed threats of the U.S. Congress to withhold funding prompted the Bank to issue a new information policy in September 1993. But little is new: at the critical stages leading up to loan approval, all Bank documents are still secret, with the exception of a cursory, two- or three-page sanitized "project information document." Thomas Jefferson wrote, "Were it left to me to decide whether we should have a government without newspapers, or newspapers without a government, I should not hesitate a moment to prefer the latter."[64] It would be better not to have a World Bank, than to have one that continues to function without freedom of information.

In practice, accountability in an institution such as the Bank will require more than just full public access to information. Max Weber emphasized the importance of the function of parliamentary review and inquiry, with full investigative powers, "independently of the officials' good will." For the World Bank, the Morse Commission was just such a body, an unprecedented event in the history of international institutions. Its effectiveness as a truly independent inquiry was based on its full access to the internal files of the India country department and its total independence from the administration of the Bank. But its terms of reference were limited, and, to worldwide consternation, the Bank's management ignored its recommendations.

A reformed World Bank would have to be overseen by a kind of permanent Morse Commission, one which could be made up of representatives from civil society around the world, including environmentalists, academics, church representatives, human rights groups, social equity groups, and others. Such an "independent appeals commission"* would have full powers to investigate specific complaints of environmental and human rights abuses in Bank operations, and would have full access to Bank files. In the fall of 1993 the Bank was preparing—once again in response to growing international criticism—a proposal for a watered-down "inspection panel" which would have even less independence and resources than the existing Operations Evaluation Department. The recommendations of the "inspection panel" would have no force, and its reports on problems in ongoing projects would not be made public until after management and the executive directors had decided what action to take. The Bank's major shareholding governments should be pressured to instruct the Executive Board to amend the Bank's bylaws to set up a truly independent appeals commission that could require management to follow its directives.

Another aspect of accountability involves the responsibility of Bank staff for project performance. No matter how poorly designed and implemented the project, no matter how tragic the human and environmental consequences, no matter how blatant and cynical the violation of Bank policies and covenants, no one is held responsible. Indeed, many of the Bank staff members who were deeply involved in the planning and execution of its greatest social and ecological debacles over the past decade have been promoted, even in the face of internal Bank reports documenting their suppression of dissenting views and 'a pattern of misleading the senior management and the Bank's Executive Board.

To cite two examples which are not atypical: The individual responsible for the Bank's public relations efforts to downplay the problems in the Polonoroeste program during the mid-1980s was promoted to as envi-

* The phrase was first used in this context by Lori Udall of the Environmental Defense Fund.

ronmental officer in the Bank's India country department in the late 1980s; he subsequently and successfully promoted the continuation of Bank support for the Sardar Sarovar dam in the face of growing internal criticism by the Bank's environmental staff and growing popular protest in India and around the world. He played a key role in helping to draft the responses of Bank management defying the recommendations of the Morse Commission report. In late 1992, the Bank promoted him to head an environmental division overseeing Bank lending to eight former Soviet republics. The Bank's country director for Brazil in the late 1980s played a central role in the implementation of the Carajás project, and was the principal Bank staffer charged with attempting to push through the second Brazil Power Sector loan in 1987–88, as well as the Rondônia Natural Resources Management project in 1990. He was appointed in October 1992 to a newly created post as vice-president for human resources, a promotion that further demoralized the Bank environmental staffers whose warnings the Brazil country de-partment ignored.

Besides lack of accountability, we have seen and analyzed how the Bank has been plagued throughout its existence by a second sin—the pressure to lend, driven from the beginning by a dearth of "bankable projects," and exacerbated in later years by the Bank's unique net negative transfer quandary, posed by its limited set of developing-country borrowers. The 1992 Wapenhans report, discussed in the preceding chapter, reveals a damning picture of an institution virtually out of control, where the pressure to lend has overwhelmed all other considerations.

There are recent signs that the pressure to lend may be so deeply rooted in the Bank's institutional culture as to be irradicable. The Bank's first response to the Wapenhans report was not to strengthen its existing policies to ensure project quality (the policies, we noted earlier, are known as "operational directives" or ODs), but to conclude that they were too complicated and difficult to carry out. Consequently, Bank management in early 1993 announced to staff that it will reissue all of the major ODs— for example on forced resettlement, environmental assessment, protection of tribal peoples—as new, simplified, less specific "operational policies."

It took Bank management nearly a year to formulate a more comprehensive plan of action to address the problems described by Wapenhans. The proposed actions, presented in spring 1993 to the executive directors in a document entitled "Next Steps," were so inadequate that they sent "Next Steps" back to management, demanding major revisions. The U.S. executive director complained at a board meeting in early May 1993 that "the expected actions are not concrete enough to be monitorable." "Those hostile to the Bank," he warned, would seize on "Next Steps" "as not a serious response to critical issues of project implementation."[65]

Beneath the eddies and whirlpools of new policies and action plans that catch the attention of outside observers, the driving undercurrent of the Bank's bureaucracy silently flowed on with inexorable continuity. According to one executive director quoted in the *Economist*, "Next Steps" had "Ernie [Stern's] fingerprints all over it."[66]

The pressure to lend, we may recall, is both internal and external: it comes from the Bank's member countries, and is strongly reinforced by the institution's natural proclivity toward bureaucratic self-aggrandizement. This pressure will not lessen without strong, clear directives from the Bank's major shareholding countries. Even more important, these countries must take measures to alleviate the tremendous international economic constraints on poorer countries—constraints that provide the alibi for the Bank's mega-lending. The Bank's charter requires it to lend mainly for projects, but over the past decade the industrialized nations, led by the United States, encouraged it to increase lending as an alternative to forgiving large portions of private commercial debt. The foreign exchange component of mega-projects has been used to help hold off default to private international banks and governments, a goal, we have seen, that totally subverts all considerations of project quality.

The Bank should no longer be used as a money-moving machine to address global macroeconomic imbalances for which the real solution lies in a new global economic bargain between North and South. Key elements of this bargain include debt forgiveness and the lowering of protective barriers to exports from developing countries. These two measures alone would transfer more than $110 billion annually back to the South. Debt-related net negative transfers to the North amount to more than $50 billion annually, and industrialized-country tariffs and other trade restrictions deprive developing countries of at least another $60 billion annually in export income. Trade barriers to developing-country textile exports alone cost developing nations an estimated $24 billion annually.[67]

Even without debt forgiveness and massive trade reform, net negative transfers to the World Bank would not be a problem for borrowers if the Bank's lending really helped them to "develop." Presumably, Bank projects would more than earn back the cost of repayment. But the Bank's haste to lend has meant that the quality of the projects it finances has been declining for years. We've seen that even in purely conventional economic terms an alarming number of these projects have been failures, not to speak of the enormous ecological and social damage they have inflicted. It would be only just if the Bank were to forgive the debts owed by many nations with net negative transfer problems, especially since many of these countries—such as Brazil—have also been the sites of some of the worst Bank-financed fiascos. Writing down Bank loans and credits in Africa would also be fitting, if the interest of the poor were really a priority. In Africa, loans from the Bank and the IMF account for 36 percent of the total foreign debt; basket case Uganda owes 62 percent of its debt solely to the World Bank. This debt is eating up more than ten percent of the export earnings of eight sub-Saharan countries, and more than a third of the earnings of Zambia and Uganda.[68]

The Bank has opposed vehemently any debt forgiveness on its own part, pointing out that the credit rating of the IBRD would then drop, and its cost of borrowing in international capital markets would increase—something it claims it would have to pass on to future borrowers. But the credit rating of the Bank does not depend on the repayment of all of its loans by developing members; it depends on the guarantees (the callable capital) of its industrialized members to back up every dollar it borrows in the event of default or debt forgiveness.

In fact, the World Bank could retire billions of dollars of borrowing-country debt without touching the callable capital of the Group of Seven. The Bank has some $18.5 billion in liquid reserves which it maintains in a semi-permanent investment fund, placed in government and high-grade corporate bonds. The interest alone that the Bank earned on this portfolio was about $1.13 billion in 1993.[69] This fund has existed for decades, and since 1985 has never sunk below $17 billion. The World Bank is the single largest institutional bond investor on earth, a global Midas without equal.

The major shareholding countries of the Bank could easily direct it to allot $10 billion of this fund to its poorest and most economically strapped borrowers for relief from the burden of their World Bank debts.* Indeed, Oxfam has proposed this for Africa, having witnessed first hand the social damage precipitated by Bank-Fund adjustment programs.[70]

All of these issues—the need for project quality in existing aid, and the need for a fair deal for developing countries in terms of trade and debt relief—are ones that public opinion and global civil society will have to force the Group of Seven to face rather than ignore, as was the case at the Earth Summit.

If the Bank were to focus on project quality, with full public consultation, participation, and access to information, there would be far fewer loans, and smaller but better ones. It would be a much more modest institution, but one that might be able to make a real difference through example. We have seen that the technological approaches that are envi-

---

* The Bank argues that it needs a substantial bond portfolio "to ensure flexibility in its [the IBRD's] borrowing decisions should borrowing be adversely affected by temporary conditions in the capital markets" (World Bank, *Annual Report 1993* [see endnote 69], 67). But half or a third of $18.5 billion for these purposes would be more than sufficient.

ronmentally more sustainable—end-use energy efficiency and alternative agriculture, for example—all involve greater inputs of information, skilled staff work, and fine-tuning to local circumstances, and less money for energy and capital. All of this means a rather simple, but total, reversal of perspective: instead of the Bank focusing on its own needs, on seeking the "comparative advantage" of big loans with the least amount of staff work possible, it would have to identify its priorities in terms of the real needs of local communities and ecosystems in developing nations. The small core of Bank lending that has gone for education, health, and population programs in recent years—about 13 percent in 1992—should be retained. But even these loans have been criticized for their top-down approach and lack of sensitivity to local needs, and would need to have their basic approach revisited.

There would still be a role for non-project policy loans, as well as for adjustment loans, but again the perspective would have to be reversed. These loans should encourage balanced budgets and the setting of internal priorities and policies to create a constructive, coevolving partnership between the state and civil society—rather than turning economies inside out to remake them as export machines to service debt at the cost of damage to the environment, social services, and civil rights.

Could multilateral development banks ever be effective in such an approach? A few mechanisms and precedents exist. Several years after the creation of the Inter-American Foundation, the Inter-American Development Bank established a small-projects facility to demonstrate that it too was capable of handling small projects for nongovernmental entities. For over twenty years, the small-projects facility has disbursed about $10 million annually to finance approximately twenty small projects of NGOs, small enterprises, and cooperatives. The Inter-American Bank's former chief legal counsel, Jerome Levinson, notes that the World Bank and other MDBs already have a mechanism at their disposal, the so-called global loan, which allows them to lend "to an intermediary financial institution which then on-loan[s] the resources to final users, for example, small industrial or agricultural enterprises."[71] (Obviously, such loans require careful preparation and supervision, and some in the past—like large loans to agricultural credit institutions—have exacerbated ecological problems and social inequity rather than alleviating them.)

There is no reason, either, why the World Bank and its sister institutions could not make end-use efficiency and conservation a priority in negotiations with energy ministries, or alternative agriculture and local farmer empowerment priorities in dealing with agriculture ministries. Bank officials may fear that demand for loans would drop precipitously if it took this approach, and that the loans that would go through would be smaller and involve much more staff work. If this turns out to be the case, there is no clearer sign that the long-term interests of global ecology and global civil society are directly at odds with the current institutional incentives and priorities of the World Bank.*

This brings us to the Global Environment Facility. It is ironic that at the very moment when other forms of hyper-centralized planning and management have collapsed or are in crisis all around the world, the industrialized nations have endorsed just such an approach through the GEF. We have already seen how the GEF has been subverted from the beginning as a means to "top-off" mainstream Bank lending with grants. As the youngest but vigorously growing offspring of the World Bank, it seems so far to have inherited with a vengeance its parent's genes for moving money quickly and ignoring quality, for withholding information, and for lack of accountability in decision making.**

Even in the context of international conventions, specific solutions to environmental problems can best evolve, and be tested and adapted, in more flexible, local contexts. A case in point that nongovernmental groups presented at a GEF meeting in Beijing in May 1993 is indicative of

* The Bank issued a new energy efficiency policy paper in early 1993, in which it claimed that it would "be more selective in lending to energy-supply enterprises" and that "approaches for addressing demand-side management (DSM) and end-use energy intermediation issues * The Bank issued a new energy efficiency policy paper in early 1993, in which it claimed that it would "be more selective in lending to energy-supply enterprises" and that "approaches for addressing demand-side management (DSM) and end-use energy intermediation issues will be identified, supported, and given high-level in-country visibility" (World Bank, *Energy Efficiency and Conservation in the Developing World* [Washington, D.C.: World Bank, January 1993], 12). But the policy paper lacks specific commitments for actually increasing lending for end-use efficiency—which, according to the Bank's 1991 energy sector review will account for only 1 percent of Bank energy lending for the period 1992 to 1995. In mid-1993, the Bank approved a $400-million loan to begin a 3,750-megawatt expansion of coal-fired power production in the Singrauli region of India (see discussion in Chapter 2)—with no consideration of end-use efficiency and "demand-side management" alternatives. Germany, the United States, and Belgium refused to vote in favor of the loan on environmental grounds.

** In May 1993, representatives from more than sixty participating countries met in Beijing and discussed contributing over $2 billion to replenish the GEF. The Chinese had originally proposed the fourth anniversary of the massacre at Tiananmen Square as the date for the meeting, but this was too much to stomach for some Western donors and the date was changed. U.S. proposals for greater public participation and access to information were poorly received by other countries, including several European nations and Japan. It appears that the GEF will continue its links to the World Bank, though probably as a more autonomous body.will be identified, supported, and given high-level in-country visibility" (World Bank, *Energy Efficiency and Conservation in the Developing World* [Washington, D.C.: World Bank, January 1993], 12). But the policy paper lacks specific commitments for actually increasing lending for end-use efficiency—which, according to the Bank's 1991 energy sector review will account for only 1 percent of Bank energy lending for the period 1992 to 1995. In mid-1993, the Bank's biggest energy loan in preparation was a $400-million IDA credit to begin a 3,750-megawatt expansion of coal-fired power production in the Singrauli region of India (see discussion in Chapter 2)—with no consideration of end-use efficiency and "demand-side management" alternatives.

continuing problems rooted in the GEF's flawed approach. A proposed GEF biodiversity project to protect endangered primate species along the Tana River in northeastern Kenya envisages the forcible resettlement of the local human population in the area. In preparing the project the World Bank ignored studies of the East African Wildlife Society that showed that the endangered primates lived in symbiosis with the local population, and were more numerous around human settlements. Indeed, according to the East African Wildlife Society, upstream construction of dams and irrigation schemes has contributed to the degradation of the Tana River ecosystem and primate habitat. Some of these projects were financed by the World Bank. The GEF primate project is to be linked to a new Bank agriculture loan.[72]

Once again, we see that the Global Environment Facility's viability is connected to the need for far-reaching reforms in the Bank as a whole, as well as in other international development assistance agencies. Currently, the GEF serves to propagate the profound fallacy that addressing global environmental problems is a matter of industrialized nations contributing an additional few billion dollars for more projects (in this case, "green" ones), while $60 billion annually (in 1993) for official development assistance continues business as usual. The whole approach of more money for more projects is a totally perverse one from the standpoint of ecological balance. What is needed is not "more," but "different"—a different approach to economic development in the South and North that emphasizes local ecology and community, that increasingly replaces raw inputs of physical capital and energy with human capital; that is, information, skill, and locally attuned and flexible approaches.

Such an approach still increases, albeit more slowly, the absolute level of global ecological stress, however, and there are real limits to endless material growth. The main debate appears to be whether we have a few decades or a century before we reach these limits, or whether (as some researchers maintain) we have already reached or overshot them.* This possibility that these more pessimistic ecological assessments are even partially on target underscores the need to halt the collective denial of our global predicament by governments and international organizations. This denial is based on the strange faith that the future will always provide

* We might recall Harvard biologist E. O. Wilson's observation that "human beings . . . have become a hundred times more numerous than any other land animal of comparable size in the history of life. By every conceivable measure, humanity is ecologically abnormal. Our species appropriates between 20 and 40 percent of the solar energy captured in organic materials by land plants. There is no way that we can draw upon the resources of the planet to such a degree without drastically reducing the state of most other species" (Edward O. Wilson, *The Diversity of Life* [Cambridge, Mass.: Belknap Press of Harvard University Press, 1992], 272).

technological escape hatches, provided there is enough money to pay someone to pry the hatch open.

Finally, to reinvent the World Bank as an accountable and responsible institution would require changing its charter to incorporate other goals and values, ones commensurate with the values of global civil society. Former IDB chief counsel Jerome Levinson has suggested that the charters of the World Bank and other multilateral financial institutions be changed to commit them to promote the values of democracy, human rights, and social equity, as well as economic welfare.[73] Ecological balance and conservation of the other life forms with which we share this planet should also be added as guiding commitments. The charter of the European Bank for Reconstruction and Development (EBRD), a multilateral bank established in 1990 to finance the reconstruction of Eastern Europe and the republics of the former Soviet Union, commits the EBRD to "the fundamental principles of multiparty democracy, the rule of law, respect for human rights and market economics," and specifies as one of its major functions "promot[ing] in the full range of its activities environmentally sound and sustainable development."[74]

But several caveats are in order here. Reforming the World Bank charter to incorporate these goals would be only a necessary first step and by no means a sufficient one towards infusing it with the values of global civil society. Changing the Bank's charter is not an easy task: amendments to the Articles of Agreement require the assent of 85 percent of its voting shares and three-fifths of its members.

More troubling, the EBRD in practice has turned out to be the worst of possible models for multilateral bank reform. Despite its progressive charter, its bureaucracy has refused to incorporate practical measures for public participation and freedom of access to information. Its member governments, after setting up the institution only two years ago, are already complaining about its lack of openness and accountability.[75] And this newest kid brother of the World Bank has become a subject of scandal and embarrassment. Its first president, Jacques Attali, and management squandered some $300 million on ostentatious staff perks including a private jet for Attali, lavish Christmas parties, and the installation of opulent art works and sculpture-quality marble in an $80-million refurbishing of what was already a perfectly serviceable building. This is twice as much money as it has lent in its brief history.[76]

Where does this leave us? Is the World Bank so flawed in its fundamental conception, so unresponsive to outside pressures for change, so rent by contradictions in its underlying organization that it may not be possible, or worth the effort, to try to radically restructure it? The Bank's history to date points towards this conclusion, but the prospect of more organized international public pressure for change means it is not inevitable. For the moment, the most feasible strategy appears to be a three-pronged one of decreasing Bank funding, supporting a variety of more flexible institutions and networks, and calling upon the world's governments to address the agenda suppressed at the Earth Summit—a new global bargain on debt relief and fair trade between North and South. Cuts in funding will be the greatest spur to reform. It is the only external pressure that World Bank management appears to take really seriously.

The mid-1990s will mark a number of important fifty-year anniversaries in the history of the entire system of public international institutions set up after World War II. We should remember that this system was created with great hopes in the ruins of the greatest man-made cataclysm in history. But it is failing. These are appropriate occasions for launching a worldwide citizens' campaign to reassess and revamp the World Bank. If reform is impossible, every effort must be made to pressure governments to channel resources permanently away from the Bank into alternative investments, domestic and international. There is no other choice. A sustainable world system will be possible only if it recognizes and is based on local ecological and social concerns.

Development, Freedom, Care

> Perhaps it has never been more necessary than now, to say what the myths say: that a well-ordered humanism does not begin with itself, but puts things back in their place. It puts the world before life, life before man, and the respect of others before love of self. This is the lesson that the people we call "savages" teach us: a lesson of modesty, decency and discretion in the face of a world that preceded our species and will survive it.[77]
> —Claude Lévi-Strauss, 1972

There are 5,100 languages spoken on earth. Within a generation all but about a hundred may perish.[78] "Language is world," Wittgenstein wrote, and it is the insane pride of our age to be the accomplice of the relentless annihilation of almost all of the human worlds that have ever come to be. This is the great dying of thousands of cultures and histories—millions of thoughts, feelings, and ways of being in the world that were created and existed within the social space of the languages and the societies that bore them. Countless species of living beings named only in indigenous tongues will also die, species unidentified by science and forever lost, whole natural worlds that gave birth to many of these thousands of languages and societies. Indeed, according to E. O. Wilson of Harvard, 20 percent of the earth's species may perish in a generation, and "50 percent or more there after," the greatest mass extermination since the later Cretaceous extinction, 65 million years ago.[79] We hardly realize that the planet is now enveloped by this great dying of worlds human and natural—after all, death matters initially only to those who perish.

In the state of Mato Grosso do Sul in Brazil, there is a tribe of Indians called the Kaiowa, whose members—particularly the young—uprooted from a forest that is no more, their natural and cultural worlds obliterated, are committing suicide out of total despair. In the Dourados reservation, home to 7,200 Kaiowa, twenty killed themselves in 1992, and more than a hundred since the late 1980s; they hang or poison themselves. Only a few years ago they thought of themselves as descendants of the sun—before, in the words of one of their leaders, "the forest was cut, the birds flew away, the fish died."[80] They do not seem to have much faith in market-driven forces of substitution and structural change.

Most of what is vanishing does not appear to be of much immediate use to much of the world as it is now organized; we have seen that this form of organization views the entire planet as raw material, expendable for transformation, substitution, and exchange. We encounter this world as if it were in the thrall of an uncannily impersonal force; "autonomous technology" or a worldwide process of "development [that] cannot be halted." To describe this historically unusual state of affairs as an "enframing" that encloses and transforms all beings into "standing reserve," as Heidegger does, makes us think about what is going on in a more original way, but appears to offer no solution.

Much of the discourse on development, sustainable or otherwise, has focused almost exclusively on means, as if the ends were understood. But the ends rightly considered will guide us towards the appropriate means. The ultimate end is freedom, not just to survive but to unfold and realize human potentialities, to live in the fullest sense of the word. The United Nations Development Program, in its first human development report, in 1990, defined development as "the process of enabling people to have wider choices."[81] H. W. Arndt, at the conclusion of his treatise on the history of the idea of development, cites the dictum of "the wisest of development economists" that "the case for economic growth is that it gives man greater control over his environment and thereby increases his freedom."[82] And herein lies the fatal fallacy.

How true it is that the project of economic growth—development as it has been practiced to date—is a project of greater, indeed ultimately total control over the environment, the project of modernity. But paradoxically, the more we pursue control in this way the more we encounter evidence that we are losing it; whether in alarming indicators of global ecological crisis, or in the twentieth century's frightening eruptions of political and social violence—violence often a hundredfold more lethal than previous episodes in history, thanks to the administered, instrumental efficiency of modern technology and bureaucracy.

The problem lies in pursuing freedom through a process that destroys its possibility. Economic growth in its current form has reached the point where it has unleashed a tremendous, almost unimaginable *impoverishment* through the destruction in a short time of most of the human worlds and a significant proportion of the life forms that have evolved and survived on earth. Concretely, increasing humankind's freedom entails conserving and creating possibilities for individuals and societies to choose among different futures; it means living and working in the present in such a way as to conserve and create as many future options as possible.

Making possible different futures—sustaining and building the real circumstances in which human possibilities can flourish—must start with, must be based on, the conservation and enhancement of existing natural and social diversity. If we destroy the diversity bestowed on us by the past, we also destroy the future and create a present that is little more than a prison. For peoples whose world lies in ruins, like the Kaiowa, the sense of imprisonment, of no future, is total, a sentiment that increasingly festers in other social spaces ground up and discarded by the global economy, like the urban ghettos of the industrialized North.

And so the paradox: any social enterprise to secure and expand future human choices and freedom, if it is to succeed, has to conserve and secure as much as possible the wealth and variety of what already exists, which is the past. Such an approach creates a present rich in possibilities and concrete choice. It is important to conserve biodiversity not because it may be useful or profitable (though in some cases it will be), but because in the act of conserving we will begin to save ourselves from what has become an all-engulfing planetary nihilism, one that ultimately threatens humankind itself. Conservation is not just about conserving different species, or conserving different human cultures, but about making possible different futures and different worlds. It is a foundational act of freedom—for ourselves and other beings.

The guardian and enabler of this freedom is care—care as an attitude and a way of being in the world that saves the natural and human past, thereby securing a future of manifold possibilities. Such care embodies an approach to technology and development that transcends Cartesian dualism, that bases social and economic practice on the dependence and interconnectedness of humans with ecosystems and social systems, and implies a less aggressive, more subtle and considered approach to human interventions in the biosphere. It looks to science as a source of comprehension, understanding, and adaptation, rather than to the chimera of universal prediction and control.

Goethe, in writing the second part of Faust, was inspired by an old Latin myth on the creation of humankind by Care.[83] Care (Cura) one day was crossing a river, when she saw some clay and picked up a piece and began to shape it. Jupiter passed by, and Care asked him to animate the clay with spirit, which he did. Jupiter and Care each wanted to name the new creature, when Earth intervened and claimed it should be named after her. To resolve their dispute, the three deities turned finally to Saturn, god of time, and thus the wisest of gods and final arbiter of the fate of all things. Saturn decreed that since Jupiter gave the creature spirit, he would receive the spirit at death; from Earth came the body, to Earth the body would return, and it would be named *homo,* man, since it was close to *humus* (earth). "But," Saturn concluded, "since Care first shaped this creature, she shall possess it as long as it lives."[84]

Care has two primordial senses, meanings that are not unrelated: anxiety, worry, and concern; and solicitude, devotion, attentiveness, with connotations of responsibility, trusteeship, and protection. In fact the first meaning, properly construed, engenders the second. The second part of *Faust,* we recall, is among other things a parable of the tragedy of modern development. Care appears to Faust; he scorns her and is blinded. He continues to direct what he thinks are gigantic development works, while in reality he oversees the excavation of his own grave.

In the emergence of global civil society there is a call that is simultaneously local and global, a call for a long transformation of human attitudes and practices. This evolution provides hope, but no certainty, that the accountability crisis of world technological civilization can be overcome, that the iron bars of instrumental reason need not be the confining cage of human destiny, that humankind's collective surrender to anthropophagus technophilia can be confronted and overcome.

The project of global civil society is freedom, freedom concretely rooted in myriads of campaigns to save the biological and cultural inheritance of the planet, freedom of information and choice among alternatives, a project to conserve and create options for those who will inherit this earth. This freedom, after all, is the real purpose of what humankind pursues through development. And it is secured through actions imbued with care—the care manifested one day in November 1973, when the women of the village of Reni, in the Indian Garwahl Himalayas, marched into the forest, in front of the logging contractors, to embrace the trees.

Notes

1 • The Dwelling Place of the Angels

1. "Special Health Unit on Alert," *Bangkok Post,* 15 October 1991, 28; Dr. Pongsak Bidayakorn, the director of Bangkok General Hospital, is quoted in the same article.

2. For Bangkok nightlife and the AIDS situation, see Richard Rhodes, "Death in the Candy Store," *Rolling Stone* 618 (28 November 1991), 62.

3. Laura Tyson, "Mr. Condom Hands Out Bangkok Survival Kit," *Annual Meeting News* (published by International Media Partners, New York, N.Y. and *The Nation,* Bangkok, Thailand), 13 October 1991, 3; Tulsathit Taptim, "AIDS— 1 in 50 by 1996," *Annual Meeting News,* 15 October 1991, 63; Mechai Viravaidhaya (health minister), "AIDS in the 1990s: Meeting the Challenge," Bangkok, Thailand, 12 October 1991 (unpublished).

4. "Slums Near World Bank Venue to Be Relocated," *Nation,* 18 June 1991; "Slum Scenery to Be Improved," *Bangkok Post,* 22 June 1991, 2; "Slum Dwellers Pressured to Move before WB-IMF Meet," *Bangkok Post,* 22 August 1991; "Squatters Wait in Confusion as WB Conference Nears," *Nation,* 29 July 1991, A2; "NHA Tackles 'Eye-Sore' by Relocating Slum Dwellers," *Bangkok Post,* 4 August 1991. *The Nation* is a Bangkok English-language daily newspaper.

5. Nopporn Wong-Anan and Piyanart Srivalo, "PM Inspects WB Conference Hall," *Nation,* 2 August 1991, A3.

6. "Life Under the Expressway," *Bangkok Post,* 15 October 1991, 15.

7. On Thai NGOs, see Ernst W. Gohlert, *Power and Culture: The Struggle Against Poverty in Thailand* (Bangkok, Thailand, and Cheney, Washington, U.S.A.: White Lotus Co., Ltd., 1991).

8. The opening of the People's Forum is described in "Poor Reveal Their Fears, Misery at People's Forum," *Bangkok Post,* 9 October 1991, 3.

9. "Watching 'Angels' from the Edge of the Slum," *Nation,* 9 October 1991, 2.

320 • Notes to Pages 6–13

10. See Jacques Attali, *Millennium: Winners and Losers in the Coming World Order* (New York: Times Books, 1991).

11. Ibid., 4–5, 14.

12. German NGOs published an extensive illustrated account of the 1988 meeting and the German and international alternative activities: Buero fuer unge-woehnliche Massnahmen und Bundesconferenz entwicklungspolitischer Actions-Gruppen (BUKO), *Wit, Witz, Widerstand: Die IWF/Weltbank-Kampagne in Bild und Wort* (Berlin: Schmetterling Verlag, 1989).

13. "Poor Reveal Their Fears, Misery at People's Forum," *Bangkok Post*, 9 October 1991, 3; Ann Danaiya Usher, "Villagers Still Stranded from First WB Hydro Dam," *Nation*, 9 October 1991, A4.

14. Sources for EGAT World Bank loan totals: International Bank for Recon-struction and Development, *Statement of Loans*, 31 August 1991, vol. 1 (Africa and Asia re-gions); International Development Association, *Statement of Develop-ment Credits, July 31, 1991*.

15. See Edward S. Mason and Robert E. Asher, *The World Bank Since Bretton Woods* (Washington, D.C.: Brookings Institution, 1973), 689.

16. "Gunmen Fire on Villagers Protesting Dam Project," *Bangkok Post*, 2 June 1991.

17. The chronology of these events can be found in a study by the Project for Ecological Recovery, "Critical Analysis of World Bank Responses to Issues Raised by Thai NGOs Concerning the Pak Mun Hydroelectric Project," 31 October 1991 (unpublished).

18. Walt Rainboth, professor of biology, University of California at Los Ange-les, letter to Dr. George Davis, Department of Malacology, Academy of Natural Sciences of Philadelphia, 4 December 1991, 6.

19. Ibid., 4.

20. See, for example, Mark Rentschler, "Affirmative Investigation of the Pak Mun Dam," U.S. Agency for International Development memorandum, 29 August 1991 (unpublished), 8; "Rural Doctors' Group Oppose Pak Mool Dam," *Nation*, 22 August 1991, A2.

21. Porntip Boonkrob et al., "Local Water Resource Management, Thailand," in *1991 People's Forum International Case Study, Topic: Water* (bound volume available from the Project for Ecological Recovery, Bangkok, Thailand). By the early 1970s it was already evident that Bhumibol was an economic failure because of its large shortfall in providing anticipated power and irrigation benefits (see Mason and Asher, *Since Bretton Woods*, 687).

22. Eric D. Larson, ed., "Report on the 1989 Thailand Workshop on End-Use-Oriented Energy Analysis," International Institute for Energy Conservation, Washington and Bangkok, April 1990; see Sonny Inbaraj, "Plan Offers to Save '15 Pak Mools,'" *Nation*, 15 October 1991, A2.

23. See Rentschler, "Affirmative Investigation of the Pak Mun Dam," 2–3.

24. Oranuch Anusaksathien and Vatchara Charoonsantikul, "A Lending Leg-acy," *Nation*, 6 October 1991, B1.

25. See Art Van de Laar, *The World Bank and the Poor* (Boston, The Hague,

and London: Martinus Nijhoff Publishing, 1980), 35; J. Howard et al., *The Impact of International Organizations on Legal and Institutional Change in the Developing Countries* (New York: International Legal Center, 1977). On Thailand, see Mason and Asher, *Since Bretton Woods,* 687–89.

26. Sanitsuda Ekachai, "Is It Growth or Decline?" *Bangkok Post,* 3 October 1991, 27.

27. Ann Danaiya Usher, "Forum Raps 'Green Revolution,'" *Nation,* 10 October 1991, A2.

28. Suda Kanjanawanawan, "Shrimp Farms Spoiling Ecosystems," *Nation,* 10 October 1991, A1.

29. These are Thai Agriculture Ministry figures, cited in Sanitsuda Ekachai, "Is It Growth or Decline?" *Bangkok Post,* 3 October 1991, 27.

30. Thai Royal Forest Department statistics, in *Thai Development Newsletter* (published by Thai Development Support Committee, Bangkok), no. 18 (1990), 10.

31. Paul Handley, "The Land Wars," *Far Eastern Economic Review,* 31 October 1991, 15–16; Larry Lohman, "Commercial Tree Plantations in Thailand: A Continuation of Deforestation by Other Means," *Thai Development Newsletter,* no. 18 (1990), 20–21.

32. Lohman, ibid.

33. "Soldiers Set to Move on Pa Kham Villagers," *Nation,* 28 February 1991.

34. Larry Lohman, "Trees Don't Grow on Money: Thai Forests and the World Bank," *Bangkok Post,* 10 October 1991, sec. 3, 1; see also Larry Lohman, "The Scourge of Eucalyptus in Thailand," *Ecologist,* vol. 20, no. 1 (January/February 1990), 14. According to Lohman,

Jaakko Poyry has served at least 40 forest-industry projects in Brazil, including the Jari complex; various logging operations in the Amazon; pulp mills; plantations run by Shell and other companies; and schemes to use tropical forests to fuel aluminum refining and wood gasifying projects. . . . It has worked with PICOP [a World Bank-funded project] in the Philippines; PT Indorayon and transmigrasi [Transmigration] officials in Indonesia . . . government logging operations in Malaysia; and eucalyptus and pulp companies in Burma, Thailand, Vietnam, Chile, the U.S. and dozens of other countries. (Lohman, "The Scourge of Eucalyptus," 17, n. 57.)

35. "People's Forum Discuss Irony of Prostitution," *Bangkok Post,* 12 October 1991.

36. The discussion of *muang phai* irrigation is based on the following sources: Porntip Boonkrob et al., "Local Water Resource Management, Thailand," in Project for Ecological Recovery, *1991 People's Forum International Case Study, Topic: Water* (1991); Larry Lohman, "Who Defends Biological Diversity?" *Ecologist,* vol. 21, no. 1 (January/February 1991), 5–13; Nantiya Tangwisuttijit, "Arguments That Hold Water," *Nation,* 5 October 1991, C1–C3; Kitti Thungsuro et al., "The People and Forests of Thailand," in Project for Ecological Recovery, *1991 People's Forum International Case Study, Topic: Forests* (1991). See Chatchawan

Tongdeelert and Larry Lohman, "The Muang Faai Irrigation System of Northern Thailand," *Ecologist,* vol. 21, no. 2 (March/April 1991).

37. "Forum Urges Shift from Economic Growth Focus," *Nation,* 11 October 1991; "Forum Urges Bigger Role for People in Development," *Bangkok Post,* 11 October 1991, 3.

38. Kevin Rafferty, "Kurosawa," *Annual Meeting News,* 15 October 1991, 18. Kevin Rafferty, "The Rotten Core of Japan Inc." *Annual Meeting News,* 14 October 1991, 49.

39. Kevin Rafferty, "Kurosawa," *Annual Meeting News,* 15 October 1991, 18.

40. Peter Truell and Larry Gurwin, *False Profits: The Inside Story of* BCCI, *the World's Most Corrupt Financial Empire* (Boston and New York: Houghton Mifflin Co., 1992), 165–66.

41. John Ring Adams and Douglas Frantz, *A Full Service Bank: How* BCCI *Stole Billions Around the World* (New York: Pocket Books, 1992), 92.

42. Treull and Gurwin, *False Profits,* 97–98.

43. Interview with Jack Blum, former chief investigator for BCCI matters with the Senate Foreign Relations Committee Subcommittee on Narcotics and Terrorism, 31 December 1992. This subcommittee, chaired by Senator John Kerry, Democrat from Massachusetts, carried out path-breaking investigations of BCCI in 1988 and 1989.

44. Treull and Gurwin, *False Profits,* 166.

45. "Address by Lewis T. Preston to the Board of Governors of the World Bank Group," World Bank press release, 15 October 1991.

46. Ibid.

47. Ibid.

48. Ibid.

2 • Decade of Debacles

1. Jaime da Silva Araújo, President of the Union of Rural Workers of Novo Aripuana, Amazonas, President of the National Council of Rubber Tappers, statement before the World Commission on Environment and Development, São Paulo, 28 October 1985.

2. Friends of the Earth, International, "The Brazilian Amazon Is Burning at the Fastest Rate Ever," press release, 16 October 1991. The Friends of the Earth press release accurately cites the INPE figures for the number of fires burning in 1991, but wrongly concludes that in 1991 the forest was burning at "the fastest rate ever."

3. Philip M. Fearnside, "Deforestation in Contemporary Brazilian Amazonia: The Effect of Population and Land Tenure," draft manuscript in preparation for publication in *Ambio,* vol. 22, late 1993, p. 7. Amazon deforestation figures are a matter of considerable political and scientific dispute. World Resources Institute (WRI) in Washington, for example, estimated annual Amazon deforestation to be as high as 80,000 square kilometers for 1987. (*World Resources, 1990–91* [New York: Oxford University Press, 1990], 102–3.) The WRI estimates were similar to

those of Brazil's National Institute for Space Research (INPE); both relied on data from weather satellites of the U.S. National Oceanic and Atmospheric Administration (NOAA). But researcher Philip M. Fearnside has persuasively argued that these figures may be too high by more than 100 percent, because the data used by INPE and NOAA monitors burning, and it is difficult to reliably extrapolate what area of deforestation each fire may represent. (See Philip Fearnside, "The Rate and Extent of Deforestation in Brazilian Amazonia," *Environmental Conservation*, vol. 17, no. 3 [Autumn 1990], 213–26.) In 1987, Fearnside estimates total deforestation in the Amazon was probably closer to 35,000 square kilometers, rather than 80,000. Brazil's Ministry of Science and Technology, using more accurate Landsat 5 satellite data, came up with Amazon deforestation figures of 17,871 square kilometers in 1989, and 13,818 square kilometers in 1990. (Sergio Garschagen, "Goldenberg anuncía redução do desflorestamento na Amazônia," *Gazeta Mercantil*, 7 March 1991.) Fearnside's current (1993) estimate of 11,000 square kilometers deforested annually is still a huge area, representing a square about 105 kilometers on each side.

4. Philip M. Fearnside, personal communication, 12 May 1993. See Philip M. Fearnside and Judy M. Rankin, "Jari and Carajás: The Uncertain Future of Large Silvicultural Plantations in the Amazon," *Interciencia*, vol. 7, no. 6 (November–December 1982), 326.

5. Numerous studies in recent years have linked World Bank–financed infrastructure investments in Rondônia, Mato Grosso, and Pará with the high rate of deforestation in these regions. See, for example, Jean-Paul Malingreau and Compton J. Tucker, "Large-Scale Deforestation in the Southwestern Amazon Basin of Brazil," *Ambio*, vol. 17, no. 1, 49–55; Philip Fearnside, "Spatial Concentration of Deforestation in the Brazilian Amazon," *Ambio*, vol. 15, no. 2, 74–81; Philip Fearnside, "The Charcoal of Carajás: A Threat to the Forests of Brazil's Eastern Amazon Region," *Ambio*, vol. 18, no. 2; A. Setzer, "Relatório de Atividades do Projeto IBDF-INPE 'SEQE'—Ano 1987," Instituto National de Pesquisas Espaciaies (INPE), Brasília, 1988. A particularly useful discussion of the dynamics of deforestation in the Brazilian Amazon can be found in David Cleary, *The Brazilian Rainforest: Politics, Finance, Mining and the Environment* (London: The Economist Intelligence Unit, Special Report No. 2100, May 1991).

6. Fearnside, "The Rate and Extent of Deforestation in Brazilian Amazonia," 216; Fearnside, "Deforestation in Contemporary Amazonia: The Effect of Population and Land Tenure," 25 (figure 3: Percentage of Original Forest Lost by 1991).

7. Linda Greenbaum, "The Failure to Protect Tribal Peoples: The Polonoroeste Case in Brazil," *Cultural Survival Quarterly*, vol. 8 (December 1984), 76–77.

8. Kido Guerra and Cléber Praxedes, "Bird Relata Incompetência da Funai no Polonoroeste," *Jornal do Brasil* (Rio de Janeiro), 23 July 1987, caderno 1, 5.

9. Meri McCoy-Thompson, "Brazil Enlists DDT Against Malaria Outbreak," *Worldwatch*, vol. 3 (July/August 1990), 9–10.

10. A good, comprehensive review of the environmental consequences of

Carajás can be found in Anthony Anderson, "Smokestacks in the Rainforest: Industrial Development and Deforestation in the Amazon Basin," *World Development,* vol. 18, no. 9 (1990), 1191–1205. Anderson obtained his data as part of a World Bank mission. Philip Fearnside has published several excellent articles on the Carajás situation.

11. Environmental Defense Fund et al., letter to Barber Conable, President, World Bank, 6 August 1987.

12. Armean M. Choksi, Director, Brazil Department, World Bank, letter to Environmental Defense Fund et al., 15 September 1987.

13. One of the most damning indictments of the Carajás Iron Ore Project and the role of the World Bank can be found in the draft report of the European Parliament's Committee on the Environment, Public Health, and Consumer Protection, "Environmental Problems in the Amazon Region," doc. B3-13/89, Rapporteur H. J. Muntingh, 29 January 1990 (hereafter cited as European Parliament, "Environmental Problems").

14. Philip M. Fearnside, personal communication, 12 May 1993. See Fearnside and Rankin, "Jari and Carajás," 326.

15. Francisco F. de Assis Fonseca, Environmental Superintendent CVRD, internal memorandum, 7 April 1987, "Steel Industry Along the Carajas Railway—The Korf Metallurgy Technology Ltd. Study," reference code SUMEI/SUPES–186/87 (Portuguese original and English translation in files of the Environmental Defense Fund, Washington, D.C.).

16. European Parliament, "Environmental Problems," 9, citing a May 1989 resolution of the European Parliament condemning the CVRD Iron Ore Project.

17. European Parliament, "Environmental Problems."

18. Philip M. Fearnside, personal communication, 12 May 1993.

19. For a well-documented analysis of the socially perverse effects of the Carajás development model, such as increased malnutrition and landlessness among the poor, see Anthony Hall, "Agrarian Crisis in Brazilian Amazonia: The Grande Carajás Programme," *Journal of Development Studies,* vol. 23, no. 4 (July 1987), 533–52.

20. Ken Serbin, "Marabá: Welcome to the Fourth World." *National Catholic Reporter,* 14 December 1990, 18.

21. World Bank, *Indonesia Transmigration Sector Review* (Washington, D.C.: World Bank, 24 October 1986), 157.

22. Ibid., 162; International Bank for Reconstruction and Development, *Statement of Loans, August 31, 1991,* vol. 1 (Africa and Asia regions), 165–206.

23. See generally, "Indonesia's Transmigration Programme: A Special Report in Collaboration with Survival International and Tapol," *Ecologist,* vol. 16, no. 2/3 (1986). The Bank's position is set out in World Bank, *Indonesia Transmigration Sector Review,* and in "Transmigration in Indonesia," a January 1990 briefing paper of the Indonesia country department (unpublished, available from World Bank).

24. The average 1986 cost in Sumatra ranged between $5,310 and almost $8,000, depending on the remoteness of the site; swamp reclamation sites averaged $7,154. (World Bank, *Indonesia Transmigration Sector Review,* 41.)

25. See World Bank, *Indonesia Transmigration Sector Review,* 3, 156. See also

World Bank (Indonesia country department), "Transmigration in Indonesia," prepared in 1990, which probably underestimates somewhat the number of "spontaneous" transmigrants and does not include transmigration sponsored by "nucleus estates" loans.

26. See World Bank *Indonesia Transmigration Sector Review,* 94–97, 102. For the period 1980–85 of the third five-year plan (Repelita III), the Bank estimates that 10,000 square kilometers were deforested, "an important loss of tropical rain forest" (op. cit., 96). The January 1990 briefing paper of the Bank's Indonesia country department cited above estimates that Transmigration cleared 20,000 square kilometers of land in the decade of the 1980s, "not all in forested areas." These Bank figures are extremely conservative, since they average out (roughly) to less than three-quarters of a hectare of forest clearing per household. A 1985 study by three Indonesian ministries and the London-based International Institute for Environment and Development (IIED) noted "the amount of land converted for farm plots is, in fact, the minimum amount lost. The failure of the Transmigration Program to establish sustainable farming systems on these newly opened lands results in many families abandoning these sites after two to three years only to join the ranks of the shifting cultivators or illegal loggers" (Government of Indonesia, Department of Forestry, State Ministry of Population, Environment, and Development, Department of the Interior, and IIED, "A Review of Policies Affecting Sustainable Development of Forest Lands in Indonesia" [November 1985], vol. 2, 64 [hereafter cited as Government of Indonesia and IIED, "Review of Policies"]).

27. See Natural Resources Defense Council (NRDC) and the Indonesian Environmental Forum (WALHI), "Bogged Down: The Tragic Legacy of the World Bank and Wetlands Transmigration in Indonesia" (June 1990, unpublished, available from NRDC).

28. World Bank, *Indonesia: Sustainable Development of Forests, Land, and Water* (Washington, D.C.: World Bank, 1990), xx–xxi.

29. NRDC and WALHI, "Bogged Down," 7.

30. World Bank, *Indonesia Transmigration Sector Review,* xiv–xv.

31. The French consulting study on transmigrant sites is cited in Carolyn Marr, "Uprooting People, Destroying Cultures, Indonesia's Transmigration Program," *Multinational Monitor,* October 1990, 12–15.

32. Number of transmigrants in Irian Jaya from George Monbiot, "The Transmigration Fiasco," *Geographical Magazine,* May 1989, 30 (this article provides a summary of major problems with Transmigration in Irian Jaya); and World Bank (Indonesia country department), "Transmigration in Indonesia."

33. See Marcus Colchester, "The Struggle for Land: Tribal Peoples in the Face of the Trasmigration Program," *Ecologist,* vol. 16, no. 2/3 (1986), 99–110; Carmen Budiardjo, "The Politics of Transmigration," *Ecologist,* vol. 16, no. 2/3 (1986), 11–116. For a journalist's critical account of Transmigration in Irian Jaya, see George Monbiot, *Poisoned Arrows* (London: Michael Joseph, 1989).

34. Amnesty International, "Indonesia: Continuing Human Rights Violations in Irian Jaya" (April 1991), Amnesty International Secretariat, London.

35. Government of Indonesia and IIED, "Review of Policies," vol. 2, 117.

36. Indonesian Journalists Association seminar reported in *Warta Economi* (Economic reports), a Jakarta weekly economic magazine, 2 December 1991 summarized in "Indonesia News Service," December 1991 (available from Indonesia Publications, Lanham-Seabrook, Maryland).

37. Shahnaz Anklesaria Aiyar, "Singrauli Fall-Out in U.S. Congress," *Indian Express,* 21 April 1987.

38. Much of the information on Singrauli, including the quote from Nirendra Nirau, is based on the joint "Trip Report of the Environmental Defense Fund and Lokayan to the Environs of the World Bank–Financed Singrauli Super Thermal Power Plant and the Dudhichua Coal Field, February 25–27, 1987." (Lokayan is an Indian NGO that focuses on ecological and social issues.) The trip report was submitted for the record in testimony presented by EDF and six other national environmental groups before the House Subcommittee on International Development Institutions and Finance, Committee on Banking, Finance, and Urban Affairs, 100th Cong., 1st sess., 8 April 1987 ("Statement of Bruce M. Rich"). See also Smitu Kothari, "Displaced," *Illustrated Weekly of India,* 24 April 1988, 43–45.

39. International Bank for Reconstruction and Development, *Statement of Loans, August 31, 1991,* vol. 1 (Africa and Asia regions), 165–81; International Development Association, *Statement of Development Credits, July 31, 1991,* 238–60.

40. Singrauli is one example where the Bank admitted that it "agrees with many of the [NGO] criticisms" (World Bank, *The World Bank and the Environment: First Annual Report, Fiscal 1990* [Washington, D.C.: World Bank, 1990], 69). Regrettably, this theoretical agreement has been of no concrete benefit to the 23,000 people directly displaced by the Singrauli Super Thermal Plant, or to hundreds of thousands of others displaced by the other Singrauli plants and by as many as eight additional Bank-financed thermal power facilities all over India.

41. Kavaljit Singh, "The Chandil Nightmare," October 1991 (unpublished manuscript, available from the Public Interest Research Group, New Delhi, India), 1.

42. Ibid.

43. Most of the information on Subernarekha is based on the following sources: Kavaljit Singh, "The Chandil Nightmare" and "Subernarekha Multipurpose Project: For Whose Benefit?" (unpublished manuscripts, available from the Public Interest Research Group, New Delhi, India); Lori Udall et al., letter to Heinz Vergin, Director, India Department, World Bank, 16 May 1991 (unpublished, available from Environmental Defense Fund, Washington, D.C.); Senate Committee on Appropriations, Subcommittee on Foreign Operations, "Statement of Bruce M. Rich on Behalf of Environmental Defense Fund et al.," 102nd Cong., 1st sess., 25 June 1991; Clarence Maloney, "Environmental and Project Displacement of Population in India, Part I: Development and Deracination," Universities Field Staff international field staff report, 1990–91/No. 14 (Indianapolis: University Field Staff International); Probe International, "Subernarekha Project in India: Uproots Tribal People, Transforms River Basin," press release, Toronto, Canada, September 1991.

44. Singh, "Subernarekha Multipurpose Project," 8.
45. Ibid., 10.
46. World Bank office memorandum, "India-Subernarekha Irrigation Project (Cr. 1289-IN)—Resettlement Emergency Action," 16 June 1988.
47. Maloney, "Environmental and Project Displacement."
48. Kavaljit Singh (Public Interest Research Group, New Delhi), Anil Singh (Voluntary Action Network, New Delhi), et al., "Police Arrest Peaceful Demonstrators," statement of ten Indian nongovernmental organizations, New Delhi, 6 May 1991(available from the Public Interest Research Group, New Delhi), 2.
49. Jaime da Silva Araújo, statement before the World Commission on Environment and Development, São Paulo, 28 October 1985.
50. This section draws in part on the arguments of several leading Indian ecological and social thinkers, particularly Shiv Visvanathan and Smitu and Rajni Kothari. A representative sampling of their writings can be found in the *Lokayan Bulletin,* which is published at least quarterly by the Indian NGO Lokayan in Delhi; of particular importance is a special issue on "Survival" (vol. 3, nos. 4/5 [1985]). The concept of "two distinct epistemological cultures" is discussed in a document of the Consultative Group on the Environment, led by Rajni Kothari, called "An Approach to Environment in the Eighth Plan," *Lokayan Bulletin,* vol. 8, no. 3 (1991), 9. Rajni Kothari speaks of global trends toward "global integration" and "local destitution" in "On the Non-Party Political Process: The NGOs, the State, and World Capitalism," *Lokayan Bulletin,* vol. 4, no. 5 (1986), 22. Shiv Visvanathan discusses the "insurrection of local groups across the world" and the revolt of local knowledges in "Brundtland's Lovely Non-Magical Cosmos," *Lokayan Bulletin,* vol. 9, no. 1 (1991), 47–54.

3 • Brave New World at Bretton Woods

1. Belgian delegate Georges Theunis, submitting the World Bank charter for approval to the Bretton Woods Conference, from U.S. Department of State, *Proceedings and Documents of the United Nations Monetary and Financial Conference, Bretton Woods New Hampshire, July 1–22, 1944,* vol. 1, 1101 (hereafter cited as *Bretton Woods Proceedings*).
2. John Maynard Keynes, addressing the closing plenary session of the Bretton Woods Conference, 22 July 1944, ibid., 1110.
3. Robert W. Oliver, *International Economic Co-operation and the World Bank* (London and Basingstoke: Macmillan Press, Ltd., 1977), xvi, 110–11; this is the single best account of the origins of the World Bank. Alfred E. Eckes, Jr.'s account, cited in note 4 below, is indispensable and particularly useful for its insights into the thinking of the U.S. government; its bibliography is also excellent. Edward S. Mason's and Robert E. Asher's official history of the first twenty-five years of the World Bank, *The World Bank Since Bretton Woods* (Washington, D.C.: Brookings Institution, 1973), commissioned by Robert McNamara, is also a key source.
4. Armand Van Dormael, *Bretton Woods: Birth of a Monetary System* (New York: Homes & Meier Publishers, Inc., 1978), 5–7; Alfred E. Eckes, Jr., *A Search*

328 • Notes to Pages 50–60

for Solvency: Bretton Woods and the International Monetary System, 1941–1971
(Austin and London: University of Texas Press, 1975), 33; Sir Roy Harrod,
"Problems Perceived in the International Financial System," in A. L. K. Acheson,
J. F. Chant, and M. F. J. Prachowny, eds., Bretton Woods Revisited (Toronto:
University of Toronto Press, 1969), 10. Funk quoted in Van Dormael, op. cit.,
5–6.

5. Keynes quoted in Van Dormael, *Bretton Woods*, 7; see Oliver, *International Economic Co-operation*, 46–47; the British official is Sir Roy Harrod, the quote from Harrod, "Problems Perceived," 12.

6. Eckes, *Search for Solvency*, 38–40.

7. F. A. Hayek, *The Counter-Revolution of Science: Studies on the Abuse of Reason* (Indianapolis: Liberty Press, 1952), 164.

8. Oliver, *International Economic Co-operation*, 28–31, 43–46.

9. Ibid., 52–53. See Edward Jay Epstein, "Ruling the World of Money," *Harper's*, November 1983, 43–48.

10. Eckes, *Search for Solvency*, 34–35, 56–57; see Oliver, *International Economic Co-operation*, 92–99; Mason and Asher, *Since Bretton Woods*, 15–16.

11. Eckes, *Search for Solvency*, 56–57.

12. Ibid., 52–53; Mason and Asher, *Since Bretton Woods*, 15–19; see Oliver, *International Economic Co-operation*, 111–154. Treasury memorandum quoted in Eckes, *Search for Solvency*, 56.

13. Eckes, *Search for Solvency*, 62.

14. Ibid., 114.

15. Van Dormael, *Bretton Woods*, 168.

16. *Bretton Woods Proceedings*, 79–83.

17. Ibid.

18. Ibid.

19. Ibid., 88.

20. Ibid., 1116.

21. Ibid., 1116–18.

22. Ibid., 1120.

23. Van Dormael, *Bretton Woods*, 222.

24. Georges Theunis of Belgium, in *Bretton Woods Proceedings*, 1103.

25. World Bank, *Annual Report 1993* (Washington, D.C.: World Bank, 1993), 202.

26. See World Bank, *International Bank for Reconstruction and Development Articles of Agreement* (as amended effective 16 February 1989) (Washington, D.C.: World Bank, 1989), Article V, Sections 1–5; Article VIII (a).1.

27. Ibid., Article IX, Section 1.

28. *Bretton Woods Proceedings*, 1110; see, generally, Eckes, *Search for Solvency*, 165–209.

29. Quoted in Oliver, *International Economic Co-operation*, 160.

30. Editorial, *New York Times*, 4 December 4 1943.

31. Eckes, *Search for Solvency*, 168–69.

32. Ibid., 191.

33. Quoted in Oliver, *International Economic Co-operation*, 286.

34. See the definitive biography of Robert Taft by James T. Patterson, *Mr. Republican* (Boston: Houghton Mifflin, 1972).

35. Eckes, *Search for Solvency*, 182.

36. John H. Crider, "Taft Starts Fight to Bar World Bank," *New York Times*, 13 July 1945, 1; quotes from *Congressional Record*, 79th Cong., 1st sess., 12 July 1945, 7440.

37. Ibid., 7442.

38. Ibid., 7441.

39. Senate Committee on Banking and Currency, *Participation of the United States in the International Monetary Fund and the International Bank for Reconstruction and Development*, S. Report 452, part 2, "Minority Views," 79th Cong., 1st sess., 1945, 8.

40. Ibid., 17.

41. Ibid., 9.

42. *Congressional Record*, 79th Cong., 1st sess., 18 July 1945, 7689.

43. See Patterson, *Mr. Republican*, 294; and Eckes, *Search for Solvency*, 307, n. 86. Eckes argues that "neither Taft nor his revisionist defenders fully understood the process of international investment or the advantages of multilateral lending over bilateral government or private loans" (Eckes, ibid.). One can argue with equal force to the contrary—that in an atmosphere of generalized optimism, whipped up by Treasury, about the virtues of the new multilateral financial institutions, Taft was the only one who understood and pointed out some of the possible long-term problems.

44. See Jeffrey D. Sachs, "New Approaches to the Latin American Debt Crisis," paper prepared for the Harvard Symposium on New Approaches to the Latin American Debt Crisis, Institute of Politics, Kennedy School of Government, Harvard University, 22–23 September 1988.

45. See, for example, the discussion of Robert McNamara's tenure in Chapter 4. For a devastating French critique of the World Bank, see the writings of René Dumont; for example, *Finis Les Lendemains Qui Chantent . . . 3 Bangladesh-Nepal: "l'aide" contre le developpement* (Paris: Édition du Seuil, 1985), especially pp. 63–79, 106–20; and *Pour l'Afrique, j'accuse* (Paris: Plon, 1986), Annex X, "René Dumont Contre La Banque Mondiale," 373–85.

46. Quoted in Mason and Asher, *Since Bretton Woods*, 699.

47. The best discussion of the Savanah meeting, and the issues at stake, is found in Robert N. Gardner, *Sterling Dollar Diplomacy: The Origins and Prospects of Our International Economic Order*, rev. ed. (New York: McGraw-Hill, 1969), 257–67; see also Van Dormael, *Bretton Woods*, 287–303.

48. Van Dormael, *Bretton Woods*, 293.

49. Gardner, *Sterling Dollar Diplomacy*, 257.

50. Quoted ibid., 258.

51. Mason and Asher, *Since Bretton Woods*, 30.

52. Quoted in Van Dormael, *Bretton Woods*, 291; 292.

53. Gardner, *Sterling Dollar Diplomacy*, 265.

54. Mason and Asher, *Since Bretton Woods,* 34.

55. U.S. Senate, *Breton Woods Agreement Act, Hearings on H.R. 3314,* 79th Cong., 1st sess., 12–28 June 1945, 14.

56. Oliver, *International Economic Co-operation,* 226; Van Dormael, *Bretton Woods,* 286.

57. Oliver, *International Economic Co-operation,* 82–83; Eckes, *Search for Solvency,* 44.

58. Mason and Asher, *Since Bretton Woods,* 50.

59. Eckes, *Search for Solvency,* 220–21; Mason and Asher, *Since Bretton Woods,* 26.

60. International Bank for Reconstruction and Development, *Annual Report 1947–48* (Washington: International Bank for Reconstruction and Development, 1948), 10 (hereafter cited as IBRD, *1948*).

61. Eckes, *Search for Solvency,* 225.

62. Ibid., 101–2.

63. IBRD, *1948,* 16.

64. Raymond F. Mikesell, "The Emergence of the World Bank as a Development Institution," in Acheson, Chant, and Prachowny, *Bretton Woods Revisited,* 72.

65. Quoted in Mason and Asher, *Since Bretton Woods,* 235.

66. Oliver, *International Economic Co-operation,* 243; Mason and Asher, *Since Bretton Woods,* 58. On the Dutch war and economic blockade in Indonesia, see George McTurnan Kahin, *Nationalism and Revolution in Indonesia* (Ithaca and London: Cornell University Press, 1970), 212–30, 332–51, 391–446.

67. Morse quoted in Kahin, *Revolution in Indonesia,* 419–20.

68. See Kahin, *Revolution in Indonesia,* 404–18.

69. Mason and Asher, *Since Bretton Woods,* 57.

70. Quoted ibid., 58.

71. Ibid., 66.

72. Ibid., 587–90.

73. Quoted ibid., 589.

74. Oliver, *International Economic Co-operation,* 239, 259.

75. Gerald M. Meier, "The Formative Period," in Gerald M. Meier and Dudley Seers, eds., *Pioneers in Development* (New York: Oxford University Press, 1984), 8, citing Dudley Seers, "The Birth, Life and Death of Development Economics," *Development and Change,* vol. 10 (1979), 708.

76. IBRD, *1948,* 14–15, 17–18.

77. See, generally, Meier and Seers, *Pioneers in Development,* 205–72; on Rosenstein-Rodan, see Oliver, *International Economic Co-operation,* 272–73.

78. See Mason and Asher, *Since Bretton Woods,* 190.

79. Albert O. Hirschman, "A Dissenter's Confession: 'The Strategy of Economic Development' Revisited," in Meier and Seers, *Pioneers in Development,* 90–91.

80. Meier, "The Formative Period," 19.

81. Walt Whitman Rostow, "Development: The Political Economy of the Marshallian Long Period," in Meier and Seers, *Pioneers in Development,* 242.

82. Ibid., 240
83. Mason and Asher, *Since Bretton Woods,* 701–2.
84. John Howard, Introduction to John Howard, ed., *The Impact of International Organizations on Legal and Institutional Change in the Developing Countries* (New York: International Legal Center, 1977), 1–4; see Fernando Cepeda Ulloa, "Colombia and the World Bank," ibid., 80 ff.
85. Dragoslav Avramovic, "Comment [on Paul N. Rosenstein-Rodan]," in Meier and Seers, *Pioneers in Development,* 225.
86. Mason and Asher, *Since Bretton Woods,* 326–30.
87. See ibid., 493–525.
88. Ibid., 432.
89. Ibid., 434.
90. See ibid., 350–51.
91. See Aart Van de Laar, *The World Bank and the Poor* (Boston, The Hague, and London: Martinus Nijhoff Publishing, 1980), 56–59; Mason and Asher, *Since Bretton Woods,* 380 ff.
92. See Mason and Asher, *Since Bretton Woods,* 88.
93. Ibid., 755.
94. See Van de Laar, *The World Bank and the Poor,* 15–16.
95. See Mason and Asher, *Since Bretton Woods,* 218–19; World Bank 1963–1964 annual report quoted on p. 221.
96. Ibid., 221, 223.
97. I. P. M. Cargill, "Efforts to Influence Recipient Performance: Case Study of India," in John Prior Lewis and Ishan Kapur, eds., *The World Bank Group, Multilateral Aid, and the 1970s* (Toronto and London: Lexington Books, 1973), 94.
98. Mason and Asher, *Since Bretton Woods,* 228.

4 • The Faustian Paradox of Robert McNamara

1. Robert McNamara, "Address to the Board of Governors, September 30, 1968," in *The McNamara Years at the World Bank: Major Policy Addresses of Robert S. McNamara, 1968–1981* (Baltimore: Johns Hopkins University Press, 1981), 7 (hereafter cited as *McNamara*).
2. Faust, directing a massive land reclamation scheme, in the last act of Goethe's play: Johann Wolfgang von Goethe, *Faust,* trans. Walter Arndt, ed. Cyrus Hamlin (New York and London: W. W. Norton & Company, 1976), lines 11,559–566, pp. 293–94.
3. Robert L. Ayres, *Banking on the Poor* (Cambridge, Mass., and London, England: MIT Press, 1984), 4.
4. Robert McNamara, "Speech Before the Bond Club of New York, May 14, 1969," *McNamara,* 55.
5. Robert McNamara, "Speech to the UN Conference on the Human Environment, June 8, 1972," *McNamara,* 196.
6. Ibid., 198–200.

7. Quoted in Deborah Shapley, *Promise and Power: The Life and Times of Robert McNamara* (Boston: Little, Brown and Company, 1993), 515.

8. Ibid., 527.

9. Robert McNamara, "Address to the Board of Governors, September 24, 1973," *McNamara*, 240.

10. Robert McNamara, "Address to the Board of Governors, September 25, 1972," *McNamara*, 217.

11. Robert McNamara, "Address to the Board of Governors, September 24, 1973," *McNamara*, 246–48.

12. Ibid., 249.

13. Ibid., 261.

14. Ayres, *Banking on the Poor*, 79.

15. Ibid., 232, 4.

16. Quoted in Edward S. Mason and Robert E. Asher, *The World Bank Since Bretton Woods* (Washington, D.C.: Brookings Institution, 1973), 306.

17. Ayres, *Banking on the Poor*, 66–67.

18. William Clark, "Robert McNamara at the World Bank," *Foreign Affairs*, vol. 60 (Fall 1981), 174.

19. René Lemarchand, *The World Bank in Rwanda: The Case of the Office de Valorisation Agricole et Pastorale du Mutara (OVAPAM)* (Bloomington: African Studies Program, Indiana University, 1982), 71. Mr. Lemarchand was a consultant to a World Bank poverty project in Rwanda.

20. Ibid., 90.

21. Ibid., 80.; see Aart Van de Laar, *The World Bank and the Poor* (Boston, The Hague, and London: Martinus Nijhoff Publishing, 1980), 201.

22. See, for example, Ayres, *Banking on the Poor*, 123–24.

23. Rainer Tetzlaff, *Die Weltbank, Machtinstrument der USA oder Hilfe fuer die Entwicklungslaender?* (Muenchen: Weltforum Verlag, 1980), 511–12; Tatjana Chahoud, *Entwicklungsstrategie der Weltbank: Ein Beitrag zur Ueberwindung von Unterentwicklung und Armut?* (Saarbruecken and Fort Lauderdale: Verlag breitenback, 1982), 207–11; Zaki Laidi, *Enquête sur la Banque Mondiale* (Paris: Fayard, 1989), 119.

24. Betsy Hartmann and James Boyce, "Bangladesh: Aid to the Needy?" *International Policy Report* (Center for International Policy), vol. 4, no. 1 (May 1978), 6, cited in Cheryl Payer, *The World Bank: A Critical Analysis* (New York: Monthly Review Press, 1982), 235.

25. Cheryl Payer, "The World Bank and the Small Farmer," *Monthly Review*, November 1980, 41–42.

26. Robert Wade, "The System of Administrative and Political Corruption: Canal Irrigation in South India," *Journal of Development Studies*, vol. 18, no. 3 (April 1982), 288.

27. Ibid., 314.

28. Ibid., 317.

29. Ibid.

30. Ibid., 326, n. 55.

31. Robert Wade, "The World Bank and India's Irrigation Reform," *Journal of Development Studies,* vol. 18, no. 2 (January 1982), 171, 175, 179, 180–82.

32. Mick Moore, "Institutional Development, the World Bank, and India's New Agricultural Extension Programme," *Journal of Development Studies,* vol. 20, no. 4 (July 1984), 304.

33. Ibid., 310.

34. Ibid., 309.

35. Ibid., 307.

36. Ibid., 304, 312, 314.

37. See Payer, "The World Bank and the Small Farmer"; and Payer, *A Critical Analysis,* 237.

38. Tina Wallace, "Agricultural Projects and Land in Northern Nigeria," *Review of African Political Economy,* January–April 1980, 59.

39. The World Bank figures are cited in James C. Scott, *Weapons of the Weak: Everyday Forms of Peasant Resistance* (New Haven: Yale University Press, 1985), 65.

40. Ibid., 80.

41. Ibid., 79.

42. Ibid., 56.

43. Ibid., 248–49, xvii.

44. Ibid., xvii.

45. Pieter J. M. Robben and Pieter A. van Stuijvenberg, "India's Urban Housing Crisis: Why the World Bank's Sites and Services Schemes Are Not Reaching the Poor in Madras," *Third World Planning Review,* vol. 8, no. 4 (1986), 335–51.

46. Horace Campbell, "Tanzania and the World Bank's Urban Shelter Project," *Review of African Political Economy,* no. 42 (1988), 5–18.

47. Lemarchand, *The World Bank in Rwanda,* 18.

48. Ibid., 5.

49. Ibid.

50. Christian Kleinert, "Settlement Pressure and the Destruction of Forests in Rwanda," *Applied Geography and Development: A Biannual Collection of Recent German Contributions* 29 (1987), 101–3.

51. Detailed information on these projects unfortunately can be found only in World Bank documents that the Bank holds as confidential, "for official use only." The author relied on the following: International Bank for Reconstruction and Development, Operations Evaluation Department, *Project Performance Audit Report, Malaysia-Johore Land Settlement Project (Loan 967-MA)* (Washington, D.C.: World Bank, 13 December 1982); *Project Performance Audit Report, Malaysia-Jenka Triangle Project I (Loan 533-MA)* (Washington, D.C.: World Bank, 30 June 1978); *Project Performance Audit Report, Malaysia-Second Jenka Triangle Land Settlement Project (Loan 672-MA)* (Washington, D.C.: World Bank, 18 June 1980); *Project Performance Audit Report, Malaysia-Third Jenka Triangle Project (Loan 885-MA)* (Washington, D.C.: World Bank, 25 June 1982); World Bank, *Malaysia FELDA VI Land Settlement Project (Report no. 1863-MA)* (Washington, D.C.: 27 April 1978).

52. IBRD, OED, *PPAR, Malaysia-Johore Land Settlement Project,* 7.

53. I am estimating an average forest cover of around 20 million acres for peninsular Malaysia at the beginning of the 1970s. By 1980, forest cover was reduced to 16.9 million acres out of a total land area of 32.5 million acres. (Sahabat Alam Malaysia [Friends of the Earth, Malaysia], *The State of the Malaysian Environment 1983/84* [Penang, Malaysia: Sahabat Alam Malaysia, 1983], 26.)

54. IBRD, OED, *PPAR, Malaysia Jenka Triangle Project I,* 4.

55. IBRD, OED, *PPAR, Malaysia-Johore Land Settlement Project,* 7.

56. Ibid., 2, 4–6.

57. See International Bank for Reconstruction and Development, Operations Evaluation Department, *Project Performance Audit Report, Colombia-Caqueta Land Colonization Project (Loan 739-CO)* (Washington, D.C.: World Bank, 30 June 1978).

58. International Bank for Reconstruction and Development, Operations Evaluation Department, *Project Performance Audit Report, Cameroon-Niete Rubber Estate Project (Credit 574-CM)* (Washington, D.C.: World Bank, 22 June 1981), 27, 33.

59. International Bank for Reconstruction and Development, Operations Evaluation Department, *Project Performance Audit Report, Brazil Alto Turi Land Settlement Project (Loan 853-BR)* (Washington, D.C.: World Bank, 29 December 1982), 17–20, 52–53.

60. International Bank for Reconstruction and Development, Operations Evaluation Department, *Project Performance Audit Report, Nepal Settlement Project (Credit 505-NEP)* (Washington, D.C.: World Bank, 20 June 1983), 23, 32, 41, 58.

61. Ibid., 58–59.

62. World Bank, *Annual Review of Project Performance Audit Results, 1978* (Washington, D.C.: World Bank, February 1978) (hereafter cited as *PPAR Review 1978*); see discussion in Tetzlaff, *Die Weltbank,* 461–64.

63. Tetzlaff, *Die Weltbank,* 464.

64. World Bank, *Annual Review of Evaluation Results for 1989* (Washington, D.C.: World Bank, 14 August 1989), v, vii, 2-7 (hereafter cited as *Evaluation Results 1989*).

65. World Bank, Operations Evaluation Department, "Environmental Aspects of Selected Bank-Supported Projects in Brazil: Environmental Aspects and Consequences of Bank-Assisted Projects in the Middle and Lower Sao Francisco Valley," draft confidential report (unpublished, 1990), 9–10.

66. World Bank, *India Irrigation Sector Review* (Washington, D.C.: World Bank, Agriculture Operations Division, India Department, Asia Region, 27 June 1991), 9–10.

67. Ibid., i.

68. Ibid.

69. Ibid., iv.

70. *Congressional Record,* 95th Cong., 1st sess., 18 July 1977, 23,601.

71. Ibid., 23,601–602.

72. Ibid., 23,603.

73. Andreas C. Tsantis and Roy Pepper, *Romania: The Industrialization of an Agrarian Economy under Socialist Planning*, report of a mission sent to Romania by the World Bank (Washington, D.C.: World Bank, 1979), 37.

74. Van de Laar, *The World Bank and the Poor*, 40.

75. Valerie J. Assetto, *The Soviet Bloc in the IMF and the IBRD* (Boulder: Westview Press, 1988), 147.

76. Van de Laar, *The World Bank and the Poor*, 40.

77. International Bank for Reconstruction and Development, *Statement of Loans, July 31, 1991*, vol. 2 (EMENA and LAC regions) (Washington, D.C.: World Bank, 1991), 325.

78. Assetto, *The Soviet Bloc*, 149, 152, 157.

79. Ibid., 144–45.

80. Tsantis and Pepper, *Romania*, 32, 12.

81. Ibid., 15, 385.

82. Ibid., 4.

83. Ibid., 357.

84. See, for example, the *Wall Street Journal*'s scathing editorial on the World Bank and Romania, "Resurrection of the Dead," 10 August 1979, 10.

85. Van de Laar, *The World Bank and the Poor*, 146.

86. S. Shahid Husain (formerly World Bank Senior Vice-President for Operations Policy and currently Vice-President for Latin America and the Caribbean), quoted in Shapley, *Promise and Power*, 543.

87. Ayres characterizes "learning by doing" rather innocuously as the simple process of trying to improve future projects by learning from past experience—something the Bank has not been notably successful at. (Ayres, *Banking on the Poor*, 144–46.) Indeed, the reverse was often true: the Bank often repeated the same mistakes, but used its approach to development as an experiment to justify its financing of highly risky, unproven, environmentally and socially disastrous schemes like the ones described in Chapter 2.

88. Marshall Berman, *All That Is Solid Melts into Air: The Experience of Modernity*, "Part I: Goethe's Faust: The Tragedy of Development" (New York: Penguin Books, 1988, first published by Simon & Schuster, Inc., 1982), 37–71; the second quote is from Cyrus Hamlin, "Interpretive Notes," in the Arndt translation of *Faust* (New York: W. W. Norton & Company, 1976), 343.

89. See Berman, *All That Is Solid Melts into Air*, 60–86.

90. Johann Wolfgang von Goethe, *Faust*, translated and with an introduction by Walter Kaufmann (New York: Doubleday, Anchor Books, 1963), lines 11,125–30, pp. 434–37.

91. *Faust*, Arndt translation, lines 11,248–50, p. 285.

92. *Faust*, Kaufmann translation, line 11,349, pp. 450–51.

93. *Faust*, Arndt translation, lines 11,555–56, p. 293.

94. *Faust*, Arndt translation, lines 11,567, 11,569; 11,579–86, p. 294.

95. *Faust*, Kaufmann translation, lines 11,544–50, pp. 464–67.

5 • Greens Lay Siege to the Crystal Palace

1. Fyodor Mikhailovich Dostoyevsky, *Notes from Underground,* in *Existentialism from Dostoevsky to Sartre,* ed. and trans. Walter Kaufmann (New York, London, and Scarborough, Ontario: New American Library, 1975; first published by World Publishing Co., 1956), 71.

2. Marshall Berman, *All That Is Solid Melts into Air: The Experience of Modernity* (New York: Penguin Books, 1988; Simon & Schuster, 1982), 236.

3. I owe much of this discussion on the symbolism of the Crystal Palace—but not all of the conclusions I draw—to Marshall Berman's provocative discussion in *All That Is Solid Melts into Air,* pp. 219–48. It is important to note the distinction between the Crystal Palace as a perceived, somewhat ominous symbol of modernity, especially in Dostoyevsky and nineteenth-century Russian literature, and the actual building. According to Berman, "for Dostoyevsky and his anti-hero [in *Notes from Underground*], too, the Crystal Palace stands for . . . everything that is ominous and threatening about modern life, everything against which modern man must stand *en garde*" (p. 220). The structure itself, from all contemporary descriptions, was not architecturally oppressive, and created a space to integrate man and nature with industry, rather than crushing them; it was a graceful, light building, a marvelous oversized greenhouse, evoking a "late Turner painting . . . fusing nature and industry in a vividly chromatic and dynamic ambience" (Berman, op. cit., 237).

4. Dostoyevsky, *Notes from Underground,* 69.

5. Ibid., 79.

6. See, for example, Arthur Mitzman, *The Iron Cage: An Historical Interpretation of Max Weber* (New York: Grosset and Dunlap, 1971).

7. Edward S. Mason and Robert E. Asher, *The World Bank Since Bretton Woods* (Washington, D.C.: Brookings Institution, 1973), 250–51.

8. A. W. Clausen, "Address to the Board of Governors," Washington, D.C., 29 September 1981, in World Bank, *The Development Challenge of the Eighties, A. W. Clausen at the World Bank, Major Policy Addresses 1981–1986* (Washington, D.C.: World Bank, 1986), 7 (hereafter cited as *Clausen*).

9. Ibid., 5.

10. These figures are adapted by Cheryl Payer from the Inter-American Development Bank (IDB) publication *External Debt and Economic Development in Latin America* (Washington, D.C.: IDB, 1984), table 4, p. 19, in Cheryl Payer, *Lent and Lost: Foreign Credit and Third World Development* (London and New Jersey: Zed Books, 1991), 12.

11. A. W. Clausen, "Sustainable Development: The Global Imperative," Fairfield Osborn Memorial Lecture in Environmental Science, Washington, D.C., 12 November 1981, in World Bank, *Clausen* (1986), 29–30.

12. Quoted in Aart Van de Laar, *The World Bank and the Poor* (Boston, The Hague, and London: Martinus Nijhoff Publishing, 1980), 5.

13. Van de Laar, ibid., 7.

14. House Committee on Banking, Finance, and Urban Affairs, Subcommittee on International Development Institutions and Finance, *Environmental Im-*

pact of Multilateral Development Bank-Funded Projects, 98th Cong., 1st sess., 28 and 29 June 1983.

15. Ibid., 503–13.

16. The information on the history of the Nambiquara, including the statement of the International Red Cross doctors, is taken from a letter concerning the Nambiquara sent by the Núcleo de Direitos Indígenas and twelve other Brazilian indigenous rights groups to Mr. Lewis T. Preston, President, World Bank, 15 April 1992.

17. House Subcommittee on International Development, 28 and 29 June 1983, 475–94; quotation from p. 478.

18. Ibid., 487.

19. Ibid., 490.

20. Ibid., 521.

21. Ibid., 525.

22. Ibid., 535.

23. Ibid., 533.

24. Ibid., 524.

25. U.S. Congress, House Committee on Banking, Finance, and Urban Affairs, Subcommittee on International Development Institutions and Finance, *Draft Recommendations on the Multilateral Development Banks and the Environment,* 98th Cong., 2nd sess., 11 and 13 September 1984, 11. James Conrow was deputy assistant secretary of the treasury for developing nations.

26. World Bank, "Response to Statements of Environmental Organizations Sent by the U.S. Executive Director," (Washington, D.C.: World Bank, 11 January 1984, unpublished), 2 (hereafter cited as World Bank Response).

27. Ibid.

28. World Bank office memorandum from Luis de Azcarate to files, 30 March 1984.

29. World Bank Response, 1.

30. Ibid., 7.

31. Ibid., 8–9.

32. Ibid., 32.

33. Ibid., 7.

34. Ibid., 8.

35. This individual has to remain anonymous.

36. House Subcommittee on International Development Institutions and Finance, 11 and 13 September 1984.

37. House Committee on Banking, Finance, and Urban Affairs, Subcommittee on International Development Institutions and Finance, *Multilateral Development Bank Activity and the Environment,* 98th Cong., 2nd sess., Committee Print No. 98–20.

38. House Committee on Science and Technology, Subcommittee on Natural Resources, Agriculture Research, and Environment, *Tropical Forest Development Projects: Status of Environmental and Agricultural Research,* 98th Cong., 2nd sess., 19 September 1984, 17.

39. Ibid., 17, 26–30.

40. Ibid., 20–22.

41. Ibid., 22.

42. Bruce Rich et al., letter to A. W. Clausen, 12 October 1984 (available in files of the World Bank and the Environmental Defense Fund).

43. Roberto Gonzalez Cofino, letter to Bruce Rich, 7 November 1984 (available in files of the World Bank and the Environmental Defense Fund).

44. Robert W. Kasten, Jr., letter to A. W. Clausen, 24 January 1985.

45. Robert W. Kasten, Jr., letter to the Honorable Donald T. Regan, 13 January 1985.

46. This quote, and the following paraphrase, is the author's recollection of Stern's statement.

47. Quoted in Marlise Simons, "Brazilian Who Fought to Protect Amazon Is Killed," *New York Times,* 24 December 1988, 1.

48. See, for example, the letter of Ailton Krenak, National Coordinator of the Union of Indigenous Nations (UNI), to Barber Conable, President, World Bank, 10 October 1986. Krenak, writing on behalf of both UNI and the National Council of Rubber Tappers, sent to Conable a resolution endorsed by both organizations condemning "the disastrous effect of many World Bank loans in Amazonia," and called upon the Bank to "cease loans to all projects" that did not "clearly protect the rights of people already living in the forest."

49. Ernest Stern, Senior Vice-President for Operations, World Bank, office memorandum to Robert B. Keating, U.S. Executive Director, 2 April 1987.

50. See Erna Witoelar, "NGO Networking in Indonesia," in Sahabat Alam Malaysia (Friends of the Earth, Malaysia), *Environment, Development and Natural Resource Crisis in Asia and the Pacific,* proceedings of the symposium organized by Sahabat Alam Malaysia held at Recsam Complex, Penang, 22–25 October 1983 (Penang, Malaysia: Sahabat Alam Malaysia, 1983), 412–22.

51. See: Emmy Hafild, Executive Secretary of SKEPHI, Agus Pernumo, Executive Director WALHI, et al., letter to Barber Conable, President, World Bank, 10 September 1986; Bruce Rich et al., letter to Barber Conable, 10 October 1986; Barber Conable, letter to Bruce Rich, 15 December 1986; Bruce Rich et al., letter to Barber Conable, 3 June 1987 (all available from the files of the Environmental Defense Fund).

52. See Edourdo Lachica, "Indonesia Is Curbing Relocation Plan; World Bank Will Cut Loans as Result," *Wall Street Journal,* 24 December 1986, 12.

53. See Daryl D'Monte, *Temples or Tombs?* (New Delhi: Center for Science and Environment, 1985), 29–61.

54. Howard Geller, "Options for Investments in End-Use Efficiency and Conservation in Developing Countries" (Washington, D.C.: World Bank Energy Department Paper No. 34, October 1986). This was one of several studies published by different independent institutions over the coming years that would reach essentially the same conclusions.

55. Hugh W. Foster, U.S. Alternate Executive Director, statement to the

World Bank's Board of Executive Directors regarding the Brazil Electric Power Sector loan, 19 June 1986 (typewritten, U.S. Treasury Department).

56. Ibid.

57. Ibid.

58. Max Weber, "Bureaucracy," in *From Max Weber: Essays in Sociology,* trans. and ed. H. H. Gerth and C. Wright Mills (New York: Oxford University Press, 1946), 197.

59. James A. Lee, World Bank office memorandum to Mr. V. Rajagopalan, 8 January 1980.

60. J. C. Collins, World Bank office memorandum to R. Goodland, 25 February 1980.

61. D. C. Pickering and J. A. Lee, World Bank office memorandum to D. J. Mahar, 20 May 1980.

62. J. C. Collins, World Bank office memorandum to D. Mahar, 9 July 1980.

63. James A. Lee, World Bank office memorandum to Donald Pickering, 19 November 1980.

64. Enrique Lerdau, World Bank office memorandum to Nicolas Ardito Barletta, "BRAZIL—Proposed Northwest Region Development Program Amerindian Issue: Problem with Bank Consultant David Price," 9 December 1980.

65. James A. Lee, World Bank office memorandum to OEA (Office of Environmental Affairs) files, 19 December 1980.

66. James A. Lee, World Bank office memorandum to Warren C. Baum (through Mr. Rajagopalan), 9 June 1981.

67. V. Rajagopalan, note to James A. Lee, 9 June 1981.

68. W. B. Peters, World Bank office memorandum to John C. Collins, 21 July 1981.

69. World Bank, "Summary of Discussions at the Meeting of the Executive Directors of the Bank and IDA, and the Board of Directors of IFC, December 1, 1981," 15 December 1981, p. 2.

70. J. C. Collins, World Bank office memorandum to S. Shahid Husain (through J. B. Hendry), 29 July 1983.

71. James A. Lee, World Bank office memorandum to V. Rajagopalan, 4 August 1983.

72. N. O. Tcheyan, telex to Minister Mario Andreazza, Minister of the Interior, Brazil, "Subject: Amerindians—Polonoroeste," 17 March 1983.

73. World Bank, press release: "World Bank Loan of $65.2 million to Assist Settlements in the Amazon Region of Brazil," 27 October 1983.

74. Kasten and Conrow interviewed by Nicholas Claxton, producer and director, *The Price of Progress,* documentary film (London: Central Independent Television, 1987).

75. Address of Barber B. Conable, President, World Bank and International Finance Corporation, to the World Resources Institute, Washington, D.C., 5 May 1987 (printed version of the speech released to press).

76. Ibid.

77. Gus Speth, President of World Resources Institute, quoted in Philip Shabecoff, "World Bank Offers Environmental Projects," *New York Times,* 6 May 1987.

78. Address of Barber B. Conable to World Resources Institute, 5 May 1987.

79. Ibid. When Conable's major policy speeches were published by the World Bank more than four years later, this statement was somewhat altered to read, "A . . . basic truth learned from Polonoroeste is that where development is taking place, it cannot be halted, only directed. The Bank cannot influence progress from the sidelines. It must be part of the action." This revision of the actual words Conable spoke (and of the text of the speech that circulated for several years after) refers the general principle—that "development cannot be halted, only directed"—to a specific case, Polonoroeste. Making the general "basic truth" more specific shows how truly disastrous an assumption it is in practice: even with hindsight of what became a disaster, Conable asserts in this revised version that Polono-roeste was inevitable and unstoppable, and that the Bank was justified in being "part of the action." Barber B. Conable, World Bank, *The Conable Years at the World Bank: Major Policy Addresses of Barber B. Conable, 1986–91* (Washington, D.C.: The World Bank, 1991), 23.

6 • The Emperor's New Clothes

1. Max Weber, "Bureaucracy," in *From Max Weber: Essays in Sociology,* ed. and trans. H. H. Gerth and C. Wright Mills (New York: Oxford University Press, 1946), 228.

2. Representative James H. Scheuer, in hearings of the House Committee on Science, Space, and Technology, Subcommittee on Natural Resources, Agriculture Research, and Environment, *Sardar Sarovar Dam Project,* 101st Cong., 1st sess., 24 October 1989, 96.

3. World Bank, *The World Bank and the Environment: First Annual Report, Fiscal 1990* (Washington, D.C.: World Bank, 1990), 52–53.

4. Barber B. Conable, President, World Bank, "Remarks at the Conference on Global Environment and Human Response Toward Sustainable Development, Tokyo, Japan, September 11, 1989," (printed version of the speech released to the press), 6; *The World Bank and the Environment, 1990,* 6.

5. U.S. Congress Human Rights Caucus, *Briefing on Forced Resettlement by Development Projects,* 27 September 1989.

6. A good summary of the history of the Kedung Ombo situation can be found in "Statement of Peter Van Tuijl, on Behalf of the International NGO Forum on Indonesia, Concerning the Consequences of Forced Resettlement in the World Bank Financed Kedung Ombo Dam in Indonesia," made before the U.S. Congress Human Rights Caucus, 27 September 1989 (unpublished, available from the Human Rights Caucus or the Environmental Defense Fund, Washington, D.C.). Other sources include the *Tapol Bulletin* (bulletin of the Indonesia Human Rights Campaign, published by TAPOL, Thornton Heath, Croydon, Surrey, U.K), nos. 82 and 83 (August and September, 1987); and

---

Setiakawan (published by SKEPHI, the NGO Network for Forest Conservation in Indonesia, Jakarta).

7. The World Bank's defense of its role in Kedung Ombo is set forth in a letter of its Indonesia country director, Russell J. Cheetham, dated 5 May 1989, addressed to the International NGO Forum on Indonesia. The Bank asserts that contrary to charges of journalists and NGOs, "Bank supervision missions have regularly supervised the project since its inception, and reviewed the progress in resettlement during these missions." The letter maintains that allegations that the Bank did not ensure a resettlement and environmental plan for the dam, that the local population was not consulted, and that the Bank ignored the issues raised by its own consultants are all incorrect. Concerning allegations of coercion, the Bank replied, "The [Indonesian] government has a clear policy of non-coercion in these matters." The letter then states that the Bank raised the allegations of coercion with the government and "understands that Government has taken steps to curb such actions." Dialogue with several remaining villages, the letter noted, "has been extremely difficult due to the apparent group attitude of non-cooperation with the Government." The six-page, single-spaced letter concluded, "The resettlement component of Kedung Ombo has obviously had problems. The Government, with the help of the Bank, is addressing these problems."

8. The description of the Harsud rally, and the quote from Srilata Swaminadhan, can be found in Rusi Engineer, "The Sardar Sarovar Controversy: Are the Critics Right?" in *Business India,* 30 October–12 November 1989, 90–104.

9. *Lokayan Bulletin,* vol. 8, no. 1 (1990), 69–73.

10. World Bank, Operations Evaluation Department, "Environmental Aspects of Selected Bank-Supported Projects in Brazil: Environmental Aspects and Consequences of the Polonoroeste Program" (draft confidential report, typewritten), 26 November 1990, 14–15 (hereafter cited as OED, Polonoroeste Draft Report).

11. Clarence Maloney, "Environmental and Project Displacement of Population in India, Part I: Development and Deracination," University Field Staff International, field staff report 1990–91, no. 14 (Indianapolis, Ind.: University Field Staff International), 1.

12. OED, Polonoroeste Draft Report, 15.

13. Lori Udall, "Statement on Behalf of the Environmental Defense Fund Concerning the Social Impacts of Forced Resettlement in World Bank–Financed Development Projects," made before the U.S. Congress Human Rights Caucus, 27 September 1989 (available from the Environmental Defense Fund, Washington, D.C.), 4.

14. World Bank, Agriculture and Rural Development Department, "Involuntary Resettlement in Bank-Assisted Projects: A Review of the Application of Bank Policies and Procedures in FY79-85 Projects" (typewritten internal document), February 1986, 42.

15. Thayer Scudder, quoted in Nicholas Claxton, producer and director, *The Price of Progress,* documentary film (London: Central Independent Television, 1987).

16. World Bank, Operations Evaluation Department, "Environmental Aspects

and Consequences of Bank-Assisted Projects in the Middle and Lower Sao Francisco Valley" (draft confidential report, typewritten), 1990, p. 90 (hereafter cited as OED, São Francisco Valley Draft Report).

17. Ibid., 95.

18. Ibid., 93.

19. Ibid., 94.

20. Ibid., note 50, pp. 93–94, citing an internal World Bank memorandum of 24 July 1990.

21. Ibid., 52.

22. Ibid., vii.

23. *The World Bank and the Environment, 1990,* 6.

24. Kevin Cleaver, chief of the Africa Country Department 1 Agriculture Division, World Bank, defending an $80-million forestry loan for the Côte d'Ivoire, in World Bank office memorandum to Mr. André Milongo, Executive Director, 26 March 1990, 3.

25. Address of Barber B. Conable, President, World Bank and International Finance Corporation, to the World Resources Institute, Washington, D.C., 5 May 1987 (printed version released to press), 4.

26. Barber B. Conable, "Remarks at Tokyo, Japan, September 11, 1989," 10.

27. Environmental Defense Fund, "Memorandum: The Tropical Forest Action Plan for Cameroon, 1990" (typewritten manuscript); see also Korinna Horta, "The Last Big Rush for the Green Gold: The Plundering of Cameroon's Rainforests," *Ecologist,* vol. 21, no. 3 (May/June 1991), 142–47.

28. Marcus Colchester and Larry Lohman, *The Tropical Forest Action Plan: What Progress?* (Penang, Malaysia and London, England: World Rainforest Movement, 1990).

29. ARA (Working Group on Rainforests and Species Conservation) and INFOE (Institute for Ecology and Action Anthropology), "Memorandum on the Responsibility of the Federal Republic of Germany for the Destruction of Tropical Rainforests and Her Obligation to Take Action for Their Protection" (Bielefeld, Germany: ARA, 1989).

30. Rainforest Information Centre, "Memorandum on Australia's Responsibility for the Destruction of the World's Rainforests and Its Obligation to Take Action for Their Protection" (Lismore, New South Wales, Australia: Rainforest Information Centre, Inc., 1991).

31. See, for example, World Bank, Latin America and Caribbean Region, *Environment and Development in Latin America and the Caribbean: The Role of the World Bank* (Washington, D.C.: World Bank, 1992), 17–20.

32. Francisco Alves Mendes Filho (Chico Mendes), letter to Barber Conable, 13 October 1988 (translation and original available from the Environmental Defense Fund, Washington, D.C.).

33. Bruce Rich, Environmental Defense Fund, Osmarino Amancio Rodrigues, National Council of Rubber Tappers, et al., letter to Mr. E. Patrick Coady, World Bank Executive Director, United States, 9 January 1990.

34. Steve Schwartzman, Environmental Defense Fund, et al., letter to Mr. E.

Patrick Coady, World Bank Executive Director, United States, 1 February 1990; Jerónimo Garcia de Santana, Governor of Rondônia, letter to José Sarney, President of Brazil, 14 September 1988.

35. Telephone conversation with José Lutzenberger, March 1990; telephone conversation with Adrian Cowell, March 1990.

36. José A. Lutzenberger, Secretary of the Environment, Brazil, letter to Barber Conable, President, World Bank, 22 March 1990.

37. Juan de Onis, *The Green Cathedral: Sustainable Development of the Amazon* (New York: Oxford University Press, 1992), 217.

38. Eighteen nongovernmental groups in Rondônia sent an open letter to the executive directors of the World Bank on March 12, 1992, asking them to delay consideration of the Rondônia Natural Resources Project until various irregularities and problems in the project could be corrected ("Carta Abierta do Fórum das Organizações Não-Governamentais de Rondônia, Brasil para Diretores Executivos do Banco Mundial, Porto Velho, Rondônia, 12 de Março de 1992"). Their concerns were amplified—including the issue of new land settlements planned by INCRA—in a memorandum sent on May 12, 1992, to Luis Coirolo, the World Bank task manager for the project. Most of the same groups wrote the president of Brazil, Fernando Collor de Mello, on May 29, 1992, to express further concern about the project, particularly the flagrantly illegal INCRA land colonization plans. Copies were sent to Lewis Preston, president of the World Bank, as well as to the new Brazilian secretary of the environment, José Goldemberg, and a number of other Brazilian officials.

39. Articulation of Indigenous Peoples of Rondônia and Northern Mato Grosso (APIR) et al., letter to Lewis Preston, President, World Bank, 29 April 1993.

40. Barber B. Conable, "Remarks at Tokyo, Japan, September, 11, 1989," 5.

41. World Bank, *Annual Report 1992* (Washington, D.C.: World Bank, 1992), 193; World Bank, *Annual Report 1993,* 165.

42. The figure on India's energy investment comes from an internal report written by Peter Miller (currently with the Natural Resources Defense Council in San Francisco), energy specialist, for the Environmental Defense Fund, "Energy Efficiency and the World Bank in India," 1990.

43. Besides the studies cited in other footnotes and endnotes in this section, see Howard S. Geller, *Efficient Electricity Use: A Development Strategy for Brazil* (Washington, D.C. and Berkeley: American Council for an Energy-Efficient Economy, 1991). Geller estimates that an alternative energy investment scenario for Brazil, using currently available, economically viable technologies, would avoid constructing between 26,000 and 33,000 megawatts of generating capacity through the year 2010. He estimates the cost of building 26,000 megawatts of dams and coal-fired plants at around $52 billion, and the maximum cost of the requisite efficiency investments at $20 billion, saving $32 billion. (Geller, op. cit., 120–24). See also José Goldemberg et al., *Energy for Development* (Washington, D.C.: World Resources Institute, September 1987).

44. Michael Philips, *The Least-Cost Energy Path for Developing Countries: Energy-Efficiency Investments for the Multilateral Banks* (Washington, D.C.: International Institute for Energy Conservation, September 1991).

45. World Bank, International Development Association, "Additions to IDA Resources: Ninth Replenishment" (confidential document prepared for executive directors' meeting, Tuesday, 23 January 1990), 5 January 1990, para. 18, p. 6.

46. "Implementing Energy Efficiency Activities in Developing Countries, A Cross-Country Examination of Energy and Environmental Issues, Constraints and Options," World Bank Energy Sector Management Assistance Program, activity initiation brief, April 1990, pp. 3–4.

47. Aart Van de Laar, *The World Bank and the Poor* (Boston, The Hague, and London: Martinus Nijhoff Publishing, 1980), p. 208, note 33.

48. For the terms of reference of the OED study, see World Bank, Operations Evaluation Department, "Approach Paper: The Bank's Role in Environmental Issues in Brazil" (Washington, D.C.: World Bank Joint Audit Committee, 2 June 1989, internal memorandum).

49. OED Polonoroeste Draft Report. See especially the report's "Summary" and "Conclusions," pp. v–xxxi.

50. World Bank, Operations Evaluation Department, "Environmental Aspects of Selected Bank-Supported Projects in Brazil; Environmental Aspects and Consequences of the Carajas Iron Ore Project" (draft confidential report, typewritten), 21 March 1990, p. xiv (hereafter cited as OED, Carajás Draft Report).

51. Ibid., 173.

52. OED Polonoroeste Draft Report, p. 55.

53. World Bank, "Brazil and the World Bank: Into the Fifth Decade" (Washington, D.C.: World Bank, 1990), 17.

54. World Bank Latin America and Caribbean Region, "Environment and Development in Latin America and the Caribbean: The Role of the World Bank" (Washington, D.C.: World Bank, 1992), 30.

55. See the World Bank, "Funding for the Global Environment" (discussion paper, February 1990), 1–2.

56. United Nations Development Programme, "Fonds Pour l'Environnement Global (Global Environment Facility—GEF), Projet d'Amenagement et de Gestion des Aires Protégées du Congo, Commentaires Techniques du Consultant PNUD, New York, Septembre, 1991," p. 7.

57. M. Balcet, World Bank office memorandum, 13 June 1991.

58. United Nations Development Programme, "GEF, Projet d'Amenagement," 3.

59. Ibid.

60. John G. Sidle, U.S. Fish and Wildlife Services, Nebraska/Kansas Field Office, Grand Island, Nebraska, letter to Jean-Claude Balcet, Environment Department, World Bank, Washington, D.C., 12 May 1992; John G. Sidle, letter to Dr. Walt Reid, World Resources Institute, Washington, D.C., 17 June 1992.

7 • The Castle of Contradictions

1. Representative James H. Scheuer, in hearings of the Committee on Science, Space, and Technology, Subcommittee on Natural Resources, Agriculture Re-

search, and Environment, *Sardar Sarovar Dam Project,* 101st Cong., 1st sess., 24 October 1989, 97.

2. World Bank, *Annual Report 1993* (Washington, D.C.: World Bank, 1993), 111, 117, 143.

3. Ibid., 137.

4. Melvyn Westlake, "Negative Transfers to Zoom in 90s," *Annual Meeting News,* 15 October 1991, 7 (published by International Media Partners, New York, N.Y. and *The Nation,* Bangkok, Thailand).

5. This analysis reflects a similar analysis for the Bank's FY 1988 loan portfolio cited by Paul Mosley, Jane Harrigan, and John Toye, *Analysis and Policy Proposals,* vol. 1 of *Aid and Power: The World Bank and Policy-based Lending* (London and New York: Routledge, 1991), 71, based on a paper by Robert Wade, "Unpacking the World Bank: Lending versus Leverage" (unpublished paper, March 1989).

6. World Bank, *Annual Report 1993,* 205, 192, 190.

7. United Nations Economic Commission for Africa, *African Alternative Framework for Socio-Economic Recovery and Transformation* (Addis Ababa: United Nations Economic Commission for Africa, 1990).

8. Giovanni Andrea Cornia, Richard Jolly, and Frances Stewart, *Protecting the Vulnerable and Promoting Growth,* vol. 1 of *Adjustment with a Human Face* (Oxford: Clarendon Press, 1987), 34, 287–88.

9. Oxfam (U.K.), "Africa Make or Break: Action for Recovery," 38-page printed report (Oxford: Oxfam, 1993), 2.

10. David Reed, ed., *Structural Adjustment and the Environment* (Boulder, Colorado: Westview Press, 1992), 151.

11. Ibid.

12. Wilfredo Cruz and Robert Repetto, *The Environmental Effects of Stabilization and Structural Adjustment Programs: The Philippines Case* (Washington, D.C.: World Resources Institute, September 1992), 6.

13. Oxfam (U.K.), "Africa Make or Break," 7–8. For a discussion of the failures of the Bank's approach to adjustment in the Caribbean, see Kathy McAfee, *Storm Signals: Structural Adjustment and Development Alternatives in the Caribbean* (Boston: South End Press in association with Oxfam America, 1991).

14. Cruz and Repetto, *Environmental Effects,* 60.

15. Marguerite Michaels, "Retreat From Africa," *Foreign Affairs,* vol. 72, no. 1, 93–198.

16. Oxfam (U.K.), "Africa Make or Break," 25.

17. See Robert L. Ayres, *Banking on the Poor* (Cambridge, Mass. and London, England: MIT Press, 1984), 123–24, 251.

18. Philip M. Fearnside, "Deforestation and International Economic Development Projects in Brazilian Amazonia," *Conservation Biology,* vol. 1, no. 3 (October 1987), 219.

19. Ibid., 214–21, 218.

20. World Bank, *World Development Report 1992: Development and the Environment* (New York: Oxford University Press, 1992), 9.

21. Max Weber, "Bureaucracy," in *From Max Weber: Essays in Sociology,* trans. and ed. H. H. Gerth and C. Wright Mills (New York: Oxford University Press, 1946), 233–34.

22. International Bank for Reconstruction and Development, *Articles of Agreement,* Article III, Section 2.

23. Hollis Chenery, "The Developing Economy" (unpublished manuscript), quoted in Edward S. Mason and Robert E. Asher, *The World Bank Since Bretton Woods* (Washington, D.C.: Brookings Institution, 1973), 484.

24. Mason and Asher, *Since Bretton Woods,* 485.

25. Ibid., 446.

26. K. B. Griffin and J. L. Enos, "Foreign Assistance: Objectives and Consequences," *Economic Development and Cultural Change* 18 (1970), 319–20, cited in Cheryl Payer, *Lent and Lost: Foreign Credit and Third World Development* (London and New Jersey: Zed Books, 1991), 29.

27. See Polly Hill, *Development Economics on Trial: The Anthropological Case for a Prosecution* (Cambridge, England: Cambridge University Press, 1987).

28. R. H. Coase, "The Lighthouse in Economics," *Journal of Law and Economics,* October 1974, 357–76.

29. World Commission on Environment and Development, *Our Common Future* (Oxford and New York: Oxford University Press, 1987), 43.

30. Walt W. Rostow, "The Marshallian Long Period," in Gerald M. Meier and Dudley Seers, eds., *Pioneers in Development* (New York: Oxford University Press, 1984), 261.

31. Ibid.

32. Barber B. Conable, President, World Bank, "Address as Prepared for Delivery to the World Resources Institute, Washington, D.C., May 5, 1987" (version released to press), 3.

8 • From Descartes to Chico Mendes

1. René Descartes, *Discourse on Method and The Meditations,* trans. and with an introduction by F. E. Sutcliffe (London: Penguin Books, 1968), 78.

2. Václav Havel, "The End of the Modern Era," *New York Times,* 1 March 1992, sect. 4, p. 15.

3. World Bank, *World Development Report 1992: Development and the Environment* (New York: Oxford University Press, 1992), 1.

4. Walt W. Rostow, *How It All Began: Origins of the Modern Economy* (New York: McGraw-Hill Book Company, 1975), 2.

5. Gunnar Myrdal, *Asian Drama: An Inquiry Into the Poverty of Nations,* vol. 1 (New York: Twentieth Century Fund, 1968), 54–55, quoted in H. W. Arndt, *Economic Development: The History of an Idea* (Chicago and London: University of Chicago Press, 1987), 175; see also 111–13.

6. Myrdal, *Asian Drama,* 57–63.

7. Nehru, cited ibid., p. 57, note 3; also quoted in Arndt, *Economic Development,* 112.

8. Marshall Sahlins, *Stone Age Economics* (New York: Aldine Publishing Company, 1972), 34–35.

9. Claude Lévi-Strauss, *The Savage Mind* (La pensée sauvage) (London: Weidenfeld and Nicolson, 1966), 89–90.

10. Sahlins, *Stone Age Economics,* 36.

11. Ibid., 37.

12. Rostow, *How It All Began,* 21, 31, 132.

13. Max Weber, *Religions of China,* trans. H. Gerth (New York: Free Press, 1964), 248, quoted in Harry Redner, *In the Beginning Was the Deed: Reflections on the Passage of Faust* (Berkeley: University of California Press, 1982), 167.

14. Louis Dumont, *From Mandeville to Marx: The Genesis and Triumph of Economic Ideology* (Chicago and London: University of Chicago Press, 1977), 5.

15. See Tom Sorell, *Descartes* (Oxford and New York: Oxford University Press, 1987), 1–26.

16. Quoted in William Barrett, *The Illusion of Technique* (Garden City, N.Y.: Anchor Books, 1979), 126.

17. Philip J. Davis and Reuben Hersh, *Descartes' Dream: The World According to Mathematics* (San Diego: Harcourt Brace Jovanovich, 1986), 3.

18. Descartes, *Discourse on Method and The Meditations,* 35.

19. Ibid., 40.

20. Ibid., 41.

21. See F. E. Sutcliffe, Introduction to Descartes, *Discourse on Method and the Meditations,* 16–17; and Albert Borgman, *Crossing the Postmodern Divide* (Chicago and London: The University of Chicago Press, 1992), 35.

22. Descartes, *Discourse on Method and the Meditations,* 78.

23. The sources that assert this are too numerous to mention; in the nineteenth century they include Hegel and Saint-Simon. For a relatively recent, popular account see Barrett, *The Illusion of Technique,* 123–28.

24. Descartes, *Discourse on Method and the Meditations,* 109.

25. Ibid., 43.

26. Ibid.

27. See Robert N. Proctor, *Value Free Science? Purity and Power in Modern Knowledge* (Cambridge, Mass. and London, England: Harvard University Press, 1991), 39–53.

28. Cited by Claude-Henri de Saint-Simon, *Lettres d'un Habitant de Genève à Ses Contemporains,* in *Oeuvres de Claude-Henri de Saint-Simon* (Paris: Éditions Anthropos, 1966), vol. 1, 321.

29. Barber Conable, "Address to the Board of Governors of the World Bank, Berlin (West), Germany, September 27, 1988," in *The Conable Years at the World Bank: Major Policy Addresses of Barber B. Conable, 1986–91* (Washington, D.C.: World Bank, 1991), 63.

30. Francis Bacon, *New Atlantis and The Great Instauration,* ed. Jerry Weinberger (Arlington Heights, Illinois: Harlan Davidson, Inc., 1980), 16.

31. Francis Bacon, *Novum Organum,* in *Selected Writings of Francis Bacon,*

with an introduction and notes by Hugh G. Dick (New York: Modern Library, 1955), book 1, aphorism 2, p. 461.

32. Ibid., aphorism 5, p. 462. See also aphorism 18, p. 464; aphorism 19, p. 465.

33. Ibid., *Novum Organum,* "Preface," 56.

34. Bacon, *New Atlantis and The Great Instauration,* 21.

35. Ibid., 23.

36. Ibid., 21.

37. Bacon, *Novum Organum,* aphorism 113, p. 525.

38. Bacon, *Selected Writings,* 285.

39. Bacon, *Novum Organum,* aphorism 3, p. 462.

40. Ibid., aphorism 124, p. 534.

41. See Jatinder Bajaj, "Francis Bacon, the First Philosopher of Modern Science: A Non-Western View," in Ashis Nandy, ed., *Science, Hegemony and Violence: A Requiem for Modernity* (Delhi: Oxford University Press, 1990), 24–67.

42. Bacon, *Novum Organum,* aphorism 127, p. 536.

43. Bajaj, "Francis Bacon," 43, 63.

44. Bacon, *Novum Organum,* aphorism 129, p. 538.

45. See Bajaj, "Francis Bacon," 49.

46. Bacon, *New Atlantis and The Great Instauration,* 58–59.

47. Ibid., 71.

48. Ibid., 82,

49. See Bajaj, "Francis Bacon," 24–25. Bajaj bases much of his criticism of the betrayal and corruption that characterized Bacon's public life on a well-known essay by the nineteenth-century English historian Thomas (Lord) Macaulay, that is well worth reading even 155 years after it was written: Thomas (Lord) Macaulay, "Lord Bacon" (*Edinburgh Review,* July 1837), in Macaulay, *Critical, Historical, and Miscellaneous Essays,* vol. 3 (New York: Hurd & Houghton, 1871), 336–448.

50. Macaulay, "Lord Bacon," 392.

51. Martin Heidegger, *The Question Concerning Technology and Other Essays,* trans. and ed. William Lovitt (New York: Harper Torchbooks, 1977), 22; Martin Heidegger, *Die Technik und Die Kehre* (Pfullingen, Germany: Verlag Gunther Neske, 1962), 22.

52. Clarence Glacken, *Traces on the Rhodian Shore: Nature and Culture in Western Thought from Ancient Times to the End of the Eighteenth Century* (Berkeley: University of California Press, 1967), 476.

53. Ibid.

54. Bacon, *Novum Organum,* aphorism 129, p. 538.

55. C. S. Lewis, *The Abolition of Man* (New York, N.Y.: Collier Books, 1962), 87–88.

56. See Keynes's letter to his father on the auction, dated 15 July 1936, in *The Collected Writings of John Maynard Keynes,* ed. Donald Moggridge, vol. 21, *Activities 1931–1939 World Crises and Policies in Britain and America* (London and

Cambridge, England: Macmillan, Cambridge University Press for the Royal Economic Society), 381–82.

57. See Morris Berman, *The Reenchantment of the World* (New York: Bantam Books, 1984, originally published by Cornell University Press, 1981), 108; see especially Betty Jo Teeter Dobbs, *The Foundations of Newton's Alchemy* (Cambridge, England: Cambridge University Press, 1975).

58. Frank E. Manuel, *A Portrait of Isaac Newton* (Washington, D.C.: New Republic Books, 1979, reprint of 1968 edition published by the Belknap Press, Harvard University Press), 162–63.

59. John Maynard Keynes, "Newton the Man," and "Bernard Shaw and Isaac Newton," in *Collected Writings*, vol. 10, *Essays in Biography*, 363–64; 377.

60. Manuel, *Portrait of Isaac Newton*, 176, 178.

61. *The Correspondence of Isaac Newton*, ed. H. W. Turnbull, vol. 2, *1676–1687* (Cambridge, England: Cambridge University Press, 1960), p. 2, letter 157, Newton to Oldenburg, 26 April 1676.

62. See *Correspondence of Isaac Newton*, vol. 3, *1688–1694*, pp. 215–19: letter 389, Newton to Locke, 7 July 1692; letter 390, Locke to Newton, 26 July 1692; letter 391, Newton to Locke, 2 August 1692. See also Manuel, *Portrait of Isaac Newton*, 176–78; 183–87.

63. Richard S. Westfall, *Never At Rest: A Biography of Isaac Newton* (Cambridge, England: Cambridge University Press, 1980), 285.

64. Manuel, *Portrait of Isaac Newton*, 231.

65. Henri Saint-Simon, *Introduction to the Scientific Studies of the Nineteenth Century* (1808), in *Henri Comte de Saint-Simon, Selected Writings*, ed., trans., and with an intro. by F. M. H. Markham (Oxford: Basil Blackwell, 1952), 13.

66. See George Lichtheim, *The Origins of Socialism* (New York: Frederick A. Praeger, Publishers, 1969), 39–59; F. A. Hayek, *The Counter-Revolution of Science: Studies in the Abuse of Reason* (Glencoe, Ill.: Free Press, 1952), 165–67.

67. Lichtheim, *The Origins of Socialism*, 40–42.

68. Keith Taylor, introduction to *Henri Saint-Simon: Selected Writings on Science, Industry, and Social Organization*, ed., trans., and with an introduction by Keith Taylor (New York: Homes and Meier, Inc., 1975), 15.

69. Claude-Henri Saint-Simon, *L'Organisateur*, in *Oeuvres de Saint-Simon et d'Enfantin* (Paris: Dentu, 1865–76; E. Leroux, 1877–78), vol. 20, 126–27 fn., quoted in Frank E. Manuel, *The New World of Henri Saint-Simon* (Cambridge, Mass.: Harvard University Press, 1956), 306.

70. Ibid.

71. Saint-Simon, *L'Industrie*, in *Oeuvres de Saint-Simon et d'Enfantin*, vol. 18, 188, quoted in Manuel, *The New World of Henri Saint-Simon*, 240–41.

72. *The Doctrine of Saint-Simon: An Exposition, First Year, 1828–1829*, trans. George G. Iggers (Boston: Beacon Press), 106–7.

73. Frank E. Manuel, *The Prophets of Paris* (Cambridge, Mass.: Harvard University Press, 1962), 177.

74. Taylor, introduction to *Henri Saint-Simon: Selected Writings*, 15–16.

75. Lichtheim, *The Origins of Socialism*, 236, n. 2.

76. Manuel, *The New World of Henri Saint-Simon*, 188.

77. Claude-Henri Saint-Simon, *De la réorganization de la société européenne*, in *Oeuvres choisies de C.H. Saint-Simon, précédées d'un essai sur sa doctrine*, ed. Lemonnier (Brussels: Van Meenen, 1859), vol. 2, 293, quoted in Manuel, *The New World of Henri Saint-Simon*, 176.

78. Manuel, *The New World of Henri Saint-Simon*, 236.

79. Mathurin Dondo, *The French Faust: Henri de Saint-Simon* (New York, Philosophical Library, 1955), 109; Saint-Simon, *Lettres au Bureau des Longitudes*, in *Oeuvres de Claude-Henri de Saint-Simon*, vol. 6, 273.

80. Marshall Berman, *All That Is Solid Melts Into Air: The Experience of Modernity* (New York: Penguin Books, 1988), 72–74.

81. Lichtheim, *The Origins of Socialism*, 53.

82. Markham, introduction to Saint-Simon, *Selected Writings*, xxxix–xl; Dondo, *The French Faust*, 212–13 (including Enfantin quote).

83. Dondo, *The French Faust*, 213.

84. Hayek, *The Counter-Revolution of Science*, 165.

85. Ibid.

86. Quoted ibid., 166.

87. Dondo, *The French Faust*, 214.

88. Lichtheim, *The Origins of Socialism*, 40; see Manuel, *The Prophets of Paris*, 274.

89. Hayek, *The Counter-Revolution of Science*, 164.

90. See Manuel, *The Prophets of Paris*, 287.

91. See ibid., 274.

92. Saint-Simon, letter to Henri-Jean Victor, quoted in Dondo, *The French Faust*, 112.

93. Max Weber, *The Protestant Ethic and the Spirit of Capitalism*, trans. Talcott Parsons (New York: Charles Scribner's Sons, 1958), 181.

94. Quoted in J. B. Bury, *The Idea of Progress* (New York: Dover Publications, 1932), 330.

95. C. S. Lewis, *The Abolition of Man*, 83.

96. Ibid., 84.

97. Fyoder Dostoyevsky, *Winter Notes on Summer Impressions*, trans. Kyril FitzLyon (London: Quartet Books, 1985), 45–46.

98. Max Weber, *Economy and Society*, ed. Guenther Roth and Claus Wittich (Berkeley: University of California Press, 1978), vol. 2, 225, quoted in Martin Albrow, *Max Weber's Construction of Social Theory* (New York: St. Martin's Press, 1990), 183.

99. On the distinction between formal and substantive rationality in Weber's thought, see Rogers Brubaker, *The Limits of Rationality: An Essay on the Social and Moral Thought of Max Weber* (London: George Allen & Unwin, 1988), 4, 36–37, 42–43, 110–111. See, generally, Albrow, *Max Weber's Construction*, and Arthur Mitzman, *The Iron Cage: An Historical Interpretation of Max Weber* (New York: Grosset and Dunlap, 1971).

100. Weber, *The Protestant Ethic and the Spirit of Capitalism,* 181.

101. Weber, *Economy and Society,* vol. 2, 1402.

102. Ibid., 1418–19.

103. Ibid., 1417–18.

104. Ibid., 1417.

105. Robert Moses, quoted in Robert Caro, *The Power Broker: Robert Moses and the Fall of New York* (New York: Vintage Books, 1975), 218.

106. Caro, *The Power Broker,* 859.

107. Ibid., 859–63.

108. Ibid., 862.

109. Ibid., 859.

110. Ibid., 19–20.

111. Ibid., 19.

112. Quoted ibid., 12.

113. Ibid., 624.

114. Ibid., 15–16; 623–24.

115. Ibid., 623.

116. Ibid., 13.

117. Ibid., 17.

118. Ibid.

119. Marc Reisner, *Cadillac Desert: The American West and Its Disappearing Water* (New York: Penguin Books, 1987, first published by Viking Penguin, 1986), 141.

120. Michael Robinson, *Water for the West* (Chicago: Public Works Historical Society, 1979), no page cite given, quoted by Reisner, *Cadillac Desert,* 141.

121. Reisner, *Cadillac Desert,* 142.

122. The original appraisal report for the Sardar Sarovar dam states that

the binding rules of society as formulated by the NWDT [Narmada Water Disputes Tribunal] state . . . that consumptive water uses have priority over power generation. . . . Therefore, power generation, although contributing a large share of total benefits, is a residual benefit, taking advantage of undiverted flows during the buildup period of basin diversions. Consequently [*sic*], no project is conceivable without the irrigation and M&I [municipal and industrial] water supply components. . . . Given GOG's [Government of Gujarat] decision that the main objective is providing irrigation and municipal/industrial water supply, it is unrealistic to conceive an alternative project satisfying this objective, as required by the classical method of appraising multi-purpose projects, because any alternative means of providing such water is prohibitively expensive. (World Bank, staff appraisal report, "India Narmada River Development—Gujarat, Sardar Sarovar Dam and Power Project," 12 February 1985, report no. 5107-IN, pp. 56–57.)

123. Reisner, *Cadillac Desert,* 181.

124. Ibid., 185–86.

125 Ibid., 201.

126. Ibid., 194.

127. Quoted ibid., 196.

128. Ibid., 195–98.

129. Ibid., 199.

130. Quoted ibid., 188. Ickes was referring specifically to the role of the Corps in the Kings and Kern irrigation development in California.

131. See Reisner, *Cadillac Desert,* 211.

132. U.S. Bureau of Reclamation, *Assessment '87,* quoted in Richard W. Wahl, Office of Policy Analysis, U.S. Department of the Interior, "New Roles for the Bureau of Reclamation," University of Colorado School of Law, Natural Resources Center, Occasional Papers Series, 1989, p. 1.

133. Lt. Gen. Henry J. Hatch, quoted in Alan Atkisson, "Green Engineering and National Security: An Interview with Lt. General Henry J. Hatch," *In Context: A Quarterly of Humane Sustainable Culture,* no. 32 (Summer 1992), 40–44.

134. John Gunther, *Inside U.S.A.* (New York and London: Harper & Brothers, 1947), 733, 748.

135. William Chandler, *The Myth of TVA: Conservation and Development in the Tennessee Valley, 1933–83* (Cambridge, Mass.: Ballinger Publishing Co., 1984), 117–18.

136. Gunther, *Inside U.S.A.,* 731.

137. Ibid., 744.

138. Richard Hamilton, "Damodar Valley Corporation: India's Experiment with the TVA Model," *Indian Journal of Public Administration,* vol. 15 (1969), 86–109; Thomas G. Sanders, "Northeast Brazilian Environmental Refugees: Part I: Why They Leave," University Field Staff International, Latin America, field staff reports 1990–91, no. 20 (Indianapolis, Ind.: University Field Staff International), 8.

139. Quoted in Gunther, *Inside U.S.A.,* 738.

140. See Gunther, *Inside U.S.A.,* 944, where he summarizes his sources for chap. 43, "Model TVA."

141. Chandler, *The Myth of TVA,* 7; see chap. 4, "The Myth of Cornucopia."

142. Ibid., 8.

143. Ibid.

144. Quoted ibid., 129.

145. Ibid., 98.

146. Michael J. McDonald and John Muldowney, *TVA and the Dispossessed* (Knoxville: University of Tennessee Press, 1982), 62–64, quoted in Chandler, *The Myth of TVA,* 79.

147. Figure cited in Chandler, *The Myth of TVA,* 78–79.

148. Ibid., 11; see also Reisner, *Cadillac Desert,* 338–41.

149. Chandler, *The Myth of TVA,* 11.

150. Quoted in Caro, *The Power Broker,* 218.

151. Zygmunt Bauman, *Modernity and the Holocaust* (Ithaca, N.Y.: Cornell University Press, 1989), 28, 192.

152. Ibid., 158.

153. Ibid., 193.

154. Langdon Winner, *Autonomous Technology: Technics-out-of-Control as a Theme in Political Thought* (Cambridge, Mass. and London, England: 1977), 100–101.

155. Ibid., 104.

156. Max Horkheimer, *The Eclipse of Reason* (New York: Oxford University Press, 1947), 97.

157. Ibid., 21.

158. Ibid., 93.

159. Ibid., 20–21.

160. Heidegger, *The Question Concerning Technology*, 17–18.

161. Ibid., 18.

162. Ibid., 19.

163. *Oxford English Dictionary*, compact edition (New York: Oxford University Press, 1971), 859.

164. "The Encompassing Web," *Ecologist*, vol. 22, no. 4 (July/August 1992), 149.

165. Ibid.

166. Heidegger, *The Question Concerning Technology*, 27.

167. See Konrad Lorenz, *The Waning of Humaneness*, trans. Robert Warren Kickert (Boston: Little, Brown and Company, 1987), 165–68.

168. Heidegger, *The Question Concerning Technology*, 27.

169. Havel, "The End of the Modern Era," 15.

9 • Who Shall Rule the World—and How?

1. Julia Preston, "U.N. Earth Summit Marred by Corruption Charges," *Washington Post*, 6 May 1992, A23.

2. "Brazilians Umweltkrise und der Gipfel von Rio," *Neue Zuercher Zeitung*, 25/26 April 1992, 7.

3. Anne-Lise Hilty, "Auf den schlechtesten Platz in der hintersten Halle verbannt," *Die Weltwoche* (Zurich), nr. 18, 30 April 1992, 105.

4. United Nations Development Program, *Human Development Report 1992* (New York and Oxford: Oxford University Press, 1992), 1.

5. Ibid., 52.

6. Paul Lewis, "Environment Aid to Poor Nations Agreed at U.N.," *New York Times*, 5 April 1992, 1.

7. José Lutzenberger, Secretário do Meio-Ambiente da Presidência da República, Brasília, Brazil, letter to Mr. Laurence [sic] Summers, Vice President Research and Policy, World Bank, Washington, D.C., February 1992 (day missing; copy available in files of the Environmental Defense Fund, Washington, D.C.).

8. See World Bank, *World Development Report 1992* (New York: Oxford University Press, 1992), 9–10.

9. Lawrence H. Summers, World Bank office memorandum, 12 December 1991, 5.

10. Ibid.

11. Michael Prowse, "Save Planet Earth from Economists," *Financial Times,* 10 February 1992.

12. José Lutzenberger, letter to Laurence [*sic*] H. Summers, February 1992.

13. Lawrence H. Summers, World Bank office memorandum, 13 December 1991, 5.

14. *Sardar Sarovar: Report of the Independent Review,* Chairman, Bradford Morse, Deputy Chairman, Thomas Berger (Ottawa, Canada: Resource Futures International, Inc., 1992), xxiv.

15. Ibid., xxii.

16. Ibid., 226, 233–34.

17. Ibid., xxiii.

18. Ibid., 329.

19. Ibid., 336.

20. In the autumn of 1983, after appraisal, the Bank belatedly sent a mission to "attempt to evaluate the social impacts of the projects," headed by Professor Thayer Scudder of the California Institute of Technology; "the Bank's India Country Department opposed this mission." (*Sardar Sarovar: Report of the Independent Review,* 43). Six years later, in 1989, with the Narmada Valley aroused in protests, Scudder returned with Bank staff to evaluate the resettlement situation, concluded that the chances of successful resettlement and rehabilitation were lower than ever, and recommended the halting of all loan disbursements; the India country department's formal mission report stated virtually the opposite conclusion and "appeared to conclude that a corner had been turned [concerning resettlement]" (ibid., 128).

21. *Sardar Sarovar: Report of the Independent Review,* 64.

22. Ibid., 250.

23. Ibid., 238.

24. Ibid., 237.

25. Ibid., 335–39.

26. Ibid., 53.

27. Ibid., 54.

28. Ibid., 36.

29. Ibid.

30. International Bank for Reconstruction and Development, "India: The Sardar Sarovar (Narmada) Projects Management Response" (internal document SecM92-849), 23 June 1992, 16, 11–12.

31. These allegations have been confirmed by several sources within the World Bank, who, to retain their jobs, must remain anonymous.

32. Susan Reed, "Enemies of the Earth," *People,* 27 April 1992, 53, 56.

33. In August 1990, Preston met with representatives of several environmental groups in the offices of the World Resources Institute in Washington. In the course of the meeting, he expressed his skepticism about whether there were enough bankable projects in developing countries for the Bank's current levels of

lending. (Telephone discussion with Deborah Bleviss, International Institute for Energy Conservation, Washington, D.C., 1 June 1993.)

34. Willi A. Wapenhans et al., "Report of the Portfolio Management Task Force, July 1, 1992" (internal World Bank document), 1.

35. Ibid., 4.

36. Willi A. Wapenhans, "Oral Briefing of the JAC [Joint Audit Committee] at its Meeting on June 22, 1992 on The Portfolio Management Task Force" (draft notes, internal World Bank file document), 22 June 1992, 1.

37. Wapenhans et al., "Report of the Portfolio Management Task Force," 4.

38. Ibid.

39. Ibid., ii.

40. Ibid., 8.

41. Ibid.

42. Ibid., 12.

43. Ibid.

44. Ibid., 14.

45. Ibid.

46. "Festival der Heuchelei," *Der Spiegel*, no. 21, 18 May 1992, 246.

47. Lewis T. Preston, President, World Bank Group, "Reducing Poverty and Protecting the Environment: A Call to Action, An Address to the United Nations Conference on Environment and Development, Rio de Janeiro, Brazil, June 4, 1992" (Washington, D.C.: World Bank, June 1992), 5.

48. "Global Environmental Facility under Fire," 1992 Global Forum, press release no. 174, 8 June 1992.

49. "Rio Under Siege," *Terra Viva* (the independent daily of the Earth Summit, Rio de Janeiro), 11 June 1992, 2.

50. "Strong 'Personally Insulted' by Charges against Lindner," *Terra Viva*, 11 June 1992, 7.

51. "High Security for NGO Protest at Riocentro," 1992 Global Forum, press release no. 203, 9 June 1992.

52. "'Oppressed by Life' March Brings 50,000 Demonstrators Together," *Terra Viva*, 11 June 1992, 6.

53. Don Marti, "Mwango's Speech Lights Fire: NGO Youth Rally against UNCED," *Earth Summit Times*, (official newspaper of record for the United Nations Conference on Environment and Development, published in cooperation with *New York Times* and *Jornal do Brasil*), 12 June 1992, 3; "Youth 'Forcibly Removed' from Rio-Centro," 1992 Global Forum, press release no. 252, 11 June 1992.

54. Gerson da Cunha, "Castro Supplies a Moment Electric," *Earth Summit Times*, 13 June 1992, 3.

55. David E. Pitt, "Atmosphere and Finance Wind Up Negotiations," *Earth Summit Times*, 14 June 1992, 16.

56. See David Runnals, "An Open Letter to the Assembled World Leaders at the Summit," *Earth Summit Times*, 12 June 1992, 1.

57. "Festival der Heuchelei," *Der Spiegel,* no. 21, 18 May 1992, 224.

58. Anil Agarwal and Sunita Narain, *Global Warming in an Unequal World: A Case of Environmental Colonialism* (New Delhi: Center for Science and Environment, 1991), 36.

59. David C. Korten, "Development, Heresy and the Ecological Revolution," *In Context: A Quarterly of Humane Sustainable Culture,* no. 32 (Summer 1992), 31.

60. World Bank, *World Development Report 1992,* 9.

61. Ibid.

62. Paul C. Stern, Oran R. Young, and Daniel Druckman, eds., *Global Environmental Change: Understanding the Human Dimensions* (Washington, D.C.: National Academy Press, 1992), 56.

63. Ibid.

64. Ibid., 59.

65. World Bank, *World Development Report 1992,* 10.

66. Jan Tinbergen and Roefie Hueting, "GNP and Market Prices: Wrong Signals for Sustainable Economic Success that Mask Environmental Destruction," in Robert Goodland, Herman Daly, and Salah El Serafy, eds., *Environmentally Sustainable Economic Development: Building on Brundtland* (Washington, D.C.: World Bank Sector Policy and Research Staff, environment working paper no. 46, July 1991), 37–38; page numbers cited hereafter are for this original collection. The essays in *Building on Brundtland* were subsequently published as a book, *Population, Technology, and Lifestyle: The Transition to Sustainability,* Robert Goodland, Herman E. Daly, and Salah El Serafy, eds. (Washington, D.C., and Covelo, Calif.: Island Press, 1992).

67. Paul Ekins, "The Sustainable Consumer Society: A Contradiction in Terms?" *International Environmental Affairs,* vol. 3, no. 4 (Fall 1991), 250.

68. World Resources Institute, in collaboration with the United Nations Environment Program and the United Nations Development Program, *World Resources 1990–91* (Oxford and New York: Oxford University Press, 1990), 144, quoted in Ekins, "Sustainable Consumer Society," 251.

69. Ekins, "Sustainable Consumer Society," 251.

70. Goodland, Daly, and El Serafy, *Building on Brundtland.*

71. Emil Salim and José Lutzenberger, "Preface," ibid., i.

72. Tinbergen and Hueting, "GNP and Market Prices," 41.

73. See Robert Goodland, "The Case That the World Has Reached Limits," in Goodland, Daly, and El Serafy, *Building on Brundtland,* 5–17; and Herman Daly, "From Empty-World to Full-World Economics: Recognizing an Historical Turning Point in Economic Development," ibid., 18–26.

74. Trygve Haavelmo and Stein Hansen, "On the Strategy of Trying to Reduce Economic Inequality by Expanding the Scale of Human Activity," in Goodland, Daly, and El Serafy, *Building on Brundtland,* 31.

75. Daly, "From Empty-World to Full-World Economics," 23.

76. Ambassador Rhazali of Malaysia, quoted in "Government Representatives

and NGOs discuss 'Who Will Rule the World,'" 1992 Global Forum, press release no. 273, 12 June 1992.

77. Ibid.

78. Candido Grzybowskiu, Brazilian Institute for Social and Economic Analysis, quoted ibid.

79. "As U.N. Expands, So Do Its Problems," *Washington Post,* 20 September 1992, A26.

80. Ibid.

81. Ibid.

82. Ibid.

83. Jean Chesneaux, *Brave Modern World* (New York: Thames and Hudson, 1992), 150.

84. "Global Management," *Ecologist,* vol. 24, no. 4 (July/August 1992), 180–82.

85. B. N. Dhondiyal, quoted in Steve Coll, "A Plan to Save the Globe Dies in a Village," *Washington Post,* 24 May 1992, A46.

86. See Peter F. Drucker, *The New Realities* (New York: Harper & Row, 1989), 164–70; David Ruelle, *Change and Chaos* (Princeton, N.J.: Princeton University Press, 1991), 80–85.

87. M. Mitchell Waldrop, *Complexity: The Emerging Science at the Edge of Order and Chaos* (New York: Simon & Schuster, 1992), 37–38, 145–47, 329–34.

88. Drucker, *The New Realities,* 165–66.

89. Michael Redclift, *Sustainable Development: Exploring the Contradictions* (London and New York: Routledge, 1989), 80.

90. Hilary F. French, *After the Earth Summit: The Future of Environmental Governance* (Washington, D.C.: Worldwatch Paper 107, March 1992), 28; see also Patricia Birnie, "International Environmental Law: Its Adequacy for Present and Future Needs," in Andrew Hurrell and Benedict Kingsbury eds., *The International Politics of the Environment: Actors, Interests, and Institutions* (New York and Oxford: Clarendon Press of Oxford University Press, 1992), 70–78 (sections on "Enforcement," "Scientific Research," and "Monitoring").

91. French, *After the Earth Summit,* 28.

92. For an account of what international environmental law expert R. Michael M'Gonigle calls the "distressing history" of the International Whaling Commission from its founding in 1946 through 1980, see R. Michael M'Gonigle, "The 'Economizing' of Ecology: Why Big, Rare Whales Still Die," *Ecology Law Quarterly,* vol. 9 (1980), 119–237; on threats of Norway and Iceland to resume whaling, see T. R. Reid, "World Whaling Body Riven by Dispute," *Washington Post,* 15 May 1993, A17.

93. Don Hinrichsen, review of *Saving the Mediterranean: The Politics of International Environmental Cooperation,* by Peter Haas, *International Environmental Affairs,* vol. 3, no. 3 (Summer 1991), 235.

94. French, *After the Earth Summit,* 10.

95. Peter M. Haas, *Saving the Mediterranean: The Politics of International*

Environmental Coorperation (New York: Columbia University Press, 1990), 130–31.

96. Stern, Young, and Druckman, *Global Environmental Change,* 19.

97. Ibid., 59.

98. Jean Carriere, "The Crisis in Costa Rica: An Ecological Perspective," in David Goodman and Michael Redclift, eds., *Environment and Development in Latin America: The Politics of Sustainability* (Manchester, England, and New York: Manchester University Press, 1991), 194.

99. Ibid., 195.

100. World Resources Institute, *World Resources 1990–91,* 102.

101. Carriere, "The Crisis in Costa Rica," 188.

102. Ibid., 192–93.

103. Ibid.

104. Anthony Giddens, *The Consequences of Modernity* (Stanford, Calif.: Stanford University Press, 1990), 65.

105. Václav Havel, *Living in Truth* (London, England, and Boston, Mass.: Faber and Faber, 1989), 114.

10 • What on Earth Is to Be Done?

1. Peter F. Drucker, *The New Realities* (New York: Harper & Row, 1989), 13.

2. Jean Chesneaux, *Brave Modern World: The Prospects for Survival* (New York: Thames and Hudson, 1992), 176.

3. "The most conspicuous features of the postmodern condition: institutionalized pluralism, variety, contingency, and ambivalence—have been all turned out by modern society in ever increasing volumes; yet they were seen as signs of failure rather than success, as evidence of the insufficiency of efforts so far, at a time when the institutions of modernity, faithfully replicated by the modern mentality, struggled for *universality, homogeneity, monotony,* and *clarity.* The postmodern condition can be therefore described, on the one hand, as modernity emancipated from false consciousness; on the other, as a new type of social condition marked by the overt institutionalization of the characteristics which modernity—in its designs and managerial practices—set about to eliminate, and, failing that, tried to conceal" (Zygmunt Bauman, *Intimations of Postmodernity* [London and New York: Routledge, 1992], 187–88).

4. Drucker, *The New Realities,* 10.

5. David C. Korten, *Getting to the 21st Century: Voluntary Action and the Global Agenda* (West Hartford, Conn.: Kumarian Press, 1990), 156–62.

6. See, for example, Doug Brown, "An Institutionalist Look at Postmodernism," *Journal of Economic Issues,* vol. 25, no. 4 (December 1991), 1089–1101; *Development and Change,* vol. 23, no. 3 (July 1992), special issue, "Emancipations, Modern and Postmodern," guest editor, Jan Nederveen Pieterse.

7. Julio Barbosa, President of the Brazilian Council of Rubber Tappers, at the first public hearing in history to debate proposed forest clearing in the Amazon (Rio Blanco, Acre, 11 May 1990), quoted in Juan de Onis, *The Green Cathedral:*

Sustainable Development of the Amazon (New York and Oxford: Oxford University Press, 1992), 203.

8. Climate Alliance of European Cities with the Amazonian Peoples, "Working Paper for the Meeting on 4 August 1990," Umwelt Forum Frankfurt (Xerox copy), 2–4.

9. Alan Durning, "People Power and Development," *Foreign Policy,* no. 76, (Fall 1989), 66.

10. Robin Broad, with John Cavanagh, *Plundering Paradise: The Struggle for the Environment in the Philippines* (Berkeley: University of California Press, 1993), 135; see, generally, 132–57.

11. See, generally, Ramachandra Guha, *The Unquiet Woods: Ecological Change and Peasant Resistance in the Himalaya* (Berkeley: University of California Press, 1990).

12. Ibid., 173.

13. Denise Stanley, "Demystifying the Tragedy of the Commons: The Resin Tappers of Honduras," *Grassroots Development,* vol. 15, no. 3 (1991), 27–35.

14. David Barton Bray, "The Struggle for the Forest: Conservation and Development in the Sierra Juarez," ibid., 12–25.

15. Broad, *Plundering Paradise,* 56–72.

16. See, for example: Stanley, "Demystifying the Tragedy of the Commons"; Rita Brara, "Are Grazing Lands 'Wastelands'?" *Economic and Political Weekly* (Bombay, India), 22 February 1992, 411–18; "Regaining the Commons," *Ecologist,* vol. 22, no. 4 (July/August 1992), special issue, *Whose Common Future?* pp. 195–204.

17. Fikret Berkes and Carl Folke, "A Systems Perspective on the Interrelations between Natural, Human-Made and Cultural Capital," *Ecological Economics,* vol. 5, no. 1 (March 1992), 5. See also E. Ostrom, *Governing the Commons: The Evolution of Institutions for Collective Action* (Cambridge, England: Cambridge University Press, 1990).

18. Eduardo Viveiros de Castro, "Prefácio," in Ricardo Azambuja Arnt and Stephen Schwartzman, *Um Artifício Orgânico: Transição na Amazonia e Ambientalismo* (Rio de Janeiro, Brazil: Editora Rocca, 1992), 19.

19. Marianne Schmink and Charles H. Wood, *Contested Frontiers in Amazonia* (New York: Columbia University Press, 1992), 8.

20. Arnt and Schwartyman, *Um Artifício Organico,* 115–117.

21. See, generally, Arnt and Schwartzman, *Um Artifício Orgânico.*

22. Schmink and Wood, *Contested Frontiers,* 8.

23. Eduardo Viveiros de Castro, "Prefácio," 10.

24. For a description of the spread of information technologies and the empowerment of grass-roots groups in Latin America, see Sheldon Annis, "Giving Voice to the Poor," *Foreign Policy,* no. 84 (Fall 1991), 93–106.

25. Article 2, Resolution 001 (23 January 1986) of the National Environmental Council of Brazil.

26. Juan de Onis, *The Green Cathedral,* 203–4; Henri Acselrad, *Environment and Democracy* (Rio de Janeiro: Brazilian Institute for Social and Economic Analysis [IBASE], 1992), 46–51.

27. Gumercindo Rodriguis, quoted (but misidentified as Gumercindo Garcia) in Juan de Onis, *The Green Cathedral,* 203.

28. Ibid., 204–5; Acselrad, *Environment and Democracy,* 46–51.

29. Juan de Onis, *The Green Cathedral,* 222.

30. Ibid.

31. "Klima-Buendnis der europaeischen Staedte mit indigenen Voelkern der Regenwaelder zum Erhalt der Erdatmosphaere," Umwelt Forum Frankfurt, Stadt Frankfurt am Main (pamphlet, August 1992); Gerda Stuchlik and Roland Schaeffer, "The Preservation of the Environment and the Alliance Between European Cities and the Indigenous People of the Amazon," Umwelt Forum Frankfurt, Stadt Frankfurt am Main (Xerox copy, December 1991); Climate Alliance, "Working Paper for the Meeting on 4 August 1990."

32. Stuchlik and Schaeffer, "The Preservation of the Environment," 7–8 (the English-language text has been slightly modified to make it read more smoothly).

33. David C. Korten, *Getting to the 21st Century,* 106.

34. Thomas Hines, *Facing Tomorrow: What the Future Has Been, What the Future Can Be* (New York: Alfred A. Knopf, 1991), 198.

35. M. Mitchell Waldrop, *Complexity: The Emerging Science at the Edge of Order and Chaos* (New York: Simon & Schuster, 1992), 293–94.

36. Sheldon Annis, "Can Small-Scale Development Be a Large-Scale Policy? The Case of Latin America," *World Development,* vol. 15 supplement (1987), 129–34; Sheldon Annis, "The Next World Bank: Financing Development from the Bottom Up," *Grassroots Development,* vol. 11, no. 1 (1987), 24–29.

37. Annis, "The Next World Bank," 28–29.

38. See the five-part front-page series by *Washington Post* reporters John Ward Anderson, Molly Moore, Caryle Murphy, et al. on the deteriorating status of women in developing countries, "Third World, Second Class," *Washington Post,* 14–18 February 1993, A1.

39. Waldrop, *Complexity,* 332.

40. Ibid., 333.

41. Ibid.

42. Ibid., 333–34.

43. Albert Borgman, *Crossing the Postmodern Divide* (Chicago and London: University of Chicago Press, 1992), 61.

44. John Sculley, interview by Rich Karlgaard, *Forbes ASAP,* a technology supplement to *Forbes Magazine,* 7 December 1992, 95.

45. David Harvey, *The Condition of Postmodernity* (Cambridge, Mass. and Oxford, U.K.: Blackwell, 1990), 141–72; 177–79.

46. Borgman, *Crossing the Postmodern Divide,* 72–75. Borgman bases much of his analysis on Michael J. Piore and Charles F. Sabel, *The Second Industrial Divide: Possibilities for Prosperity* (New York: Basic Books, 1984), 165–220 (Borgman, n. 47, p. 157).

47. Borgman, *Crossing the Postmodern Divide,* 72–75; Drucker, *The New Realities,* 115; Harvey, *The Condition of Postmodernity,* 147.

48. Borgman, *Crossing the Postmodern Divide,* 61.

49. Sculley, interview by Karlgaard, *Forbes ASAP*, 96.

50. Michael Rothchild, "How to be a High IQ Company," *Forbes ASAP*, 7 December 1992, 18.

51. Ibid.

52. Drucker, *The New Realities*, 173.

53. Borgman, *Crossing the Postmodern Divide*, 78.

54. National Research Council, Board on Agriculture, Committee on the Role of Alternative Farming Methods in Modern Agriculture Production, *Alternative Agriculture* (Washington, D.C.: National Academy Press, 1989), 9.

55. Stephen B. Cox, "Citizen Participation and the Reform of Development Assistance in Central America," in Sheldon Annis, ed., *Poverty, Natural Resources, and Public Policy in Central America* (New Brunswick, N.J., and Oxford, U.K.: Transaction Publishers, 1992), 66–67.

56. Morse letter cited in Gautam Appa, "Narmada Projects without World Bank Backing?" *Economic and Political Weekly* (Bombay), vol. 27, no. 48 (28 November 1992), 2577–80.

57. Board statements and positions cited in Appa, "Narmada Projects," 2577–80.

58. See Milton D. Esman and Norman T. Uphoff, *Local Organizations: Intermediaries in Rural Development* (Ithaca and London: Cornell University Press, 1984).

59. Oxfam (U.K.), "Africa Make or Break: Action for Recovery," 38-page printed report (Oxford: Oxfam, 1993), 5.

60. See Drucker, *The New Realities*, 80–81.

61. See Korten, *Getting to the 21st Century*, 159–60.

62. *The Universal Declaration of Human Rights of the United Nations*, Article 21, Section 3, cited ibid., 161–62, n. 5.

63. See David Sarokin and Jay Schulkin, "Environmentalism and the Right-To-Know: Expanding the Practice of Democracy," *Ecological Economics*, vol. 4, no. 3 (December 1991), 175–89.

64. Quoted ibid., 177.

65. "Statement by E. Patrick Coady, U.S. Executive Director, to an Excutive Board Seminar, May 4, 1993" (U.S. Treasury Department, typewritten document, 4 pages).

66. "H-Street Blues," *Economist*, 1 May 1993, 87.

67. United Nations Development Program, *Human Development Report 1992* (New York and Oxford: Oxford University Press, 1992), 66–67.

68. Oxfam, "Africa Make or Break," 15.

69. World Bank, *Annual Report 1993* (Washington, D.C.: World Bank, 1993), 67.

70. Oxfam, "Africa Make or Break," 15.

71. Jerome I. Levinson, "Multilateral Financing Institutions: What Form of Accountability?" paper presented at the Conference on Human Rights, Public Finance, and the Development Process at American University, Washington College of Law, 24 January 1992, 20.

72. Senate Committee on Foreign Relations, Subcommittee on International Economic Policy, Trade, Oceans and Environment, hearing on *Authorization of the Tenth Replenishment of the International Development Association*, "Statement by Korinna Horta, Staff Economist, Environmental Defense Fund," in "Statement of Lori Udall on Behalf of Environmental Defense Fund," appendix 1, 103rd Cong., 1st sess., 27 May 1993.

73. Levinson, "Multilateral Financing Institutions," 41.

74. *Agreement Establishing the European Bank for Reconstruction and Development*, preamble, quoted in "Multilateral Financing Institutions," 41; ibid., Article 2, "Functions," Section (vii).

75. Judy Dempsey, Robert Peston, and Andrew Hill, "Attali Is Told EBRD Must Be Operated More Openly," *Financial Times* (London), 21 April 1993, 1.

76. In mid-April 1993, the *Financial Times* of London ran a series of articles exposing the EBRD's spending. See Charles Leadbeater, Robert Peston, and Andrew Hill, "Britain Will Call For Curbs on EBRD Spending," 15 April 1993, 1; Robert Peston and Kevin Brown, "EBRD Is Told to Provide Spending Details," 18 April 1993, 1.

77. Claude Lévi-Strauss, interview by Andre Akoun, "A Sort of Pope," *Psychology Today*, May 1972, 80.

78. Wolfgang Sachs, "One World against Many Worlds," *New Internationalist*, no. 232 (June 1992), 23.

79. Edward O. Wilson, *The Diversity of Life* (Cambridge, Mass.: Belknap Press of Harvard University Press, 1992), 278.

80. Carilito de Oliveira, "a leader of the Guaranis on the Dourados reservation," cited in Julia Preston, "Despair of Brazilian Tribe Reflected in Suicides: As Development Erodes Traditional Life, Youths Turn to Alcohol, Violence and Death," *Washington Post*, 20 April 1991, A12. See also James Brooke, "For Brazil's Indians, a Final Way Out," *New York Times*, 1 June 1991, 4; Conselho Indigenista Missionario, "Vinte Indios Guarani Kaiova No Brasil Suicidaram-Se Em 1992," electronic mail message from the Conselho Indigenista Missionario (the Indigenist Missionary Council), São Paulo, Brazil, 21 December 1992.

81. Cited in United Nations Development Program, *Human Development Report 1992*, 13.

82. H. W. Arndt, *Economic Development: The History of an Idea* (Chicago and London: University of Chicago Press, 1987), 177.

83. Martin Heidegger, *Being and Time*, trans. John Macquarrie and Edward Robinson (New York: Harper-Collins, 1962), 492, n. 5. Heidegger came across the fable, and its connection to *Faust*, in K. Burdach, "Faust und die Sorge," *Deutsche Vierteljahrschrift fuer Literaturwissenschaft und Geistesgeschicte*, vol. 1, 1923, pp. 1 ff.

84. Heidegger, *Being and Time*, 242, translating from the Latin poet Hyginus.

Index